12/26/75

TWELVE · TWENTY-SIX · SEVENTY-FIVE

Tony Reid

Milwaukee Wisconsin USA

12/26/75

Published by:
Genius Book Publishing
PO Box 250380
Milwaukee Wisconsin 53225 USA
GeniusBookPublishing.com

ISBN: 978-1-947521-86-5

220616 Trade

Table of Contents

Dedication

This book is dedicated to John Vaughan, former Sergeant with the Visalia Police Department, who started work on this case as the lead investigator in the homicide investigation of Claude Snelling on September 11, 1975.

While many others shared insight and crucial information, nothing can compare with John's guidance. Of course, his firsthand knowledge of the case was invaluable—after all, he was proven to have been right all along. He carefully explained why the theory that an early Ransacker suspect, a man who many had used to disconnect the Visalia cases from the rest of the series, was not only incorrect, but just comically wrong. In describing the Visalia crime scenes, he described a sense of evil that was unlike anything else he had ever encountered.

For the years that followed his time on the force, even into retirement, John noted that this case was the one that would never leave his mind until it was solved. This was the sole reason he gave so freely of his time.

It was a truly great moment to share the news with him the morning of the arrest. John Vaughan exemplifies a rare blend of courage, creativity, and honesty. After reviewing the facts of the case, Vaughn offered me his favorite analogy: "*Investigator's minds are like parachutes: they function only when they are open.*" For these things, and more… thank you, John.

Acknowledgments

First and foremost, I need to acknowledge the contribution of one person above all to this book: Margie Smith of Visalia. Margie's firsthand knowledge helped bring my attention to the case in the first place. Her demands for inquiry and justice rang like a church bell. Far more significantly, she connected me with the holders of the critical evidence and information. From there to the Clifton family members, and so many others… she gave me a home away from home, complete with meals, and an endless stream of coffee. A million thanks are still not enough.

Next, I want to acknowledge the original investigators who did some fabulous work in their own right: Richard Shelby, one of the original lead detectives and author of "*Hunting A Psychopath,*" and Jim Bevins, who led the department's sexual assault task force in the subsequent years. Both of these officers from the Sacramento Sheriff's Department (SSD) were fully haunted by the case into retirement, and their significant work has not been fully appreciated. Despite the initial misgivings he held about the evidence from Tulare County, Richard always listened and came to be a great investigative partner. He ultimately presented my information to his successors, and reconnected with Sgt. Vaughan. In this same light, I want to thank Larry Pool (formerly with Orange County), Larry Crompton (Contra Costa) and author of "*Sudden Terror,*" and the current members of the Major Crimes Unit, Visalia PD. In particular, Larry Pool took a tremendous amount of time to examine the Exeter connection, and made efforts to present information to his successors.

There are several contributors who deserve some of the greatest acknowledgement, yet cannot be personally identified. These people include direct witnesses, victims, law enforcement officers, and their surviving family members. These brave individuals agreed to be interviewed, provided critical information, and helped me make even more connections. Your bravery and insight are forever appreciated, and you all had one thing in common: your support in a quest for the truth that was your sole motivation. I appreciate the trust you had in me, and I promise to honor your confidentiality.

I also want to acknowledge a few reporters, namely Lew Griswold, formerly of the *Fresno Bee*, and Lilia Luciano and Mike Bunnell of ABC-10, Sacramento. I met Lew after a presentation on the Visalia Ransacker to the Visalia Rotary that I did with Margie more than five years ago. Following that presentation, Lew took great interest in the case, and one of his last articles with *The Bee* (before his retirement) came after the arrest of Joe DeAngelo, in which he gave much-deserved acknowledgement to Sgt. Vaughan, in a *Fresno Bee* article entitled "*Sweet Vindication.*" Lilia and Mike first took interest in the case after hearing the 12/26/75 podcast, and during their independent investigation, they received full access to my case files and evidence. They worked diligently for more than a year, and ended up with a five-part series (still accessible on YouTube) titled "*Framed By The Golden State Killer.*" We spent countless hours together reviewing the transcripts, forensic evidence, and finally for the on-site filming of the series. Your work stands as one of the only solid efforts by the media to reveal exactly what happened in Exeter on December 26, 1975.

Any researcher that fails to acknowledge our public libraries fails to acknowledge our most valuable common resource. Whether it is old phone directories, microfilmed newspapers, local genealogy directories, maps, photos… and so much more—our public libraries deserve so much more support than they receive. In particular, I need to thank the staff at The Visalia History Room, and the city libraries in Exeter, Porterville, and Tulare.

Thanks to Steven and Leya Booth, the people behind Genius Books, for believing in this project, and for allowing me the freedom to create such an enormous manuscript to address this topic with the level of detail it requires.

I also want to thank the thousands of people who have followed the developments of the investigation as they unfolded in real time, and followers of the 12/26/75 social media sites and the podcast. Your many questions, your support, and your assistance will not be forgotten.

Thank you to my friends and family who supported me, and even pushed me, to complete this work. Finally, I want to thank you, the reader. I ask that if you have more questions, please refer to the website about the case: ***12-26-75.com*** for links to shared Google maps, color photos, additional evidence, and links to the podcast and social media sites.

Foreword

In 1906, Hans Gross wrote the first manual for law enforcement officers: *Criminal Investigation: A Practical Handbook for Magistrates, Police Officers, and Lawyers.* In it, he advises that we always keep an open mind:

> *How often do we not come across inquiries where the Investigating Officer has started on an excellent plan, but has adhered to it with desperate tenacity even when the data upon which it was based have long since changed? Thus, to continue to follow a line, the falsity of which has been demonstrated, may sometimes prove more fatal and more dangerous than to grope about with no plan at all: in the latter case it is still possible to hit the right clue, in the former it is absolutely impossible. The case where an inquiry runs the greatest risk of failure is when the scheme supposes a certain person to have been the author of the crime; and, after having worked entirely with this idea, it suddenly becomes evident that that person is innocent.*
>
> *The greater difficulty there is in securing anything, the more one holds on to it; that is why fools are so obstinate. They never willingly abandon an idea, because they have had trouble in getting it into their heads. Now the scheme of an inquiry is difficult to follow out, and, when one has already worked in conformity therewith, it is not willingly abandoned; but still pursued unthinkingly and almost automatically. There is only*

one way to obviate such a danger, never to allow himself to be dominated exclusively by one idea and never to follow exclusively that sole idea.

Introduction

What is justice? Is it when the police arrest a man for a crime, or when a judge and jury send him to prison? Does it occur when he dies in custody, or is put to death by the state? The local candidate running for Sheriff, District Attorney, or Judge will tell you that it's one or all of these things—and only they can deliver it to the victim and community. They also tell us that the finality of conviction is the only goal. If the appeals courts overturn the conviction, or the parole board releases him, justice is denied.

This system relies on perfection. No police officer, prosecutor, witness, scientist, juror, or court can ever make a mistake. This also assumes that the police never tamper with or destroy evidence, pressure witnesses, or lie. Finality requires that the scientific experts are never wrong, and even their vague opinions are always perfectly formed. There is no room to consider evidence that was intentionally withheld by the prosecutor that the jury didn't get a chance to hear or weigh. According to our system of justice, all convictions should be stamped closed, the prison door shut, and the defendant made to serve every single day of his sentence without further consideration of his actual innocence. That is what justice demands.

This view of the system is one of superheroes that fight bad guys and protect the innocent. They are brave, kind, honest, and smart. They risk their lives to keep us safe, and their word is beyond reproach. Who are you going to believe, the man in uniform, the learned scientist, and the district attorney you voted for, or the rotten lying criminal defendant? It is presented as a choice—you are either for "law and order" or for anarchy. Of course, they aren't really superheroes, they are humans with the exact same motivations and frailties as the rest of us. They can be wrong. They can lie. Sometimes they are actually the criminal themselves. We don't like to think about what happens when the system convicts the wrong man, and lets the real killer go free to murder again, and we definitely don't want to ponder the idea that the police and District Attorney would cover for the killer to keep the truth from coming out.

In Exeter, California in 1975, the real killer was not just a police officer, but he was more educated, better trained, and smarter than most of the law enforcement tasked with catching him. He had a given name, Joseph James DeAngelo, Jr., but it was the other names bestowed on him by the police and press that made him infamous. The Cat Burglar that struck Rancho Cordova and east areas of Sacramento in 1972-73; The Cordova Meadows Burglar in 1973; The Visalia Ransacker from April 1974-December 1975; The East Area Rapist starting in June 1976 until he became The Original Night Stalker from December 1979 until May 1986. Finally, on June 29, 2020, they all became one man. DeAngelo stood up in court and admitted what some investigators had long suspected—that he had committed hundreds of crimes including stalking, peeping, car theft, burglary, robbery, kidnapping, assault, rape, and homicide—and that he got away with everything for more than forty years.

In court, Joseph DeAngelo was a frail-looking man in his seventies, pushed in a wheelchair by deputies. He barely whispered "yes" when prompted by his attorney. Like the characters he created, the courtroom version of DeAngelo was another act. Video from his jail cell showed a spry man. A few times during his hearing his eyes flashed black, and he muttered angry protests to his main defense counsel. For example, he said, "She can't say that," when one of his victims suggested that the judge should ignore the plea agreement and send him to the state hospital for the criminally insane. This DeAngelo courtroom character was a mild old man, but his more well-known side still lurked just under the surface.

Back in 1972, DeAngelo was 26 years old, and was just finishing his criminal justice Bachelor of Arts program at Sacramento State. He lived in an apartment in Citrus Heights with a man who would later become his brother-in-law. At that time, DeAngelo was also a prolific cat burglar who struck at least fifty homes in Citrus Heights, Carmichael, and Rancho Cordova—all suburban neighborhoods on the east side of Sacramento, in the jurisdiction of the Sacramento Sheriff's Department (SSD). He entered middle class homes after the owners were asleep, opened doors and windows for quick escape, and then spent a long time going through each room. His preferred point of entry was the garage/kitchen, or a sliding glass door at the rear of the house. He ate and drank from the refrigerator like he lived there, and usually only took purses and wallets—or maybe just one earring from a pair, a gun, camera, piggy bank, or Blue Chip trading stamps. He liked to hit several houses in the same night, and he left the emptied purses together in a pile for the police to find. He kept the money, and sometimes victims' photos and/or identification cards.

Some of the cat burglar's behavior was very odd, and specific, like turning off the A/C or furnace, putting the chain on the front door, and stacking women's undergarments in the hallway or kitchen. SSD also noted that many of the burglary victims received hang up or threatening phone calls and letters. Most distressing of all, dogs were killed (beaten to death or shot) during burglaries in Cordova Meadows in March 1972. In mid-1973, the cat burglar disappeared from Rancho Cordova. He had moved to Exeter, CA to start his new career as a police officer.

In April 1974, he turned his attention to the neighboring city of Visalia, and the new single story ranch homes on cul-de-sacs that housed the town's middle class professionals. The Visalia Ransacker (VR) took up right where the Rancho Cordova burglar left off, with the only tweak being a focus on evening break-ins of empty homes. All of the odd behaviors and petty thefts were a perfect match to the Cordova Meadows cat burglar. By the time the VR stopped in December 1975, a resident was dead, and a Visalia police officer injured. He didn't reappear in Ranch Cordova until June 1976. He had taken a new position as an officer with the Auburn Police Department.

DeAngelo's return to Rancho Cordova, Carmichael, and Citrus Heights in 1976 brought a new name, The East Area Rapist (EAR). He went back to the same homes and streets he had burgled in 1972-73, and stalked, harassed, and raped girls and women in what should have been the safety of their own homes. These attacks incorporated his same past behaviors, including ransacking the homes, taking little of value, and eating and drinking from the kitchen. At the same time, these neighborhoods also suffered dozens and dozens of burglaries, and neither dogs nor armed homeowners seemed to be a deterrent.

Eventually, he also starting attacking in Stockton, Modesto, Davis, San Jose, San Ramon, Danville, Concord, and Walnut Creek. Every new EAR attack garnered newspaper and TV headlines across the state, with a running total of his attacks front and center.

The first two hundred known cat and ransacking burglaries from 1972-September 1975 received almost no media attention, and the catchy names were used only by the police within their own files. Although both SSD and Visalia PD (VPD) were aware that they were dealing with a serial offender, they were opposed to creating community "panic," and incorrectly believed they had a better chance of catching the burglar if the cases were kept out of the press. When VPD publicly admitted that they were hunting the VR, and vowed to catch him, it set off a pattern of "call and response" that continued between DeAngelo and the police for the next decade. It also started a deep wounding divide between investigators who believed that they were playing a cunning game of cat and mouse with one of their own and others who were looking for a moronic, compulsive, disordered sex offender.

To him, it was all a "game," and it was played by communicating with the police—through words or direct action—leaving them clues that were meant to be followed. DeAngelo called the police in Visalia and Sacramento on the non-recorded phone lines (which he knew), and taunted that he was going to attack; he left "notes" with threats and clues; he gave some rape victims verbal messages and instructions for the police to follow; and, in December, 1977 he sent a poem to *The Sacramento Bee*, the Mayor of Sacramento, and television station KVIE:

"***Excitement's Crave***"
All those mortal's surviving birth
Upon facing maturity,
Take inventory of their worth
To prevailing society.

Choosing values becomes a task;
Oneself must seek satisfaction.
The selected route will unmask
Character when plans take action.

Accepting some work to perform
At fixed pay, but promise for more,
Is a recognized social norm,
As is decorum, seeking lore.

Achieving while others lifting
Should be cause for deserving fame.
Leisure tempts excitement seeking,
What's right and expected seems tame.

"Jessie James" has been seen by all,
And "Son of Sam" has an author.
Others now feel temptations call.
Sacramento should make an offer.

To make a movie of my life
That will pay for my planned exile.
Just now I'd like to add the wife
Of a Mafia lord to my file.

Your East Area Rapist
And deserving pest
See you in the press or on T.V.

The poem combined DeAngelo's direct messaging to the police with his "call and response" that used the press as a go-between for his communications. He made it explicit—he was following the press coverage of his crimes, and would respond to the statements made about him.

"*Excitement's Crave*" may have been the result of DeAngelo's frustration with SSD. They clearly had missed or ignored his barely subtle messaging to them. VPD had not made this mistake two years earlier with the VR. They strategically used their statements to the press to push the VR out into the open in the hope that he would make a mistake—which he did.

In addition to his communications, DeAngelo carefully laid out clues to be followed by law enforcement. It's not a real game if it's not possible for either side to win—that means rules, hints, and a direct matchup of skills between the competitors. Smart criminals know that they can be more successful if the police don't connect their crimes to each other. Every activity provides a bit more information: possible descriptions of the offender and his vehicle, neighborhoods hit, physical evidence, and frequency patterns like time and day of the week. The more crimes the police could connect, the more complete the picture was available for the investigators.

Back in the 1970s the Criminal Investigation and Identification (CII) system allowed California police agencies to have an offender's *Modus Operandi* (MO) entered into a database for possible matches to similar crimes in other jurisdictions. That is how VPD matched their cases to Sacramento.

DeAngelo, being a police sergeant on the multi-jurisdictional burglary task force, would have known about, and even used, CII. Why didn't he change his MO, and signature actions to avoid detection? Because the game with law enforcement was one of his primary motives. He didn't need to leave empty cans and bottles on patios, steal Blue Chip trading stamps, stack women's underclothes in hallways, or move and plant items between scenes. DeAngelo didn't have to keep burglarizing the same blocks and neighborhoods, or steal one earring or cufflink from a pair—he did those things so the police would be positive that it was him, and connect his crimes. That's completely irrational behavior for any normal criminal, and some of the less savvy investigators misinterpreted this as a sign that DeAngelo was compulsive, and couldn't stop his signature patterns. They were wrong. It was just part of the game.

It is no surprise that a man who was obsessed with the legendary status of "Jesse James" and "Son of Sam" would want to make sure that all of his crimes were properly credited to him. He longed to read or hear his names—Visalia Ransacker, East Area Rapist, and Original Night Stalker—in the paper or on television. He was infamous as a master criminal that the police couldn't identify, or stop. DeAngelo created terror in entire communities, and made his fellow police officers look like incompetent fools. That was the game, and DeAngelo had the high score against a dozen different police agencies for more than forty years. The press coverage never stopped, and even grew. There were multiple television specials that covered his decade-long crime spree, and his identity became debated around the world.

One question that still hasn't been answered, and may never be, is why DeAngelo targeted certain police jurisdictions and avoided others. In five minutes of looking at his crimes it was crystal clear that the then unknown offender was highly aware of police agency boundaries, patrol schedules, and stakeouts. Creating multiple scenes for the same crime, and placing them in different towns or counties was a brilliant strategy. Most police agencies hate sharing information and working together, and details are always going to be missed. That is a huge benefit to the criminal, and helps them avoid detection. Some of his decisions may have been based on personal animosity between DeAngelo and other members of law enforcement that he met, or with whom he worked.

I noticed that the VR burglaries were in a fairly small area of Visalia. Was DeAngelo trying to outwit and embarrass a particular VPD patrol officer or burglary investigator? There were several violent crimes assigned to the same Tulare County Sheriff's Sergeant, and this almost had to be a deliberate taunt or challenge from DeAngelo to that officer. Why did DeAngelo commit dozens of rapes in Sacramento County, but only a couple in the city itself? Clearly, he was targeting the Sheriff's department. Although DeAngelo had two college degrees in policing, he took positions with tiny departments with a starting salary less than half of what most agencies in Northern California were paying. I don't know if DeAngelo applied at bigger and more prestigious police or sheriff's departments and was rejected, but this could be important to understanding his MOs and motives.

After DeAngelo's arrest in 2018, one of the other Exeter officers who worked with him for three years said that he could never understand why someone as intelligent, educated, and well-trained as DeAngelo would be working in Exeter. He said that DeAngelo looked down on the other officers, and acted like the entire department, and his job were beneath him. That made me wonder about the qualifications required to be hired as a police officer in California in 1973. It varied by department, but the minimum standard was a high school diploma or GED, criminal background check, and a medical exam. Most agencies also had an IQ test (for fluid intelligence, the ability to reason and problem solve—not learned knowledge). The medical exam screened for physical, emotional, and mental conditions. Until 1974 most departments gave a ten-point bonus on the civil service exam for veterans, which DeAngelo would have received.

Larger, more professional departments, including VPD, used the new POST standards, which required additional training, classes, interviews, and exams for hiring and promotions. The necessity for these more rigorous standards is explained in the California Peace Officers Psychological Screening Manual:

> Peace officers operate in a high-risk environment where failure to make quick and effective decisions can result in devastating life-or-death consequences. Their vested power gives them the authority to restrain others' freedom of movement, use justified physical force, and restrict privacy rights by effecting lawful searches and seizures and detaining or arresting individuals. With this power comes many opportunities for its misuse of authority, including excessive and unjustified use of force, witness intimidation, evidence planting and tampering, false arrest and perjury, kickbacks, bribes, theft, illegal seizures, extortion, etc. Such acts result in unwarranted harm to citizens and lead to a community's loss of trust in its law enforcement officers.

I wanted to understand how each of these various requirements could have impacted DeAngelo's job search, and eventual hiring. He may have failed some aspect of a more rigorous POST hiring process, like the psychological evaluation, and been relegated to less picky agencies. One thing is certain, it made absolutely no sense for a combat Navy veteran with a BA in Criminal Justice to accept a job for less than $500 per month. Evidence shows that DeAngelo was intelligent, certainly somewhere above average, and that seemed to me like it should have been a huge advantage. Hiring for all public service jobs in California relied upon some form of IQ test. However, I soon discovered that this may have actually worked against DeAngelo.

Growing up on TV shows about detectives at the LAPD, I thought that only the smartest applicants were hired, and the best of the best became detectives. I was horribly wrong—TV has lied to us. In 2016, the average IQ of a U.S. police officer was 104. In 1970, it was 100. That is exactly average, and it's by design. That is the IQ that has been considered optimal for hiring officers who can do the job, but won't get bored and quit due to the monotony of routine police work. This issue came to a head in the courts in 1999 after a Connecticut police department turned down an applicant who had scored too high—his IQ was 125. The applicant sued, claiming discrimination, but the appeals court ruled for the police. The court's logic was that the department was allowed to limit turnover and minimize the cost of training new officers.

One thing is certain, DeAngelo graduated from college in June 1972, but was not hired as a police officer until May 1973. His career dreams and degrees were entirely focused on law enforcement, and presumably he applied to work at multiple departments, including the California Highway Patrol. He had completed a months-long internship with Roseville PD, but they didn't hire him. What happened? One possibility is that DeAngelo's IQ was too high for small departments that were focused on limiting turnover, and those that used the new POST standards refused him due to oddities with his personality, or mental health issues. The result may have been particularly tragic. DeAngelo was frustrated with his low status job, and when he resumed his criminal activities, a group of men with average IQs and training were tasked with catching him.

The game DeAngelo "played" with police in Tulare County in 1974-75 had clearly defined opponents—VPD and the Tulare County Sheriff's Office (TCSO). In 1970, Visalia got a new police chief, Raymond Forsyth, and he started recruiting the best and brightest officers from neighboring jurisdictions. He sent them for advanced training, and by 1975, there were a few new outstanding investigators.

However, Sheriff Wiley rewarded loyalty, not professionalism. His deputies were hired for their ability to not "overthink" their job. During the years DeAngelo lived in Exeter, the local papers covered serious issues within Wiley's department:

> An angry Cesar Chavez, backed by about 700 United Farm Workers Union (UFWU) supporters, called Friday for an investigation of Tulare County Sheriff Bob Wiley for alleged organized law enforcement brutality.

> Chavez' remarks came at the climax of a noisy demonstration outside Tulare County Jail, Visalia. "Wiley's special riot Gestapo squad beat up our people. The deputies came with absolutely no regard for the law," Chavez said, describing deputy sheriffs as "mad dogs."
>
> "Wiley is not dumb," said Chavez. The union leader asserted it was to Wiley's political benefit to help keep farm workers' wages down because every time their wages go up the "deputy sheriffs get ideas" about raises. He said Tulare County deputies are paid less than most deputies in California.

TCSO deputies were great at breaking up bar fights, investigating tractor battery thefts, and busting the heads of striking farmworkers, but those tasks don't require advanced reasoning skills or complex problem solving. It appears DeAngelo wanted to prove to himself, and the community, that he could outsmart the officers and deputies he worked with on a daily basis.

By sticking to the recommended "optimal" IQ, agencies like TCSO missed out on the benefits of investigators who were more creative, curious, and questioned their own assumptions. Deputies that were satisfied doing nothing but routine, assigned tasks brought with them an array of undesirable traits, including:

- Not being receptive to new information, ideas, and conflicting opinions
- A lack of humility—they were unaware that there were things that they didn't know
- Disinterest in learning new things, asking questions, and expressing curiosity
- Fear of change
- Inability to reflect on the past, or see older events in a different light
- Viewing situations as black and white, with two opposite choices (good/bad, right/wrong) and no subtleties

- Not being able to imagine win-win outcomes. Seeing only winners and losers, and fear of being perceived as the loser
- Inability to handle criticism, see another person's point-of-view, be empathetic, weigh pros and cons, and/or understand sarcasm
- Favoring short term rewards and instant gratification. The more complex and frustrating a case, the faster they wanted it to end
- Difficulty understanding the difference between opinion and fact—what they think vs. what can be objectively proven
- Inflexibility. Cannot change their mind, or admit a mistake. Once an opinion is formed, it is immovable
- Lack of critical thinking. Facts that do not support existing beliefs are simply ignored or discarded, leading to confirmation bias, tunnel vision, anchor traps, selective perception, stereotyping, overconfidence, and blind spots

The policies of policing in America determined that all of these traits are acceptable in a functioning justice system. They should be disqualifying, but instead they're seen as tradeoffs to lower officer turnover rates and training costs. By setting the optimal IQ at exactly average, half of the population was (and is) smarter than law enforcement. Right on the surface that sounds like a terrible idea, but it is terrifying if you consider some of the investigative advantages smart criminals have over the police. Criminals:

- Remember everything, and have the ability to incorporate new information or experiences rather than being stuck in old knowledge or patterns
- Solve new and unexpected problems quickly

- Are creative—they can make something totally unique and not immediately obvious. This includes staged scenes, and false clues
- Prepare, plan, and pay attention to details when evaluating risk, and rely upon skill more than luck
- Have better intuition about people and situations—their brains process information without the need for conscious logic or reasoning
- Worry about what they don't know, and constantly study and learn new skills to stay ahead of the police
- Are curious about new people, experiences, and the way things work
- Don't accept things at face value, are more skeptical. They are likely to seek proof before relying on facts and conclusions, including their own

Why did we, as a society, knowingly create a system where criminals can so easily outwit the police? Because we wanted the officers to take orders without question, make quick (often wrong) decisions, be willing to shoot citizens, and be satisfied with monotonous work. We have hired good soldiers, not Sherlock Holmes. It's no surprise that when you hire Barney Fife, you arrest innocent men, and let real killers go free.

In California, these questionable hiring practices were compounded by the country's most secretive system for covering up police misconduct, and the lack of an officer decertification process. The public, including criminal defendants, has not been able to access the disciplinary portion of police personnel records. Was a deputy caught destroying evidence, beating a suspect, or lying? Nobody knows because that information has been protected by state law for the officer's "privacy." If an officer was fired for misconduct—even a crime—he was free to be hired by another department. Some agencies (like McFarland, CA) have actively recruited and hired these "bad cops." Many communities still favor head busters over problem solvers.

What happened when DeAngelo came up against a few highly intelligent, well-trained investigators? They immediately figured him out. The detectives could see that the offender was repeating his signature activities to taunt them, communicating with them directly and indirectly, and leaving false evidence to misdirect their investigations. In fact, in early 1977 the lead detectives in Visalia and Sacramento were working together on the theory that they were hunting a fellow member of law enforcement. By the summer of 1978, Sacramento Sheriff Lowe had successfully gotten both investigators removed from the case.

At the same time, an aggressive cover-up was underway in Exeter. When the TCSO Sergeant heard that the suspect being hunted was described as a police officer who had left Tulare County in the summer of 1976, he knew exactly who it was—his neighbor and co-worker for more than three years, Exeter PD Sgt. Joseph DeAngelo, Jr. Turning in DeAngelo would have exposed the investigator's own misconduct, and caused a community uprising of anger and distrust in Exeter. Instead, this sergeant destroyed every item of physical evidence that could be used against DeAngelo, covered up a wrongful conviction, and sat silently by and watched as DeAngelo continued on his rape and robbery rampage, and then killed twelve innocent women and men across California.

DeAngelo wasn't missed as a suspect; the Sheriff's departments in Sacramento and Tulare Counties let him go. It wasn't just incompetence, it was an aggressive cover-up, and silencing of the truth. Investigators from VPD, SSD, Orange County, and Ventura connected the crimes, and developed a shockingly accurate suspect profile, but SSD, TCSO, and the "EAR Task Force" belittled them, and successfully discredited their work to the press. Admitting that an innocent man had been sent to prison, and that one of their own had tricked and fooled them was not an option. They doubled down on getting everything wrong, and bragging about it.

There is no question that arresting an active duty police officer would have shaken citizens' trust and belief in law enforcement. It would have been awful and damaging, and would have taken a lot of bravery. Unfortunately, the decisions were made by a group of insecure cowards, incapable of being seen as "losers." They sacrificed DeAngelo's victims to protect their fragile egos. He could have been stopped—some investigators loudly tried, but they were yelled down time and time again for more than forty years. DeAngelo wasn't the only criminal, police officer, or monster responsible for his crimes, he's the only one who has been prosecuted.

CHAPTER ONE

"We'll catch the guy"

"I'll be driving my wife's orange Jeep, you won't be able to miss me." Retired VPD Sgt. John Vaughan is a master of understatement.

I chose the Black Bear Diner because it seemed like the kind of place where cops eat. They serve all-day breakfast, steaks, and bottomless cups of coffee in their signature white mugs. I was afraid that if I suggested a place more suited for a vegan from Los Angeles, I might make an already awkward meeting totally unbearable for both of us.

The Jeep was the brightest thing in the parking lot, maybe in the entire county, now turned brown after years of endless drought. As I drove into town, the only color was the green from irrigated groves of citrus trees. Although it was still early, the day was quickly heading over 100 degrees. Visalia is a small city stuck in time. It prides itself on pretending that it is still 1950. The A&W brews its own homemade root beer, and sells it in jugs that you can take home. However, it was impossible to miss the racist graffiti scrawled on the wall of the Indian grocery store on the edge of the A&W parking lot.

I understood Visalia, and its power structure. My great-grandparents chased the American farming dream across the country at the turn of the 20th century, going from Kansas to North Dakota, then to the newly planted orange trees of Southern California. My great-grandfather was a pacifist, and they fled to Canada during WWI, finally returning to the apple and cherry trees of northeastern Washington State. My great-uncle, "Buck," was the police chief of a small farming city a lot like Visalia. Rumors were that he ran the town as his own personal criminal empire. He took a cut of every illegal enterprise, and black and brown suspects ended up dead in the river, rather than in a jail cell or courtroom. According to my mother, the rumors were all true. As soon as she could, she left for Seattle, and never looked back. Her sister took the other path, became a police dispatcher, and married the son of a homicide detective in Spokane.

I never planned on becoming an attorney, but somehow my internal need for fairness found a practical profession. Handling criminal appeals immediately put me in direct conflict with law enforcement, prosecutors, and judges. It's a specialized area of the law that requires endless hours of research on each case. The best appellate attorneys start at the beginning, with the events leading up to the crime, not the trial itself. That means digging into original police reports, witness statements, and forensic lab bench notes. Overworked and underfunded public defenders are rarely granted money for investigators and forensic experts, and critical details can easily be missed.

Although my office is staffed by licensed attorneys and private investigators, we each bring unique life experiences and skills. I spent summers on drilling rigs in the Arctic Circle and in Montana. Guns were a necessity in camps accessible only by helicopter, and stalked by grizzly bears and wolves. We have dirt bike riders, and a pilot who can conduct surveillance via small plane or drone. One of our attorneys is a forensics expert, who studied criminology at Oxford University, and can build a complete family tree for a subject while you wait in the field for the next address to check out or vehicle to follow. Two of us lost close friends to serial offenders, and we are guided by what we know they would want us to do if we were pursing their killers. Terri and Laurie would want the truth—no matter how long it takes, or how difficult it may be to accept.

My first phone call to John Vaughan went pretty much exactly as I expected. John had retired as a sergeant with VPD in 1996 after 35 years of service, and 20 years later, he had little interest in revisiting a 40-year-old unsolved crime spree. However, I wasn't calling about just *any case*—it was the longest and most expensive investigation in VPD history, and Sgt. Vaughan had been the lead detective. I asked him if I could just email a few documents, and he finally agreed to let me mail him an envelope. The day he got the documents he called back, and asked if we could meet to discuss the information. Now here we were in the parking lot of the Black Bear Diner.

Even twenty years after retirement, John still looked like he could topple his wife's Jeep with one hand, and the expression on his face as I pulled up made me think he was considering it. Walking into the restaurant together, we made small talk, and the mood hadn't really improved by the time we were done ordering. John was a wall of skepticism, built over 40 long years of listening to an endless number of overly excited "theories" about his biggest case. Between March 1974 and December 1975, a man dubbed the "Visalia Ransacker" had terrorized his city. There had been over 150 residential burglaries with a very weird and specific MO.

The burglar ignored expensive jewelry and electronics, and instead stole Blue Chip trading stamps, piggy banks, food, coins, cameras, two dollar bills, knives, and single earrings from a pair. He took guns, but only if they were older or foreign, and therefore lacked traceable registration numbers. Immediately upon entering the home, he opened multiple escape routes, and placed the window screens in odd places, like on the bed. He also put chain locks across doors, or blocked them with chairs, to delay the homeowner should he return during the burglary. He displayed undergarments and jewelry boxes on beds and pillows, and stole photos of the attractive teen girls who lived in the rooms. All areas, including the kitchens, were heavily ransacked. Drawers were left pulled out, or contents dumped on the floor. Sometimes he placed stacks of undies and nightgowns in rows down the hallway.

The VR always struck in the early evening, while the residents were out to dinner, a movie, or the local football game. He confined his activities to a small area of single story homes, often on cul-de-sacs, owned by middle class professionals. The houses were usually locked, and the VR favored prying and chiseling locks on sliding glass doors or back doors to garages, then going into the kitchens. The VR traveled almost exclusively through backyards, ditches, open spaces, alleys, and greenbelts—always careful to avoid sidewalks and streets. The burglaries got little press attention or police investigation, and were treated like a nuisance, not a threat.

At 2:24 am on Thursday, September 11, 1975, VPD received an emergency call to respond to a shooting at the Snelling home. When they arrived two minutes later they found Claude Snelling lying mortally wounded inside his front door. His wife explained that he had been shot by a man who had kidnapped their 16-year-old daughter, Beth. Forty-five year-old Claude, a journalism professor at nearby College of the Sequoias, was pronounced dead upon arrival at the hospital.

The killer had entered the house by removing the screen on an open window, and unlocking the back door. The air conditioning unit had stopped working that evening, likely due to intentional tampering. Beth awoke to find the masked man on top of her, pinning her arms, and holding his hand across her mouth. In a clenched teeth whisper, he ordered her to get up and go with him, or he would stab her. As they walked through the house, Beth struggled with the kidnapper, and her father got up to investigate the noise. Claude called out: "Where are you taking my daughter?" Rather than running away, the man let go of Beth, and walked back a few feet to get a clear shot at Claude as he exited the back door. As he stepped into the yard, the man fired two shots, both hitting Claude. The kidnapper then pointed the gun at Beth's head, kicked her three times in the face, and calmly walked away towards the street. He just disappeared into the darkness.

Sgt. Vaughan was assigned as lead investigator, and his team quickly determined that the gun used to kill Claude had been stolen in a recent VR burglary. The gun owner was able to show them where he had done some target practice, and ballistics examination of the spent rounds matched the bullets that killed Claude. The investigation showed that the VR had arrived on a stolen bike, which he left in a yard a block away, and departed on foot, using a landscaped ditch along the highway. Sgt. Vaughan quickly realized that Beth, and her friends at Mt. Whitney High School, had been the Ransacker's targets all along. They had been stalked and terrorized for nearly two years by a man whose true plan was kidnapping and murder. The VR was suddenly front page news, but the more that Sgt. Vaughan and his team promised to catch him, the more brazen the VR became.

On October 21, 1975, The *Visalia Times-Delta* published an update story on the Snelling homicide:

> Presently, Sgt. John Vaughan and agents William McGowen and Duane Shipley are handling the investigation. All are confident they will succeed. "We are getting a lot of leads and tips. Lots of things are being worked on," Vaughan said. "We'll catch the guy," McGowen said.

Just as that story hit newsstands and porches that afternoon, the most recent VR burglary victim, Ruth Swanson (a pseudonym), returned home for the day to an empty house. Suddenly, she heard someone trying to open the front door. When she checked the peephole, all she saw was a hand covering it. She ran to the living room window, but saw nobody on the front porch. A few minutes later, she received a couple of hang up phone calls, followed by an obscene one, using her name. VPD responded, and installed a trap on her phone.

On Friday, October 24th, the VR committed four burglaries. It appeared from witness reports and footprints that he started with two homes on W. Campus Avenue. At around 10:30 pm, while Sgt. Vaughan and his team were responding to those burglaries, the VR moved on to Whitney Lane. A neighbor saw the VR cutting through yards to S. Redwood, where he committed a third burglary—325 feet from the Snelling house. The VR then crossed Redwood to the house where he had left the stolen bike on the night of the Snelling homicide, passed through that yard, and across the back fence. He then burglarized the home on the other side of the fence.

The burglaries seemed to serve no real purpose other than to commit signature ransacking, sure to be recognized by VPD: kitchen drawers were pulled out evenly, but not disturbed; women's undergarments were displayed with jewelry boxes on the bed pillows; lotion was left out; and the chain was thrown across the front door. Sgt. Vaughan noted in his report that the only motive for much of the ransacking appeared to be to "draw attention" and "to leave his calling card." Sgt. Vaughan believed that they were being taunted for their comments to the newspaper.

It quickly became clear to Vaughan's team that the VR was working with a deep knowledge of police procedure, their patrol rotation schedule, and even their planned stakeouts. He knew exactly when and where to strike to avoid all of the police efforts to catch him. The only advantage they had was their newfound knowledge of the VR's true motive—he was stalking particular girls and young women in a set zone. Earlier that year, another teenage girl, Debbie Ward, had encountered the masked VR after he had just burglarized the apartment of their tenant, who lived over the garage. He pushed Debbie aside to escape, but she was unharmed.

Agent Bill McGowen was assigned to contact the Ward family and several other prior VR victims. He told them to look for signs of a prowler in their yards, and to report any strange noises. It paid off. Mrs. Ward found fresh footprints under Debbie's bedroom window, and upon further investigation, Agent McGowen saw a circular impression next to the prints. He found a matching flowerpot in the neighbor's yard that had been used as a step stool to look in Debbie's window, and then had carefully been put back in place.

Sgt. Vaughan was heading to Los Angeles for PERT training, but he was able to plan the stakeout of Debbie's house. It was agreed that Agent McGowen would hide in the neighbor's garage, next to Debbie's bedroom window. Agent Duane Shipley would be placed across the street to watch from that angle. The rest of the team would be positioned in the surrounding area to look for the VR, and create a net around the neighborhood should he appear. Sgt. Vaughan said that he was worried about not being there, but he trusted Agent McGowen. McGowen had been chosen because of his honesty and morality; he didn't cut corners, swear, or drink. McGowen's father, C.E. McGowen, was a police captain in the city of Tulare, and his brother, Richard, was a sergeant with the Tulare County Sheriff's Office (TCSO). Sgt. Vaughan said that he knew Bill McGowen would always do the right thing, no matter how dire the circumstances.

The biggest change in the Ward stakeout was its silence. Not only were the officers ordered to stay off the radio, their entire operation was kept top secret within the department. The only people who knew what they were doing were the team members themselves, and they were not allowed to discuss it with anyone. Sgt. Vaughan had become convinced that the VR was a member of law enforcement, who not only listened to their radio frequency but also talked directly to officers on his squad—it was the only possible way he could have avoided all of the prior stakeouts.

At 7:00 pm on Wednesday, December 10, 1975, the stakeout of the Ward house began. Agents McGowen and Shipley were in place, while four other officers in two cars and on foot covered the surrounding neighborhood. Agent Hartman oversaw the operation in a roving, unmarked car. At 8:38 pm, a frantic call broke radio silence, "Shots fired, officers need assistance."—Agent McGowen was down.

A few minutes before, the VR had been spotted at Debbie Ward's window, and McGowen had confronted him at gunpoint in the side yard. The VR was wearing a mask, which he took off, and put in his right jacket pocket to show McGowen that he was complying. He then turned, jumped the gate, and ran into the backyard screaming, "Please don't hurt me, oh my god, no." McGowen fired a warning shot into the ground to try to make the VR stop moving, and to attract the attention of Agent Shipley. The VR then jumped the fence into the Ward yard, raised his right hand, and said, "See, my hands are up." As he reached his left hand into his pocket, he pulled out a gun, and fired at McGowen through the fence slats, hitting his flashlight dead center. Mr. Ward looked out of his patio door just in time to see the VR hop over his back fence, and disappear into the night.

Agent Shipley found Bill McGowen on the ground, saw blood on his face, and thought he was dead. Glass from the flashlight lens had hit McGowen's eye, knocking him to the ground, but he had not been shot. Agent Hartman then called in the California Highway Patrol, TCSO, and all VPD units to help seal off the area and try to prevent the VR from escaping. It did no good—he was gone. Investigators found a sock full of loot dropped by the VR on the Ward's patio. The stolen items were quickly tied to a nearby home burglary that had occurred shortly before the shooting. There was no doubt, the man who had killed Claude Snelling, shot at McGowen, and committed the VR burglaries was the same offender.

McGowen created a composite sketch of the suspect. Sgt. Vaughan's team investigated and eventually cleared nearly one hundred suspects, but by September 1976 they had run out of new clues to follow. Then the Criminal Investigation and Identification (CII) system notified them of an MO and suspect match to a serial rapist in Sacramento who had started his crimes in June 1976. John immediately saw the connection. He requested the burglary and rape case reports from the SSD for the offender whom media had dubbed the "East Area Rapist." (EAR). In May 1977, Detectives Shipley and McGowen traveled to Sacramento and met with EAR investigator Detective Richard Shelby, who felt the VR was a good lead. Unfortunately, nobody else in Sacramento agreed, and Shelby was taken off the case a month later. In 2001, DNA connected the EAR to ten murders in Orange, Ventura, and Santa Barbara Counties (Original Night Stalker-ONS); that killer had never been caught.

The EAR/ONS crimes were profiled on the A&E show "*Cold Case Files*" in 2000, and that led to multiple online discussion boards dedicated to the cases. A&E eventually shut down their board after users started naming and harassing "persons of interest" in real life. Several of the people involved in the discussions were convinced that they were experts, and repeatedly contacted different members of law enforcement to tell them how they should be running their investigation and exactly who they should consider as suspects. Generally, five minutes' worth of research could prove that their "suspect" could not have committed the crimes. Although law enforcement officers tried to be patient and have an open mind so that they didn't miss an important tip, many of these case theories from internet investigators proved to be exhausting.

It would be wrong to put all internet sleuths or armchair detectives into the same group. Some individuals who become interested in a cold case bring unique research skills, or real life investigative experience, while others simply like to go with crowd sourcing, guesses, or theories, rather than with hard facts. As an attorney and private investigator, I didn't fit into either group. I was relying on original police and forensic reports, witness statements, and court records, not the internet. Also, I was looking for evidence that could meet a higher standard—evidence that could support probable cause for a search warrant, arrest, and conviction.

I could tell that John Vaughan was not entirely convinced that my ideas were grounded in facts rather than hunches, and he asked me if I had ever talked to some of the other people who had approached him about the case. I hadn't, and he seem relieved. He was not in the mood for a manic recitation of disconnected stories that added up to nothing. He was also a bit suspicious of my work as a defense attorney—generally a cop's natural enemy. Nobody likes to have their work scrutinized, criticized, and second-guessed.

I opened our conversation by telling him how impressed I was with the forward thinking, professionalism, and thoroughness of his original investigation into the VR. It was textbook police work, with complete canvasses of the neighborhoods, and no potential suspect off limits. My only criticism was the hypnosis of Beth Snelling and Agent McGowen, which seemed to have changed their original suspect descriptions and thrown the case off track. Making "suggestions" to witnesses creates false memories that feel real, which is why hypnotized witnesses cannot testify in court. However, in 1975, it was considered cutting edge science. I also pointed out to John that his team was the only one to ever catch the suspect; nobody else had even come close. It turned out that he was a lot harder on himself than I ever could have been.

Sgt. Vaughan expressed an enormous amount of regret for being in Los Angeles during the McGowen shootout. He felt responsible for letting the VR get away, and later hurting and killing so many innocent people. Even after 40 years he was still immensely frustrated that he hadn't been able to convince Sacramento that they were looking for the same suspect. He believed that Sacramento should have focused on men who had been in Tulare County between 1974-1976, with law enforcement training. John also thought that if Sacramento had utilized secret stakeouts, the VR/EAR could have been caught in 1977, and... *at least* twelve homicides could have been prevented.

To John, it wasn't just a theory; he knew that the VR was the EAR. He explained the uniqueness of the MO, and the utter creepiness that he never felt or saw in any other case. If I had doubted the connection before, I didn't after I looked into John's eyes. I also had complete certainty that the Visalia Ransacker and East Area Rapist were the same person.

We finally got to the reason for our meeting—the information in the envelope I had mailed to him. I was worried and hesitant to start, but he had no problem barking out questions faster than I could answer them. I asked him what his working relationship with TCSO had been during the VR investigation, and he said simply that there hadn't been one. They never worked cases together if they could help it—the feelings of dislike were mutual. I asked about a particular officer, TCSO Sgt. Bob Byrd. John's eyes flashed. He recited a couple of unflattering names for Byrd, including "DBO" (Ditch Bank Okie), and said Byrd wasn't an educated or trained police officer, and he had no business investigating real crimes. I carefully suggested that perhaps Byrd had manipulated and destroyed evidence, and John said, "Oh, it must have been a Tuesday."

I felt a huge weight off my shoulders as one of my biggest fears lifted. If John had not been willing to believe that Byrd was both a terrible investigator and a rule breaker, our meeting would have been over. Instead, we moved on to discussing the homicide of Jennifer Armour, a name he barely recognized. At 7:30 pm on Friday, November 15, 1974, Jennifer, a 15 year old sophomore, disappeared while walking from her house to the Visalia K-Mart. She was meeting friends for a ride to the homecoming football game between her school, Mt. Whitney, and the rival Redwood High. Jennifer's friends waited an extra fifteen minutes, then headed to the game. When they were unable to locate her there, they figured she hadn't gotten permission from her mom and had stayed home.

When Jennifer didn't return home that night, her mother assumed she was staying with a friend, and it wasn't until Saturday morning that she realized that Jennifer had been missing for more than 12 hours. She called VPD, but in the 1970s, possible runaway teen cases got little attention. There was no sign that Jennifer had been harmed or was in danger. Had she told her mom she was meeting her girlfriends, but really run off?

The answer came on the morning of Sunday, November 24, 1974. A rancher found Jennifer's body in the Friant-Kern canal, just north of Exeter. TCSO made it sound like an accidental drowning, and when Sgt. Vaughan got the Snelling case ten months later, Jennifer was not listed as a missing person or a homicide victim.

In the Black Bear Diner, John and I went over some maps I had printed out for the meeting. I showed him the two November 1974 VR burglaries that had immediately preceded Jennifer's disappearance—they were three blocks from where Jennifer was last seen. We discussed how Jennifer and Beth Snelling were the same age, physical type, in the same class at Mt. Whitney High School, and were kidnapped just four blocks apart. Had Jennifer been one of the VR's Mt. Whitney stalking victims? I asked John how many other Mt. Whitney students had ever been kidnapped in their homes, or off the street, in all of the years he had lived in Visalia. He didn't know of any others. John had always assumed that Beth Snelling's kidnapping was going to end in rape and murder in some remote, dark location—just like an orange grove out in Exeter.

I asked John about something else that was the hallmark of both the EAR and VR— his taunting of police. The EAR was perhaps most infamous for responding to two different public "challenges." The first was in March 1977, when *The Sacramento Bee* published a story stating that the EAR "has never attacked while there is a man in the home." The next attack, on April 2nd, was on a sleeping couple, and that soon became his signature. Then, on May 17, 1977, the EAR attacked a couple in the Del Dayo neighborhood. Detective Shelby immediately realized that the husband was the same man who had stood up and yelled at him at a community meeting on November 3, 1976. The man had berated Shelby for not catching the EAR, and said that in his native Italy, the men would never let their wives get hurt like that. Clearly, the EAR had been at that meeting, took the man's comments as a challenge, and targeted him. In fact, almost every single time that SSD issued a statement to the press about the EAR, he would respond with another rape. It was a constant call and response.

I had noticed that the VR had done the same thing after Sgt. Vaughan and Agent McGowen had made statements to the press about "catching" him. In fact, the VR went right back to the Snelling neighborhood, and burglarized their block again. John confirmed that the VR had clearly taunted them after every public statement, and gone out of his way to embarrass his team. That took me back to the days after Jennifer Armour was found. Tulare County Sheriff, Bob Wiley, declared to the press that "there is no reason to believe that the girl may have been murdered." Jennifer's public service was on that Friday, November 29th, and that night the VR hit five homes in Visalia, and thirteen on Saturday night. This was an insane spree, even by VR standards—there was nothing else like it in the series, before or after. Eighteen burglaries in two nights. Clearly the VR was trying to get the attention of VPD, but it fell flat. It was almost a year before John took over the case, and the officers working the burglaries back in 1974 didn't catch on to it—at all.

I took out some additional maps. Now we were looking at the Friant-Kern Canal, just north of the Exeter city limits. The area where Jennifer had been killed was easily accessed from the highway, yet totally secluded, with no homes or lights nearby. The killer kidnapped Jennifer right by the highway on-ramp in Visalia, drove east eleven miles, turned left and headed north, then right heading east again, and finally a left onto the same grove siding road the rancher was driving when he found Jennifer's body. Those actions were deliberate, specific, and planned by someone who knew the area *extremely* well. Most of the agricultural property close to Exeter surrounds the owners' ranch homes. When you turn off the road onto a dirt drive, you don't know if you're heading into trees or are on a driveway leading to a home full of people—and a shotgun.

I showed Sgt. Vaughan the grove, siding road, and spot in the Friant-Kern Canal where Jennifer was killed in November 1974. Then, I moved my finger just slightly to the southeast on the map to a different orange grove along the same canal, Neel Ranch. "And, *that's* where Donna Richmond was killed in December 1975," I told John. The distance was less than two miles, with a straight line of sight between the two groves.

Neel Ranch was owned by Hank Neel, who lived in Ventura. The property was purely agricultural, with no ranch house, and it could be accessed from the siding road along the Friant-Kern Canal. Like Jennifer, Donna had disappeared while she was alone on a Friday evening. Both girls had long blonde hair and blue eyes. Donna was a 14-year-old freshman at Exeter High, and like Jennifer, she had simply disappeared into a vehicle without any witness seeing or hearing a kidnapping.

At this point, I was expecting an eye roll, sigh, or some sign of frustration from John, but the moment passed quickly. A man named Oscar Clifton had been convicted of Donna's murder, and had died in prison three years earlier, but John was unfazed: "So that guy Clifton didn't do it." He asked how Clifton had been eliminated in Jennifer's murder, and I said that he and his family lived in Las Vegas—TCSO had fully checked his alibi since they really wanted to clear both cases with one suspect if they could. John agreed that it was now apparent that the same person had killed both Jennifer and Donna, and that the evidence in Exeter seemed to point *directly* back to Visalia and the VR.

I had originally wanted to talk to John because I believed that there were four things about Donna's murder that were meant to be tied to the VR but had been totally missed by TCSO in their rush to convict an innocent man. The first was a ski mask that was collected into evidence on Neel Ranch. It was described by the forensics tech as a "multi-colored 'ski cap' with possible hairs adhering." The description of the ski mask worn by the VR, as described by Beth Snelling, was "having white stripes and having multi-color zigzag design." Obviously, there was no photo of the VR's ski mask, but there is one from Neel Ranch. It is crumpled on the ground, but it clearly has white stripes, a zigzag pattern, and what appear to be eye holes. There would be no reason for Donna's killer to leave the mask at the homicide scene unless he wanted it to be found and matched back to the Snelling case, and to the VR.

There was also no question that TCSO investigators were supposed to connect Jennifer and Donna's murders, and then follow the cases back to Visalia and the VR. Kidnapping similarly aged blonde girls, in safe public areas on a Friday evening, and then leaving their bodies in orange groves on the Friant-Kern Canal, just north of Exeter, was a highly specific MO, and a lead that was meant to be seen and pursued. Sgt. Vaughan agreed, and said that it felt exactly like the offender he had been chasing for so many years—always taunting the police, and daring them to catch him. That brought me to a quote of John's from *The Sacramento Union* newspaper: "Both men have been known to have this peculiarity of taking things—not of special value—from one house—and leaving them at other houses."

He was correct. In October 1976, the EAR had even gone so far as to plant a bag of jewelry (stolen from EAR victims) in a house, then he attacked the next door neighbor and made statements to her indicating that he lived nearby. Sacramento Detective Shelby had the innocent neighbor, John Dority, put under surveillance, and that helped clear him when he was seen at home during the next EAR attack. The EAR had framed Dority with planted evidence, and it almost worked.

I had two more sets of maps for John to see, and I put them side by side. One showed the area where Donna's bike had been found, three miles from Neel Ranch, at what appeared to be a staged kidnapping scene. The other map showed an area John knew well, an irrigation ditch on Ave 256, between Visalia and Exeter. About a week after the Snelling kidnapping and homicide, a man called VPD to report finding a gun in an irrigation ditch on Ave 256. It was *not* the missing murder weapon, but it was a Taurus revolver, identified by its serial number, that had been stolen by the VR from a residence on Mountain Drive in May 1975. That prompted John's team to search the other irrigation ditches along the same road, where they found a large screwdriver and some ammunition wrapped in a clear raincoat. The gun had been located near a large fertilizer plant. John checked out those employees, and a few of them stayed on the suspect list. However, the location of the raincoat items was more of a mystery, and no suspects were developed there.

I told John I thought I knew the suspect that the VR was trying to frame with the raincoat—the same person he implicated with an invoice book found next to Donna's bike at the staged kidnapping scene. John had found the raincoat across the road from a small dead-end street called Hypericum, a name I had seen in Donna's homicide case file. One of the homes on Hypericum belonged to the parents of Oscar Clifton, and had been staked out by TCSO on the night they found Donna's bike. According to TCSO, they found the invoice book used for Clifton's repair business near the bike. I told John I believed the VR had tried to frame Clifton after the Snelling homicide, and then again after Donna's murder. The VR was hoping that Clifton would be convicted of Snelling, McGowen, Jennifer, Donna, and all of the burglaries, and… the VR would be in the clear.

I asked John how he had eliminated Clifton as the VR, and he just laughed. Clifton was 6′2″ and 150 pounds dripping wet—"*he was a beanpole.*" He also had a distinctive limp from a ruined knee, wore a metal brace, and had a thick Okie accent. The VR was more like 5′10″ and 170 pounds, with strong arms and shoulders. John said that he gave Clifton one glance, and knew that he could not have been their suspect. Obviously, when the EAR attacks started six months later, John was proven right. Why the VR would choose to frame Clifton was more of a mystery, but clearly he didn't know about the bad knee or his recent return after eight years of living out of state. It seemed like a question that couldn't be easily answered until we identified the VR.

Sgt. Vaughan and I talked about TCSO Sgt. Byrd a bit more, and I detailed the misconduct I had found, and the total and complete lack of physical evidence. There was nothing that tied Clifton to Donna or the homicide scene. She had not been kidnapped where her bike was found, so the planting of Clifton's invoice book (stolen from his unlocked truck) near the bike was just more staging. Clifton had a solid alibi, with multiple witnesses, and the state's case and timeline were physically impossible—barring time travel and cloning.

I told John that when he identified the VR as being the EAR, and gave the timeline for the suspect leaving Tulare County as the summer of 1976, Sgt. Byrd had immediately ordered the destruction of the case evidence in Donna's murder. It had only been five months since Clifton had been sent to death row. Not only was that highly illegal, it violated multiple court orders in place to preserve the evidence pending Clifton's appeal.

I had finally told John something that truly shocked him. He simply could not believe that any police officer would intentionally destroy case evidence, especially evidence that would be needed if Clifton won his appeal and a retrial was ordered. Clifton would have walked free. John and I agreed that whatever truth Sgt. Byrd was hiding had to be worth the risk of getting fired, going to jail, or letting Clifton out of prison. We came to the same conclusions—Byrd knew who really killed Donna, was covering for him, and was afraid that either Sacramento or Visalia would match their suspect to the evidence in Donna's murder.

We also agreed that we should be looking for VR suspects *in Exeter*. In 1975, the town had a population of 5,000 residents. Roughly half were men, and many were Latino. We knew we were looking for a white male, within a specific height and weight range, 20-30 years old, left-handed, with blue eyes. He was either active duty law enforcement in Tulare County, or was very close to someone who was. He seemed to want both Jennifer's and Donna's homicides investigated by TCSO, so we felt that he likely lived within the city limits of Exeter, not in TCSO jurisdiction. The man went unnoticed in solidly middle-class, professional neighborhoods, so he didn't look like an obvious creep or criminal.

John said he would contact Detective Shelby, the EAR Task Force, VPD major crimes, and the TCSO forensics officer who worked Donna's homicide. I agreed to work on a list of people of interest that fit our criteria. They had a solid suspect DNA profile, so all we needed to do was go down the list and eliminate them, one by one. It was going to be hard going without more help. The *Exeter Sun* newspaper microfilm reels had been sent for digitization, and nobody could find a copy of the local 1975 Exeter census. The phone books had to be accessed in person, during library hours. Assistance from law enforcement, with their vast resources, could really speed things up. John and I didn't think it would be easy, but we never imagined the force and effectiveness of the backlash we would face.

Chapter One Sources

1. VPD Reports 1974-1977
2. VPD Report - Gomes September 11, 1975
3. VPD Reports - Shipley & Arnold September 15, 1975
4. Visalia Times-Delta - October 21, 1975
5. VPD Report - Shipley October 24, 1975
6. VPD Report - Vaughan October 28, 1975
7. VPD Report - McGowen October 2, 1975
8. VPD Report - McGowen December 19, 1975
9. VPD Report - Hartman December 13, 1975

10. VPD Report - Vaughan December 17, 1975
11. VPD Report - Vaughan November 20, 1975
12. Visalia Times-Delta - May 18, 1977
13. Sacramento Bee - April 5, 2001
14. Visalia Times-Delta - November 26, 1974
15. Visalia Times-Delta - December 2, 1974
16. VPD Report - Vaughan October 8, 1975
17. Sacramento Bee - March 20, 1977
18. SSD EAR Report - April 2, 1977
19. Sacramento Bee - April 5, 1977
20. SSD EAR Report - May 17, 1977
21. TCSO Report - Johnson December 26, 1975
22. Sacramento Union - July 22, 1978
23. SSD EAR Reports - October 9 & 18, 1976
24. VPD Report - Vaughan September 25, 1975
25. VPD Report - McGowen September 28, 1975
26. TCSO Report - M. Richmond December 28, 1975
27. Mt. Whitney Yearbook 1975
28. Photo of ski mask at Neel Ranch

CHAPTER TWO

"It's about time you got here."

December 26, 1975, was a chilly Friday in Exeter, CA. The town woke to a freezing fog, and the day had little hope of reaching 60 degrees. The kids had the day off from school for the Christmas holiday, but most of the adults were back at their jobs. The economy in Exeter runs on the crop schedule, and it was orange picking season. The groves and packing houses were full of workers. Donna Richmond lived on the Swearingen Ranch, owned by her grandparents. Their citrus trees were some of the oldest in town.

Donna was a 14-year-old freshman at Exeter Union High School. She was active in 4-H, and played the flute, piccolo, and tenor saxophone in the school band. Donna's mother was a PE teacher in Visalia, and her dad, Don, worked as a county land assessor. Her sister had recently married, and her brother, David, was a high school junior.

Donna started her Friday by riding her bike, a root beer brown Schwinn 10 speed, to the home of her best friend, Carol. Donna arrived between 11:00-11:30 am, and stayed to have lunch—leftover turkey sandwiches, a day after Christmas tradition. The girls talked about what they had received for Christmas, and made plans for the day. Shortly after noon, Carol and Donna started the bike ride to Donna's house, about a mile and a half away. The shortest route was along the railroad tracks, which were strictly off limits. Both the railroad workers and the Exeter Police Department enforced this law, but the girls decided to take the risk, and they rode their bikes to Donna's house on the dirt path next to the tracks.

Shortly after arriving home, Donna asked her father if she and Carol could go out and ride their bikes for a few hours. They planned to stop first at the home of the Fieldings, who were out-of-town for the holiday, and had asked Donna to feed their animals. Mr. Richmond later remembered the last exchange he had with his daughter:

> I told her to be home by 3 o'clock. She walked out from the family room into the garage and then you could kind of hear them whispering a little outside, and she stuck her head back in and said, "Three o'clock's awful early." And I said, "Okay, Donna, four o'clock, but not any later than four." And I emphatically said four, and so they left in jubilation because they were granted another hour.

Donna and Carol left for the Fielding residence shortly after 1:00 pm. Donna was wearing a dark green pantsuit she got as a Christmas present. Over the suit, she wore a blue nylon jacket, and a large pink and orange scarf. She had striped knee socks, high platform sandals, a special gold and pearl heart necklace, and several leather strap bracelets. The girls' route took them two and a half miles past ranches of orange, lemon, and grapefruit groves, grapevines, and walnut trees. The fields were full of workers and trucks, racing to get the crop to the packing houses.

The next time Donna and Carol were seen was at 2:00 pm, at the home of their friend Heidi, who lived near the Fielding house on S. Belmont, just outside Exeter. Heidi hadn't been expecting the girls, and she wasn't able to join them on the bike ride. Carol and Donna only stayed for a few minutes, then headed north, back up Belmont, towards the home of another friend, Judy.

Meanwhile, 11 miles west of Exeter, Oscar Clifton had been busy making repairs on a house in Visalia. He had been hired by a local realtor, Bill Rose, to fix up an investment property on Garden Street.

Oscar was 35 years old, and had been married for 17 years. He and his wife had both come from Oklahoma with their families as part of the Dust Bowl migration to California's Central Valley farms. Oscar joined the Army as a cook when he was 17 years old, and after his honorable discharge, served another eight years in the Army Reserves. Following that, in the late 1960s, he operated his own trucking company. His trucking career was ended by an accident with a drunk driver—he suffered a severe knee injury that left him with a pronounced limp, and a custom-designed knee brace. He had won a judgment for $123,000 from the driver, and was still in the process of collecting the money.

In 1975, Oscar was self-employed as a carpenter, and painter. He had regular work from several real estate agents in the area; he fixed up houses to flip and maintained their rentals. On November 19th, he and his wife purchased some vacant land with real estate agent Bill Jordan. They planned to subdivide the property and build homes on the lots. It was right across the road from the home of Sheriff Bob Wiley. In addition to his business, Oscar had two teenage daughters and a young son. His life wasn't flashy, but it was going well.

At the Rose house, Oscar was waiting for the city building inspector, who was due at the site by 10:00 am. That morning, Oscar's wife had set out his clothes for the meeting: a plaid western shirt, dark blue double knit slacks, and the white crewneck fisherman's sweater she had given him for Christmas. Oscar's knee brace had a shoe built in, so he wore that pair, a black slip-on style. Oscar's wife and her sister decided to shop the after-Christmas sales, and stopped by to see Oscar on their way to the mall. They arrived during the building inspection, but Oscar was able to give them a quick tour, and show them the rest of the work to be done on the job.

The house didn't have a phone line hooked up yet, so after the inspection Oscar drove to Bill Rose's real estate office to give him an update. The house had been without power and gas for some time, and both men were anxious for the inspector to approve the reconnections. Although the meeting was mundane and wholly routine, an offhand comment by Rose was soon to change the entire course of Oscar's life. Bill Rose mentioned that he might bring an investor over to look at the Garden Street house at 2:00 pm that afternoon. Rose later recalled:

> We set up a tentative appointment to meet at a property where he was doing some repair work at two o'clock, but our meeting there was a very informal thing, and I really didn't need him. So, I had indicated to him that he could be there, or not be.

The tour of the property didn't involve Oscar, but Oscar indicated that he expected to be working at the house, and would see if he could learn any more about the utilities before then. It really didn't seem terribly important.

Oscar then went home for lunch in rural Visalia, on Ave 264. He called the building inspector, and learned that the gas and electricity to the Rose house would be turned on the following Monday. Oscar went across the road to the home of his brother-in-law, Avery Dula, helped him install a boat battery, and then returned to Garden Street at about 1:15 pm.

Oscar saw a concrete contractor he knew, Danny Boland, working nearby, and walked over to ask if Danny could give a bid on the walkway replacement at the Rose house. Danny noticed, and later described, Oscar wearing the same outfit his wife had laid out that morning, right down to the unique black shoes. Danny lived in Exeter, and was close friends with Donna and her family. Eventually, he would find himself caught between the truth and intense pressure to change his story.

Oscar returned to the job site to wait for Bill Rose to arrive at 2:00 pm, so he could tell him about the utilities. By about 2:15 pm, Oscar decided that Rose wasn't coming, and drove back to the real estate office. When he arrived there, he noticed that Rose's car wasn't in his designated parking spot, so Oscar drove on to the home of his wife's niece, Deborah. They had spoken at Christmas dinner about a dryer problem, and Oscar had offered to see if he could fix it.

Deborah lived in a rural area in north Visalia, opposite Sequoia Field, on a dead-end dirt road. Her father-in-law, Gene Owens, lived next door. As Oscar drove by in his white pickup, with its distinctive black and white "***F O R D***" lettering on the tailgate, Gene stopped working on his tractor and walked down his driveway to get a better look. Gene knew that his son and daughter-in-law weren't home, so he wasn't surprised to see the truck driving back by a few minutes later. Gene placed the time right about 3:00 pm.

Oscar Clifton's Truck in Impound—December 27, 1975
Photo: TCSO

There was never any debate about where Donna and Carol were at 3:00 pm—they had just arrived at the home of their friend Judy, off Belmont and Ave 277. The time that the girls arrived was set by Judy's mom, who said that she sent them to find Judy out riding her horse. Judy agreed to join Donna and Carol for a bike ride to the nearby home of Donna's boyfriend of three months, Don Lee. The girls were all freshmen at Exeter High, and Don was a junior. Although he had already turned 16, he didn't have his driver's license, only a learner's permit. In fact, he was on a practice drive with his dad when the girls arrived at his house, so they waited for him in the front yard.

What time was it when Donna, Carol, and Judy arrived at the Lee home? Nobody is exactly sure. The hours between 3:00-5:00 pm on December 26, 1975 have created a giant sinkhole that has swallowed five years of my research, and forty years of work from the other attorneys and private investigators who worked on the case. This knowledge gap didn't form because the information was unknowable, but rather from a shockingly inadequate police investigation. TCSO simply failed to build an evidence-based timeline for that two-hour period.

There was nothing more than brief statements from her friends:

> "Carol advised that she, Judy and Donna rode to Don Lee's residence leaving Judy's house at approximately 3:00 pm, arriving at Don Lee's residence at approximately 3:00-3:30 pm."

> "Contacted Judy. Carol and Donna left her residence at 3:00. Riding to Don Lee's residence on bicycles, arrived at approximately 3:30 pm."

> "Don Lee advised that Donna and friends arrived after 3:00 pm on bicycles."

These reports from Donna's friends were all taken by TCSO McKinney early the next morning, but the time of the arrival of the girls at the Lee home never got any closer than this vague half hour. The imprecision is maddening. "When" is the most fundamental question in any investigation, and the failure to determine what time the girls rode up to the Lee house, how long they waited for Don to arrive home, and when they left, turned out to be critical pieces of the puzzle:

> "Carol advised she and Judy, after talking a few minutes, no more than ten, left en route back to Judy's residence. No further contact with Donna."

> "Judy advised that Donna stated that she would have to hurry as she would be late getting back to her residence."

> "Don Lee advised that after a very short time, Judy and Carol left for their homes leaving Donna Richmond talking to him. Don Lee advised, Donna talked for a few minutes then left his residence on her bicycle for her residence at approximately 3:45 pm, advising him she would have to hurry or she would be late. Don Lee advised this was his last contact with Donna."

Jeanie Esajian, a journalist with the *Visalia Times-Delta*, learned a bit more than TCSO, by interviewing Judy's and Carol's mothers:

> Judy's mother said Carol and Judy wanted to leave, but Donna didn't. The two girls started away slowly, riding down the road and waiting for Donna for a while. Then they went home. This was sometime between 3:00 and 3:30 pm. They never saw her again. Carol and Judy rode their bikes to Judy's house, where Carol visited until returning home at about 4:45 pm. Carol's mother said Donna's mother had called her earlier to ask if she knew where the girls were, and at that time, Carol's mother said, she didn't know they had split up.

After Don arrived home with his dad, he and the three girls stood in the yard talking for a few minutes, and then Carol and Judy left. All three of the kids mentioned that Donna was worried about being late for the 4:00 pm curfew set by her dad, so it had to be at least 3:30 pm when Carol and Judy left Donna alone with Don. Donna had bought Don a "Pet Rock" for Christmas, and she wanted to give it to him. Don said that they talked for ten to fifteen minutes, and then Donna rode away on her bike, headed for home. He said that he stayed in his yard, and did not watch to see if she continued straight on Anderson Road, or turned left onto Marinette.

While Donna and her friends were talking in the Lee yard in Exeter, Oscar arrived back at the Rose house on Garden Street in Visalia. He didn't know it, but he had just missed Bill Rose and his investor's visit to the site. Later, Rose explained what happened:

Rose: We arrived at the property in the neighborhood of 2:30 pm.

Q: Was Mr. Clifton there?

A: No.

Q: Did you wait for Mr. Clifton?

A: No. We were at the property for about half an hour.

Q: After staying there for about 30 minutes, did you and this other gentleman leave?

A: Yes.

Bill Rose left Garden Street at about the same time that Gene Owens saw Oscar's truck drive by his house. Oscar's drive back to the job site was 11 miles, and would have taken no more than 20 minutes, placing him back on Garden Street around 3:15 pm. The Rose house sits very oddly on its lot *(*see diagram *below— "Exhibit W")*. In 1975, there were no neighbors across from the home's front door—excavation on a new set of apartments had just started. The houses on Garden Street faced an open intersection, so the Rose house was out of view unless the neighbors were outside in their driveway. Garden Street also dead ends right there, so there isn't much traffic.

When Oscar arrived, he backed his truck up the front walkway to the front door so he could load some grease-crusted stove parts into the bed of his truck. He was planning to give them a good soak, and clean them at home over the weekend. As he got out of his truck, Oscar's attention was drawn to two pickup trucks pulling up to one of the houses on the other side of Garden Street. The owner of the house, Frank Thomas, was standing at the end of his driveway, and Oscar clearly heard him say: "*It's about time you got here.*" Oscar put on his JC Penney Big Mac coveralls and got busy loading the stove parts into his truck, preparing the gas line for the new meter, and trying to fix the lock on the front door.

As he worked, Oscar noticed more activity across the street:

Oscar: The one pickup was red and it had a deep freeze, or an ice box of some sort in it. They moved it to a side, loaded a big long green, pea green or something, deep freeze beside of it, and then they loaded some bicycles into the other pickup.

Q: Approximately how long did you remain there at the Garden Street property, Mr. Clifton?

A: Somewhere around ten to four or maybe a little—maybe fifteen till.

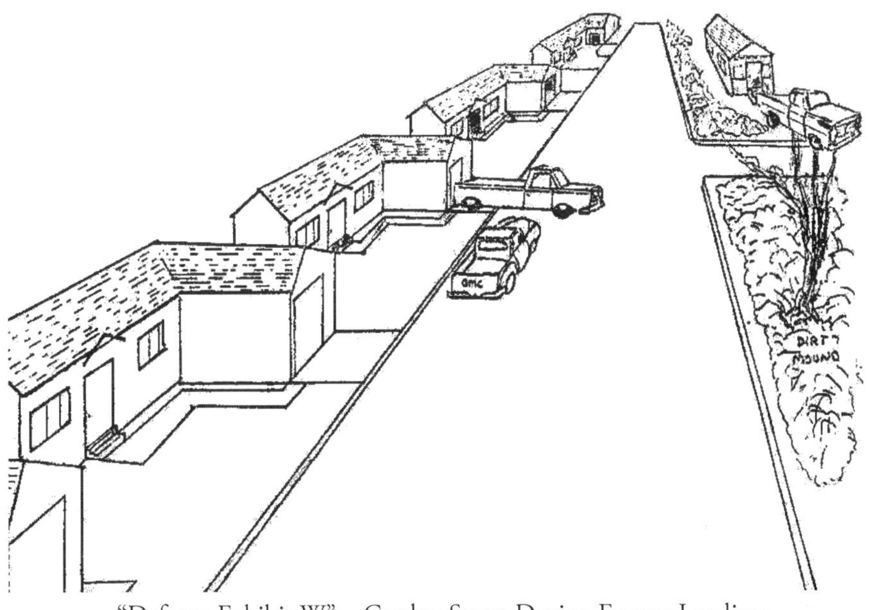

"Defense Exhibit W"—Garden Street During Freezer Loading
Image: Octagon Associates, March 1976

When he left Garden Street, Oscar went to the hardware store to get a key made, but the key guy was off until Monday, so he just got gas in his truck and drove home. He estimated that he walked into his house around 4:25 pm, after unloading his air compressor and locking it in the garage. That was confirmed by his two teenage daughters and a family friend, Rick Carter, who had been staying with the Cliftons. Oscar made some phone calls, took his knee medication, and left in the family sedan to meet his wife and son at the Dula house. He arrived there shortly before 5:00 pm. He was wearing the same clothes his wife had laid out for him that morning.

Donna's father, Don Richmond, returned home from work at 5:00 pm. He remembered it as every parent's worst nightmare:

Q: When you returned home, was Donna there?

Don Richmond: No, Sir.

Q: And were you concerned at that point?

A: Yes.

Q: All right. And what did you do?

A: Well, at that point I didn't do anything right then. My wife had made some calls to friends and church and different places and she was preparing dinner, and oftentimes the children on their way home, their grandparents live very close, and they'd stop by their grandparent's [*sic*] and we have had animal projects—they had sheep and a hog and such—that they could be right there at home and not be visible.

Q: So you say your wife was checking. Then what did you do?

A: [*My wife*] Nancy and I went to the Fieldings to see if perhaps Donna was there, and she wasn't. So we returned home and then I asked Nancy who did she call, and what kind of responses were there and she said she called Judy's family, and she had called Carol's family, and she had called down at the church that we go; especially the girls, frequently, and she had called Heidi's family. And so then, minutes kept clicking away, and I'm kind of short tempered, and I said "what exactly went on?"

Then, we got in the truck and went on out to the Don Lee family home, which is north and east [Note: *west*] of Exeter. We went one direction out there and didn't see her anywhere or her bicycle, thought perhaps she could have had a flat tire. We came back another direction and did not find her and immediately went in, and called the Exeter Hospital and they had no report of any youngsters there, so I called the Sheriff's Office. My son and a friend of his had already commenced the search in the friend's vehicle and hardly, just practically instantaneously, after I hung up from talking to the Sheriff's Office, these two boys came back to the house and said they found Donna's bicycle.

Donna's brother, David, and his friend, Jim, had found Donna's bike near their home on a dirt road used by workers tending to the orange trees and grapevines. It was a shortcut used by the kids in the area, and Donna's parents hadn't thought to check it. The night was cool and foggy, and the grove was pitch black when Donna's father arrived at the scene with the boys. The bike was off the road near some orange trees, but there was no sign of Donna. Don Richmond and the boys walked around with flashlights, calling Donna's name, but quickly decided that they needed more help, and returned to the house. TCSO McCarthy had just arrived, and was interviewing Donna's mother:

7:00 pm. Received from Nancy Richmond, mother. Missing person Donna Jo Richmond, female, white, age 14, height 5 foot, weight 86 lb, hair blonde, eyes blue, wearing dark green pants with matching jacket. Missing since Friday December 26th 1975, at 3:30 pm. Attends Exeter HS. Whereabouts unknown. R/O contacted Richmond about her missing daughter. She related that subject's bike was found 3/4 miles NW of residence. She also related that dew was on the bike, and it seemed as if the bike was there for some period of time. She related that her daughter had absolutely no reason to run away, and that she had left the residence at approximately 3:30 when her girlfriends last saw her. R/O believes foul play is involved, and that subject may have been picked up by unknown suspect(s).

Exeter PD Sgt. Gomez heard the radio call, and arrived shortly after TCSO McCarthy. He agreed to call in every Exeter PD officer

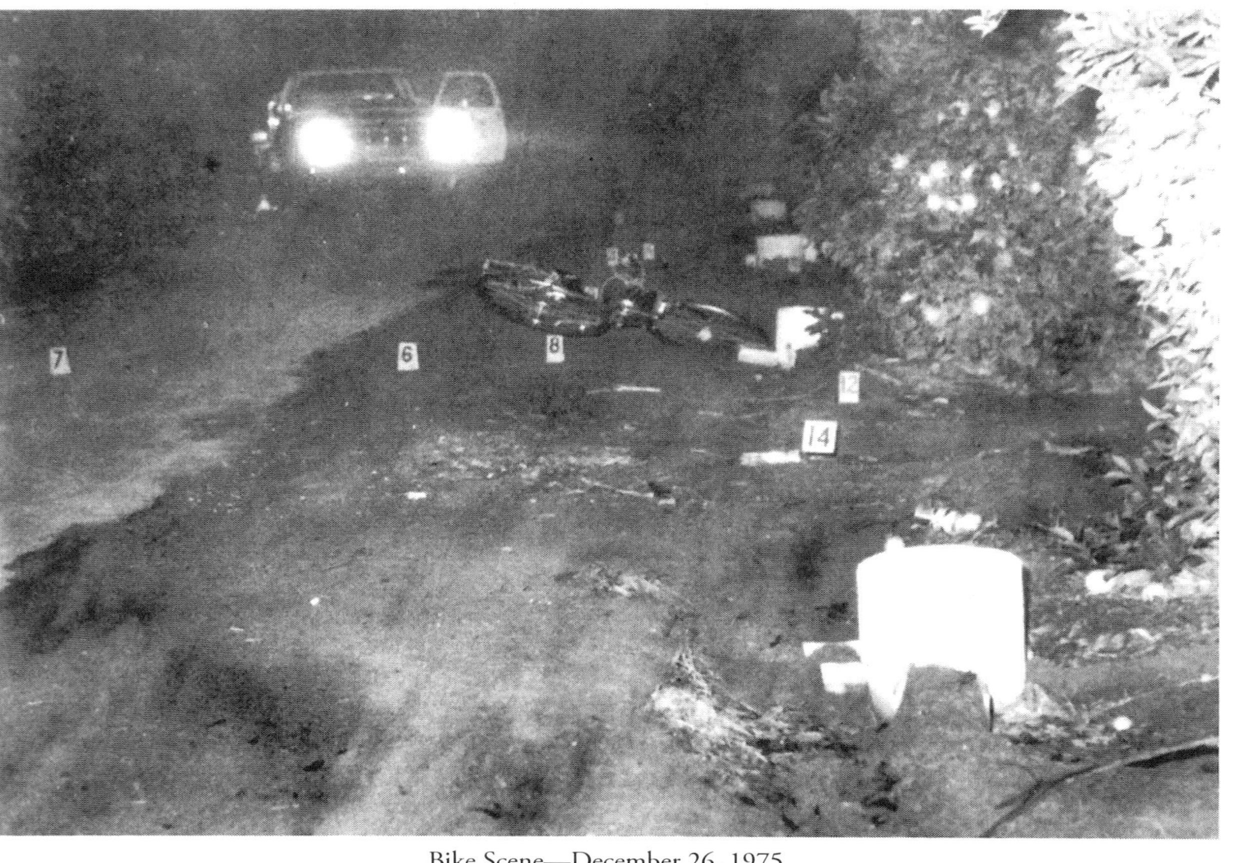

Bike Scene—December 26, 1975
Photo: TCSO

to search within the city limits. It was now 7:15 pm. Donna had not been seen for three and a half hours. Meanwhile, Oscar, his wife, and his in-laws were just arriving at Lyons Restaurant in Visalia for dinner.

Chapter Two Sources

1. **Visalia Times-Delta - December 29, 1975**
2. **Testimony of Don Richmond, June 25 1976**
3. **TCSO Report - McKinney December 28, 1975**
4. **Testimony of Bill Rose, June 26, 1976**
5. **Stmt taken by PI Pettyjohn - Avery Dula January 2, 1976**
6. **Stmt taken by PI Pettyjohn - Danny Boland December 30, 1975**
7. **Stmt taken by PI Pettyjohn - Danny Boland March 24, 1976**
8. **Stmt taken by PI Pettyjohn - Gene Owens December 30, 1975**
9. **Testimony of Don Lee, June 26, 1976**
10. **Testimony of Bill Rose, June 28, 1976**
11. **Diagram of Garden Street, Visalia**
12. **Testimony of Clifton, July 6, 1976**
13. **Donahue Intake Notes**
14. **Testimony of Don Richmond, June 26, 1976**
15. **TCSO Report - McCarthy December 26, 1975**
16. **Photo of Bike Scene off List**
17. **Photos of Clifton Truck in Impound**
18. **Area Maps**

CHAPTER THREE

"They found her shoe."

After TCSO McCarthy reported what had happened, there was a frenzy of activity. Lt. Peabody arrived at the Richmond house, and sent McCarthy back to the bike to secure the scene. He gathered more information from the Richmonds, and passed it along to the Sheriff and Captain Ollie Farris. McCarthy also wrote in his report that Capt. Farris requested that he "notify Sgt. Byrd of the situation, and have him respond." By 9:00 pm, Byrd was at the scene and quickly took lead of the investigation. At this time, dozens of citizens had already arrived to help search for Donna.

The involvement of Lt. Farris and Sgt. Byrd was inherently bad news for Oscar Clifton. Their history was filled with personal disputes over union organizing at the fruit packing houses, and an attempted rape case in 1965 that both Oscar and the victim claimed never happened—at least not the way Byrd wrote in the typed statement that he forced her to sign. Farris and Byrd made so many threats to "get" Oscar and his family that they left California for eight years, and had only moved back to Visalia in early 1975. Sgt. Byrd had known Donna her entire life, and he was an extremely close family friend. He lacked the objectivity, education, skills, temperament, honesty, experience, and training necessary to lead the investigation into Donna's disappearance.

The first mention of an invoice book appeared in Sgt. Byrd's report from the bike scene, after he arrived at about 8:45 pm. He stated that near Donna's bike, he found an invoice book with the name "A. Clifton" and a small notepad. There was no mention of the items in the initial reports from the Richmonds—the first people on the scene. Like every one of the prior attorneys who have examined the evidence, I began with the assumption that the invoice book was found exactly as Byrd described it in his report. However, as the years of work on the case went by, it became crystal clear that Byrd could never be a reliable source of information.

The first officers on the scene were McCarthy, McDonald, Peabody, Barnes, and Farris. McCarthy and Peabody did not mention the invoice book in their reports, and there are no reports from McDonald, Barnes, or Farris. None of those TCSO members were called to testify at trial, which is highly suspicious. Deputy Hart was mentioned tangentially in other reports, but we have no details from him. TCSO Deputy Holguin and Detective Melton Richmond arrived later, and prepared their own reports, but did not mention seeing the invoice book, and did not testify about the bike scene. The only source for the information that the invoice book was at the scene is Sgt. Bob Byrd—if you take him at his word.

By 9:25 pm, TCSO forensics technician Brian Johnson arrived. As later reports and testimony would show, Sgt. Byrd *personally* directed the evidence documentation and collection around Donna's bike. Johnson photographed the invoice book and a small jotter notepad with the bike, as Byrd claimed they were found. Johnson also photographed and collected nearby bottles and cans, and specific tire tracks, pointed out by Sgt. Byrd. There were two sets of footprints near the bike, but Johnson was directed not to photograph them, nor most of the nearby tire tracks. Both confirmed this fact in their own testimony.

After photographing the invoice book and notepad, Johnson placed them in a paper evidence bag and gave them to another deputy for immediate transport to the crime lab in Visalia for fingerprinting. For some reason, Johnson did not document the notepad in his final written report:

A photograph was also taken of a receipt book lying near the bike on the east side. The name A. Clifton was observed in the book. The book retained by reporting officer and sealed in the evidence bag at 10:00 pm, 12-26-75. The receipt book was turned over to Dep. Hart for transport back to the crime lab.

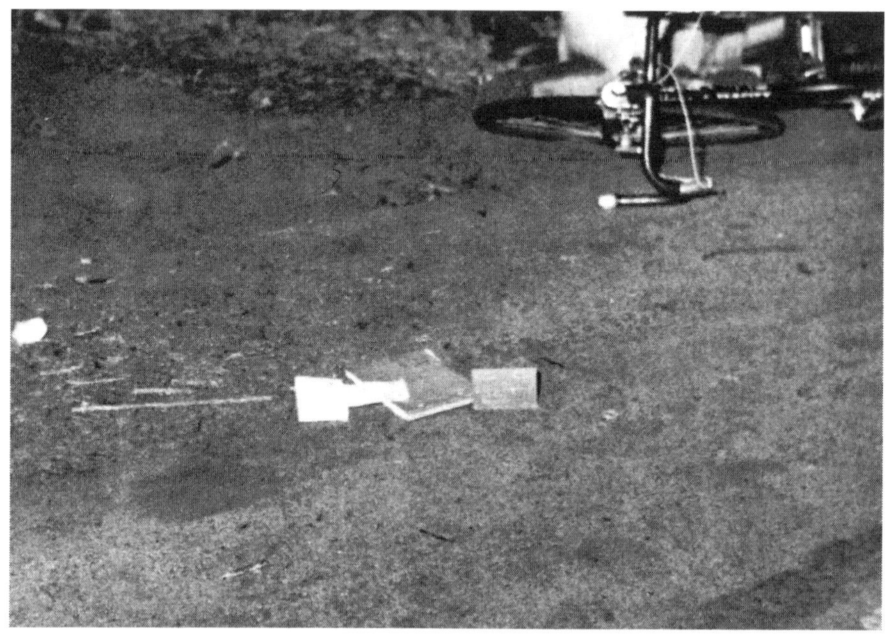

Donna's Bike With Invoice Book and Notepad—December 26, 1975
Photo: TCSO Johnson

At 10:00 pm, TCSO Sgt. Hensley received the bag at the crime lab, and removed the items for fingerprinting. If Hensley had not documented that examination in his report, the notepad would have completely disappeared from the case after it was photographed by the bike. By January 1976, the notepad had become a problem that both TCSO and the Tulare DA, Jay Powell, were desperately trying to hide:

Reporting officer was instructed by Lt. Peabody to come to headquarters to process some physical evidence on this case. The items were one receipt book bearing some used and some unused pages, one small notebook bearing some used and some

> unused pages, one piece of carbon paper. Reporting officer processed the items for latent prints using the Chemprint brand of ninhydrin spray. Usable latent prints were developed on the used pages of the receipt book.

In his report, Sgt. Byrd claimed that he immediately recognized "A. Clifton," with a Visalia PO Box written in the invoice book, as Oscar Clifton, a man he had known ten years earlier living in Farmersville. This is not believable on its face, and reading through the other TCSO reports from that night solidified that some (or *all…*) of Byrd's story was a lie. TCSO Holguin reported that they identified Oscar by contacting one of the realtors named on an invoice in the book, but TCSO Chamberlain's report stated that Byrd gave him Oscar's name as soon as he arrived at the bike scene, and Byrd sent him to TCSO headquarters in Visalia to pick up Oscar's 1965 booking sheet.

Sgt. Byrd's own reports told multiple different stories about how he found Oscar's home address, making it appear as if it were a big mystery that needed to be solved. The problem with lying about one thing is that it makes it impossible to trust anything else the person says. It is clear from the record that Sgt. Byrd immediately associated Oscar with the invoice book, and simply got his address by calling directory assistance. So why all the lies and pretending?

At about 7:00 pm, Oscar, his wife, and the Dulas left their two young sons at the Clifton house with the three teenagers, and drove into Visalia for dinner. The five kids were alone watching TV, and both Oscar's truck and Carter's truck were parked out near the garage, on the edge of the dark, foggy fields. After dinner, the adults went to the mall to look at a few sale items, then returned home around 9:30 pm. The family went to bed early. Sleeping in the house were Oscar, his wife, his 15 and 13 year old daughters, his 8 year old son, and their family friend, 18 year old Rick Carter. Oscar hadn't taken a shower after work, washed any clothes, or his truck. According to the entire extended family, it had been a completely normal, routine—even boring day.

At 1:15 am Saturday, December 27, 1975, the entire Clifton house was awakened by a crowd of TCSO deputies coming through the front door yelling. Oscar's daughter Annette still has a very specific memory of that night:

> I was 15 years old. What I recall when they walked into our house, and I mean they filled our living room—there was a lot of them. They yanked him around, and when they were finished putting the handcuffs on, I heard a man, who was later associated with Bob Byrd, say: "We didn't get you last time, and we're gonna get you this time," and I'd had no clue what it meant.

Oscar and his wife were livid. They immediately accused Lt. Farris of continuing the unwarranted harassment that had caused them to move away almost a decade earlier. Neither of the Cliftons was worried, just angry. They firmly believed that Byrd and Farris were simply attempting to terrorize them as part of their long-running revenge for past disputes. As he was arrested, Oscar stated that he would not speak to TCSO about anything, and they could talk to his attorney. He got dressed in his blue slacks and western shirt he had worn the prior day, a coat, and his knee brace with the integrated black shoes. He also took his reading glasses from the nightstand. His white sweater and coveralls were taken into evidence from his bedroom later that day.

At the jail, TCSO Johnson collected Oscar's clothing, and hair and blood samples. Oscar refused to sign the Miranda waiver, and was placed in a holding cell. After some time, Sgt. Byrd removed Oscar from the cell, and took him to an interrogation room. Although Oscar clearly saw the interview tape running, Byrd later refused to produce it, and claimed that it was turned off. At some point, Oscar gave a brief outline of his afternoon, but the only record of his answers ended up being contradictory statements from the different TCSO deputies present.

Everyone agreed that Oscar recounted his time on Garden Street, with a trip to the Roberts home between 2:15-3:15. The only dispute centered around the exact words heard. TCSO King said that Oscar stated "***at*** Bill Rose's, or ***with*** Bill Rose," Holguin said "***with*** Bill Rose, or ***gone by*** Bill Rose's house." Sgt. Byrd claimed that Oscar said that he was with Rose, and he wasn't, so that proved he lied about his alibi, and had something to hide.

There are extremely good reasons why today, in 2021, police may not ask a suspect any questions if they have invoked their right to counsel. If they do so, all answers are inadmissible in court, including any evidence the police obtained based upon those answers. Additionally, if a Miranda waiver is signed, *all questioning* must be recorded. Under no circumstance may the suspect's answers be admitted to court based on the memory and hearsay testimony of the police. In the end, it didn't matter that King and Holguin told the truth—the only narrative that survived was Byrd's statement that Oscar "lied" about his alibi.

TCSO also arrested Rick Carter, who had been sleeping in the living room. Sgt. Byrd took him out to his patrol car, and began questioning Carter about his activities on Friday and document his contact with Oscar over the entire whole day. Carter had started living with the Cliftons about six months earlier. He'd previously been involved in a single car drunk driving accident, and that had led to criminal charges and a serious dispute with his stepmother. Since Carter had full access to Oscar's invoice book, he was a viable suspect. Carter could not read—at all, and had severe learning disabilities. He had no parent or attorney with him, and readily answered TCSO's questions in the police car, and again at the station, after waiving his Miranda rights.

Carter's story was pretty simple. In the morning, he did some work for his dad at his store in Woodlake, went back to the Clifton house for lunch, then went and raked leaves for a member of the Dula family for a couple of hours. He was at the Clifton home with Oscar's daughters when he saw Oscar enter the driveway around 4:15 pm, and then Oscar went into the house shortly after. Carter said he didn't notice anything unusual about Oscar or his clothing, and didn't talk to him other than a basic greeting. TCSO had Carter sign his statement and take a polygraph examination administered by Gary Hood. Hood was a Porterville firefighter, but he had received extensive training and certification as an examiner, and was the only polygraph expert in the county. Hood found Carter to be truthful, and TCSO released him from custody on the morning of Saturday, the 27th.

One thing that has taken me years to understand is just how unconcerned Oscar was when he was also released from custody that Saturday morning. He had moved out of the state for a decade for no reason other than to escape the constant threats and harassment led by Sgt. Byrd and Lt. Farris. Apparently, Oscar truly thought that they were just angry that he had dared to move back into their jurisdiction. He believed that they were trying to scare him. Oscar later explained that Saturday morning in a letter to his attorney:

> I only wish I had gone and talked to them [potential alibi witnesses] the four hours I was out. But I just believed the girl had run off, and they would find her at someone's house. I just went to sleep, but I should have used those few hours for my life.

Oscar didn't know Donna or the Richmond family, and he assumed that she had run away from home, and that Byrd had taken the invoice book from Oscar's unlocked truck and lied when he said he found it by Donna's bike. If you knew you hadn't been to Exeter or kidnapped a girl, you would know that there was no way they could prove a case against you, *right?*

At 7:50 am, TCSO Johnson was back at the bike scene, where he noted in his report that he collected soil samples from under a couple of the orange trees. Although the report is dated December 26th, it covers police activities through the 31st, so it was actually prepared in January, then backdated. There are a few things that the report left out; I assume intentionally. Johnson's twenty-seven mile round trip to the bike scene came between collecting evidence from Oscar at the jail and processing his truck at the impound yard. It appears that the only purpose was to get soil and leaves from the orange trees. The leaves were logged into evidence but not included in the report that went to the defense, presumably at Sgt. Byrd's direction. I had to question this: *Why didn't Byrd want the defense to know about the notepad and the leaves?*

At 9:00 am, Johnson joined TCSO Vern Hensley at Jackson's Towing in Visalia, where Oscar's truck was parked in the impound yard. They photographed the truck—inside and out, processed it for fingerprints, and collected items of evidence. Their main goal was to try to connect the truck to Donna or the grove where her bike was found. That meant trying to find Donna's fingerprints, hair, or blood, or some soil or tire evidence. They collected good comparable fingerprints on the outside of the passenger door and its wing window, and on the glovebox door. They found no blood or hairs, but they swept the truck floor and underside for further examination at the crime lab, along with taking inked impressions of the tires. Hensley said that he found a leaf stuck in the side mirror of the truck, and right there I got suspicious. *They collected dirt and a leaf from the truck?* That happened right after Johnson made a strange, unscheduled drive all the way back out to Exeter for soil and leaves, and then quickly returned to Visalia? *Hmm...*

A closer look through the entire collection of TCSO reports tells a complicated story about the search of Oscar's truck. Hensley's and Johnson's work was being directed, at the yard, by Sgt. Byrd *and...* the Tulare DA Jay Powell. This is one of many facts of the case that only sound alarming in retrospect. What is wrong with the lead investigator and prosecutor making sure that evidence searches are executed properly, and will stand up in court? Absolutely nothing—until a critical piece of physical evidence disappears, and the DA lies about ever seeing it.

As Visalia residents awoke on Saturday morning, they stepped out on to their porches to a front page news story from *Visalia Times-Delta* staff writer Miles Shuper, who was covering the search for Donna:

> When she failed to arrive at home, her parents began a search around the residence. The bicycle was found in an orange grove along with a shoe. Officers said they are unsure if the shoe belongs to the missing girl.
>
> "I don't want to talk about it," Mrs. Richmond said in a telephone conversation. "Somebody's got her. ***They found her shoe.*** They've [*sheriff's deputies*] been here all night. I just don't want to talk about it." [*emphasis added*]

The information had been rushed to press right at the 2:00 am deadline, with no time to include a photo of Donna, a description of her clothing, or the last place she had been seen. An arrest was mentioned, but no suspects were named. Similar stories ran on Sunday and Monday in other newspapers:

> "When she failed to arrive at the family home north of Exeter, a brother set out along the route she normally took to go home. He spotted her bicycle, according to the sheriffs [*sic*] office, in a grove of trees. Nearby were a shoe and a feminine undergarment." [*Fresno Bee*]
>
> "Approximately 150 persons, including about 15 Tuleareans, joined the search for the girl after her brother found the girl's bicycle and some of her clothes in a grove of trees. … Nancy Richmond, who telephoned the sheriff's office at 7:15 p.m. Friday, reporting that her missing daughter's bicycle and some clothing was found after a search by family and friends." [*Tulare Advance Register*]
>
> "The girl was declared missing Friday afternoon after one of her shoes and her underwear were found lying near her bicycle on a pathway that she normally took to get from her rural home in Exeter." [*Long Beach Press-Register*]
>
> "The family began searching about 4 pm Friday. Her bicycle and some clothing were located, and sheriff's officers were called." [*Porterville Recorder*]

> "The tragic course of events began Friday afternoon when Donna failed to come home at the time agreed upon with her mother.
>
> "Knowing Donna to be a responsible girl, the mother became concerned and evoked a search by authorities who found Donna's bicycle and a shoe in the grove near her rural home." [*Exeter Sun*]

There is a *high degree* of specificity in those stories—Donna's shoe and panties/pad were found in the grove with her bike on the night of the 26th. The first of those stories turned out to be critical evidence in the case. Miles Shuper's news story cited both "officers" and Donna's mother as saying that Donna's shoe had been found ***prior*** to the Times-Delta's 2:00 am press time. Miles still has a vivid memory of that first night, and the certain horror told by the finding of Donna's clothing—there was no possibility that she was a runaway; something terrible had happened. The reporters typically pulled the information directly from the "hot sheet" posted on a clipboard at the Sheriff's station, and then followed up with Mrs. Richmond to confirm the details.

Just after the newspapers were delivered on Saturday morning, someone took Donna's shoe, and underwear, and planted them next to the road along the route between the Clifton house and the grove where Donna's bike was found. Presumably the items were in TCSO custody, and the person who planted them worked for the Sheriff's Office. There is no doubt that it happened, and evidence points to the involvement of TCSO Brian Johnson and Mike King, but clearly they would have been acting on the direct order of Sgt. Byrd, Lt. Farris, Lt. Barnes, Sheriff Wiley, and/or Tulare DA Jay Powell. A report from TCSO Logan, signed by David Richmond, Jim Dyatt, and Jere Runciman, tells the rest of the story:

12-27-75, 09:40 Hrs. "We were traveling eastbound on Ave 264 approximately 1/2 mile west of Rd 176 when we spotted a sandal type shoe near the ditch on the south side of the roadway. Dave, victim's brother, tentatively identified the shoe as belonging to his sister Donna Richmond."

Did a member of TCSO, present at the Richmond house that morning, direct the boys to a location where they would find the shoe that had just been planted on Ave 264? Was it just dumb luck, or maybe a coincidence? The fact is, after leaving the Richmond house, the boys found their way to Donna's shoe—the same shoe that the *Visalia Times-Delta* had already reported being found in the orange grove with Donna's bike the night before. When Miles Shuper heard the news, he assumed that the boys had found Donna's other shoe the following day, and didn't give it another thought. Why would he?

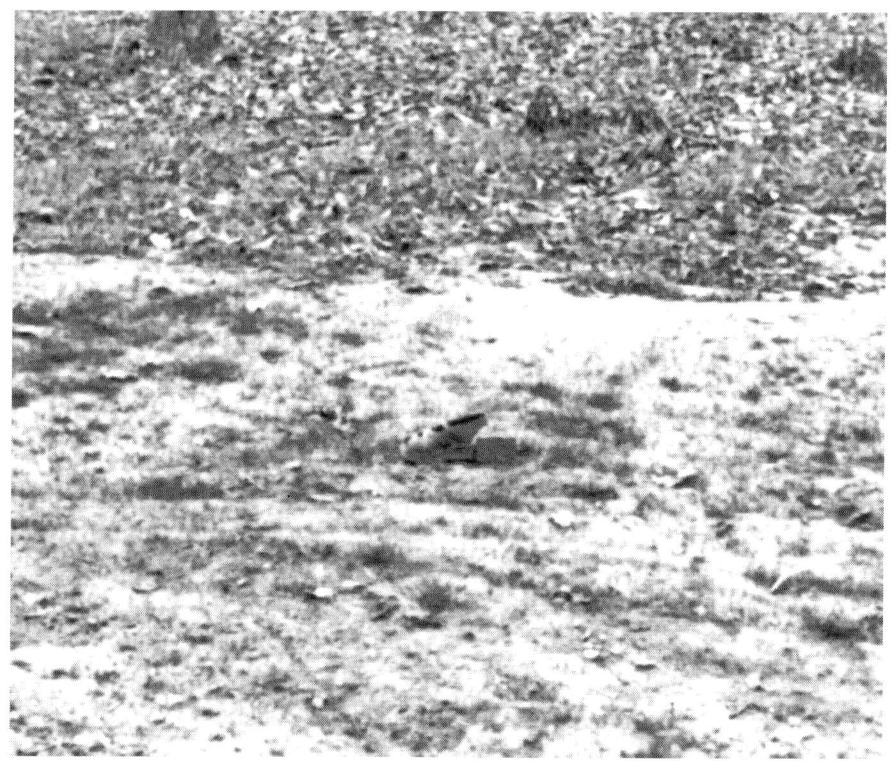

Donna's Shoe Photographed on Ave 264—December 27, 1975
Photo: TCSO

At 10:10am, a call came over the radio saying that Donna's underwear and sanitary belt had been found in a nearby irrigation ditch on Road 176. These were the same undergarments/underwear/clothing that multiple newspapers reported were found with the shoe, in the grove with Donna's bike, on Friday night. The story about exactly who supposedly found the underwear has always been murky and shifting. In the end, TCSO King testified that he found the items while driving along a siding road, but his contemporaneous report made no mention of Road 176, the ditch, or finding any items of clothing. TCSO clearly planted the underwear in a location between the bike scene and the Clifton house. This may have made some sense on Saturday morning, but that was short-lived.

Within less than a day, Sgt. Bob Byrd and other TCSO deputies had committed multiple felonies in violation of the 1975 California Penal Code, including filing false police reports (§ 115 and § 134), perjury in the search warrant affidavit (§ 118), filing backdated police reports (§ 132), planting false evidence (§ 134), concealing and destroying evidence (§ 135), and criminal conspiracy to falsely and maliciously cause another to be charged or arrested for a crime (§ 182.2)—as well as several misdemeanors, including making arrests without lawful authority (§ 146), retaking goods from the custody of an officer (§ 102), maliciously procuring a search/arrest warrant (§ 170), and deceiving witnesses (§ 133).

Although it's impossible to know exactly who would be implicated if an evidentiary hearing were held today, the planted evidence was in the custody of Brian Johnson and Vern Hensley. Warren Logan and Mike King testified at trial that they found the shoe and underwear after it was moved, and that other deputies were aware of the fraud—but said nothing. Byrd ordered the creation of the backdated, false TCSO reports, and was clearly involved in framing Oscar. Some of these men should have gone to prison and could still be charged with felony perjury today. From the morning of December 27th forward, there was no way for TCSO to turn back. Someone was going to prison, and they had to make sure it was Oscar, not the deputies.

The most shocking thing about the fact that TCSO planted evidence in an attempt to implicate Oscar is that nobody seems even remotely surprised. Lying, falsifying evidence, and tainting witnesses were literally considered business as usual for TCSO and the Tulare DA's office in 1975. The stories are endless, and well documented. Unfortunately, this time their misconduct was about to help a brutal killer escape.

Chapter Three Sources

1. TCSO Report - Peabody December 30, 1975
2. TCSO Report - Byrd December 29, 1975
3. TCSO Report - Holguin December 28, 1975
4. TCSO Report - Richmond December 28, 1975
5. TCSO Report - Johnson December 26, 1975
6. TCSO Report - Hensley January 2, 1976
8. TCSO Report - Chamberlain December 27, 1976
9. ABC10's "Framed by the Golden State Killer?" Pt. 2 @ 1:20
10. Transcript of Rick Carter's First Statement - December 27, 1975
11. PI Pettyjohn's Report, January 8, 1976
12. Oscar to Donahue Correspondence
13. Visalia Times-Delta - December 27, 1975
14. VisaliaTimes-Delta - Certification of Publication Times - Ron Goble
15. Fresno Bee - December 28, 1975
16. Tulare Advance-Register - December 29, 1975
17. Long Beach Press-Register - December 29, 1975
18. Porterville Recorder - December 30, 1975
19. Exeter Sun - December 31, 1975
20. TCSO Report - Logan December 27, 1975

CHAPTER FOUR

"4:15… I mean 4:40-4:45."

Jeanie Esajian, a twenty-five year-old reporter for the *Visalia Times-Delta*, arrived at Donna's house near the bike scene just before noon on Saturday the 27th. She had her camera and notepad. She was hoping to get some news on the search, and more details about the suspect arrested earlier that morning. Donna's house was nestled in among her grandparents' orange trees, and the area was chaotic with a mix of workers picking oranges and TCSO deputies coming and going from the makeshift search command center.

Ms. Esajian noticed Sheriff Bob Wiley standing at the edge of the field, talking to a family of workers. She took a photo of him showing a picture to 20-year-old Gloria Mascorro and her parents, while Gloria's little sister played at their feet. A short while later, Ms. Esajian was told that Gloria had informed TCSO that she had seen Oscar Clifton in the grove next to Donna's house while she had been picking oranges the day before. At about 2:30 pm, Gloria returned to the field, and Ms. Esajian approached her for an interview. Ms. Esajian recalled: "I asked her if the man she saw was Oscar Clifton, and she said, 'I think it was him. He looked just like the picture.' I then asked her if they showed her a picture of him to which she replied, 'Yes.'"

On Monday, December 29th, Ms. Esajian's photo was on the front page of the *Times-Delta* with the caption: "*Tulare County Sheriff Bob Wiley shows a photograph of Oscar A. Clifton, suspect in the kidnap-slaying, to Gloria Mascorro of Tulare, a field worker, near the Richmond home Saturday.*"

Investigation Nets Suspect In Exeter Slaying Times-Delta Photos by Jeanie Esajian

Tulare County Sheriff Bob Wiley shows a photograph of Oscar A. Clifton, suspect in the kidnap-slaying, to Gloria Mascarro of Tulare, a field worker, near the Richmond home Saturday afternoon.

"Defense Exhibit U"
Photo: Jeanie Esajian

I've stared at that photo and caption a hundred different times, and it is always surreal. I've never encountered another case where you can actually see the moment that law enforcement tainted an eyewitness identification. It should be in police investigation manuals as the example of what should never, ever happen. DNA testing has given us a lot of insight into the causes of wrongful convictions, and over seventy percent of those cases involve an eyewitness who identified the incorrect suspect. Those aren't witnesses who lied or did anything intentionally dishonest. In almost every instance, a police officer or prosecutor directed or encouraged the witness to identify a particular suspect.

Today, in 2022, there is a very specific procedure that must be followed when showing photographs to witnesses. The officer conducting a suspect identification with a witness cannot know which person is the suspect, or be familiar with the other subjects in the lineup. If the officer doesn't know who the witness is "supposed" to pick, they can't intentionally or accidentally signal that to the witness with verbal prompts or looks. Witnesses go into identifications believing that the guilty person will be presented to them, and they want to be helpful by picking the right one. It's easy to feel approval or disapproval from the officers and be unduly influenced.

Obviously, this process is a million miles away from the county sheriff coming to your workplace, showing you a man's mugshot, saying he's been arrested for kidnapping your employer's granddaughter, and asking if you saw him the previous afternoon.

At this point on December 27, 1975, events get murky. TCSO Johnson's and Sgt. Byrd's reports tell two very different versions of their activities between 12:30-2:00 pm on that Saturday.

According to Johnson, he was working with TCSO Byrd, Holguin, and Hensley on Road 176, where he was directed to collect the underwear and sanitary belt into evidence. His report states that at 1:50 pm he left Hensley at the scene taking photographs, and he:

> Accompanied Sgt. Byrd and Det. Holguin to victim's residence where Mrs. Richmond was shown the 2 items collected from the ditch. She stated she was as positive as she could be that the items collected were her daughters. She also showed R/O similar pairs of feminine panties which belong to her daughter.
>
> Received 1 platform shoe tan in color from Sgt. Byrd.

However, looking at the reports from both Byrd and Holguin, there is no mention of Mrs. Richmond. Instead, Byrd's report states that at 12:35 pm he and Holguin interviewed Gloria Mascorro, and she gave a statement placing Oscar in the grove next to the Richmond house at 3:30 pm the day before. I believe that Byrd and Holguin were on Road 176 at 12:30, as Johnson stated, and that Byrd and Holquin's reports were created later, to take Sheriff Wiley out of the story of how Gloria came to identify Oscar.

At some point, TCSO Holguin hand-wrote a statement, and Gloria Mascorro signed it. The statement said that Gloria was working near the corner of List and Spruce just before 3:30 pm, and saw a man in a white pickup pass her going west on List. Then about five minutes later it passed again going east, stopped at the corner, and turned left, going north on Spruce. Gloria then returned to her tree, and encountered the same man masturbating while looking at her. She said she ran and told her father, who tried to chase the man's truck on Spruce, but failed to catch it. Holguin's statement described the man as 5' 10" to 6' with blond hair, a white turtleneck sweater, light gray pants, and black framed glasses. The truck was a plain white pickup, of *unknown make and model.*

Gloria did not write anything in her own words, or sit for a taped interview. Holguin prepared the statement to match Oscar's activities as much as possible based on the information they had at the time, and that occurred after Sheriff Wiley had already been photographed showing Oscar's booking photo to Gloria. Reading Sgt. Byrd's report, it's clear that he was creating a story to counter Ms. Esajian's photo:

> She [Gloria] was advised that there would possibly be a line-up for possible identification as the description was similar to the one of the suspect we had in custody on the 207 [P.C. §207—kidnapping].

Without a recording of the interview, it's impossible to guess how much of the story was made up by Sgt. Byrd, and how much

Gloria was either enticed or threatened into making the words her own. Knowing Byrd's interrogation techniques, and hearing from other witnesses he pressured, my guess is that it was a combination of both. Gloria was likely told that she had to help make sure the bad guy didn't get away and hurt another girl, and that if she didn't help, she and her entire family might not be able to keep their jobs with Donna's grandparents.

There is one point of agreement among the TCSO reports: At 2:00 pm the deputies started to receive radio calls to rush to the grove two miles directly north of the Richmond house on Spruce. Neel Ranch is fifty-five acres of orange trees that sits between the Friant-Kern Canal to the west and Marinette Avenue to the south. It is just northeast of the Exeter city limits, which puts it under the jurisdiction of the Sheriff, not Exeter PD. The owner of the ranch was Hank Neel, a citrus grower from Ventura who had purchased the property in 1964. The Neels had a manager to run the property during the work day, but there was no home or family living there.

Jesus Renteria Lara worked on Neel Ranch, and he started that Saturday morning driving a spray rig. The tank was filled with Gibberellin and 2,4-D at the central pump house, and sprayed onto the trees on both sides of the narrow rows as the rig drove by. Those trees had fruit that had not yet been picked, and this combination spray was applied to give the oranges more time to ripen, instead of just falling off the trees. Jesus had finished five tanks by the time he took his lunch break. It was 1:30 pm when he refilled and started on row #17; he was five trees from the end of the row when he found Donna:

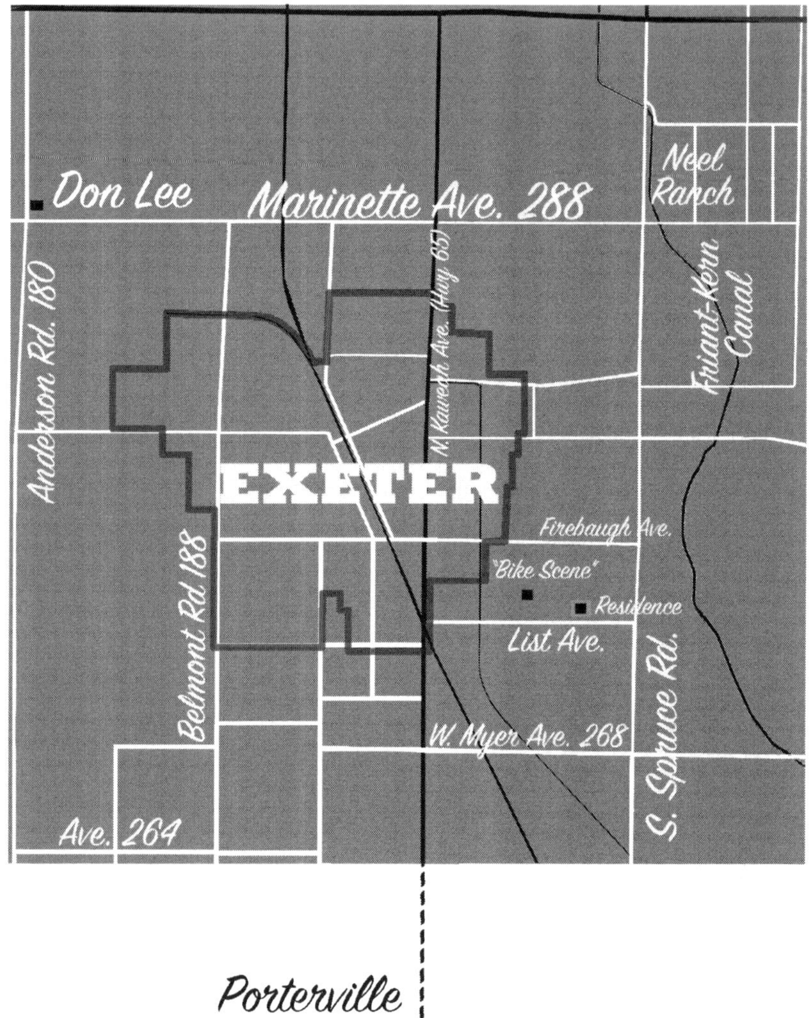
Visalia
Woodlake
Don Lee
Marinette Ave. 288
Neel Ranch
Anderson Rd. 180
N. Kaweah Ave. (Hwy 65)
Friant-Kern Canal
EXETER
Firebaugh Ave.
"Bike Scene"
Residence
List Ave.
Belmont Rd 188
W. Myer Ave. 268
S. Spruce Rd.
Ave. 264
Porterville

Renteria-Lara: I was spraying when I came next to her. I turned to the side and I saw her there laying a little bit under the trees.

Q: Did you get off your spray rig?

A: No. I did not get off.

Q: What did you do?

A: I continued spraying to finish the material that I had in the tank, and then I made a turn to come back and see if it was true what I had seen and then I went on ahead to notify… the fellow that acts as a foreman there… neither of us went in. We stayed on the edge of the field.

Q: When you drove your spray rig by and you first observed the little girl, how close to her were you at that time?

A: I passed right next to her. Actually, the tires almost touched her… I didn't stop because I felt some horror, some fear to see a dead body there.

Homicide Scene, Neel Ranch—December 27, 1975
Photo: TCSO

Just like the bike scene the night before, Neel Ranch quickly dissolved into barely controlled chaos. Forensic deputies Hensley and Johnson soon arrived and started documenting the scene with photos and collecting evidence.

The homicide scene photos are indescribably horrible and sad. My conscious mind tells me that Donna was killed by a human, but the only thing that makes sense to my eyes is that it was an animal, monster, or demon. I know that the man who killed her left Neel Ranch and walked around looking like a normal person, but he was the boogeyman wearing a human face. The cruelty is unbearable, and I just cannot imagine such evil living casually among us.

The complete investigation into the homicide scene at Neel Ranch was documented by TCSO Johnson:

> 2:35 pm: Assisted in taking scene photos, collecting evidence and photographing foot and tire track. Evidence collected included soil samples, possible blood samples, leaf samples, and pieces of victim's clothing. Took measurements of crime scene.
>
> After completing scene walked south and located a multi-colored ski cap "with possible hair" adhering to it. This was photographed and collected by R/O. Completed 5:30 pm, 12-27-75.

Sunset was at 4:49 pm that night. It was fully dark by the time Johnson left Neel Ranch. TCSO did not hold the scene for daylight, or to wait for assistance from the California Department of Justice investigators and forensics teams in Fresno—they never called them. DOJ would have taken plaster casts of the tires and footprints, and conclusively determined which ones belonged to the killer versus grove workers and law enforcement. Their investigators would have carefully diagrammed the body area and learned the exact sequence of events. Was Donna killed there or someplace else? How many people

Multi-Colored Ski Mask, Neel Ranch—December 27, 1975
Photo: TCSO

were involved? DOJ divers could have been sent in to search the canal for the murder weapon or other evidence. There could have been a complete search of the grove and complete canvass of the workers present on Neel Ranch on the 26th. None of that happened.

The handling of Donna's body was even worse. Her uncle was allowed into the crime scene to identify her, and he requested that the funeral home be allowed to take her body rather than the coroner. Shockingly, Sgt. Byrd agreed, and two men from the funeral home arrived, collected Donna's body, and went to the hospital for X-rays to be taken. There was no documentation of the workers' names, and no record of anyone from TCSO traveling with her body and maintaining chain of custody. Because of this, no evidence collected at the funeral home or at autopsy should have been admissible at trial. None of it implicated Oscar Clifton, but the lax handling raises unanswerable questions about most of the forensic evidence in the case.

TCSO Johnson drove directly from Neel Ranch to the funeral home, where Donna's body had already arrived. He photographed her on the autopsy table as he collected every item of her clothing and jewelry into evidence, including the shoe and panties he already had in his custody. The only clothing items not documented at this point, and presumably collected at the funeral home, were Donna's pants and second shoe. Johnson also photographed the autopsy and took custody of the biological samples, which he drove to the forensics lab in Visalia and secured for the night.

At autopsy, Dr. Miller documented 17 stab wounds, several of them penetrating Donna's lungs and abdomen, and a closed wound to the back left side of her head. There was also severe bruising in her lower left back area, likely from kicking or punching. There were abrasions and bruises on the right side of her face, in the cheekbone area. She had no defensive wounds on her hands. There were no signs of sexual assault, and all microscopic examinations for spermatozoa/semen were negative.

It was believed that Donna was killed where she was found, shortly after she was last seen. Neel Ranch is exactly three miles east of Don Lee's house, on the same road, Marinette. It was more than three miles north of the location where her bike was found near her home. That raised the question: Was Donna actually kidnapped on Marinette *shortly after* she left the Lee home, and the killer then planted the bike near her house; *or,* did she make it most of the way home, and was forcibly kidnapped, then transported *back to* Marinette?

Another unexplained mystery was the removal of Donna's shoes, underwear, and pants, but the total lack of a sexual assault. There is no indication that the killer was interrupted or prevented from carrying out his intended plan. Was the murder staged to look like rape was the motive? What other reason would there have been to stab Donna? When a scene is staged, the purpose is to tell a story about the motive for the crime, and to make the police believe it. For instance, if a husband murders his wife for the life insurance money, he might stage a fake burglary and rape attempt to make it look like a random stranger broke in and killed her. What story was Donna's homicide trying to tell?

The other option is that the removal of clothing was a type of posing. In that situation, the motive for leaving her unclothed and exposed would be to upset someone else—a person that the killer knew would view her body in that condition. Sgt. Byrd had known Donna her entire life. Was Donna stabbed on Neel Ranch, just inside TCSO jurisdiction, so that Byrd would be the one to view her body in a particularly shocking and upsetting manner? Was it some kind of taunting meant to embarrass TCSO, and make it look as if they couldn't keep their community safe?

When my office initially read the TCSO reports from the first twenty-four hours, we were struck by the sense that we were reading from an investigative sciences textbook used to train law enforcement… Scene staging and posing are in chapter one, and every educated investigator learns to look for exactly this kind of scenario—in fact, staging a homicide to look like a sexual assault is the *most common* type of faked evidence. However, it wasn't just Neel Ranch that caught our attention. The bike location also appeared to be a classic "premeditated diversion scene." The sole purpose of this type of secondary location is to confuse the investigation with false evidence, and divert police away from the real story. Again, the bike site looked like a case study from a textbook.

The bike area is on private property—a road used by grove workers that parallels the nearby street, List Avenue. This same road runs behind Donna's house, and is used by kids riding their bikes. The remote location itself points to a killer who knew the farmland extremely well. He was aware that the kids used this shortcut, as well as the schedule of the orange picking crews. The items planted there were Donna's bike, her shoe, her panties and sanitary belt, and Oscar's invoice book last seen in his truck on December 23rd. That leaves the mystery of the unidentified notepad, which was the same kind used by Exeter PD. Was that planted on purpose, or accidentally dropped in the dark? Did someone lose it during the initial search?

The presence of Oscar's invoice book would make the scene premeditated, since it is most likely that it was stolen ahead of Donna's murder. Most diversion scenes are done in hasty panic, after the crime. Making a plan to steal an item and frame an innocent man ***before*** the crime is highly unusual, and very specific—but, common enough to be included in police training texts. The story told by the bike scene was clear: Donna was riding home on the shortcut to her house; encountered a stranger who grabbed her and assaulted her; then, forced her into his vehicle, causing the invoice book to fall out. He then took her to Neel Ranch to kill her.

The first thing that confused me about this narrative was why Donna's underwear and one shoe would be there without her pants and other shoe. It was nonsensical, but highly effective. The items near the bike glowed like a neon sign—a sex maniac disrobed Donna, kidnapped her, and dropped his invoice book, and his name was Oscar Clifton. Besides framing Oscar, this diverted attention away from Marinette and Neel Ranch. The searchers spent all night looking in the *wrong spot*, and the next morning TCSO took Oscar's photo and showed it near the bike scene. The delay in finding Donna's body left open a time window that made it more difficult for Oscar to prove his alibi. It worked perfectly, exactly as the killer intended.

Not only did Sheriff Wiley taint Gloria Mascorro's identification of a possible suspect, he was asking the wrong question, in the wrong location. TCSO should have been canvassing the area where Donna was last seen, near the Lee house, asking if anyone had seen Donna, her bike, a vehicle, or a man around 3:45 pm the previous afternoon. Even just asking the witnesses who had been working near the bike scene could have been useful—if they had asked about ***any*** vehicle or person seen, not just Oscar. They might have learned about a different suspect. The killer clearly understood TCSO and knew that they would follow the misdirection right to Oscar without a pause or second thought. This immediately indicated an experienced, intelligent, and highly organized killer.

Several pieces of evidence point to Donna getting into a car shortly after leaving the Lee house, or at the Lee house. Her bike was found with the front wheel turned completely backward, as if to fit in the trunk of a car. Donna was wearing distinctive platform sandals, and no prints from those shoes were found at the bike scene. There was no sign of a struggle in the dirt. Nobody saw Donna after her friends left her at the Lee house. If she had ridden to where her bike was found near her home, the route would have taken her straight through Exeter. It was a busy Friday afternoon, full daylight, and she would have passed dozens of cars, homes, and businesses along the way. Donna and her family were well known in town, yet not one person reported seeing her along the 4.3 mile route.

TCSO did not let any of these questions distract them from Oscar. As soon as Donna's body was found, Oscar and Rick Carter were re-arrested on suspicion of murder, kidnapping, and rape. Again, these were warrantless arrests in their home. Oscar was booked into jail, and Carter was taken to headquarters in Visalia for questioning by TCSO King and Holguin. They had already verified Carter's alibi, and knew for a fact that he was unavailable to commit any crime against Donna. He had passed a polygraph, and there was no probable cause to arrest him. At 5:45 pm, Carter gave a second taped interview with the same basic facts as the first one, given twelve hours earlier. It was not the statement that King and Holguin wanted, and they booked Carter into jail, told him that he was being charged and that DA Powell was seeking the death penalty against him.

The next morning, at 9:00 am, Carter was brought from the jail back to TCSO headquarters. King and Holguin resumed their "questioning" of Carter for another two hours, with no interview tape running. After the tape was started at 11:00 am, Carter then gave a significantly different statement, claiming that he had remembered new details, including: Oscar had been wearing cowboy boots, and had not been wearing his knee brace; he was wearing "multi-colored" pants; he had locked himself in his bathroom for an "extended" period of time; he had changed his clothing before leaving the house; and, he had even arrived home later than Carter "remembered" in his original statement.

Although TCSO and DA Powell claimed that Carter changed his time estimate of Oscar's arrival home, the actual tape said "***4:15… I mean 4:40-4:45.***" Carter had been coached to say 4:45, but that was not his actual statement. After giving this changed statement, Carter was released from custody.

While King and Holguin had been busy with Carter, Sgt. Byrd and Deputy Johnson had miraculously located Donna's missing shoe and pants. Knowing the truth makes it difficult to repeat the lies told in TCSO reports that morning. TCSO Johnson was meticulous with every single piece of evidence documented in his reports. I can look at the evidence tag and chain of custody card for each item he indicated that he collected and took into evidence on Neel Ranch—except the "pieces of victim's clothing." Those had to be Donna's second shoe and her pants. The conclusion is inescapable; instead of logging in those items with the other evidence from Neel Ranch and autopsy, Johnson allowed them out of his custody, and they were planted to implicate Oscar.

The story told in the TCSO reports is that at 8:55 am on Sunday, December 28th, TCSO Logan and Hoffman were driving on Ave 264, searching near Oscar's house, and they spotted Donna's shoe on the south side of the road, exactly as the first shoe had been found by Donna's brother the day before. At 9:10 am, TCSO McKinney and Johnson arrived, photographed the shoe, and Johnson took it into evidence—again. This location had been passed by dozens of TCSO officers, citizens, and searchers during the previous twenty-four hours. It would have been impossible for the shoe to be missed if it had been there since Friday night, but it wasn't… it was on Neel Ranch.

TCSO never released any information to the press about "finding" the second shoe on Sunday morning. Miles Shuper and Jeanie Esajian, who were reporting on the story for the *Visalia Times-Delta*, continued to believe that Donna's first shoe had been found by her bike on Friday night, and her second shoe was found on Saturday morning on the road leading to Oscar's house. Even if Miles or Jeanie had covered the trial six months later, they likely wouldn't have realized the mistake. The discussion of the second shoe was a "blink and you missed it" moment of testimony:

Powell: Now, did you have occasion to find some other piece of clothing?

Logan: Yes, sir, I did.

Q: And would you tell us what that was?

A: It was the other shoe—to the set.

Q: And when was it that you found the other shoe?

A: The 28th of December, 1975.

Q: And where did you find the second shoe?

A: It was located on the south dirt portion just off the roadway on Avenue 264, east of Road 156.

The dilemma of Donna having ***three*** shoes was documented, but no single journalist ever had all of the pieces to put it together.

Sgt. Byrd's story about Donna's pants is even more rage-inducing. In his report, he claimed that he was contacted by dispatch at 7:30 am Sunday, reporting that a woman in Farmersville, Laverne Lamb, had Donna's green pants. Byrd stated that he traveled to her home, obtained a statement, and took the pants into custody. According to Byrd, Mrs. Lamb said that at 5:45 pm on Friday the 26th, she left work heading to Exeter to deposit a check at the bank for her employer. As she headed east on Ave 264 in the dark fog, she saw a new pair of pants in the road, stopped, took them home for her daughter, and washed them.

Laverne Lamb eventually told several different versions of how she came to guess that the pants belonged to Donna, none of them believable. The purpose of the story was obvious. Not only did Byrd want to make it appear that Oscar had thrown the pants out of his truck as he drove home on Friday afternoon, he also needed to address the fact that both the *Visalia Times-Delta* and *Fresno Bee* had already published that Donna's "shoe and a feminine undergarment" had been found with her bike on Friday night, not along the road on Saturday morning. Sgt. Byrd needed Lamb's story to "prove" that the clothing was on Ave 264 ***before*** the bike was found; thus it could not have been collected and then planted by TCSO.

Why would Laverne Lamb go along with Byrd's story? One option was to protect her own family:

Scroggin-Lamb Family Reunion

> "James and Verna Scroggin expected to spend a quiet weekend at home, instead they hosted a family reunion. First of the unexpected guests to arrive was the Scroggin's son James, and his wife, Cindy. Linda, their daughter, with her husband, Stan Lamb, and daughter, Tammy, arrived next. Joining the Scroggin family for a barbecue, was Scroggin's sister, Velma Lee, her husband, Allen, and their children, Donald, Julie, Diane, and Mandy. Also attending the gathering were Lamb's father and mother, Clyde and Laverne Lamb and their children, Starla and Keirsten from Farmersville." [Exeter Sun May 15, 1974]

> "A combination birthday and farewell party for Stanley Lamb was given at the Farmersville home of his parents, Clyde and Laverne Lamb before he flew to Munich where he will be stationed. His wife Linda and their daughter Tammy will divide their time between the Lamb home and the Exeter home of Linda's parents, Mr. and Mrs. Jim Scroggin." [Exeter Sun July 17, 1974]

> "A family dinner featuring a roast pig was held at the home of Allen and Velma Lee celebrating the birthdays of Verna Mae Scroggin, and her granddaughter, Tammy Lamb… those attending were the Lee children, Donald, Julie, Mandy and Diana, Clyde and Laverne Lamb, and their children, Starla and Keirsten." [Exeter Sun September 11, 1974]

So, in short, Laverne Lamb's son was married to Don Lee's cousin, Linda Scroggin. As these three reports detail, the family spent ***a lot*** of time together, and that was newsworthy in Exeter. In 1975, the Lee and Scroggin families lived in different homes on the *same property*. Don Lee touched on this during his trial testimony:

> Q: What type of car were you driving on December the twenty-sixth, the one you came home in?
>
> *Don Lee*: Ford Pinto.
>
> Q: To whom does the car belong?
>
> A: My cousin… James Scroggin.

Since the Lee/Scroggin property was the last place that Donna was seen alive, suspicion naturally fell on Don and his cousin James as likely suspects in her disappearance and murder. People couldn't help but wonder if Donna had rejected an advance, and "things went wrong."

It is not possible that Donna rode away from Don Lee wearing the pants at 3:45 pm, and two hours later his "aunt" happened to find them on a dark foggy road, miles away, and decided to keep them. It did not happen. Of course, Sgt. Byrd knew the Lambs, Lees, and Scroggins well. They were his neighbors in both Farmersville and Exeter, and several of the men worked for Tulare County. I have no doubt that Sgt. Byrd took the pants from TCSO Johnson, or the evidence room, and asked Laverne Lamb to go along with the story to implicate Oscar and divert suspicion from Don Lee and James Scroggin.

At 11:15 am that same Sunday morning, the Vice Principal of Exeter Union High School, Wheldon "Bud" Brumley, called Woodlake PD to report an incident involving his fourteen-year-old daughter, Beth. He stated that at 3:30 pm on the afternoon of the 26th, a man had made sexual statements to Beth right by their home in Woodlake. He said that Beth described the man as "older," and said that he looked "drunk" or "mentally retarded." He was driving a white pickup. This would turn out to be more bad news for Oscar Clifton.

Chapter Four Sources

1. Stmt taken by PI Pettyjohn - Jeanie Esajian January 5, 1976
2. Testimony of Jeanie Esajian, July 7, 1976
3. Visalia Times-Delta - December 29, 1975
4. "Eyewitness Identification Reform"
5. TCSO Report - Johnson December 26, 1975
6. TCSO Report - Byrd December 29, 1975
7. TCSO Report - Holguin December 28, 1975
8. Holguin Stmt of Gloria Mascorro - December 27, 1975
9. Neel Ranch Deed
10. Holguin Stmt of Jesus Renteria Lara - December 27, 1975
11. Testimony of Jesus Renteria Lara, June 28, 1976
12. TCSO Report - Byrd December 29, 1975
13. Homicide Scene Photos
14. TCSO Report - Hensley January 2, 1976
15. Autopsy report of Donna Richmond - January 16, 1976
16. TCSO Chain of Custody Cards
17. Investigative Sciences Journal Volume 6, Number 1, January 2014: "Staged Crime Scenes: Crime Scene Clues to Suspect Misdirection of the Investigation," Arthur S. Chancellor, MCJA
18. Geberth, Vernon J., Frequency of Body Posing in Homicides, Law and Order Magazine, Vol. 58 No. 2 February, 2010.
19. Geberth, Vernon J., Practical Homicide Investigation: Tactics, Procedures, and Forensic Techniques. Fifth Edition. CRC Press, Inc., Boca Raton, Florida, 2015.
20. TCSO Report - King December 28, 1975
21. TCSO Report - Holguin December 28, 1975
22. Testimony of Richard Carter, July 7, 1976
23. TCSO Report - Hoffman December 28, 1975
24. TCSO Report - Woodcox December 28, 1975
25. TCSO Report - Byrd December 29, 1975

26. Exeter Sun - May 15, 1974
27. Exeter Sun - July 17, 1974
28. Exeter Sun - September 11, 1974
29. Testimony of Don Lee, June 25, 1976
30. Woodlake PD Report, Ortiz - December 28, 1975

CHAPTER FIVE

"Is this a put on?"

In the months leading up to Donna's murder, Sgt. John Vaughan and his team in Visalia had been working around the clock to catch the man who had kidnapped Beth Snelling and killed her father Claude. By going back and reviewing the Ransacker activity, John was able to place the first burglary in March of 1974, but could find no real pattern. Although most of the break-ins occurred on Friday or Saturday night, it wasn't a rule. Also, the ransacking behavior was fairly consistent throughout the series; until he attacked Beth, there was no obvious change in the intensity or sexual overtones of the crimes.

However, there were two noticeable trends in the cases: The killer clearly favored the homes of female students and teachers at Mt. Whitney High School as well as families who attended the First Baptist Church. When the Ransacker hit the home of the church's pastor in August 1975, he seemed particularly angry. He stole a photo of the teen daughter from the fireplace hearth, removed a Sunday School pin from the piano, smashed it, and left it in the photo's place. He also left a trail of women's underclothing on the kitchen floor and took a bottle of cherries from the refrigerator and left it in the neighbor's yard.

On the day of the Snelling homicide, VPD also received a much more direct message, that Sgt. Vaughan believed came from the Ransacker:

> She [Sandy] related that she was with several other female Letterettes and that she parked her vehicle at approximately 12:35 pm next to a white pickup in the southeast corner of the Mt. Whitney High School parking lot near the gym, and that they noted the mirror of the pickup to be turned facing their vehicle, and that she got out with some of the other female subjects, and they noted the writing:
>
> "***Beth, I'll get the rest***"
>
> The writing appeared to be made by a finger in the dust of the mirror.

The truck belonged to a teacher who had parked it in the lot before school. He confirmed that the writing had not been there, nor had the mirror been turned out when he parked. VPD Agent McGowen supervised the scene and conducted interviews. The entire side mirror was removed and booked into evidence. Vaughan and McGowen were concerned that "the rest" referred to the Letterettes, a spirit squad at school of which Beth Snelling was a member. It didn't feel like a hoax, partly because the news of what had happened in Beth's kidnapping had not reached the papers yet. Although people were hearing that Claude had been shot by a burglar, the details about Beth were only known by a handful of people, mostly police officers—and the Ransacker.

One thing was instantly clear: Claude Snelling was a true hero, in every sense of the word. He had given his life to save his daughter from a terrible fate, hadn't hesitated for a minute, and used his last breath running to cut off the man who had just shot him. The loss of Claude to his family, church, and community was felt immediately; over 600 people attended his memorial. *The Campus*, the newspaper for the College of the Sequoias where he taught journalism, devoted many pages to him:

> Claudc Snelling believed in three things, his family, his god, and his work. His family always came first. Mr. Snelling was constantly talking about his wife's accomplishments in school. He was so proud that she went back to school to get her masters [sic] degree. There was only one thing that Claude Snelling was more proud of than his wife, and that was his kids. The staff could always expect a daily report on how well his kids were doing. Church meant a lot to Mr. Snelling. He taught Sunday School because he enjoyed it, not as an obligation. Every person who really knew Claude will miss him. He always had time to talk with anyone. Snelling had a way of making you feel that he considered you the most important topic in his mind when you had something to say.
>
> The newspaper staff will have a hard time getting over this tragic loss. Mr. Snelling was THE NEWSPAPER. He was the one person I know who is practically irreplaceable. But I like to think of the situation in this light. If Claude Snelling had to die it was better he died quickly while saving his daughter. Because if he had been unable to save Beth, Snelling would have died a thousand little deaths. And that would have been much more tragic.
>
> Claude Snelling was most active in his classroom. Under his fifteen year direction, the journalism department at COS produced many outstanding publications and journalists. The CAMPUS consistently was rated as one of the top junior college newspapers in California. Mr. Snelling would enthusiastically work with his students on the production of the CAMPUS and calmly mediate any disputes among the staff. Mr. Snelling worked long and hard for the college. He had but one interest at his heart—his students.

Vaughan's team interviewed the Letterette girls, re-interviewed prior Ransacker victims, chased every lead and tip from the public, and attempted to find the store that had sold the Ransacker his shoes and ski mask. Nothing panned out. Looking at Sgt. Vaughan's list of suspects from November 1975, it's clear that absolutely no individual was off the table. The youngest was fourteen, and the oldest was thirty-eight. There were students, local professionals, and known creeps. Eventually, they were all cleared.

At that point, Sgt. Vaughan ordered a deeper investigation into the Ransacker. It is always hard for me to remember that there was no public discussion of a serial burglar, or the VR, until after the Snelling homicide. The newspaper hadn't shown any interest in the prior burglaries because the value of the stolen property was so low, and the officers working the cases had seen them as a nuisance, likely done by "kids."

Sgt. Vaughan's team was frustrated by the lack of documentation, and went through every single burglary report until they believed they had a starting point. They re-interviewed the prior victims, and tried to create a clear record of who was hit, when, what happened, and descriptions of items that were stolen. They also asked the public to report prior break-ins where the police weren't called, and they canvassed door-to-door looking for any missed burglaries.

This gave Vaughan's team a good idea of what had happened in Visalia, but it left them relying on TCSO and neighboring towns to bring their possible cases to them for evaluation. Obviously, TCSO had no interest in having VPD "meddling" in their investigations, but there also seemed to be a problem with information shared by Tulare PD—either that, or they just didn't realize that information from the fall of 1974 might be valuable to the Snelling case. Together, this led not only to Sgt. Vaughan not being aware of Jennifer Armour's kidnapping and murder, but also a serial burglar in the nearby city of Tulare and to two EAR-style attacks in the county.

The first attack was on October 9, 1974, at a home just south of the Visalia city limits, on Caldwell. It was a Wednesday afternoon, and Mary Murphy (a pseudonym) was alone. She had finished her job with the school district for the day, and was in the kitchen fixing dinner. Suddenly, a man came through Mary's unlocked kitchen door. He was wearing a mask with only eye holes, and carrying a gun. Mary noticed that he had blue eyes, and he called her by her name. He ordered her to her bedroom, for what she described as a rape attempt. Mary resisted, and the man beat her, then kicked her in the face once she was down on the floor. She suffered head injuries and serious damage to her vision. She was unable to identify her attacker because of the mask, but TCSO detectives decided that since he had used her name, and had known that she would be home alone, it must be her young neighbor. They quickly arrested him, with no investigation.

This type of masked home invasion was previously unheard of in Visalia. Mary, her husband, and children were solidly middle class churchgoers. This wasn't someone walking in on a burglary; Mary was watched, stalked, and targeted. It reminded me of both a specific VR incident and several general EAR MO points. In the VR case, it was a year later, in October 1975, when Ruth Swanson had seen the man hold his hand over the peephole on her front door. Like Mary, Ruth was employed by the Visalia School District, and had a teen daughter at home. Ruth had suffered an extensive VR burglary a month before the peephole and obscene phone call incident, and the man had tried to come through what he thought would be an unlocked door as Ruth worked in her kitchen after school.

Although the EAR is most well known for attacking couples, his attacks in 1976 and early 1977 were on girls or women with no other adults in the house. He would watch them, make calls, and then enter the house when their parents or husbands were gone. In several cases, he struck right at dinnertime when the girls were alone watching TV or playing the piano, rather than asleep in their beds. He usually wore masks with only eye holes, and was armed with a knife and a gun. He punched victims in the face and head if they offered the slightest resistance. He often used their names, and told one girl that he lived nearby and not to scream when he left or he would hear her. The EAR had blue eyes.

I pulled the court file on the prosecution of Mary's neighbor, and it turned out that he had been acquitted by the jury when they heard evidence that he had an airtight alibi, with multiple witnesses. TCSO had made the arrest with no investigation, and when his defense team gave them the alibi information, DA Powell just called the witnesses liars. After the acquittal, TCSO closed the case as "solved," and said that the jury "got it wrong." The real attacker was never caught. The young neighbor's name was forever tied to a crime he didn't commit, and Mary's daughter told me that Mary needlessly lived in fear of that neighbor for the rest of her life.

Mary was attacked on a Wednesday, and the neighbor was arrested and charged on Friday. That night, the city of Tulare had six cat burglaries. They were so unusual that Tulare PD had no doubt that they were all the same offender. The newspaper was mainly interested in the dollar value of the loss in each case, but they were in locked homes, with sleeping occupants. The cat burglar pried the locks on sliding glass doors, and back doors into garages. They were not crimes of opportunity, and pointed to a bold and dangerous burglar that seemed to appear out of nowhere. If TCSO was supposed to notice and figure out that they arrested the wrong man for Mary's attack, it didn't work.

On Sunday night that same week, Kay Nieman (a pseudonym), a young mother and teacher with the Tulare school district, was alone with her two children asleep in their bedrooms. She lived about a block from a home hit by the cat burglar two nights before, but she was four houses south of the city limits. Kay's husband was away on a hunting trip for the long Columbus Day weekend. She got into bed with her small dog and fell asleep watching *McCloud* on television. A short time later, Kay awoke to hands turning her face towards the edge of the bed. She caught a glimpse of the man standing there, but his face just looked like a dark blob. He started punching her in the face and head, and she saw from his wrist that he was white, just before she lost consciousness.

When Kay awoke, she had a concussion and couldn't see—both of her retinas had been detached from the force of the blows. She went to her phone and was able to dial the next door neighbor and ask for help. The neighbor was awake watching TV, waiting up for her husband, TCSO Sgt. Richard McGowen, who was at a work function. Mrs.

McGowen immediately headed to Kay's, met her husband pulling into the driveway, and they approached the house together.

The McGowens knocked on the front door, and Kay tried to open it, but she couldn't. She was very disoriented, and didn't understand that her attacker had put the chain across the door. Eventually Sgt. McGowen walked around to the open back door to the garage, and entered the house through the kitchen, the same way the suspect had. Tulare PD immediately connected the attack on Kay to their cat burglar, but it was TCSO jurisdiction, and Lt. Barnes assigned Kay's attack to Sgt. Byrd.

When I talked to Kay and to Mrs. McGowen, they both stressed that the chain incident was one of the weirdest parts of the night. I agreed that it was extremely odd, but also very familiar. Sgt. Vaughan recognized it as part of the VR/EAR's MO right away. Three days after the incident with Ruth Swanson and the covered peephole, the VR hit four homes near the Snelling scene, in what Sgt. Vaughan called obvious "taunting." The chain trick was carefully documented by Detective Shipley:

> It was found that the suspect gained entry by prying the lock on the glass sliding door, and after gaining entry the suspect went to the front door and locked a chain lock, apparently to detain the victim if he returned home while the suspect was inside the residence.

The *same thing* had happened during the March 18, 1977 EAR attack:

> Apparently [neither] Friend nor her father could understand what Victim was saying. Friend and her father went to the garage door and Friend knew where the house key was kept on a nail in the garage. Friend ran back to the front door with the house key and tried to unlock the door, but when she tried to open the door the suspect had placed

> the chain across the inside of the door and they couldn't open the door.
>
> Friend ran to the back door and tried to open it and found a chain had been placed across on the inside of this door too.
>
> Victim stated at this time she was able to yell "back yard—back yard" and Friend's dad came in through the sliding glass door.

This unusual MO point also matched the EAR's attack on a 19-year-old he had stalked and burglarized while she was still in high school in Rancho Cordova. The burglary occurred in March 1973, and he returned to her house while her father was out of town on October 9, 1976. The EAR woke her after he had tied all of the bedroom doors shut using clothesline from the backyard. While Sacramento Sheriff's investigators were processing the rape scene, the next door neighbor, John Dority, approached one of the deputies:

> Dority stated he thought that his residence had been burglarized also. Dority stated he had returned home at 0130 hours, 10/9/76, and found his rear door unlocked and the chain on the inside of the front door had been latched. Dority said he was the only one at home, because his parents were out-of-town for the weekend. Dority did not find anything missing from the residence and did not wish to make a report. Dority related that he did not find any windows open, or any screens removed.

The EAR had broken into Dority's house **before** the rape, and the reason soon became clear:

> *1500 hours.* "Reporting Officer was inside Victim's residence, and Dority came to the door. Dority came inside and told this officer, that he had found some jewelry in his mother's room, and that he did not believe it was his mother's

> property. Dority showed this officer about six (6) rings and three (3) coins in a plastic bag.
>
> "After Dority left, this officer asked the Victim if Dority could be the suspect. Victim said he had the build and size of the suspect, but she would have to hear Dority whisper to be more sure.
>
> "The suspect had told Victim that he lived down the street from her, and he would hear her if she screamed."

The only reason that Dority apparently looked around the house more, and then found the planted stolen jewelry, is because the EAR forgot to take the chain off the door before he left. The security chain was just one of the ways he gave himself more time to escape out of a back window if someone came home while he was in the house. Sometimes he shoved a chair under the knob, or made an alarm with dishes or bottles, so he could hear noises if the door opened.

Imagine if the EAR victim had told investigators that the attacker might live nearby, and they had searched Dority's house and found the bag of jewelry themselves… *He would have been arrested on the spot.* Instead, Dority remained a strong suspect, but Detective Shelby was cautious, and ordered that Dority be put under surveillance. The team that was watching him ended up clearing him, after reporting him home during the next EAR attack. It was the chain that made Shelby think twice. When Shelby found empty Coors beer cans at another EAR scene he wrote: "*The Bee*r cans found in the kitchen—Is the suspect a beer drinker? *Is this a put on—some type of charade*?" Not every cop fell for the staging, framing, and fake-outs.

Kay Nieman suffered injuries nearly identical to those of Mary Murphy a few days earlier, and it was obvious to everyone involved that Kay's attacker was also the Tulare Cat Burglar. However, somehow Sgt. Byrd decided to investigate Kay's case as unrelated to both Mary's attack and the cat burglar. It was odd, and nonsensical, and his reasoning is unknown. Within a month he had a new investigation to ruin, and this time the attacker had killed.

Friday, November 15, 1974 was a big football night in Visalia. It was the Mt. Whitney vs. Redwood "Cowhide" game. The game was being played at Mineral King Bowl, behind Redwood High. Jennifer Armour was a 15-year-old sophomore at Mt. Whitney, and she arrived home from school with a friend that Friday. The two girls planned to walk up to K-Mart to meet some other girlfriends for a ride to the game. Jennifer called her mom at work and got permission, but her friend's parents said no, and made arrangements to pick up their daughter at Jennifer's house.

It's unclear if Jennifer's mom knew that she would be making the walk to K-Mart alone, but Jennifer set out from her house at 7:00 pm. Sunset was at about 4:50 pm, so it was fully dark. The walk to K-Mart was about two miles, and her friends were expecting her at 7:30 pm, so she would have needed a good four mph pace to make it on time. Jennifer was last seen walking near S. Demaree St and W College Ave, almost at K-Mart. Her friends waited for her until 7:45 pm, then headed to the game.

Jennifer had disappeared somewhere in those last few blocks. It's a very weird area—busy yet desolate. One side of the street faced the back of the newly constructed strip mall, and the other had a few apartment buildings set off the street. It was the perfect spot for an unseen kidnapping. The most recent VR burglaries had occurred on Saturday, November 2, 1974. Jennifer was last seen about 4 blocks directly west, less than two weeks later.

It took Jennifer's mom until the next morning to piece together what had happened, and to confirm she had not spent the night at a friend's after the game. I desperately want the next part of the story to be about search parties, missing person flyers, and newspaper pleas for information after a young girl vanished on a dark November night, but of course that never happened. Nothing happened. Other than her family, friends, and police no one in Visalia knew Jennifer was missing.

Jennifer was found by accident, more than a week later, on Sunday November 24, 1974 in the Friant-Kern Canal. A rancher, Howard

Walter, was checking the irrigation for his orange trees, and he saw a body in the canal in rural Exeter. Jennifer was naked, and her hands were bound with her bra. The only other item of her clothing that was found was her blouse, on the canal bank at the edge of the grove. Her shoes, pants, underwear, and jacket were missing, and never found. The killer who had kidnapped Jennifer and driven her twelve miles to the secluded, pitch black grove had also taken her clothing with him.

Armour Homicide Scene, Ave 304
Photo: Reid

On Tuesday, November 26th, the Tulare County Sheriff, Bob Wiley, issued a statement regarding Jennifer, saying "there is no reason to believe that the girl may have been murdered." Jennifer's cause of death was released as "drowning," and the manner was described as some kind of unknown accident. The response from the VR was unmistakable. On Friday, the day of Jennifer's service, the VR committed five burglaries between 5:00-11:00 pm. Per his normal MO, the residents were out for the evening when he struck. However, suddenly the Tulare Cat Burglar was back in action. He broke into one house after midnight while the owner was asleep.

The next night, Saturday November 20, 1974, the VR hit thirteen houses in Visalia between 5:00-11:00 pm. It was his busiest night ever. The eighteen burglaries over two nights covered the entire VR area; he must have been literally running between houses. He was not sighted even once, and left no clues behind. The Tulare Cat Burglar was also in the mood for a spree. Between midnight and 6:00 am Sunday morning, he broke into eight homes, connecting them with very specific MO points:

- The residents were asleep in bed
- The burglar spent an extensive amount of time inside the homes
- Locks were forced on sliding glass doors, and back doors to garage/kitchens
- Some homes had nothing missing, so theft was not the only motive
- He took watches, cash, and wallets from nightstands next to sleeping residents
- Purses were moved to odd places, cash taken
- The burglar left no fingerprints
- Purses/wallets were found outside of homes
- One house was hit twice, once in October and once in November
- The last house hit had TCSO Rusty Chamberlain and his wife asleep in it. The burglar took a watch and coins from the nightstand—and Chamberlain's gun

After the wrong suspect was arrested for attacking Mary Murphy, the next-door neighbor of TCSO Sgt. Richard McGowen was burglarized, beaten, and nearly blinded. After Sheriff Wiley announced that Jennifer Armour had not been murdered, there were eighteen VR hits and nine Tulare cat burglaries, ending with the theft of Rusty Chamberlain's watch and gun as he and his wife slept nearby. The Tulare Cat Burglar never struck again. The next year when Sgt. Vaughan's team told the press that they would catch the VR, four burglaries immediately followed—they got the message, and called it taunting. TCSO, on the other hand, decided that the attacker of Mary Murphy, Kay Nieman, and Jennifer Armour, as well as the cat burglar, were all separate offenders, with different motives, and that there was no common MO or pattern, and they weren't going to discuss the cases with VPD —or ever solve any of them.

These factors contributed to VPD closing Jennifer's missing person case without ever learning the true details of her death. In fact, a year later, TCSO was still publicly debating whether Jennifer had been murdered:

> Capt. Ollie Farris and Lt. Jim Brown of the Sheriff's Office said they aren't sure if Miss Armour died as a result of foul play—but they'd like to know what she was doing in that cold canal water during a particularly cold time of the year. Whether she was picked up by a stranger and forced into a vehicle, or got into an auto driven by someone she knew, detectives just don't know. But they'd like to.

Jennifer had no drugs or alcohol in her system, and I can't imagine anything more stupid than two actual police officers suggesting that she voluntarily went out to a freezing cold, naked, hands-tied, swimming party in a concrete-lined canal in a pitch black orange grove instead of meeting her friends for the homecoming game. That TCSO statement was made two months after the Snelling kidnapping and homicide three blocks from where Jennifer was last seen. Two girls in the same class at Mt. Whitney were kidnapped by a killer, yet a swimming "accident" made more sense to TCSO. This never stops being infuriating. The opportunity to bring Exeter into the VR investigation was right there in the fall of 1975.

Reading the news coverage of the Snelling homicide, and the instant connection to the Ransacker, one would expect that he might lay low, or just pick a different nearby town or area. Instead, he waited only eleven days to commit another burglary—at a house on the same street where he had stolen the Snelling murder weapon three weeks earlier—Ruth Swanson's house. Every single member of the community was looking for him, and VPD had added extra patrols and stakeouts, but the Ransacker couldn't wait to prove that he was unafraid and unstoppable. The ransacking at the Swanson house was extensive. He clearly spent a lot of time there, despite every neighbor being on high alert.

This taunting behavior continued throughout the fall of 1975. It was a constant game of cat and mouse with Sgt. Vaughan's team helpless to stop him—but they were learning. They followed his footprints through yards, ditches, and over fences. They knew the time of night he was likely to strike, and finally caught a break with the prints outside Debbie Ward's window. They did everything right to catch him, they just couldn't hold him. The McGowen shooting incident on December 10th was finally too much. The Ransacker was done with Visalia.

By early 1976, Sgt. Vaughan began to think that the Ransacker had left town. There were no further sightings or burglaries, and it made sense because McGowen had gotten a good look at him and they had published two composites. On January 6th, McGowen also made sure that the VR's MO could be matched with other offenders in California:

> Reporting agent contacted Homer Porter, MO Burglary Analyst and Computer Operator with CII, Sacramento, and gave Mr. Porter information regarding the complete description, known characteristics, and the MO of the Snelling homicide suspect and the "Ransacker." Requested Mr. Porter to feed this information into the CII Computer, the MO section, in effort to identify other known ransack

burglars or any previous arrests on MO's similar to ours in this particular area.

Mr. Porter stated that he would feed the available information into the computer and would notify this agent in approximately one week as it would take this long to complete that task. He related further that after doing this particular area, he would attempt to do the Southern California and Bay area in effort to identify a burglar with the same description and MO as our reported Ransacker and Murder suspect.

Mr. Porter related further with the particular characteristics and MO of this particular suspect and due to the fact that we know his race, height, approximate weight and color of hair and shoe size, it was a strong possibly [*sic*] that he could more easily make a match by use of the computer.

CII analysts were also requested to search the computer for all recent recorded sales of Smith & Wesson revolvers in the Visalia area to any person matching the physical of our ransacker. [NOTE: *The term* "our ransacker" *is copied from the original text*].

Meanwhile, on September 5, 1976, Sacramento Sheriff's investigator Alan Lancaster ***also*** had the MO and suspect information from the first four EAR attacks uploaded to the CII database, and asked for possible matches. The information triggered notification to Sgt. Vaughan's team of a match between the EAR and VR MOs, and suspect descriptions. Presumably, SSD also received the notifications. In addition to the rapes, the same neighborhoods in Sacramento were experiencing ransacking burglaries, but the cases were being handled separately, by two different investigative teams within SSD. Reviewing the report details of both sets of crimes convinced Sgt. Vaughan that he was looking at the Ransacker in Sacramento.

On November 10, 1976, *The Sacramento Bee* published a front page story titled "*East Area Rapist… Fear Grips Serene Neighborhoods.*" The rapes had been occurring in Rancho Cordova, Del Dayo, and

Carmichael since June, but SSD had decided to hide the information from the community and press, hoping to catch the rapist in a stakeout. Word spread, and a community meeting had drawn 500 angry residents, who were in no mood for the Sheriff's explanations and excuses.

On May 18, 1977, the first news of the possible VR/EAR connection was published in the *Visalia Times-Delta* (written by Miles Shuper) under the headline "*Police Seeking to Link Rapist to Snelling Slayer.*"

> Lt. Roy Springmeyer said today: "Because of the degree of the similarity in the physical descriptions and the methods used, we just can't afford to overlook the possibility that the same person could be responsible for the rapes and the Visalia crimes." Detectives Bill McGowen and Duane Shipley left Visalia early today to meet in Sacramento with investigators probing the rapes in which the attacker now has threatened to kill two persons.
>
> Visalia police Sgt. John Vaughan, who has been heading the Snelling murder investigation, said today he has copies of many of the Sacramento rape investigation reports and the profiles of the crime patterns.
>
> They are being closely studied and compared to the information gathered by Visalia officers during the 20-month investigation of the Visalia slaying and the nearly four-year probe of the ransacking burglaries, Vaughan said.

There has been endless debate about exactly what happened during McGowen and Shipley's visit to SSD. VPD felt like their information wasn't taken seriously, and SSD still argues today that the information they received didn't match their suspect. In February 1978, a young couple, Katie and Brian Maggiore, were chased, shot, and killed by a masked man in Rancho Cordova while out for an evening walk with their dog. Sgt. Vaughan became even more convinced that the

EAR was the Ransacker. He went to the press. On July 22, 1978, *The Sacramento Union* printed their story headlined "*Rapist, Visalia Cases Tied*."

> Could they be the same man?
>
> "Absolutely not," says Bill Miller, Sacramento County Sheriff's Spokesman. In May 1977 Visalia Police officials met with the Sheriff's East Area Rapist Task Force, and say the department cut off contact with them after comparing both men's methods of operation.
>
> "There is no connection. We've gone over the whole case, and it isn't the same guy. If it is, he's changed his entire method of operation," says Miller. "You've got a guy down there in Visalia who's convinced. As least somebody wants to be convinced, it just isn't there."
>
> Most interesting to Visalia are the idiosyncrasies both men share according to McGowen and Sgt. John Vaughan, who say Visalia has spent more time and money on the Ransacker than any other in the city's history.

The situation really exploded after *The Union* article, and it got highly personal. SSD struck the next blow, on the front page of *The Sacramento Bee*. On July 23, 1978, the headline read "*Sheriff Department Attacks Newspaper Rapist Story*":

> The Sacramento County Sheriff's Department Saturday called the Visalia Police Department and *The Sacramento Union* "irresponsible" for suggesting the east area rapist and a burglar suspected of murder might be the same man. Sheriff's spokesman Bill Miller further charged Visalia police with being "unprofessional."
>
> "It appears to me," he charged, "that these investigators in Visalia were looking for publicity—and it's not there. That is really irresponsible," Miller said.

> He later repeated his charge against the Visalia police, adding, "What they did was unprofessional and irresponsible."
>
> He was slightly less critical of the Union, saying, "The reporter reported what she was told by McGowen and Vaughan. But it does seem irresponsible to me to scare thousands of people in Sacramento. You can't say the East Area Rapist is a killer without something more to base it on than what she got from Visalia."
>
> Union Editor Don Hoenshell said the newspaper would stand by its story.
>
> "If Miller and his agency, which has done nothing about the East Area Rapist in 2 years want to impugn the integrity of another police agency, that is their problem. We just want to report the news."
>
> Vaughan, according to the Union, also claimed that both the Ransacker and the rapist had the "peculiarity" of taking things, often items of little value, from one house, and leaving them in another. Miller said this simply is not so.

That *Bee* story was picked up the next day by the *Visalia Times-Delta*, and Miller's comments repeated for the local community. Sgt. Vaughan and his team were taken off the case. It was no wonder that Vaughan had little interest in trying to reason with SSD when we started looking at Exeter.

My office was given the entire Oscar Clifton defense file in 2016—fifteen boxes, which were soon joined by five more from his attorney's office. We were tasked with answering three questions:

1. What was the evidence of Oscar's guilt?
2. If he was innocent, how did he get convicted and lose his appeals?
3. If he didn't kill Donna, who did?

We soon added two more of our own:

1. How was Oscar eliminated in the kidnapping and murder of Jennifer Armour in November 1974?
2. Why wasn't the Ransacker investigated in either homicide?

As I later explained to Sgt. Vaughan, Jennifer's kidnapping in the VR zone, her status as a fellow Mt. Whitney student, physical type, and the apparently angry "taunting" ransacking spree were strong circumstantial evidence. The later attack on Beth Snelling a few blocks from Jennifer's kidnapping site also pointed to the Ransacker. The homicide scene in Exeter suggested a killer who knew the area well, felt comfortable there, and would have some kind of explanation for his presence in the private grove if he were seen. I felt sure that the Ransacker lived in Exeter on November 15, 1974. Oscar Clifton was then residing in Las Vegas.

Reading through Oscar's arrest records, the grand jury transcript, and talking to his family, the story tells itself. He was arrested with a Nevada driver's license; TCSO Lt. Brown testified that he personally verified Oscar's whereabouts between 1965-75, and Oscar's wife said that the invoice book was started when he moved back to Tulare County, which was March 10, 1975. Sgt. Byrd was assigned to Jennifer's case, which had finally been classified a homicide, in March 1976. There is no way that Byrd would have failed to try to blame Jennifer's murder on Oscar.

Sgt. Vaughan said that the Ransacker team hadn't looked at Jennifer's case simply because they had been told it was an accidental drowning. When TCSO reclassified it as a homicide, they did not inform VPD or ask about the original missing person file. It was pretty obvious why Sgt. Byrd hadn't wanted to tie Jennifer's case to the Ransacker—it would raise immediate questions about who really killed Donna. Not only did all of the evidence point to Donna and Jennifer being killed by the same man, it also seemed obvious that the attacker wanted law enforcement to make that connection and look back to Beth Snelling, Visalia, and the Ransacker.

On June 15, 2016, the EAR Task Force and the Sacramento FBI field agents held a press conference and made their position crystal clear: The East Area Rapist and the Visalia Ransacker were not the same offender. *Period.* They didn't want to hear another word about it. Sgt. Vaughan, VPD, and former Orange County cold case investigator Larry Pool did not agree. Clearly, only one side was correct, and it seemed critical to figure out how Vaughan had originally made the connection.

Sgt. Vaughan had been given the SSD files for the first eighteen EAR attacks, from June 18, 1976-May 3, 1977. Looking at those reports, alongside the VPD reports on the Ransacker, the Snelling case, and the McGowen shootout provided the answer. Needless to say, Sgt. Vaughan's team won by a landslide—it was not even close.

One thing that immediately stands out in the EAR reports is the difference between the way VPD tried to warn and inform the public versus the important details intentionally hidden by SSD. In Sacramento the citizens were left in the dark for five months; they had no idea that a serial rapist was in their neighborhood. When SSD finally admitted it to the press, they said that the EAR was coming in unlocked windows, and nobody had gotten hurt.

In fact, he was chiseling and prying locked doors, and two women were attacked in their driveways—one forcibly dragged out of her open car window. Several victims had been hurt including being cut with a knife, severely punched in the head/face, and beaten with a billy club—requiring stitches. The EAR exhibited extremely violent and dangerous behavior from the very first attack, and locked doors and windows did not slow him down. These were not victims of opportunity. They were stalked days, weeks, months, even years in advance of their attacks. SSD intentionally downplayed the danger and the sophistication of the attacker's methods from the beginning. As *The Sacramento Bee* reported: Publicity about the rapes was minimized because the sheriff's department feared widespread panic would result, and because they hoped to entrap the rapist.

This tactic left women and girls uninformed about the true risks, and completely vulnerable. Somehow, investigators thought it was fine to use them as "bait."

In looking at the EAR case files, the only two differences I saw between the EAR and the Ransacker were that the EAR victims were tied up, and that there were completed sexual assaults. Everything else matched exactly. Just as with Visalia, I was reading the same description: newer single story homes in professional neighborhoods, often on cul-de-sacs, backing onto open spaces or adjacent to concrete-lined ditches. The targets were attractive teen girls and young mothers. The scenes were extensively ransacked, but little of value was taken. The attacker was masked, armed with a knife and gun, white, 20-30, with strong shoulders and arms. He disguised his voice with a "*clenched teeth*" whisper, but his voice got extremely high when things didn't go to plan.

I was looking for differences, but all I found were similarities:

Physical Description:

White male
EAR = 19-25 in 1977 VR = 18-27 in 1977
EAR = 5'10"-5"11 VR = 5'10"
EAR = 140-180 lbs VR = 150-180 lbs

- Muscular, but not bodybuilder type. Strong shoulders, arms, & hands
- Agile fence jumper, walked/biked several miles per night
- Pale or very light complexion
- Left-handed or strongly ambidextrous
- Mask/Hood—various, but usually homemade, with only eye holes
- Gloves (including brown cotton in both cases)
- Dark clothing and Army green
- Armed with snub-nosed revolvers

- Growl/Whisper/Clenched Teeth covering high pitched voice when excited
- Used set commands, such as "Shut up, or I'll stab you"
- Used lotion at scene, sometimes brought the lotion with him
- Placed chains across doors and chairs under door knobs to prevent entry
- Opened multiple escape routes, including interior doors/ windows and outside gates
- Made improvised alarms including dishes, chairs, and bedroom doors tied shut
- Stopped and shot when chased
- VR and early EAR victims were moved outside after being awakened in bed. Outdoor scenes were pre-selected and prepared
- Victims woke to find the attacker on top of them in bed, hand over mouth/nose, being suffocated
- Used ditches, bike paths, canals, riverbeds, open spaces, vacant lots, orchards, railroad tracks, and power easements to travel unseen, avoid detection, and escape if chased
- Took costume jewelry, but left expensive pieces in plain view. Often took one earring from a pair, including multiple pairs at the same scene. Dumped out jewelry boxes or displayed them after moving them to odd locations
- Stole men's class rings, cufflinks—one cufflink from a pair, and favored personalized/engraved items
- Photos of residents were moved, torn up, broken in their frames, turned on their faces, and/or stolen. Attacker took the time to go through photo albums, and removed some of the photos
- Rifled through and moved purses, often found dumped out and left in backyards

- Stole coins. Emptied penny jars and piggy banks. Also targeted silver dollars, two dollar bills, collectible and foreign coins. Often left other cash in plain view or displayed
- Ransacked all rooms, including kitchen drawers/ cupboards, closets, dressers, and desks
- Stole items from attack scenes, then left them at other break-ins or in neighbors' yards
- Brought bottles and cans to the scenes, left them outside and in the kitchens. No fingerprints
- Victims received hang-up, obscene, and threatening phone calls before and after attacks
- Food was taken from the refrigerators and left in odd places, often outside or in neighbors' yards
- Used stolen bikes as transportation, and left them in front of nearby homes, not the yards of the attacks. Left the bikes and fled on foot to ditches if chased
- Window screens were removed, left on beds/unusual places, sometimes even replaced over a window with a small crack or hole to cover activities
- Depending on the scene, closed drapes were opened to warn of someone approaching, or open drapes were closed to hide his activities
- Almost all homes hit were single-story, ranch style, in solidly middle-class neighborhoods. Favored homes on cul-de-sacs, corner houses, and those that bordered ditches, parks, orchards, or fields
- Returned to hit in the same neighborhoods over a period of months or years
- Antique police billy club used in August 29, 1976 EAR attack (*matched the description of one stolen in October 24, 1975 VR case*)
- Made improvised step stools from items found in backyards

- VR targets, and almost all early EAR attacks, were teenage girls with long hair
- Victims were punched, kicked, or bludgeoned
- Turned off or disabled A/C and heating units
- Used a screwdriver to chisel around locks and remove striker plates
- Often broke in through the back door to the garage, then through the kitchen door
- The early, single victims were all threatened with a knife, and several were cut. The knife was described as having a 3-4 inch long blade
- Responded to news stories and police statements to the press in a "call and response" pattern
- Stalked victims over days, weeks, months, and years, including victims of prior burglaries

Those are the specific, documented behaviors that can be found in the EAR files reviewed by Sgt. Vaughan and in the VPD Ransacker reports. However, if they had the TCSO files on the 1974 attacks on Mary Murphy and Kay Nieman, they would have found additional specific MO point matches:

- Attacker wore a mask with only eye holes
- Attacker had blue eyes
- Attacker was armed with a gun
- Stated sexual assault motive
- Entry to the house was made through a locked back door into the garage, then through the unlocked door to the kitchen
- The bedroom doors of sleeping children were closed
- A purse was taken into the back of the house and contents dumped out
- Valuable jewelry was left in plain sight

- The dog in the bedroom did not alert
- The victim was punched in the face, in a sudden attack
- Husbands were at work or on out-of-town trip
- Jewelry box on dresser was dumped out, but nothing taken
- Attacker left no fingerprints at the scene
- Cigarettes stolen
- The Nieman attack occurred next door to the public information officer for TCSO, one day after TCSO made a press statement about the October 9th case being solved, in a "call and response."

I also noticed some EAR details that matched other specific evidence in Jennifer's and Donna's murders:

- Bras used to tie June 18, 1976 victim and Jennifer Armour on November 15, 1974
- In the July 17, 1976 attack, the EAR took a multi-colored ski cap from a bedroom closet, wore it over his mask during the assault, then placed it in a dresser drawer. This was unnecessary to hide his identity, and matched the multi-colored ski-mask/cap described by Beth Snelling and the one found at Neel Ranch.

The November 10, 1976, EAR attack had several highly unusual details that reminded me of a combination of the planning and staging at the Snelling house and Donna's murder scenes:

- It was a dinnertime attack. The victim was 16 years old, and her parents had just left the house. The EAR broke in through a living room window and confronted the girl with a knife from her kitchen as she was watching TV with her dog

- He had pre-cut bindings waiting outside, which he used to tie her up. He then replaced the window screen, turned off the TV, and locked the door behind him
- The EAR walked the girl at knifepoint, hands bound, over the neighbor's short fence, through the yard, into a culvert under the street, and one-third of a mile along a cement drainage ditch that ran in a greenbelt behind houses. They finally stopped in a clearing with a large tree stump
- He removed her lower clothing. When he left, he told her to wait for twenty minutes, leaving her bound, blindfolded, and gagged. She waited over an hour before returning home, half naked. A neighbor found her and took her to her parents who thought she had just gone out with her boyfriend. The EAR had staged the scene perfectly; they never suspected she had been kidnapped.

I also factored in the October 9, 1976 EAR attack and his attempt to frame John Dority by breaking into his house, planting evidence, and making "neighbor" comments to the victim. This was another similarity between the VR and EAR, and tied them both to the MO of Donna's killer.

After assessing all of the information Sgt. Vaughan's team had in May 1977, it was overwhelmingly clear that the EAR and the Ransacker were the same suspect. In fact, he seemed to be doing specific, unnecessary things to make sure that law enforcement saw the pattern and made the connection. I was angry. SSD had not only ignored the best clue they had, but they had gone out of their way to humiliate and discredit the very investigators who had caught him once and found him again. Why had the Sacramento Sheriff's Department spent forty years denying the truth? How many innocent rape and murder victims could have been spared? I was beginning to understand why Sgt. Vaughan was so reluctant to revisit the case, and so pessimistic about convincing the EAR Task Force to look in Exeter.

Chapter Five Sources

1. VPD Report - McGowen October 2, 1975
2. VPD Report - McGowen September 12, 1975
3. College of Sequoias "Campus" - September 19 1975
4. VPD Report - March 1976-May 1977
5. VPD Report - Vaughan November 2, 1975
6. "Murphy" Interview
7. "Murphy" Court Records
8. Visalia Times-Delta - October 12, 1974
9. Visalia Times-Delta - April 24, 1975
10. VPD Report - Shipley October 24, 1975
11. "Nieman" Interview
12. Mrs. McGowen Interview
13. Visalia Times-Delta - October 15, 1974
14. VPD Report - Shipley October 30, 1975
15. SSD EAR Report - March 18, 1977
16. SSD EAR Report - October 9, 1976
17. SSD EAR Report - July 17, 1976
18. Armour Interview
19. Visalia Times-Delta - November 25, 1974
20. Visalia Times-Delta - November 26, 1974
21. Visalia Times-Delta - January 7, 1975
22. Walter Interview
23. VPD Report - Vaughan October 8, 1975
24. Tulare Advance-Register - December 2, 1975
25. Visalia Times-Delta - November 21, 1975
26. VPD Report - Spencer September 23, 1975
27. VPD Report - January 7, 1976
28. SSD EAR Report - September 5, 1976
29. Sacramento Bee - November 10, 1976
30. Visalia Times-Delta - May 18, 1977
31. Sacramento Bee - February 3, 1978
32. Sacramento Union - July 22, 1978
33. Sacramento Bee - July 23, 1978

34. Oscar Clifton Arrest Record December 26, 1975
35. Oscar Clifton NV Drivers License
36. TCSO Arrest Report - December 27, 1975
37. Grand Jury Testimony of Jim Brown, February 5, 1976
38. Mrs. Clifton Interview
39. Invoice Book
40. TCSO Report - Lyon March 2, 1976
41. Tulare Advance-Register - March 15, 1976
42. Sacramento Bee - June 16, 2016
43. FBI EAR Website
44. SSD EAR Case Reports June, 1976-May, 1977

CHAPTER SIX

"Type A"

By Monday, December 29, 1975, TCSO had finished their "investigation" into Donna's murder, and DA Powell pretty much had Oscar convicted. The lead story and headline on that day's issue of the *Visalia Times-Delta* that day read:

> ***Powell Says He'll Seek The Death Penalty***
>
> DA Jay Powell said today he will seek the death penalty in the Friday slaying of a young Exeter girl.
>
> Powell said Oscar A. Clifton, 35, will be charged today, with murder and kidnaping in the abduction and slaying of 14-year-old Donna Richmond, daughter of Tulare County Assessor, Donald Richmond. Investigators said they believe the girl was kidnaped, raped, then slain in a rural Exeter orange grove.
>
> Clifton, according to court records, is a registered sex offender. He was sentenced in Tulare County Superior Court in 1966 [*sic*: 1965] for an attempted rape conviction. Officials said he left Tulare County for Las Vegas, Nevada several years ago, and recently returned.
>
> Powell said the suspect did not re-register as a sex offender as required by law when he returned to the county. He said that alleged failure might also result in a criminal charge by his office.
>
> A man identified as Richard A. Carter, 18, who reportedly was living at the Clifton residence, also was taken into custody.

But authorities emphasized that Carter was picked up only for questioning."

Reading that story never gets any easier, or less upsetting. DA Jay Powell knew, for an absolute fact, that Donna had ***not*** been raped, and that Oscar was ***not*** a registered sex offender who had failed to re-register. Powell also knew that he could not seek the death penalty due to the lack of aggravating factors. As horrible as Donna's murder was, the lack of rape, robbery, or another separate felony made it Murder in the First Degree—***not*** a death penalty case.

The additional information about Rick Carter is such a cold, calculated lie, it's almost unbelievable to see it in print. Reports from TCSO King and Holguin told a very different story—Carter wasn't "picked up only for questioning":

TCSO Holquin:

12-27-75 19:30 HRS. R/O and Det. King booked subject Carter for investigation of homicide.

12-28-75 0900 HRS. R/O with assistance from Det. M. King was assigned to interview suspect R. Carter after being advised by jail personnel that suspect Carter wished to talk to detectives about the above case. Suspect Carter was then removed from the area by R/O to the interview room.

TCSO King:

12-27-75 19:30 HRS. R/O and Det. Holguin took Suspect Carter to the County Jail where he was booked for investigation of homicide.

12-28-75 0900 HRS. R/O was detailed to assist in interviewing Suspect Carter who had indicated to Jail personal that he was desirous to talk about this case with the investigating Officers. Det. Holguin went to the Jail and brought Suspect Carter to the interview room at the Sheriff's Office in Visalia.

There is also a TCSO chain of custody card that shows Carter's clothing being logged in by the "Jail Division on 12-27-75."

The purpose of the lie is obvious—Carter needed to look like a voluntary cooperative witness, not a man who had been illegally arrested, jailed, and threatened with death, or even worse—a possible alternate suspect who had free access to the invoice book. In fact, Carter was arrested without probable cause, and with no warrant: he had provided his alibi, which TCSO checked and confirmed; he had voluntarily allowed a search of his body, clothing, and truck; and he had passed a polygraph examination on his truthfulness. There was no direct or circumstantial evidence to support his unlawful arrest and jailing. Holguin and King should have been charged under Penal Code §236 for false imprisonment—"the unlawful violation of the personal liberty of another." I would even argue that it was a felony, because their sole intent was to prevent Carter from offering truthful testimony, and instead feel threatened into committing perjury.

The *Visalia Times-Delta* story also carried a front page photo of Donna captioned "slaying victim" next to the booking photo of Oscar with "murder suspect" beneath it. The case was open and shut; everyone could see exactly who killed Donna, and Powell was going to make sure that he was put to death. A few hours after the paper hit newsstands, at 5:30 pm, Gloria Mascorro was brought to TCSO headquarters to attend an in-person lineup. I can only imagine how many copies of the newspaper were carefully positioned for her to view Oscar's photo as she waited in the police station—just in case she didn't remember the one Sheriff Wiley had already shown her two days before.

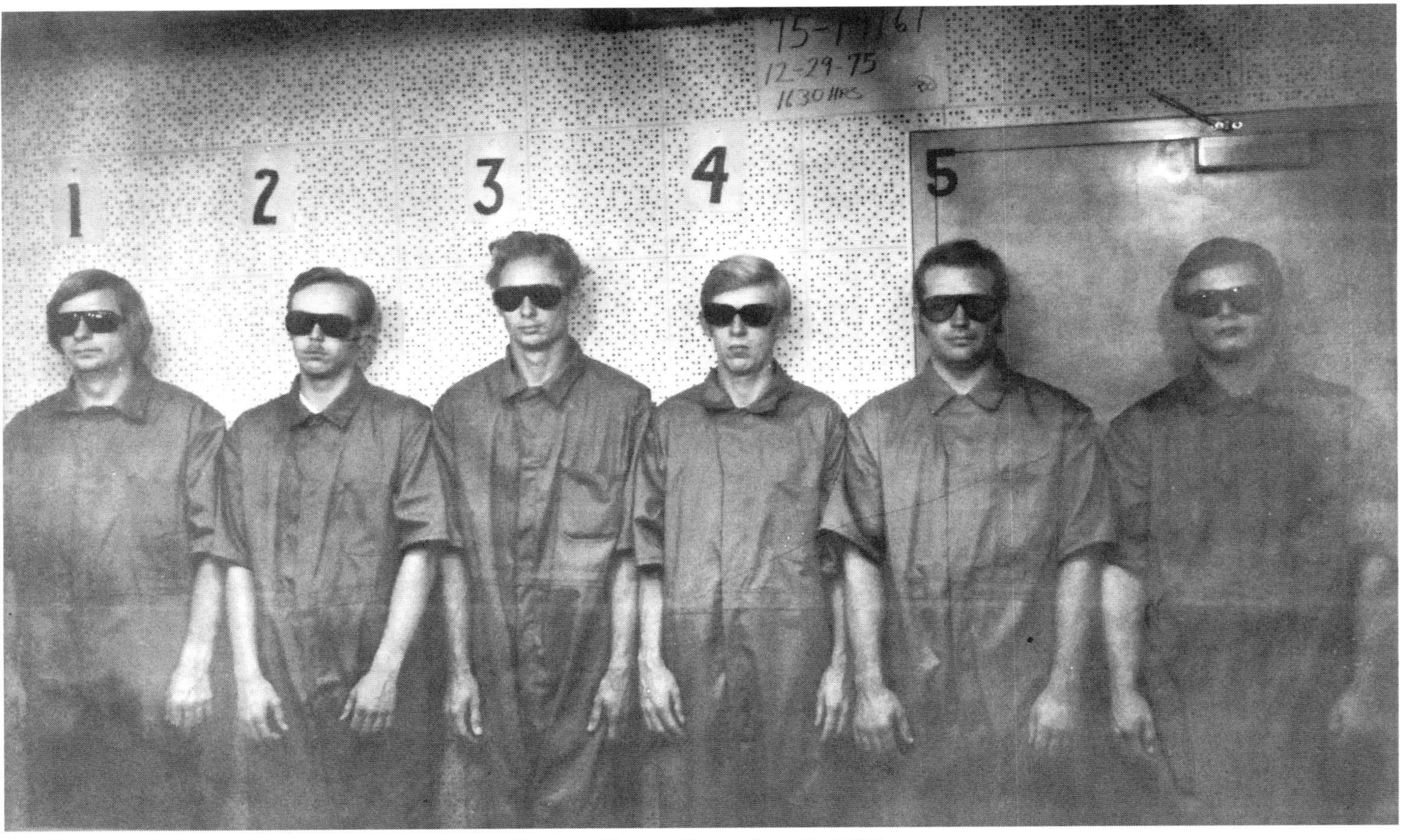

Lineup Photo—December 29, 1975
Photo: TCSO

In the lineup, Oscar was positioned in the center, number three of six. Gloria's statement said that the man she saw was blond, tall, and thin. There were only two men who could have remotely fit that description, and Oscar was half a head taller than the other option. The other five men were TCSO members, well-known to the deputies leading Ms. Mascorro in her identification. Two had dark brown hair, the one other blond guy was heavy, and one had a mustache. It would have been impossible not to pick the tallest, thinnest blond guy, placed right in the center. It was the very definition of a suggestive police lineup, and together with the prior showing of his photo and that evening's newspaper, Gloria's identification of Oscar was a clear due process and civil rights violation. It was, and is, a legal disaster. The only goal was to make sure Oscar was convicted, at any cost. It was not meant as an investigation into who killed Donna, not for one minute.

Tulare DA Jay Powell really needed a win, especially since he was not a "local." He graduated from Berkeley law school in 1959, and worked in the Bay Area until he took a public defender job in Fresno in 1964. I've seen references to his work with Melvin Belli, but I was never able to find any information to confirm or expand on that. In 1965, Powell became the City Attorney for Firebaugh, in Fresno County. He ran for judge there in 1970, but was defeated. In July 1971, he was hired to lead the Tulare County Public Defender's office. He ran that office until he was elected District Attorney in November 1974. Of the 42,962 total votes cast for the seat, Powell won by only 308 votes—less than one percent. There was a lot of skepticism about his ability to be "tough on crime." He chose to answer his critics by refusing to accept plea deals, overcharging every case, taking minor crimes to trial, and seeking the harshest penalties.

Just as in Fresno, Powell's real energy seemed to be saved for his dream of becoming a judge. At the time of Donna's murder, he had just applied to be appointed to a new Kings County Superior Court position, but the Kings County Board of Supervisors opposed him, and he did not get the post. Powell applied again in 1977 and 1978 when Tulare County ended up having three vacancies on the Superior Court bench, but the Governor passed him over all three times. Perhaps the Governor had heard about the accusations of incompetence and prosecutorial misconduct that seemed to define Powell's term as DA.

Most of the deputy prosecutors quit during Powell's first year in office, which led to the promotion of Brenton Bleier to the position of ADA, just eighteen months after he became an attorney. The *Visalia Times-Delta* covered a talk Bleier gave to the Kiwanis Club:

> Bleier offered several solutions to problems in the legal system, including doing away with prison rehabilitation programs for the 'criminal class;' limiting the number of persons eligible to be represented by a public defender; decreasing the amount of evidence that is not admissible in court; putting limits on appeals made on behalf of defendants; and eliminating credit for time served in prison for persons in jail awaiting sentencing.

Powell had decided to prosecute Oscar himself, with Bleier as his second chair.

Tulare County usually sent case samples that needed forensic examination, or testing, to the California Department of Justice (DOJ) lab in Fresno. Instead, DA Powell hired the Institute of Forensic Sciences (IFS) in Oakland instead. It was an unusual, and expensive, choice for the county, but not if you wanted to make sure that the defense didn't hire them first and didn't want DOJ offering an opinion about the evidence. Powell had just tried a double homicide case, and IFS had done an outstanding job for the defense. Their findings had been exculpatory, and failed to establish any connection between the defendant and the homicides. Powell clearly didn't want a repeat during his prosecution of Oscar Clifton.

On the morning of Tuesday, December 30, 1975, TCSO Johnson met with IFS Criminalist Charles Morton, and took him on a tour of the scenes. Morton was hoping to make plaster casts of the tire tracks and footprints, but the scenes had not been preserved, and that proved impossible. The idea that they were planning to collect "evidence" at two unsecured orange groves during harvest season, four days after the fact, is appalling. This was unbelievably substandard police work. Donna deserved so much better. Criminalist Morton did take plaster casts of the tire tracks that Byrd claimed matched Oscar's truck on Road 176. They were tracks on the shoulder, about fifty feet north of the panties, on the opposite side of the road. I try to imagine Johnson watching Morton take the casts, knowing or suspecting that the panties had been planted by his fellow deputies, and saying nothing.

Morton was also taken to the TCSO evidence room, where he examined Donna's bike, and made notes:

> Left fork, front wheel, white paint transfer up 15-16.5 inches, and a smaller one, at around 17 1/4. Pale blue transfer on steering column, looks like it is covered with dust or dirt. Small quantity of white material in right pedal cap. Dirt embedded in left pedal. Possible white transfer to edge of button on left side of handle bar.

The main area of white paint transfer was about 1.5 inches, measuring 15 inches up from the hub. Morton's notes indicate that he then went to Jackson's Towing, examined Oscar's truck, and removed a sample from an area that appeared to have "minor nicks and scratches on the paint." Although it's not documented on that page, it appears that Morton also took a sample from the TCSO vehicle that Johnson used to transport the bike to evidence. Morton returned to his lab in Oakland with the paint samples and the refrigerated evidence taken at autopsy.

When Oscar was arrested, his wife had turned to her brother-in-law, Avery Dula, for help securing a criminal defense attorney. Avery's business lawyer suggested Ray Donahue, and Oscar's wife, parents, and siblings got together enough money to pay for his retainer as well as the services of retired FBI agent turned private investigator Robert Pettyjohn. Donahue hand-wrote notes of his intake meeting with Oscar. The notes begin with Oscar's visit to the Roberts house, seeing Gene Owens, then returning to the Rose house on Garden Street in Visalia, where "people across street were loading refrigerator." He also mentioned trips to Rich Brothers to try to get a key made and the Builder's Emporium. Donahue gave this information to Pettyjohn, and told him to work on verifying Oscar's alibi for the afternoon and evening of December 26th.

Pettyjohn started with Oscar, his family, Rick Carter, and the Dulas. They confirmed seeing Oscar throughout the day in the clothing his wife had laid out for him in the morning, including seeing him out to dinner that evening. Oscar's mood seemed entirely normal. His daughters confirmed seeing him arrive at home shortly before 4:30 pm, clean and relaxed.

On December 31st, Pettyjohn went to Garden Street to talk to Frank Thomas, the man who had sold his freezer and two bicycles on the 26th. Thomas confirmed Oscar's story, including the comment about the men being late. He said that he was at the end of his driveway looking at his watch when they arrived, and placed the time at 3:15 pm. Thomas also said that the men stayed until about 3:45 pm. Oscar had said that he left Garden Street shortly after the trucks—*therefore, just before 4:00 pm.*

Pettyjohn also interviewed Gene Owens, who placed the time that he saw Oscar at the Roberts' house at 3:00 pm. Both men signed sworn statements. Pettyjohn also got a statement from Danny Boland, who confirmed Oscar had come by his job site on Garden Street to discuss working on the Rose house at around 1:30 pm. Pettyjohn felt that he had solidly confirmed that Oscar was at various locations in Visalia between 1:15-3:45 pm, stopped to get gas, and was seen in his own driveway at 4:15 pm.

Meanwhile, Woodlake PD decided to follow up on Bud Brumley's report of an "incident" with his daughter Beth on the afternoon of the

26th. The police report is strange. For some unstated and unknown reason, Beth's older sister, Jayna, made the statement to the police "for Beth." She said that between 2:00-3:00 pm, a man in a white pickup pulled up near where Beth was walking home, and asked her a sexual question. Jayna said that Beth then walked off towards home, and the man drove away.

In the December 31st report of Woodlake Officer Diaz, the suspect was listed as Oscar Clifton. Diaz's report states that the incident occurred at ***2:00 pm***, and that Beth identified Oscar:

Miss Brumley told me that the man was the same one she saw in a newspaper, meaning the suspect that was arrested for the murder of Donna Richmond in Exeter.

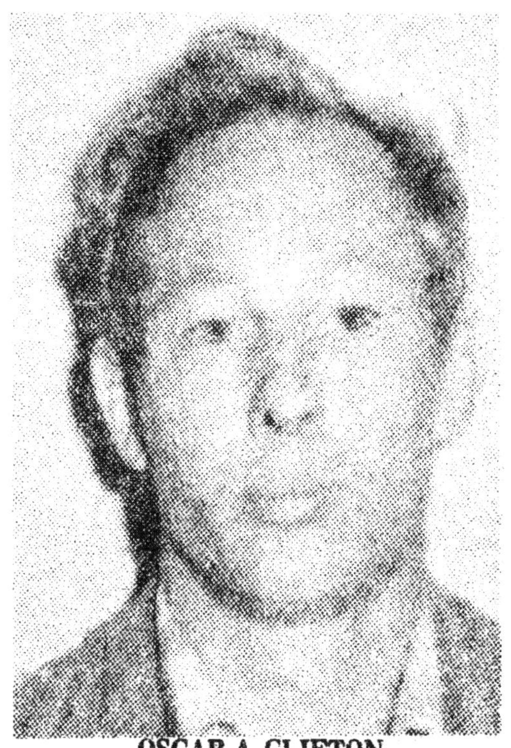

OSCAR A. CLIFTON
. . . murder suspect

TCSO Booking Photo of Oscar
Visalia Times Delta, December 29, 1975
Photo: TCSO

Beth had seen Oscar's booking photo on the front page of the *Visalia Times-Delta* from two days prior with the caption "murder suspect" prior to making her statement. Beth never gave a description of the man, his clothing, or the truck (other than white). Officer Diaz forwarded the information to TCSO.

The *Exeter Sun* is a weekly newspaper, and their first story on the case ran on that same Wednesday, December 31st [under a photo with caption "Donna Richmond, the Exeter victim of a sadistic slaying"].

> ***DA Files Five Charges in Girl's Murder***
>
> Counts of homicide, kidnap with intent to do bodily harm, rape, sodomy and failure to register as a sex offender. District Attorney Jay Powell said he will ask for the death penalty for Clifton who was arrested Saturday about 6 pm after Donna's mutilated body had been found. Personal articles were found strewn in several places west of Exeter.

Again, just as with the *Times-Delta* story, Donna was not raped or sodomized, and Oscar wasn't a registered sex offender. Although Donna was stabbed, and her death was horrible, she was not "mutilated." The autopsy confirming the lack of sexual assault had been completed by 7:30 pm on the 27th, and the conclusions were unequivocal. DA Powell was not mistaken about the facts, he was simply generating headlines for himself, trying to explain why Oscar would have randomly blown up his life and family, and making sure there wouldn't be even one potential juror in the county who didn't believe him. The statements to the press were blatant and unconstitutional prosecutorial misconduct.

On January 26, 1976, Powell silently dropped the rape, sodomy, and failure to register charges. Neither the *Visalia Times-Delta* nor the *Exeter Sun* reported the news, and the prior lies became the permanent facts of the case in the court of public opinion, and within the Tulare DA's Office. That's all it took to change reality—and history, a few lines of lies to the newspaper.

On January 2, 1976, TCSO McKinney met with Beth Brumley in her home and showed her a photo of the recent in-person lineup attended by Gloria Mascorro. Beth had already told Officer Diaz that she had seen Oscar's photo in the papers as the suspect charged with killing her classmate Donna. During the interview, McKinney also showed Beth a photo of Oscar's truck: "R/O was advised that photo of suspect's pickup looked like pickup she had observed." During *this* interview, Beth now indicated that the incident had occurred between 2:15-2:30 pm on the 26th.

Pettyjohn followed up with the man who had purchased the appliance from Frank Thomas on the 26th, Bill Irwin. Pettyjohn spoke to Irwin by phone on January 7th, and Irwin said he was supposed to be at the Thomas home between 1:00-2:00 pm, but that he was "quite late," arriving after 3:00 pm. He had dropped his wife at the Tulare District Hospital for medical care at 1:55 pm, then driven up to Visalia to purchase and load another freezer at the Kelley house, and made "a couple of stops" ***before*** they got to Garden Street. He recalled Thomas being at the end of his driveway and making a comment about the fact that he was late—Irwin said that he replied that he was "slow but sure." He said that he was at the Thomas house for thirty minutes. Unfortunately, although Pettyjohn included the interview in his report to Donahue, he did not obtain a sworn statement from Irwin.

At this point, the defense team felt confident that they had proven Oscar's alibi, and indicated in their notes that Brumley's and Mascorro's identification had been tainted by the Sheriff and the newspaper coverage, and were likely mistaken. On the flip side, TCSO had no interest in checking on Oscar's alibi or interviewing any of the defense witnesses. They believed the case was open and shut. Both sides believed that the forensic examinations would prove them correct.

The first order of business for IFS was to try to prove that Donna had been sexually assaulted. The physical examination at autopsy had found no evidence to support it: there was no sign of trauma, Donna was still virginal, and all microscopic examinations of samples taken were specifically noted as negative for spermatozoa (sperm cells). TCSO Johnson had given Criminalist Morton the "rape kit" slides and wash fluid, a sample of Donna's pubic hair, and some "crusted" dirt removed from her backside together in one evidence envelope.

The current crime lab guidelines used today for testing an item for male ejaculate are fairly simple and plainly stated:

- Seminal fluid is the secretions of the male reproductive organs not containing sperm cells.
- Semen is defined as the secretions of the male reproductive organs that contain sperm cells.
- The presumptive test for seminal fluid is based upon the detection of the enzyme acid phosphatase. This enzyme is not specific for seminal fluid.
- If acid phosphatase (AP) is present, a purple color will appear within a short period of time (30 seconds).
- A positive reaction indicates the presumptive presence of seminal fluid.
- A confirmatory examination for sperm cells should be conducted.

This procedure has remained completely and totally unchanged since AP testing was introduced in the 1950s, and on January 5, 1976 IFS Criminalist Michael Grubb followed it, to the letter.

He ran the control sample to make sure the testing chemicals were working properly and obtained the purple color in eight to ten seconds. Grubb's lab bench notes indicate that the pubic hair and anal wash were both negative for AP—taking more than forty seconds to develop any color.

The results of his last test were *inconclusive*:

> Sample from hair—some areas in sample have a dirt adherent to crusted stain. Crusted area tested observed under Stereoscope—Beginning of color developed in less than 12 seconds—strong @ 30 seconds. Indicative of S.F. [*seminal fluid*].

The *proper* crime lab procedures direct a criminologist on how to deal with this situation:

> If discoloration occurs as the test is being conducted, there may be an ***interfering substance***. The analyst should proceed with the test and determine if the test is truly AP presumptive positive, negative, or inconclusive. [*emphasis added*]

There ***was*** an interfering substance—the Gibberellin tree spray. It was covering the samples. Grubb reported the "inconclusive" result, and Morton directed him to take the evidence samples to a lab at Berkeley for further examination and testing. They were given to graduate student Edward Blake, who started with a microscopic examination of the pubic hair. He observed hair, menstrual blood, and bits of dirt, but no sperm cells. He then created a "wash" of the dirt and hairs: A small portion of clumped hair was extracted with saline and centrifuged to remove dirt and other debris. The solution was decanted for further analysis.

Blake proceeded to check the "wash" for the presence of AP. He reported to Morton that AP was present in the sample. Blake did not report the development time, so it is impossible to know if his testing was a true positive, but it seems highly unlikely given Grubb's prior negative and inconclusive AP testing of the same evidence following the proper procedures. Not only was Blake's report of the presence of AP questionable, he then drew a wholly unsupported scientific conclusion: "These determinations prove that human semen is contained on the pubic hairs that were submitted."

Not only did Blake fail to identify "semen" (which requires the presence of sperm cells), he didn't even find *any* of the necessary cellular components of seminal fluid: granulocytes, macrophages, lymphocytes, spermatocytes, or epithelial cells. Blake's statement was junk science in 1976, and is embarrassingly hot garbage today. In science, precise language matters, and in criminal cases it can mean the difference between freedom and death row. Grubb and Blake tested the same samples and got the same results, but reached different scientific conclusions. Grubb found that the possible AP reaction was "indicative of seminal fluid," and Blake stated that it "prove(s) human semen." It may seem like a wording difference or semantics, but scientifically they aren't even close. It feels like such a small, nitpicky point, but those words cost Oscar his life and let Donna's killer escape justice.

Criminalist Grubb's response to Blake's finding was completely appropriate. He picked up the evidence from Berkeley, took it back to IFS, and analyzed Blake's samples to confirm his finding of "semen" on the pubic hairs. Grubb not only failed to find "semen," what he did next scientifically proved that Oscar ***could not*** have contributed any bodily fluid to the evidence.

Before DNA testing, one of the only ways to identify a rapist was to find his blood type in the evidence. About ninety percent of men secrete their blood type in their nasal mucus, saliva, and ejaculate. If the victim and suspect had the same blood type, this testing wasn't informative, but if they had different types, the two-step ABO process could identify both:

> The forward grouping suggests the presence or absence of A and B antigens, whereas reverse grouping indicates the presence or absence of anti-A and anti-B in serum.

This can be easily visualized in Blake's own chart, prepared when he tested vials of blood from Donna and Oscar to determine their blood types.

1. Reaction of Cells

	Oscar Clifton	Donna Richmond
Anti A	-	+++
Anti B	-	-

2. Reaction of Serum

	Oscar Clifton	Donna Richmond
A cells	+++	-
B cells	+++	+++

Blood Typing by E. Blake

Oscar's type O blood contained neither the A nor B antigens, but both antibodies—his body would attack those blood types as foreign, which is why blood has to be typed before a transfusion. Donna's type A had the A antigen, and antibodies to B. ABO testing is run in "forward and reverse" to confirm the findings, and to make sure it's not a mixed sample or contaminated with another bodily fluid.

Blake had made two slides of the "wash" that he claimed contained human "semen," then Grubb examined those slides microscopically when he returned to his lab. The purpose was a "sperm search." Again, there can be no finding of "semen" in the absence of sperm cells, even with a positive AP result. That is because there are many substances that either contain that enzyme or can create a false positive test. Grubb's findings were actually conclusive—there were ***no sperm cells*** present on Blake's slides—it was not human semen.

Then, on January 26, 1976, Grubb conducted ABO testing on these samples. He found only the A antigen (forward), but no antibodies to A (reverse): It was either a mixed sample from two different individuals with blood type A, or the sample contained no male body fluids, only Donna's own. Blood types B, AB, and O were positively excluded. If Blake really did find human semen, it could not have come from Oscar.

Criminalist Grubb recorded all of this analysis and testing in his lab bench notes and it was contained on his time slips, and the later invoice that was paid by the DA's office. Further, Grubb testified to this fact under oath to the Grand Jury on February 5, 1976:

> I transported the material to Ed Blake… I then picked up the material at a later date and performed ABO typing of the material on the pubic hairs. The reaction that I received was indicative of a ***type A individual***. [*emphasis added*]

Grand Jury is a process for the prosecutor to present his witnesses and evidence, and obtain an indictment. This is done outside the presence of the defendant and defense counsel, and they are not allowed to present any evidence to the jury. Needless to say, DA Powell did not ask Grubb or Blake what Oscar's blood type was, and the jurors had no idea that the ABO testing had eliminated Oscar as a suspect.

However, I have no doubt whatsoever that the reason the "crust" on the dirt from Donna's backside got a reaction to the AP test was due solely to the fact that it was the tree spray Gibberellin. *Why?* Because that is ***exactly*** what Gibberellin is designed to do—it stimulates the activation and secretion of the naturally occurring acid phosphatase in the oranges to make them ripen faster. At the end of the season, oranges that are still green can be "pushed" by Gibberellin. Otherwise, they fall off the tree and that portion of the crop is lost. Gibberellin causes any organic matter that normally secretes acid phosphatase to "greatly increase" it. The entire function of Gibberellin is to boost the amount of AP. Obviously, a forensic sample with known Gibberellin contamination should ***never*** have been subjected to AP testing, and any results would be invalid, since it would have automatically created an increase in the amount of AP detected in a sample.

Donna was covered in Gibberellin, over her entire body, but especially where it pooled on the dirt clod stuck in the crevice of her buttocks—the exact sample that both Grubb and Blake tested. There is no mention of the tree spray in any TCSO report, the autopsy, or the lab bench notes. Although it is visible in the crime scene photos, there is no evidence that Blake, Grubb, or Morton saw those photos, or if they had, would have had any reason to suspect it was freshly sprayed Gibberellin. The AP test was never meant to be used on samples that had *known* sources of AP other than semen, like female urine, menstrual blood, citrus peel/leaves/stems, or nematodes in dirt. Generally, it is utilized on dry stains on fabrics like clothing and bedding. As forensic methodology manuals confirm, AP is a presumptive test to find areas to examine under the microscope with Christmas Tree Stain to find sperm cells, and confirm the presence of semen. It was never intended to be used on dirt clods full of citrus debris sprayed with Gibberellin. That is just ridiculous. Blake's testing was unscientific, and his conclusions factually untrue.

Morton and Grubb spent January and February of 1976 examining almost one hundred pieces of evidence collected by TCSO. They collected hairs and fibers from the items of clothing, and compared those to Oscar and Donna. On March 12, 1976, Morton spoke to ADA Bleier, and told him that they had found nothing of evidentiary value—no blood, fingerprints, semen, hairs, fibers, leaves, soil, or tire or footprint matches. *It was all a big zero.* According to a phone message for Morton taken by his assistant on March 22, 1976, Bleier did not take the news well: "Regarding Clifton case. Needs report immediately!! Evidence is going to defense because of delays. Guy is very upset."

Bleier was worried that the defense was about to learn that he had nothing, and seek a dismissal of the charges against Oscar. At this juncture, you can really feel the pressure on Criminalist Morton to give Bleier what he wanted: something, anything that connected Oscar to the homicide. Morton's private lab only stayed in business as long as they had satisfied clients who hired them again, or gave them a positive referral. If you are working for the prosecution, that is measured by convictions obtained. It goes without saying that this is not how forensic analysis is supposed to work, but in reality, any time there is room for a scientific opinion or "interpretation," criminalists feel pressured to lean towards their employer. County and state crime labs are no exception, and too often see themselves as an extension of the prosecutors' offices.

On March 25, 1976, Criminalist Morton tried to find hair evidence to connect Oscar to the homicide. He took each of the hairs collected from Donna's and Oscar's clothing and mounted them to glass slides. Each evidence slide was given a number that corresponded to the original item of evidence, so a hair collected from Oscar's sweater (item #16) was given the number 16b. The evidence number, case number, and Morton's initials were placed on a label at the edge of each slide. At the same time, Morton also prepared twenty hair reference slides for comparison purposes:

- Clifton Pubic Hair
- 2 Hairs (Head) D. Richmond
- Head Hair D. Richmond
- Pubic Hair Donna Jo Richmond (later called slide VPH)
- Clifton Back of Head x2
- Head Hair D. Richmond x6
- Clifton Right Side of Head x2
- Clifton Top of Head x2
- Clifton Left Side of Head x2
- Clifton Front of Head
- Clifton Head Hair, D.J. Richmond Head Hair

Morton made written lab notes about the slides and his microscopic hair comparison examinations, then laid out all of the slides together and photographed them as a record of the exact slides that were examined.

He looked at the hairs from Donna's clothing and the ski mask found on Neel Ranch for Oscar's hair, but nothing matched. He then looked at the hairs collected from Oscar's clothes and the sweepings from the floor of his truck, but couldn't find any similar to Donna's hair. Microscopic hair "analysis" is ridiculous junk science, long ago discredited as subjective nonsense, but in 2019, the exact history of these comparison slides turned out to be important.

The conditions under which these slides were created are appalling. One of the slides is a large, double-sized slide that contains both Donna's and Oscar's hairs—together. You can see hairs exposed, sticking out from under the covers. The slide is proof positive that Criminalist Morton had both Oscar's and Donna's hair samples out at the same time, on the same work station. Morton later testified that he didn't even bother with tweezers; he used his bare hands. He touched Oscar's hair, then Donna's hair, the slides, and the slide covers, transferring DNA from himself, the suspect, and the victim between the hair comparison slides and the evidence slides. He didn't care, and there was no reason for him to worry about sweat, spit, skin cells, menstrual blood, or urine transferring between the items because he just wanted to look at hairs under a microscope.

Modern DNA testing is so sensitive it can amplify an imperceptible level of human cellular material—a profile can be developed from a single cell. A couple of recent criminal cases have highlighted the dangers of accidental DNA transfer. A San Jose man was killed in a home invasion robbery, and DNA testing of his fingernails matched a petty criminal. The man was arrested and charged with homicide. Eventually, his attorney who was working on the accused's history of substance abuse as a mitigating factor for the death penalty discovered that the defendant had been in the hospital at the time of the murder, and the police and DA had not bothered to check his alibi. It turned out that the same paramedic had taken the defendant to the hospital and then responded to help the murder victim. Even though he had changed his gloves between calls, he still left the first man's DNA on the victim.

A similar (but opposite) problem occurred when eleven-year-old Rene Conrad went missing on her way to her neighbor's house. A month later, she was found murdered and hidden in the neighbor's backyard kiln. The neighbor, Galik, was convicted, and on appeal argued that his DNA was not found on the victim, but other male DNA was. At issue were some rape kit swabs and a piece of duct tape that covered the girl's mouth. A male profile that did not belong to Galik was found on the tape, but it turned out to be from a criminalist who had worked in the DOJ lab in Fresno. Although he had not handled the tape, and didn't even work in the same lab, somehow a few of his cells had gotten on the evidence in 1996, and were picked up by DNA testing in 2012.

In that case (*In re Keven Duane Galik*, 2021), the rape kit swabs contained male DNA, but there had been no sperm cells found and the amount of DNA was very "low level," which suggested contamination. Despite the presence of unknown and known male DNA on the evidence that didn't match Galik, his conviction was upheld. In 2021, the court found that the partial male profile was not related to the crime:

> (1) The detected DNA was found in low levels; (2) only partial Y-STR profiles were detected, and the origins are unknown; (3) the results are uninterpretable.
>
> The DNA testing now is very sensitive and can detect DNA from less than ten cells and can even detect "something from a single cell." It is absolutely imperative that the utmost care and caution be taken that exogenous cellular material is not introduced so it ends up as a DNA result.
>
> The physiological source of petitioner's new DNA evidence is unknown. The DNA from the vaginal swabs was a "low level." Touch DNA is a low amount of DNA that is transferred to an object not through a body fluid. Most of the time, it is not possible to determine how and from where touch DNA originated. Touch DNA does not establish that the person actually touched that object or had direct contact with it. Secondary transfer occurs when something you have

> on, let's say your own DNA on your own body gets picked up by an intermediary and then transferred to something else. If someone was not careful during an autopsy, transfer DNA could occur.
>
> You don't know who that profile is from, and you don't even know if it is relevant to the crime.

In truth, secondary transfer DNA is a terrifying reality for criminal defendants. Juries tend to believe that if someone's DNA is found, the only explanation is primary transfer—the defendant was at the scene and left the evidence. However, there are an incalculable number of ways DNA can transfer to an item. A 2016 study on items washed together in a washing machine is a case in point:

> For both spermatozoa and vaginal secretions, we revealed that ***sufficient amounts of DNA may transfer*** onto laundered clothing to yield complete genetic profiles. Furthermore, DNA from relatives living within the same household was found in most cuttings taken from control children's underwear. [*emphasis added*]

In late 2009, police in Europe thought they had a serial killer and burglar connected through DNA to more than 40 cases over 16 years: "*The Phantom of Heilbronn*." It turned out that the evidence swabs had all been contaminated with the same factory worker's DNA during the swab manufacturing. Every single item that comes in contact with evidence can introduce unrelated DNA, including evidence bags and gloves. None of this could have been imagined when Criminalist Morton made the hair slides in 1976. He was just trying to find something to connect Oscar to the homicide, not create contaminated hair slides—but unfortunately, he did.

Although Morton's initial forensic analysis had not found anything, he offered ADA Bleier three pieces of evidence that he felt were worth more specialized expert examination: the white paint transfer from Donna's bike, a fragment of leaf TCSO Hensley said he collected from the side mirror of Oscar's truck, and the footprints documented at Neel Ranch.

On January 27th, Morton had run tests on the paint transfer from Donna's bike, and compared it to the samples of paint he collected from Oscar's truck and the TCSO vehicle. He eliminated the paint from Oscar's truck and found the TCSO vehicle to be "similar." On March 15th, Morton called TCSO Johnson and asked him to collect more paint samples. Johnson returned to Jackson's Towing and removed paint from fourteen different locations on Oscar's truck. On March 28th, Morton tested all of those samples against the paint from Donna's bike—they were not the same. Oscar's truck had not been in contact with the bike, but a vehicle with white paint similar to a law enforcement vehicle had been.

Morton sent the leaf bit from the truck mirror, along with two leaves collected at Neel Ranch, to a research botanist at Berkeley named John Strother. On April 6, 1976, Strother wrote a report to Morton with his findings:

> In my judgement [*sic*], both samples are from plants of the genus Citrus, which includes grapefruits, lemons and oranges of commerce… the material was not sufficient to allow positive identification as to particular species.

In short, Strother could not say that the leaf from Oscar's truck had come from an orange tree or Neel Ranch.

Although two different sets of footprints were found near Donna's bike, Sgt. Byrd had ordered Johnson to ignore them. There were eight photos of footprints taken at Neel Ranch. Morton's analysis had eliminated seven of the photos—they did not match any of Oscar's footwear. However, Morton felt that one of the photos, which was only a partial heel print, could have been a match to one of the three pairs of boots collected from Oscar's house.

On March 26th, Morton called James Harris, Associate Director of the Visibility Lab, University of San Diego; he also called the Naval

Electronics Lab; and, finally, Richard Blackwell at the Jet Propulsion Lab at CalTech. He billed this work as "locating image enhancement specialist." On March 28th, Morton called ADA Bleier and received authorization to hire Harris. On the 29th, TCSO Hensley gave Johnson the original 4x5 negatives for the eight footprint images taken at Neel Ranch. Johnson then flew with the negatives to San Diego, met Harris at the airport, gave him the negatives, and flew back to Visalia. On April 5th, Morton called Sheriff Wiley and they spoke for 15 minutes about the evidence in the case. The next day, Morton called Harris and spoke to him twice, for a total of about 40 minutes, then called ADA Bleier. None of the news was good for the prosecution.

On April 8th, Morton had two more phone conversations with Harris, and another on April 12th. On April 13th, Morton sent an express package via airplane to Harris that contained a mold of the boot heel that Morton had made in his lab. On April 15th, Morton called Harris again, and on the 17th, he flew round trip from Oakland to San Diego to work on the possibility of image enhancement: *Could Harris enhance the image to the point where he could "match" the boots worn by the defendant?* The total cost of that trip was $700. On June 8th, Harris sent Morton an invoice for two days of work on the photos, at $400 per day, which Morton paid with a note that said:
"It is unfortunate that we were not more successful with the limited work which was performed."

Limited? What more could they have done? Flown it to the moon and back? The DA's office paid a couple thousand dollars to have an expert tell them that none of the footprints found on Neel Ranch matched Oscar.

Chapter Six Sources

1. Visalia Times-Delta - December 29, 1975
2. Autopsy Report - January 27-29, 1975
3. TCSO Report - Holguin December 28, 1975
4. TCSO Report - King December 28, 1975
5. TCSO Chain of Custody Card #10

6. Lineup Photo - December 29, 1975
7. TCSO Report - Deathriage December 31, 1975
8. TCSO Report - McKinney December 30, 1975
9. Tulare Advance-Register - November 23, 1974
10. Visalia Times-Delta - May 5, 1976
11. TCSO Report - Johnson December 26, 1975
12. Charles Morton Bike Paint Bench Notes
13. Donahue Intake Notes
14. Stmt Taken by PI Pettyjohn - Gene Owens December 30, 1975
15. Stmt Taken by PI Pettyjohn - Frank Thomas December 31, 1975
16. Stmt Taken by PI Pettyjohn - Danny Boland December 30, 1975
17. Stmt Taken by PI Pettyjohn - Avery/Glenda Dula January 2, 1976
18. Stmts Taken by PI Pettyjohn - Cliftons January 2, 1976
19. Pettyjohn Report - January 8, 1976
20. Brumley Statement December 31, 1975
21. Woodlake PD Report - Diaz December 31, 1975
22. Exeter Sun - December 31, 1975
23. TCSO Report - McKinney January 2, 1976
24. IFS Bench Notes
25. Forensic AP Testing November 17, 2020
26. Blake Report to Morton - February 3, 1976
27. Mujahid, Adnan, and Franz L Dickert. "Blood Group Typing: From Classical Strategies to the Application of Synthetic Antibodies Generated by Molecular Imprinting." Sensors (Basel, Switzerland) vol. 16,1 51. 31 Dec. 2015
28. IFS Timeslips
29. IFS Invoice
30. Testimony of Michael Grubb at Grand Jury - February 5, 1976

31. Bailey, K. M., et al. "Effects of Gibberellic Acid on the Activation, Synthesis, and Release of Acid Phosphatase." Journal of Experimental Botany, vol. 27, no. 97, Oxford University Press, 1976.
32. John Pehrson "Citrus Crop Load Alters Spray Plans" Fresno Bee, December 27, 1970
33. Crime Scene Photos
34. Bleier to Morton Phone Message - March 22, 1976
35. IFS Long Distance Call Records
36. IFS Hair Slide Photos
37. "Framed for Murder By His Own DNA"
38. In re Kevin Duane Galik, Sr. On Habeas Corpus, June 17, 2021
39. "The False Promise of DNA Testing"
40. "Germany's Phantom Serial Killer: A DNA Blunder"
41. TCSO Report - Johnson March 16, 1976
42. TCSO Report - Johnson March 22, 1976
43. Strother Report to Morton - April 6, 1976
44. TCSO Report - Johnson March 26, 1976
45. Receipts and Invoice Harris

CHAPTER SEVEN

"May there never be another one."

On Tuesday, February 3, 1976, Sgt. Vaughan and his team met with Dr. Joel Fort, a psychiatrist who often served as an expert witness in criminal cases. He was hired to create a psychological profile of the Ransacker. Fort was famous for his testimony that helped convict Tex Watson in the Manson Family cases. A month after the meeting in Visalia, Dr. Fort testified in the trial against Patty Hearst. Fort claimed that she had willingly joined her kidnappers in robbing banks—he called her "*The Queen of the SLA.*" He claimed that her kidnappers hadn't raped her; she had consented to having sex with them. A year after his testimony against Hearst, the State of California accused him of cheating Medi-Cal. He eventually had his medical license suspended for three months, and was put on probation for a year.

Given my prior knowledge of Fort, it was difficult for me to accept his assessment of the Ransacker. However, it was interesting, and proved to be very accurate. More importantly, Fort shaped the views of Vaughan's team, and directed their investigation:

> Pertinent information developed during this session was as follows:
>
> 1. The suspect is primarily a prowler and peeping tom with burglary being secondary.
> 2. The suspect could live in another city and come to Visalia for the sole purpose of his entertainment and gratification.

3. The suspect probably lives alone or with an elderly relative but could be married. He is a loner.
4. The suspect is a voyeur who enjoys seeing peoples' intimate possessions.
5. The suspect may very well enjoy the high risk or danger of the whole matter.
6. There is insufficient evidence to conclude that the suspect has any typical common severe mental illness. He could function effectively during the daytime but could be considered weird by neighbors or fellow workers.
7. The primary motivation for the crime is sexual.
8. The suspect has most likely peeked in hundreds of windows, most of which have not come to our attention, and then maybe weeks or months later, the suspect burglarizes some of these same homes.
9. The suspect may be achieving the simplest form of pleasure or sexual release by just looking and may then masturbate when he gets home.
10. The suspect probably hoards all of the property he has taken.
11. The suspect would most likely not leave the area and will probably continue his pattern of prowling and burglaries.
12. Most likely the suspect is back out prowling.

In telling citizens about the suspect, you should drop the physical description and tell them that the suspect lives a kind of, on the surface, ordinary existence. He doesn't call attention to himself but is kind of seclusive, isolated, and probably has no obvious or no known friendships or social relations. Someone who has lived in the neighborhood for a long time but neighbors know very little about him. A loner type.

In the days following the above session, teams of investigators were assigned surrounding cities to personally contact law enforcement agencies and extensively check on

> prowlers and voyeurs. Agencies contacted were all TCSO substations, Porterville, Lindsay, Exeter, Farmersville, Woodlake, Tulare, Dinuba, Hanford, Lemoore, Corcoran, Kingsburg, and inquires [*sic*] by phone of Fresno Police and Sheriff's Office.

At this *same* point in time—early 1976—Sgt. Byrd was already assigned to the cases of Murphy, Nieman, Armour… *and* Donna Richmond. He didn't say a single word about any of them in response to VPD's inquiries. A week later, Agents McGowen and Shipley went to Atascadero State Hospital and spent a day discussing the case and suspect with Dr. R. M. Schumann, psychiatrist, and Dr. Paul F. Branwell, psychologist. Their profile of the offender was nearly identical to the one Fort provided, but added one specific detail:

> Statistics reveal that 50% of voyeurs don't live in the area they prowl but almost half of them live within 15 to 20 minutes of the area they prowl in. This is 15-20 minutes driving time by car, or 15-20 minutes walking time.

Vaughan ended his summary report:

> As of March 3, 1976, all prowler calls are being followed up by investigators but no evidence has been found to lead officers to believe that our suspect has been active.

There are a lot of interesting insights there, but I was surprised by how many Sgt. Vaughan had already figured out on his own based upon his years in law enforcement and interviewing offenders. He already knew they were looking for a sexually motivated stalker and peeper. However, he and his team had been convinced that they were looking for someone who lived within the ransacking zone. The experts agreed that he likely lived further out, in a neighboring area or town. This was hard for Vaughan to accept. He felt that the Ransacker knew the neighborhoods and victims far too well, so he had to be a Visalia local. It was a frustrating spring for his team; they worried that they had chased him away and lost their best chance to identify and catch him.

Meanwhile, DA Powell was riding high that February. He had just obtained a conviction and death sentence in the trial of Henry Borbon for a double homicide. The case had been riddled with controversy, including testimony from one of Powell's former deputies that Borbon was being prosecuted despite Powell's belief in his actual innocence. There were also substantiated charges that key prosecution witnesses had been bribed with cash, sex, and drugs, or threatened into testifying against Borbon. The critical witness, Borbon's own cousin, who had been implicated in the murders, suddenly had "new memories" after being hypnotized, and after having pending charges against him dropped.

Why did Powell care which of the two Borbon cousins he prosecuted? Because, in June 1974, Henry Borbon had filed a one million dollar lawsuit against Tulare County for false arrest during a controversial fake drug sting meant to boost Sheriff Wiley's re-election campaign. It was all very complicated and bizarre, yet entirely true.

Powell had bolstered the circumstantial case against Oscar by adding minor charges related to Gloria Mascorro and Beth Brumley. Ray Donahue filed motions and appeals to have those charges separated from the homicide trial as unrelated and prejudicial. He lost. Donahue also filed a motion for change of venue—to have the trial moved to a different county that hadn't run the sensationalistic and completely incorrect news stories. He didn't win that motion either. Just as frustrating was the DA's refusal to provide any information on the evidence testing that had been done at IFS. The defense was completely in the dark, despite a clear order from the court that required that "reports" on all evidence tested be provided to Donahue.

Oscar's trial was scheduled to begin on April 19th, and on March 26th, Donahue was still begging the court to help him get ***any*** information on the forensic testing:

Donahue: Your Honor, I would like an order that all the reports and so forth be reduced to writing and submitted to us. I understand that they have a problem with this laboratory, and I'm not trying to lay the blame on the district attorney, but the laboratory hasn't had the work done. And, I think we must have these reports within the next week. The 19th is coming up pretty quick here.

So, I have contacted the laboratory in San Francisco, and I talked to Kenneth Parker who owns it, and he is willing if the Court makes an order that if the other laboratories don't finish it up, he'll go and pick up the items, particularly the clothing and the tires, the boot markers, the three things we're concerned with at this time. I think we have everything else.

Bleier: Well, your Honor, I thought the Court had made an order and at this time we oppose any order of the Court that the witnesses reduce their findings to writing. We think there is no authority for that. If we proceed with those basis of oral communication between us, I don't think there is any basis for forcing them to write something up constituting the basis of their testimony.

Donahue: I'm asking that any laboratory reports or any technical data any expert witness is going to be involved in this thing concerning the investigation of evidence that was picked up at the defendant's home, his car and so forth, that those items be reduced to writing.

Bleier: We oppose that for the same basis; he has no authority for that. If we choose to deal with our witnesses on a written statement, he has an opportunity to talk to them and we can't instruct them not to talk to them but to my knowledge there is no authority that these matters should be reduced to writing.

It probably goes without saying that Donahue didn't win that argument either. The judge refused to enforce his own prior discovery order, and told Donahue that he could have his expert talk to Morton, but that he wasn't going to get the lab notes or any reports from IFS.

This was utter insanity. Not only was that a due process violation, it goes against all common sense notions of fairness. Why wouldn't the defendant be entitled to see the results of the evidence testing?

It's clear from the long distance phone records, and messages between Criminalist Morton and ADA Bleier, that they were trying to stall the defense's access to the testing results for as long as possible. Although Bleier was telling Donahue and the judge that the testing wasn't done, he knew that Morton had come up with nothing incriminating, and was frantically seeking outside experts to find something to tie Oscar to Donna, the bike scene, or Neel Ranch.

In the end, Donahue was allowed to send Kenneth Parker to IFS for an "informal verbal discovery" meeting with Morton. Parker asked for copies of the lab bench notes from the analysis done by Morton and Grubb, and for a copy of Blake's report, but Morton said he couldn't provide them on instructions from the DA's office. Parker gave Donahue a summary of what Morton had told him, which wasn't much, and indicated that he expected that he would know more when he reviewed Morton's "formal discovery," which he expected to include:

> … what was examined, what tests were used, what were the results of the tests, and what do the tests mean in terms of support of opinion regarding what is at issue.

Bleier argued that the defense was not entitled to see any of that information, the judge agreed, *and* as a result, it was never provided to Parker or Donahue.

Reading through the correspondence between Donahue and Parker, it's clear that neither of them was a creative thinker. They were solely focused on the fact that none of the analyzed evidence implicated Oscar. They didn't wonder why Bleier was so insistent that they not see the lab bench notes or any written scientific conclusions from Morton or Grubb. Bleier's behavior should have made them highly suspicious that there was exculpatory evidence that pointed away from Oscar—and proved his actual innocence.

In May 1976, as Oscar's trial approached, Judge Ginsburg overturned the conviction of Henry Borbon and ordered a new trial. Ginsburg cited prosecutorial misconduct, specifically: Prosecutors made misleading statements to the jury, repeatedly referred to inadmissible evidence in front of the jury, gave the jury the impression that the defense was hiding evidence, and suppressed testimony that it was Henry's cousin (Fernando) who was the actual accomplice involved—***not*** Henry. Ginsburg said that the DA also failed to disclose information that impeached the cousin's credibility, including his own past admissions of participation in the homicides and four felony fraud charges that were pending against him. Ginsburg said he had no choice but to overturn the conviction because the prosecutors' actions were committed in "bad faith."

The Borbon case should have served as a warning to Donahue. Every account of DA Powell's office describes chaos, and definitely not a "normal" prosecutor; he was willing to do *anything* to win a conviction, no matter how unconstitutional or immoral. Yet Donahue seemed unable to adjust. He failed to react to behavior that should have been alarming, especially from ADA Bleier. When Donahue asked for discovery documents and didn't get them, he just let it slide. Meanwhile, Powell had suffered a humiliating loss in Borbon, and was becoming ever more desperate to make up for it by ensuring that Oscar Clifton ended up on death row. This resulted in a last minute panic, and a flurry of activity behind the scenes.

On June 9, 1976, TCSO Chamberlain and Detective Chambers went to Jackson's Garage—the impound yard where Oscar's truck had been since his arrest—and collected both sets of seat belts as well as the bench seat. That afternoon, Chamberlain arrived in Los Angeles at the L. A. County Sheriff's Crime Lab with the seat and seatbelts. Criminalists at the lab examined the items for evidence of blood and found nothing. Chamberlain then returned the seat and belts to Jackson's like it never happened. The results were highly exculpatory, and DA Powell had a duty to disclose the fact of the testing and the results to Donahue. Powell apparently just didn't care.

When Morton examined the white sweater Oscar had been wearing on the day of the homicide, he found a blond hair, and collected it into evidence. The hair could have belonged to Oscar, Donna, or Oscar's younger daughter. Morton conducted microscopic hair comparisons, but still could not determine who contributed the hair to the sweater.

Since Morton could not conclude that the hair belonged to Donna, he reached out to Richard Bisbing at the Michigan State Police Crime Lab. Bisbing was recognized as the leading authority on ABO typing of hairs, and had been able to get his results admitted in criminal cases. Morton obtained Bisbing's testing method, and on June 22-23, carefully ran three rounds of ABO testing on hairs from Oscar, Donna, and the sweater. The results were conclusive and consistent. Oscar's hair was O, Donna's was A, and the sweater hair was O. There is no way that the hair found on Oscar's sweater came from Donna—she was "positively excluded."

At this point, jury selection had already begun. There was no forensic evidence connecting Oscar to any crime, and Powell's "eyewitnesses," Brumley and Mascorro, were both in direct conflict with the people who placed Oscar in Visalia between 3:00-4:00 pm. It appears that the only reason that TCSO finally decided to check with the alibi witnesses was to prove a theory that PI Pettyjohn had somehow told them what to say, or tainted their statements. The idea was crazy on its face. Pettyjohn was a "Mr. Law and Order" agent with the FBI for over thirty years.

On June 21, 1976, Sgt. Byrd finally interviewed Frank Thomas, the man on Garden Street who had sold his appliance (six months earlier) on December 26th:

Byrd: This is a Friday after Christmas being, December the 26th, 1975, is that correct?

Thomas: That is right.

Q: Someone talked to you in regards to this particular date, do you recall who that was?

A: That was Pettyjohns. [*sic*]

Q: He is an investigator… did he identify himself?

A: Yes, he identified himself, investigator.

Q: I believe the interview was in regards to if you remember a particular incident on that day, is that correct?

A: Right.

Q: Would you relate what that incident was?

A: He'd asked me if I had walked out to the end of my driveway and I had made the statement as of well, it's about time that he got here, or he finally got here, or statement to that sort, and I told him that I had and he was.

Q: Do you recall how it was that you remembered making this particular statement?

A: Yeah, I remembered.

Q: Then why was it that you made this statement?

A: Well, he was about an hour and a half late getting there.

Q: Who are we referring to?

A: This was a Bill Irwin, he was supposed to be here to buy my freezer.

Q: Oh, I see, who were you talking to when you made this statement?

A: Well, nobody in particular. I mean my son and the kids were all out there, and I had been working on their bikes and stuff, to them I guess.

Q: What time was it that you think that you made this statement?

A: Somewhere in-between ten after three and twenty after three.

Q: What makes you think that it was this time?

A: Well, when I walked out there, I remember looking at my watch, and I remember one hand was on three and one it was either just before or just after three.

Q: Do you know Oscar Clifton?

A: No.

Q: Have you ever seen Oscar Clifton?

A: I have seen pictures of him, but not in real life.

Q: Prior to seeing it in the paper, did you?

A: No.

Q: This will conclude the interview, today's date being June the 21st, 1976, time at this time 9:30 pm.

Mr. Thomas gave Byrd the name of a neighbor who had been at his house on the day of the homicide. The next morning, as jury selection continued at the courthouse, TCSO Rusty Chamberlain located and interviewed that neighbor, twelve year old Brent Trueblood. Chamberlain took his taped statement, and Brent confirmed that he had been at the Thomas house on the day after Christmas, and was in the driveway when the two trucks arrived to load the freezer and bikes. He described the trucks and passengers exactly, including the special lift gate on one of the trucks. Chamberlain pointed to the Rose house, and continued:

Chamberlain: Was there anyone working at that house that day?

Trueblood: Yeah.

Q: And were they working there during the time that these people came over to get the freezer?

A: Yeah.

Q: How many people were working there, do you know?

A: One that I could see.

Q: Was there any vehicles there?

A: Yes, a white GMC.

Q: Where was it at?

A: Backed up to the front door.

Q: Did it have anything on it that would make it stand out?

A: No, it was all stock.

Q: Are you sure it was a GMC?

A: Yes. I saw the emblem on the side of the fender.

Q: You saw an emblem on the side of the fender?

A: Yes. It said GMC with a red background and then there was some numbers on the side of the engine, but I didn't see them.

Q: Did you notice the person that was working there?

A: Yeah. He walked out the front door to the back of the pickup, turned around and walked back in.

Q: In reference to the guys loading the freezer that day, was it during that time that he walked out, or was it during another time that day?

A: It was during the time that they were loading the freezer.

Q: Where were you at when you was looking at him?

A: Next door at Thomas' in the driveway.

Q: And you had a clear view of that house over there that they are remodeling?

A: Yes.

Q: Did you ever see that pickup afterwards that you can remember?

A: No.

Q: Have you ever seen that man since that you can remember?

A: No.

Q: How long was he there before the people came over with the freezer?

A: I don't know. I was in the house most of the time before the guys with the freezer came and then we were outside. That was the first time that I saw him there.

[*NOTE: Trueblood went on to describe the man as white, in his 20s, skinny, tall, blond, no glasses, no facial hair.*]

Q: Do you think you would know him if you saw him again?

A: Maybe, I don't know.

Q: I showed you some pictures here before we started this interview. Did you see the man that you saw there the day after Christmas working on the house?

A: No, but two of them resembled him a little bit.

Q: Now, you are referring to pictures numbered two and four?

A: Yes.

Q: They resembled him a little bit, is that correct?

A: Yes.

Q: Did you notice when you came in that day was the pickup still there?

A: I think it was, we came in just as they (the freezer guys) were leaving. A friend was with me and he looked over…

Q; I don't need to know what your friend knows, just what you know. Ok? Nobody told you anything that you don't remember yourself really?

A: Nope.

Q: Do you remember anything about what he was wearing?

A: Gray overalls.

Q: Do you mean like the one-piece, or with the bib in the front?

A: The one piece.

Q: They were regular overalls like you work on a car or something?

A: Yes.

Q; Is there anything that has caused you to remember or has anyone come around and talked to you or something that made you pay strict attention to what you saw that day?

A: No, I just remember stuff.

Q: Has anyone else either from the Sheriff's office or anywhere else come and talked to you?

A: No.

Q: Have you discussed removing the freezer and this man who was working over at that house, have you discussed that with your family before today?

A: No.

Q: Has anyone asked you any questions about it?

A: No.

Q: How about your mom? Did you talk to your mom at all about it?

A: No.

There is no question in my mind that by the end of day on June 22nd, ***both*** Det. Rusty Chamberlain and Sgt. Byrd knew, for certain, that Oscar was innocent—beyond *any* doubt. It was not even a lingering question. Thomas was absolutely clear and positive about when he made the comment to the freezer guys, how long they were there, and that Pettyjohn had known about the details before he arrived for the interview. He also placed Trueblood in his driveway as a possible witness.

Trueblood's statement was the final straw for me. Trueblood had no reason to lie, and had not been coached. He was completely disinterested, and had never discussed it before. He got two details slightly wrong: Oscar was 35, not in his 20s, and the truck was a

Ford, not a GMC. However, Oscar did have a "baby face," and the red emblem Trueblood described was on the front fender facing the Thomas house—the red badge just didn't say GMC, it said "*F-100.*" It's an easy mistake to make from 164 feet away.

The unique details, that had never been discussed, were spooky. Not only had Oscar's truck been backed up to the front door, but three months before Trueblood's statement the defense had hired a local architect to make a drawing of Garden Street, and it showed Oscar's truck in that exact position. Obviously, it was highly unusual for someone to back up the front walkway to the door; nobody would just randomly guess that, not in a million years. Also, "*One pair Olive Green Coveralls*"—the coveralls—were collected into evidence in Oscar's bedroom with his white sweater. The items are consecutively numbered on the search warrant receipt, numbers two and three. They were both sent to IFS, and found to be free of evidence. Oscar had put them on over his clothing to load the greasy stove parts into the back of his truck—just as Trueblood described seeing.

TCSO Chamberlain had shown Trueblood six photos, and he had picked two as possibly being the man he saw. One of them was number four, Oscar's photo, which Chamberlain indicated on the back of it. Also, there was no other man it could have been—Bill Rose clearly said that nobody other than Oscar had been hired to work on the Garden Street house. The "tall, skinny, blond man with the white pickup" ***had to be*** Oscar, and Trueblood was positive that the only time he had seen him was during the freezer loading.

Brent Trueblood told Chamberlain that he thought his friend Johnny Guerber had spoken to Mr. Clifton during the freezer loading. Chamberlain conducted a taped interview with Guerber that same day, June 22nd, and Johnny confirmed that he also saw and spoke to Oscar while he was riding his bike near the Rose house.

The next day, Sgt. Byrd sent Chamberlain to Tulare to interview Bill Irwin, the man who bought the Thomas freezer, and his wife, Iverna. They agreed that Bill had gone to Visalia after dropping

Iverna at the hospital, and Bill told Chamberlain that he had been at the Thomas house between 1:30-2:00 pm and stayed for fifteen to twenty minutes. The next day, Chamberlain checked with the Tulare hospital, and discovered that Iverna had checked in at 1:55 pm, so Bill could not have been in Visalia at that time. Additionally, Bill said his memory was better when he originally spoke with Pettyjohn six months earlier, and referenced making "a couple of stops" on his way to the Thomas house.

TCSO Chamberlain prepared a nine-page report covering his interviews on the 22nd and 23rd, which was signed by Sgt. Byrd instead of a Lieutenant, which was highly unusual. Chamberlain also gave all of the interview tapes to Byrd for transcription.

As jury selection ended that day and the trial was getting ready to start, Oscar was worried about Donahue. He explained his concerns in a later exchange of letters:

> *Letter from Oscar to Donahue on July 18, 1977:*
> Please send me a copy of the letter from Exeter, the one to your wife, that you gave Wiley and they gave me, and I gave it to you.

> *Donahue's reply on July* 27:
> I have checked my file for a copy of the letter Mrs. Donahue received, but apparently, I did not keep a copy, for I cannot find one.

[*NOTE: Years later, Oscar hand-wrote an addendum on the bottom of that response letter from Donahue:*]

> Mr. Donahue's wife had received a letter from some unknown person. This letter concerned her husband (my attorney) trying to help me, among other things. It just seemed like Mr. Donahue stopped trying after this letter, and some more things happened to his home. I received a copy

> by mistake from the Sheriff's clerk. But, Mr. Donahue took it after receiving word from my wife that I had a copy of this letter. Now, the only proof I have that there was a letter is as stated above.

This type of threat might seem like a minor point, and something that defense attorneys dismiss, but Ray Donahue didn't usually handle murder cases. In fact, he was only associated with one other high profile criminal defense, and that case may have amplified his fear of the threatening letter to his wife. It was covered in the *Tulare Advance-Register* in 1963:

> A veteran reporter looked at the packed courtroom. "They're the type who go to funerals for entertainment, or to automobile races hoping to see a wreck," he remarked.
>
> It was… one of the most sensational murder trials in the history of Tulare County, and… the courtroom was filled with the curious, the thrill seekers, the "hangmen." People weren't just there to see and hear. They were maintaining a "death watch!"
>
> A jury of seven men and five women went out to determine the fate of convicted killers Ronald Polk and George Gregg, both 23, for the brutal mutilation slaying of a 20-year-old Norwalk sailor, William Fambro.
>
> And after the jury returned its verdict—death in the chamber at San Quentin—even then they weren't satisfied. They pushed against a door at the end of a corridor to get a last glimpse of the condemned men.
>
> A father lifted his son onto his shoulders so the child could get a better look.
>
> "You could sell 'em tickets to the execution," said another reporter," and even then it probably wouldn't be enough excitement for them. How morbid can you get?"

People from all walks of life were there at one time or another, many of them day in and day out—retired pensioners, high school students on Christmas vacation, businessmen, secretaries, housewives… Charlie Whitson, who operates a coffee shop on the courthouse's ground floor, said business had never been so good. "I'd like to have the popcorn and Coke concession," cracked Special Deputy Don Gibson, Tipton [CA].

One man accosted Ray Donahue, attorney for Gregg, in the hall one afternoon and demanded, "What in h… do you mean calling those damn niggers mister?" [as in printed original]

Reporters were repeatedly asked, "When are they gonna hang 'em?" And although the "lynchers" were there, they managed to control themselves. Deputies stationed at strategic locations in the room helped them to remember restraint.

If you had taken a poll among them at any time during the trial, you could have gotten a conviction with or without evidence.

The defense attorneys were subjected to much harsh criticism, which prompted Judge John Locke to remark:

"Unpopular causes arouse great public indignation. The uninformed tend to identify the attorney with his client or the crime allegedly perpetrated by the client.

Thoughtless people tend to say the persons charged with such crimes should be hanged forthwith… The greatest danger to our American system lies in the unthinking clamor for the hanging tree and the lynch law.

Yet were their liberty in jeopardy, these over-zealous persons would be the first to demand each and all of their constitutional rights."

And what did the two defendants think of it all?

"I thought we got a fair trial… Mr. Donahue worked real hard for me. It's not his fault. I've been treated okay here."

He said he wasn't too surprised when the jury sentenced him to death. "I know that's the way Mr. Ballantyne (DA) wanted it."

Polk, unlike Gregg, feels he did not get a fair trial... he thought DA Ballantyne "went out of his way to stick me," but that his attorney, Nat Bradley, did "all he could."

Some hardened court veterans admitted they "got a queasy feeling in the stomach." The spectacle is over. May there never be another one.

It's important to note that the co-defendant's attorney in that case, Nat Bradley, was the judge at Oscar's trial. We know that Donahue's family had received at least one direct threat, and he and Bradley had firsthand experience with mob justice. The community was rightly outraged by Donna's murder, and the newspapers had publicly convicted Oscar of crimes that weren't even committed. How much did fear sneak into Donahue and Bradley's decisions during the trial? I am sure it had to have had an impact on both of them.

Polk and Gregg were freed after their convictions were overturned for *Miranda* violations by TCSO during questioning. Their supposed statements were the main evidence against them. I had to wonder if Donahue and Bradley were expecting the appeals courts to make things right for Oscar too.

Chapter Seven Sources

1. **VPD Supplemental Report - Vaughan March 5, 1976**
2. **San Francisco Examiner - November 29, 1982**
3. **Borbon News Stories - Tulare Advance-Register, Exeter Sun, Visalia Times-Delta**
4. **Pre-trial motions - People v. Clifton**
5. **Hearing March 26, 1976 - People v. Clifton**
6. **IFS Long Distance Phone Records**
7. **Parker/Donahue Correspondence**
8. **Tulare Advance-Register - May 25, 1976**

9. Tulare Sheriff Report - Chamberlain June 9, 1976
10. Bisbing phone records and notes
11. IFS Morton ABO Bench Notes
12. Byrd Interview Transcript - Thomas June 21, 1976
13. Chamberlain Interview Transcript - Trueblood June 22, 1976
14. Coveralls Record - Warrant Receipt, COC, IFS Receipt, Morton Testimony
15. Testimony of Laverne Easley, July 16, 1981
16. Testimony of Rusty Chamberlain, July 16, 1981
17. TCSO Report - Chamberlain June 25, 1976
18. Chamberlain Interview Transcript - Irwin June 23, 1976
19. Oscar/Donahue Correspondence, July 18, 1977 and July 27 1977
20. Tulare Advance-Register - January 15, 1963

CHAPTER EIGHT

"Where is the notepad?"

In thinking about how to summarize Oscar's trial, I'm always struck by what *didn't* happen much more than what did. Largely, Ray Donahue's strategy was that it was up to DA Powell to prove his case, not up to the defense to disprove it. That tactic might have worked at a bench trial, with only a judge hearing it, but Donahue had a jury full of local citizens who were going to demand that somebody pay for what happened to Donna. Worse than that, they had read false news stories saying that she had been "brutally raped, sodomized, and mutilated." How was Donahue ever going to win them over when reality had left the courtroom before the trial even started?

Donahue did a terrible job of defending Oscar. The exact reasons are a constant mystery to me. He was extremely well paid for his work. He had the resources to hire an investigator and forensic expert, and yet he did the bare minimum, and often not even that. He seemed to have no curiosity and little interest in the fundamental questions that were left unanswered by TCSO's "investigation." There was nothing in his notes or behavior that indicated that he ever read the witness testimony presented at Grand Jury. Although he occasionally seemed engaged in the fight against Powell, there is always an underlying sinking feeling that he believed that Oscar was guilty, and wanted to see him convicted. Either that, or he was afraid that if he won an acquittal, his family and law practice would pay a price measured in violence, vandalism, and community shunning.

After losing the motions to have the trial moved out of the county, and the misdemeanor charges related to Brumley and Mascorro tried separately, Donahue's number one task was to seat the best jury possible. Each potential juror was questioned about their knowledge of the case from the press, past life experiences with crime, and personal relationships with potential witnesses. If the juror said something showing a clear bias, Donahue could ask the judge to strike them "for cause." If the judge refused, Donahue could use one of his peremptory challenges—he had twenty-six. Donahue left three of those challenges unused, and accepted some highly questionable jurors.

Every single juror who said that they were opposed to the death penalty was removed "for cause" by Judge Bradley. That eliminated many jurors with strong religious faith, and some intellectuals who did not trust the justice system to be fair. Nine of the seated jurors stated that they had read about the case in the newspaper. The other three didn't admit they had read about the case, but who knows. People who would lie about their knowledge of the facts of the case are even more frightening for the defense.

On the morning of the second day of jury selection, June 22, DA Powell introduced Sgt. Byrd to some of the prospective jurors: "Seated to my right is Sergeant Bob Byrd with the Tulare County Sheriff's Office. Mr. Byrd is the investigating officer in this case and he will be with me during the trial and will be one of the witnesses." Sgt. Byrd was seated in that same position every day of the proceedings.

The opening statement in a murder trial is critical. The defense needs to counter every single argument the DA is going to make, and raise doubts in the jurors' minds before they hear the state's witnesses. For Donahue, this should have started with a large display showing where Oscar was from 3:00-5:00 pm, right next to the same timeline for Donna. Each witness should have been clearly labeled, and their disinterested status discussed. Donahue could have pointed out that both Mascorro and Brumley had already seen Oscar's booking photo, and knew who they were supposed to identify. He should have explained when and where the invoice book was likely stolen. He *needed* to tell the jury that there was no sexual assault, no motive for

Oscar to kill Donna, and no physical evidence tying him to the crime. He should have blamed Sgt. Byrd for failing to recognize the scene staging, and for conducting no investigation. At best, the local sheriff's office was in over their heads, and needed outside help.

Instead, Donahue made no opening statement at all. This left the jury believing that Oscar had no defense, and that everything DA Powell said was true. It would be easy to say this was simple incompetence, but looking at Donahue's handwritten trial preparation notes, that can't be the answer:

> "Books at scene."
>
> "String of clothing like someone drawing a map."
>
> "So stupid when consider that nothing about Clifton, clothes, truck indicate he had struggled with anyone, no blood - no fibers - no tissue - no hair - no semen."
>
> "Times and distances involved."
>
> "Reasonable Doubt - other prints - note pad, 3rd person, no prints on bicycle."

No, Donahue clearly did understand the main issues, *and* that they were important. Why didn't he tell the jury? Keeping your defense secret is not a trial tactic, it's malpractice. It is so upsetting that I find myself writing the opening statement in my head, wishing I could go back in time and do Donahue's job for him. Of course, if I could go back in time Donna would have just been a few minutes late for dinner, and Oscar wouldn't have been the one on trial.

On June 24, 1976, DA Powell's case started with the testimony of Beth Brumley. As expected, she identified Oscar as the man she said had asked her a sexual question just before 3:00 pm on the afternoon of the homicide. She said it occurred as she was walking near her home. She admitted she hadn't mentioned it to anyone until she saw the story of Donna's murder on the front of the Sunday paper, two days later. On cross-examination, Donahue didn't confront her with her prior inconsistent statements regarding the time and location—

she had never said 3:00 pm before. He also didn't tell the jury that she had seen Oscar's photo prior to identifying him. Beth's mother testified next, and her only role seemed to be to confirm that Beth arrived home at 3:00 pm, and that she hadn't called the police at the time because Beth didn't tell her that anything had happened.

Gloria Mascorro also identified Oscar as the man she had seen drive past her twice, and then "masturbating" in the grove at 3:30 pm. She denied being shown Oscar's photo by Sheriff Wiley, which was completely unbelievable given her front page interview with the *Visalia Times-Delta* stating the opposite. She was adamant that Oscar was driving a plain white pickup with no visible make, and wearing a turtleneck, light gray pants, and black framed glasses—none of which were true. She admitted that her family had not told the ranch manager, the Richmonds, or the police about the incident, and TCSO had not done any investigation of the story after she told them on the 27th.

Gloria's father testified that he saw the white pickup, didn't see a make on it, and thought it was a Dodge because of the round taillights. Clearly he did not see Oscar's distinctive Ford tailgate or tall rectangular taillights. Donahue should have been able to shred the Mascorros to bits; nobody could see the back of Oscar's truck and fail to know it was a Ford, or to describe the black and white lettering. Donahue didn't tell the jury that the Mascorros worked for the Richmond family, and were not disinterested witnesses who simply reported something they happened to see.

Donna's father, Don, testified about the search for Donna and the boys finding her bike. He identified the invoice book, but said he didn't touch it. David Richmond's testimony on direct matched his dad's, but he got a little bit rattled during Donahue's cross-examination. He said that he had picked up the invoice book to see if it belonged to Donna, but his fingerprints weren't found on it. He claimed that he hadn't picked up the notepad, but seemed to know that it contained columns of numbers. Something was off, but Donahue didn't pursue it.

Don Lee, Donna's boyfriend, took the stand next. He placed the time that Donna rode away on her bike no earlier than 3:45 pm. He said he didn't watch to see which route she took, or if anyone was at the intersection near his house. It's clear from both Donahue's notes and questioning that he was suspicious of Don and his story, but Pettyjohn's lack of investigation into the state's witnesses left Donahue without a direction to follow. He did get Don to change his story on the witness stand, first saying that he hadn't offered Donna a ride home, then saying that he had, but she declined. Don said he could have driven her home in the yellow Ford Pinto that belonged to his cousin, James Scroggin. That statement was particularly odd because it was changed, and Don didn't have his license yet.

TCSO forensics deputy Brian Johnson took the stand multiple times during the trial. The first was simply to authenticate the photo he took of Donna's bike with Oscar's invoice book, and the unidentified notepad next to it. It was clear from this moment that DA Powell was actively trying to hide the notepad. Johnson looked right at the photo and said it was the bike and invoice book, as if nobody would notice the notepad if he didn't mention it. Donahue jumped right on it:

Donahue: Where is the notepad?

Johnson: I believe it's in evidence at the Sheriff's Office. I'm not sure.

Donahue also picked up on a comment Johnson made about having taken a photo with a bike tire track in it. Donahue asserted that no such photo existed—since he had not been given a copy. Donahue asked if the bottles and cans found near the bike had fingerprints, and Johnson said no, they did not. He said he photographed "one good tire track" near the bike, but it was "overlapping." Donahue asked if Johnson found skid marks, signs of a struggle, or Donna's footprints at the bike scene, and he said no. There was *nothing* that pointed to a kidnapping there.

There was a lot of confusion about whether or not Johnson checked the bike for fingerprints, but his report shows that he did, and he found none. Why weren't Donna's own prints on her bike? Why were there no fingerprints on the invoice book, or the nearby bottles and cans? There was no explanation offered. Johnson was told to return to the crime lab to bring back the mystery photo and notepad.

DA Powell then called TCSO Hensley to testify about his identification of fingerprints belonging to Oscar and his wife (who prepared the invoices) on three used pages within the invoice book. Donahue asked why there hadn't been any fingerprints, only "smudges" on the covers of the book, but Hensley had no answer. He also could not explain the unidentified fingerprints he collected from the passenger side of Oscar's truck. They were located on the door, wing window, and glove box. The Cliftons, Donna, and Rick Carter were eliminated. If the killer took the invoice book from Oscar's truck, did he leave his prints?

Hensley's testimony blew holes in Byrd's original theory of the case—that Donna had thrown the book out of the truck to leave a clue. The invoice book was so far off the road surface, it couldn't have simply fallen out and landed where it was photographed... Additionally, the fact that someone had wiped *all* of the fingerprints off the front and back covers clearly pointed to planted evidence, not some accidental drop.

DA Powell wanted to introduce testimony from Sgt. Byrd about statements that he claimed Oscar made in custody. Donahue argued that Oscar had said that he didn't want to speak without his attorney, refused to sign the Miranda waiver, and that TCSO had failed to produce the interview tape. Oscar should have been booked into jail, not taken to TCSO and interrogated. The jury was dismissed, and the arguments were heard outside their presence. The heart of what Powell was hoping to have the jury hear was Byrd's claim that Oscar had "lied" about his alibi. Byrd said that Oscar told him that he was "with" Bill Rose between 3:00-4:00 pm. The other officers present were questioned by Powell and Donahue.

TCSO Mike King testified that Oscar said that he went to north Visalia, then he was "at Bill Rose's or had met with Bill Rose between three and four pm." On cross-examination, King said "he was at Bill Rose's house at approximately between 3:00 and 4:00 pm." That was exactly where Oscar was during that hour; the Roberts house in N. Visalia at 3:00, and at Bill Rose's house from 3:15-3:50 pm. There was no lie.

Initially, Sgt. Byrd completely denied questioning Oscar, and claimed that Oscar just "volunteered" statements about his alibi, but under Donahue's questioning he admitted:

> *Byrd:* I begged Mr. Clifton to tell me where the girl was.
>
> *Donahue:* You begged him?
>
> A: Yes, sir.
>
> Q: Why did you want to know where the girl was?
>
> A: She was a personal friend. I've known her ever since she was a baby and I've – trying to find her before… It was cold. I thought maybe she was stashed someplace and she might still be alive.
>
> Q: Did he say he had been to Bill Rose's place between three and four pm.
>
> A: Yes sir, he did.
>
> Q: And you heard that?
>
> A: You're correct.

Donahue also got Byrd to confirm what was in his written report:

> Subject Clifton had advised that he had no statements to make until he talked to his lawyer, but did make the voluntary statement which he stated he had witnesses to where he was.

Oscar explained to the judge what happened:

Oscar: They took me into the room where the lineup was, and we sat there for probably thirty, forty minutes then they brought a tape recorder in, and asked me if I wanted to make any statements and I told them no, not until I had an attorney there. And then they just kept on talking, and asked me where I was that day.

Donahue: How long were you in this room with Byrd, Holguin, and King?

A: Altogether probably an hour and a half, maybe two hours.

TCSO King was brought back onto the witness stand to explain why there was no tape of the interview:

King: Normally in a case like this when you take a taped statement you go through the statement one time with the person and then you come back and question him again on it and tape his statement. The tape recorder wasn't turned on because we hadn't gone through the statement that he wanted to make.

Obviously, that's ***not*** how police interviews are supposed to work, but it was very telling testimony. It explained exactly what had happened in the two hours before King turned on the tape during that final interview with Rick Carter, when he suddenly had tons of "new and different" memories. Coercing and coaching witness statements and then turning on the tape to be played in court is unconstitutional. That is exactly the kind of behavior that makes false confessions sound real, or forced witness statements seem voluntary.

The jury didn't hear any of the testimony from the Miranda hearing, and were completely in the dark about what had really taken place after Oscar's arrest. Judge Bradley ruled that TCSO had not violated Oscar's Miranda rights, and that Sgt. Byrd could present hearsay testimony to the jury about what he claimed Oscar had said. It was shocking even by 1976 standards, and utterly unimaginable today. Politically, it was much safer for Bradley to support TCSO's actions, and give Powell what he wanted. If he was overturned on appeal he could just blame the "liberal" courts; It was a win-win for Bradley's re-election campaign.

Prior to the Miranda hearing, TCSO Johnson had been sent back to the evidence room to get the missing photo and notepad. When he returned to the witness stand, it quickly became obvious why DA Powell had not given the missing photo to the defense—there was an unidentified footprint near the bike. It didn't match Oscar, so they hid it. It only got worse. Johnson testified that the footprint was only photographed by "accident" after Sgt. Byrd had specifically instructed him not to document any of the footprints found near the bike. In 2021, a suppressed photo and testimony of hidden exculpatory evidence would end the trial right then and there. Under current California statute (PC §141), the DA could be charged with a felony and go to prison. In 1976, there wasn't even a shrug; it was just business as usual for TCSO and the Tulare DA's office.

Donahue tried to get more answers from Johnson:

Donahue: Well, other than Sgt. Byrd telling you that two sets of tracks out there were similar to her brother or somebody, these shoes the brother was wearing, why was it that you did not take any photographs of the other shoe prints that you found out there?

Johnson: Because there was numerous people out there at that time. I felt the majority of them would probably be those people.

Q: Well, Mr. Johnson, were there any other tire tracks out there?

A: There was tire tracks from deputies' vehicles, my vehicle.

Q: How about the people that worked in the field? Didn't they leave—were there any tire tracks of theirs?

A: I wouldn't know, sir.

Q: Well, how do you know that they were tracks from the vehicles belonging to the Sheriff's office?

A: Because at the time that I arrived out there the tracks were right behind the Sheriff's vehicles.

Q; So you didn't take any pictures of any footprints?

A: No, sir.

Q: And any tire tracks that you didn't feel were connected with this situation, you ignored them; is that correct?

A: That's correct.

Q: Well, then, there were other tire tracks present, there were footprints present, but you picked and chose the ones you wanted to photograph; is that correct?

A: Yes, sir.

Q: In other words, somebody else could have been in that grove with a car, with a pickup, the tire tracks could be there, were there, and you simply chose to ignore them; is that correct?

A: The tire tracks **were there**. They were not photographed.

Q: Then there were other tire tracks out there that you did not photograph?

A: This is correct.

Q: There were other footprints out there you did not photograph.

A: Yes, sir.

Q: And you did not find one footprint from Donna Jo Richmond, did you?

A: No, sir.

Just as disturbing as the undocumented tire tracks and footprints was the fact that Johnson had still not brought the notepad to court, and seemed to be hoping that Donahue had forgotten about it. He hadn't, and Sgt. Byrd was put back on the stand to answer more questions from Donahue about the footprints, while Johnson retrieved the notepad from the evidence room:

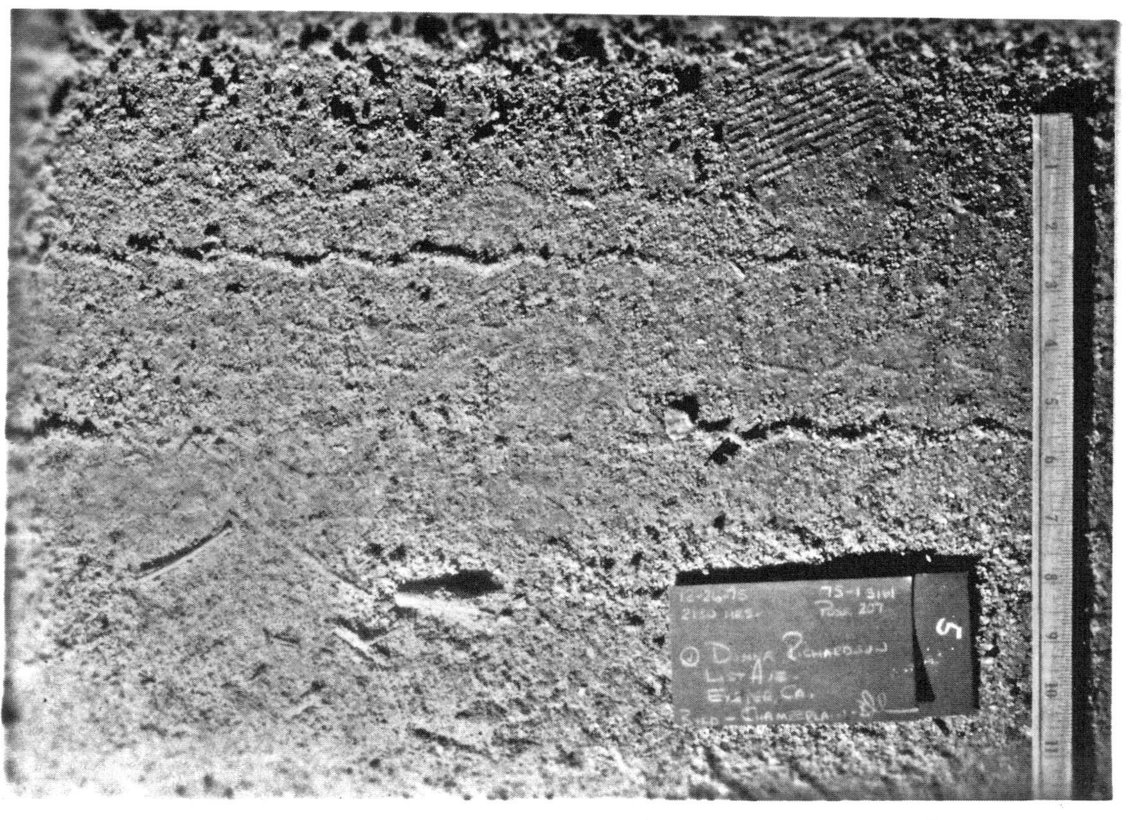

Unidentified Footprint by Bike—December 26, 1975
Photo: TCSO

Donahue: Sgt. Byrd, referring to this photograph, which shows a footprint of some kind, was anything done or attempted to be done to identify that footprint?

Byrd: Not to my knowledge, no, sir.

Q: Is it Donna Jo Richmond's footprint?

A: No sir, not to my knowledge.

Q: You don't know whose footprint it is, do you?

A: No, sir, I do not.

Q: You didn't even know there was another footprint out there, did you?

A: I knew there was a lot of footprints in the general area.

Q: And do we have any photos of those footprints?

A: No, sir.

Q: Whose footprints were they?

A: Searching parties that was in the area.

Q: Well, Sgt. Byrd, you mean to tell me that you checked everybody's footprints that was searching in that area?

A: No, sir.

Q: Well, then, how can you make the statement it was from the searching parties?

A: Because there was about 35 or 40 people walking along where the tracks were, and that's the only prints I seen, the one's they were leaving.

Q: But you don't know who left them, do you?

A: Not individually, no, sir.

Both Johnson and Byrd testified that if they saw a footprint or tire track that they thought came from a member of law enforcement, they ignored it. That was evidence found near Donna's bike, and it was completely undocumented.

Johnson finally returned with the notepad, which turned out to be a non-event. Donahue had it admitted for identification, and Johnson confirmed that it was the same notepad that was photographed next to the invoice book and bike. Donahue didn't ask if Johnson knew who it belonged to, or what kind of investigation had been done regarding its owner. There was no reason for the jury to understand that it might be important evidence that pointed to the real killer.

Next, TCSO King took the stand to talk about what Oscar had said during the illegal questioning. King told the jury that Oscar said that "he had met with Bill Rose between three and four pm," and he hadn't. It's easy to know that King was lying because he had just told the judge twice that Oscar had actually said he was ***at*** Bill Rose's, not ***with*** him. DA Powell or Sgt. Byrd clearly told him to change that testimony in front of the jury—and he did.

Byrd also took the stand to assert that Oscar had told him that "he had met with Mr. Rose between three and four at a construction site," and since Rose wasn't there at that time, that meant Oscar was a liar who lied about his entire alibi. Again, during the Miranda hearing outside of the jury's presence, Byrd had been more truthful, and admitted Oscar had actually said he was working *at* Rose's remodeling job, not *with* him. Byrd also stated that Oscar had "changed" his story when he first said he had been in N. Visalia at 3:00 pm, then said he was with Rose from 3:00 to 4:00 pm in Visalia. Obviously, it wasn't a "change"; it was a sequential telling of his activities between 3:00-4:00 pm. It would be difficult to find more dishonest, bad faith testimony from a sworn witness.

Donahue could have challenged King and Byrd with their prior statements to the court, and explained that the two locations were not an "either/or"—he was at both during that hour. Of course Donahue didn't, and Powell ran with the narrative that Oscar lied about his alibi.

Next up in DA Powell's case to the jury was the trail of Donna's clothing. Supposedly, instead of leaving the clothes at the murder

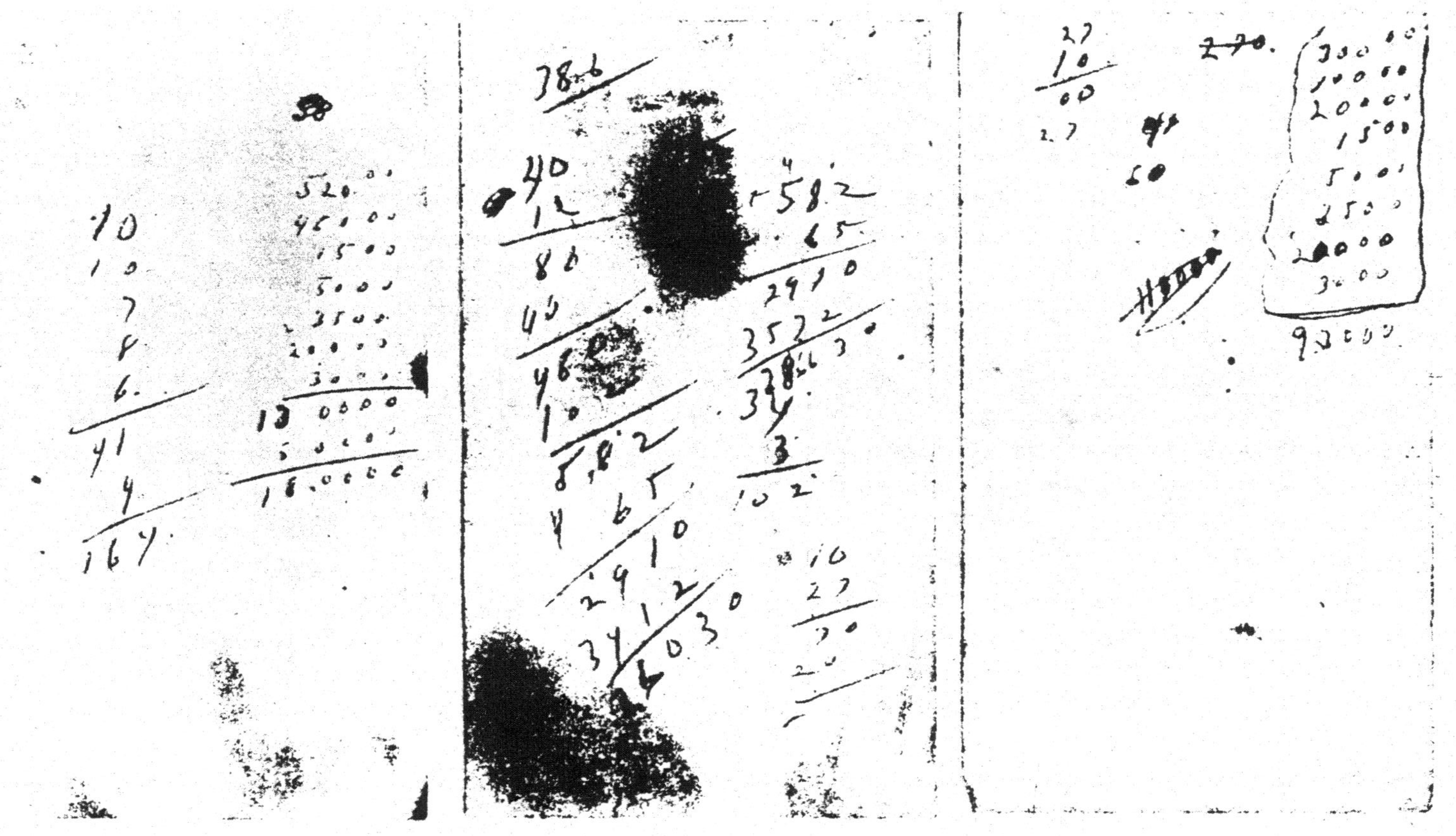

Three Pages of Notepad
Photo: TCSO

scene or dropping them in the canal on his way out of the grove, Oscar took them with him, then dropped them one by one, creating a map leading directly to his doorstep. That included a needless detour off Ave 264, then up Road 176 to drop the panties, and a U-turn back to Ave 264. Looking at Donahue's trial preparation notes, he clearly did not believe it was true. He needed three pieces of information that he hadn't noticed, and Pettyjohn didn't find for him: Laverne Lamb was Don Lee's aunt; at 2:00 am on December 27th, the *Visalia Times-Delta* published that Donna's shoe had been found with her bike; and TCSO Johnson had collected Donna's pants and second shoe on Neel Ranch, and documented it in his report.

I've scoured every document in the files, and there was no investigation into Laverne Lamb, at all. Pettyjohn didn't interview her, her employer, or the bank where she was supposedly headed that evening to verify any part of her story. He didn't do even the most basic background check on her, or her family members. He just took her at her word, even though her story was very odd and suspicious. I dug into her because it was apparent to me that she had been lying, and there had to be a reason. She either got the pants from a family member who had forcibly removed them from Donna himself—or she *never* had the pants, and agreed to help Byrd implicate Oscar to draw suspicion away from her own relatives.

Although there was a pile of newspaper stories compiled and submitted to the court in support of the motion for change of venue, yet the very first *Visalia Times-Delta* story in the Saturday morning edition was missing. There is no indication that Donahue ever saw it. Even more infuriating, he obtained a declaration from the Managing Editor of the *Visalia Times-Delta* to prove the publication times for the weekday and Saturday editions (presumably for the Esajian story). It clearly states that the presses rolled at 2:00 am for the Saturday morning paper. Donahue should have noticed that the reporter knew about the shoe at least seven hours before it was "found" by David Richmond. The evidence that the shoe was planted by TCSO was right there the entire time, in black and white, documented by a journalist directly trained by Claude Snelling. If anyone had been paying attention, Claude could have helped solve his own murder.

When I first noticed that Johnson's report stated he collected "pieces of victim's clothing" at Neel Ranch, it caught my eye because those items didn't seem to be on the chain of custody cards with the other things he took into evidence at the scene. Also, except for the pants and shoe, he documented taking each item off of Donna's body and into evidence at the funeral home. However, I couldn't be positive because I didn't have the crime scene and autopsy photos. As soon as I saw those I knew—every piece of clothing on her body at Neel Ranch was still on when she arrived for autopsy.

Miraculously, TCSO said that they then happened to locate both the pants and shoe first thing the next morning—pointing right at Oscar. The information was all there; Pettyjohn and Donahue just weren't able to put it together. They had too much trust and faith in the honesty of the officers and DA Powell to think objectively.

Continuing with the "clothing trail," DA Powell called TCSO Logan to testify about finding Donna's shoes:

> *Powell:* What was the date when you found that shoe again?
>
> *Logan:* Twenty-seventh of December, 1975.
>
> Q: What did you do with the first shoe after you had located it?
>
> A: We just secured the scene around the shoe itself.
>
> Q: Who took possession of the shoe, do you recall?
>
> A: We secured the area until Sgt. Byrd and Detective Johnson arrived and took charge of the scene itself, and I'm not sure exactly who took possession of the shoe.
>
> Q: Detective Johnson and Detective Byrd arrived?
>
> A: Yes, sir.
>
> Q: Did you have occasion to find some other piece of clothing?
>
> A: Yes, sir, I did.

Q: Would you tell us what that was?

A: It was the other shoe.

Q: When was it that you found the other shoe?

A: The 28th of December, 1975.

Q: That would be the following day?

A: Yes, sir.

Q: Where did you find the second shoe?

A: It was located on the south dirt portion just off the roadway Avenue 264, east of Road 156.

Donahue on cross-examination:

Donahue: Did you find these two shoes yourself, or did some other officer find them first?

Logan: The first shoe we received a radio transmission that a citizen had located a shoe along the roadway, and Deputy Moore and myself were the first officers at the scene.

Why didn't Donahue make sure that the jury knew that Donna's brother had found the shoe, and that TCSO and Powell were trying to hide it? Oscar asked the same question when he found out the truth. It didn't take any special training to guess that someone told David where to "find" the shoe. Donahue tried to make points with the jury by asking Logan why the shoes were resting off the road on their soles if they had been thrown from a moving truck, and how the second shoe had been missed during the Saturday search, but it wasn't plainly stated. Donahue rarely got to the point, and jurors aren't good at reading between the lines.

TCSO Johnson took the stand to establish chain of custody on the shoes. Donahue asked him about fingerprints, and Johnson said that he checked, but didn't find any. How did it make sense to the jury that Oscar had been in a frantic panic, throwing things from his truck in broad daylight, but then stopped, wiped his prints from the shoes, and placed them carefully off the road on their soles? It was a laughable story, yet somehow Powell offered it to the jury and they bought it.

Laverne Lamb's testimony was Sgt. Byrd's attempt to counter the fact that multiple newspapers had quickly published the fact that Donna's shoe and underwear had been found by her bike. The only way they could have ended up on Ave 264 and in a ditch on Road 176 was if a member of TCSO had planted them there. But wait, what if someone said that she had found Donna's pants on Ave 264 before the bike was found—that would prove that the other items weren't planted, right? No. Not at all. Lamb's story was that she was rushing to get to the bank before it closed, and her lights hit something on the center line:

> I went past a good little ways, and then I backed up because it looked like new, something new, you know, clothing, so I back up. I took them home and put them in the wash.

In a rush, on a dark, foggy two-lane road… *she did what?* I didn't believe any of it, not for a minute, and knew that there was no way she was a truly random, disinterested witness. Especially when I saw that Sgt. Byrd kept the pants for weeks, until *after* all of the other evidence was sent to IFS. He did not want them to be forensically examined or tested. Who did he think the evidence on the pants would implicate? Obviously not Oscar.

Real estate agent Bill Rose took the witness stand next for the state. Personally, he supported Oscar, but didn't think there was much he could do to help, other than simply tell the truth. Oscar had started doing work for him in May 1975, helping on rentals and investment properties that Rose owned or managed. He said that he last saw Oscar at 11:00 am on the 26th, in his office. They discussed the building inspection, and Rose told Oscar that he and his investor would be stopping by at 2:00 pm. He said that he was late, and didn't arrive on Garden Street until 2:30. He walked around the house, inside and out, for thirty minutes before leaving at 3:00 pm.

The only reason any of Rose's testimony seemed damaging was because DA Powell tried to imply that Oscar wasn't where he was supposed to be at 2:00 pm, and then lied about being "with" Rose from 3:00-4:00 pm. Obviously, that ignored Rose's own statements about not needing Oscar at the meeting, and being very late. Donahue missed a giant opportunity to use Bill Rose as an exculpatory witness because Rose was certain that the men with the trucks and freezer loading had not occurred between 2:30-3:00 pm. Rose was positive that he would have seen them if they had been there. That confirmed Frank Thomas' time estimate of their arrival at 3:15 pm—after Rose left Garden Street.

Powell next recalled TCSO Mike King to testify that he had found Donna's underwear in the irrigation ditch along Road 176 while he was driving along a siding road. I didn't believe King's testimony even before I found the newspaper reports that the underwear had really been found with Donna's bike and shoe the night before. King had submitted an extremely detailed report that covered his activities on the 26th and 27th, and there was *absolutely* no mention of being on Road 176, or finding a critical piece of evidence, not one single word. After forcing Rick Carter to change his statement and lying about Oscar's alibi statements, more perjury was hardly surprising.

Jesus Renteria Lara, the spray rig driver who found Donna's body, testified through a Spanish language interpreter. He said that he nearly touched her with his tires, and was too afraid to stop spraying. He admitted that he covered the trees, and Donna, with spray. Although Lara claimed that nobody from the grove approached her body to check on her, it sounded coached and unbelievable. TCSO was committed to pretending that only the killer, and his truck, had left prints in the area.

Chapter Eight Sources

1. Jury Selection, June 21-24, 1976
2. Donahue Trial Notes
3. Testimony of Beth Brumley, June 24, 1976
4. Testimony of Mrs. Brumley, June 24, 1976
5. Testimony of Gloria Mascorro, June 24, 1976
6. Testimony of Mr. Mascorro, June 24, 1976
7. Testimony of Don Richmond, June 25, 1976
8. Testimony of Don Lee, June 25, 1976
9. Testimony of Brian Johnson, June 25, 1976
10. Testimony of Vern Hensley, June 25, 1976
11. Testimony of Miranda Hearing, June 25, 1976
12. Testimony of Brian Johnson, June 28, 1976
13. Testimony of Bob Byrd, June 28, 1976
14. Testimony of Brian Johnson, June 28, 1976
15. Testimony of Mike King, June 28, 1976
16. Testimony of Bob Byrd, June 28, 1976
17. Testimony of Warren Logan, June 28, 1976
18. Testimony of Brian Johnson, June 28, 1976
19. Testimony of Laverne Lamb, June 28, 1976
20. Testimony of Bill Rose, June 28, 1976
21. Testimony of Mike King, June 28, 1976
22. Testimony of Jesus Renteria Lara, June 28, 1976

CHAPTER NINE

"Svengali Squad"

Anyone who wanted to know about Oscar's conviction, Jennifer Armour's murder, or the VR eventually found their way to Margie in Visalia. She had the answers, and the documents to back them up. Her interest in the cases grew from living through the ransacking burglaries in her neighborhood and the unique fear the VR created in the community. She also worked for Bill Rose, and had a chance to see Oscar right before Christmas, 1975. She couldn't reconcile that man with Donna's murder, and she knew that Rose supported his innocence.

Margie is a one woman army. She wrote to Oscar, and talked regularly with his siblings and wife. She made files and notebooks, and took her information to anyone who would listen, including VPD, the Tulare DAs, and the EAR Task Force. She posted on discussion boards, and set people straight when they had their facts wrong. She never gave up. Without Margie, Oscar's story would have died with him, and nobody would have remembered Jennifer, or what Sgt. Vaughan and his team had done. She is the true historian of the cases.

When I first met Margie, she mentioned something she called the "*Luck of the VR.*" It didn't mean just bad luck, it went further, into some kind of curse on the people trying to catch the VR, and a darkness that seemed to protect him from getting caught. I had already experienced it on the morning Margie and I first met. I had gotten up early for the three-hour drive to Exeter. I wanted to be there when the library opened, so the microfilm reader would be free. I was going to spend a few hours looking at the *Exeter Sun*. My plan was to start in 1973, and work my way through 1976. I knew I wouldn't get through all two hundred issues of the paper in a day, but I was going to read as many as I could. I went to the front desk and asked for the newspaper reels. The librarian gave me a look of dread: "We just sent all of those out for digitization yesterday; it will probably take about a year." She said that the boxes might still be at the main branch, in Visalia.

I had to wait a few hours for the Visalia Library to open, and I was able to find the person who had the boxes of microfilm, but she couldn't help. They were on their way out the door to the company that was going to scan and index them. So close, yet so very far… I'd missed them by one day. It took ten months, but finally, in February 2017, the *Exeter Sun* was available online. There was a catch—the only way to view and save them was in person, in Visalia. Luckily, any page could be saved as a PDF to an external drive. Some of the years, like 1976, the scans were almost totally unsearchable; the original microfilm quality didn't allow for text recognition. For those, I just saved a copy of the full front page or two and moved on.

I wasn't sure exactly what I hoped to find in the *Exeter Sun*, but I wanted to understand what was going on in and around Exeter during the VR years. It was a world away from Visalia, and the paper stayed focused on local events, residents, and issues that mattered to the community. I was particularly interested in the crime reports, not only to see if the VR was offending there, but also to understand who was working in law enforcement in the area. It was a mix of California Highway Patrol, TCSO, and Exeter PD. The city itself was fairly small, and many incidents of local concern actually occurred in the county, or on a state highway. I also wanted to learn more about Donna, her family, and her friends. For entire months, I got up early and went to bed late, spending my spare time reading what grew to thousands of saved pages. As I read, I started adding names to my list of men to investigate and eliminate. Now I just needed help from law enforcement to run their DNA and compare them to the known profile for the EAR.

Meanwhile, Sgt. John Vaughan hadn't wasted any time jumping out of retirement. His first two calls were to the major crimes investigator at VPD who was assigned to the Snelling homicide, and a friend who might know how to reach retired TCSO forensics deputy Brian Johnson. Vaughan had maintained a good relationship with the head of major crimes, but he was unable to do anything to help. Jennifer Armour's and Donna Richmond's homicides were in the exclusive control of TCSO, and he suggested that Vaughan contact their cold case team, two retired officers, Chris Dempsie and Dwayne Johnson. Vaughan and I met with them, and their position was clear: Oscar killed Donna, and three teen friends of Jennifer's killed her. Both cases were closed, and would not be reopened. They didn't want to hear about the VR, EAR, or any other suspects in Exeter. John just turned to me and said: "It's time to go, this meeting is over."

Sgt. Vaughan has zero patience for fools; he's a true New Yorker. His path to Tulare County and a career in law enforcement came via Porterville. John grew up in Binghampton, NY, where the two main life options were working for IBM or the railroad—his father chose IBM. Like many of the other families in upper New York, John's were immigrants from Italy and Ireland. John was a high school sports star, and his left-handed pitching skills took him to the minor leagues in Fresno, and training with the San Francisco Giants. Unfortunately, he blew out his shoulder overtraining for a tryout with the New York Yankees. He had a friend playing community college basketball in Porterville, and took the train back to California to stay with him. John had dreamed of a career with the California Highway Patrol, cruising the coast on a motorcycle, but settled for being a patrol officer in Porterville. He met his wife Gail there, and decided to make a life in Tulare County.

After three years with Porterville PD, he saw that VPD was hiring, and offering advanced training through the program at College of the Sequoias. In a recent interview, John described his background:

Ray Forsyth, who was the Chief at that time, was the best Chief I ever worked for. He required training to move up the ranks. To get up to homicide investigations, you had to join the state association, and they had high standards. Whenever I was offered training, I immediately took the opportunity. However, if I had been on the stakeout that night, instead of at PERT chart training in Los Angeles, I wouldn't have hesitated for one second to shoot to kill. I knew exactly how dangerous the VR was.

I was the first person to put in a request for a commercial burglary program. When the state granted the funding, they commented that this was the first time they had seen a program that was not for residential burglaries… I always wanted to do things differently. When out on patrol, if I turned on my search light to the left side of the street, I would look right. That's where the action was.

John said that he always stood out in Visalia. He was a big guy with a New York accent, whose ideas always went against the normal way of doing things.

John's frustration with TCSO didn't end with the cold case squad. He could not get Brian Johnson to talk to him. John called and left messages, but Johnson refused to respond. Vaughan and I had the same assessment: He had something to hide. I decided to go in person and try to talk to him. Johnson hadn't returned my phone messages asking for a meeting, and nobody answered the door at his house. I heard a noise inside, then saw his car in the driveway. As I stood on his porch, Johnson quietly came out of a side door, got into his car, and started to drive away. I ran down the front lawn and into the street in front of his car to stop him. He seemed to know who I was and why I wanted to talk. He agreed to pull back into the driveway, but didn't exit his vehicle.

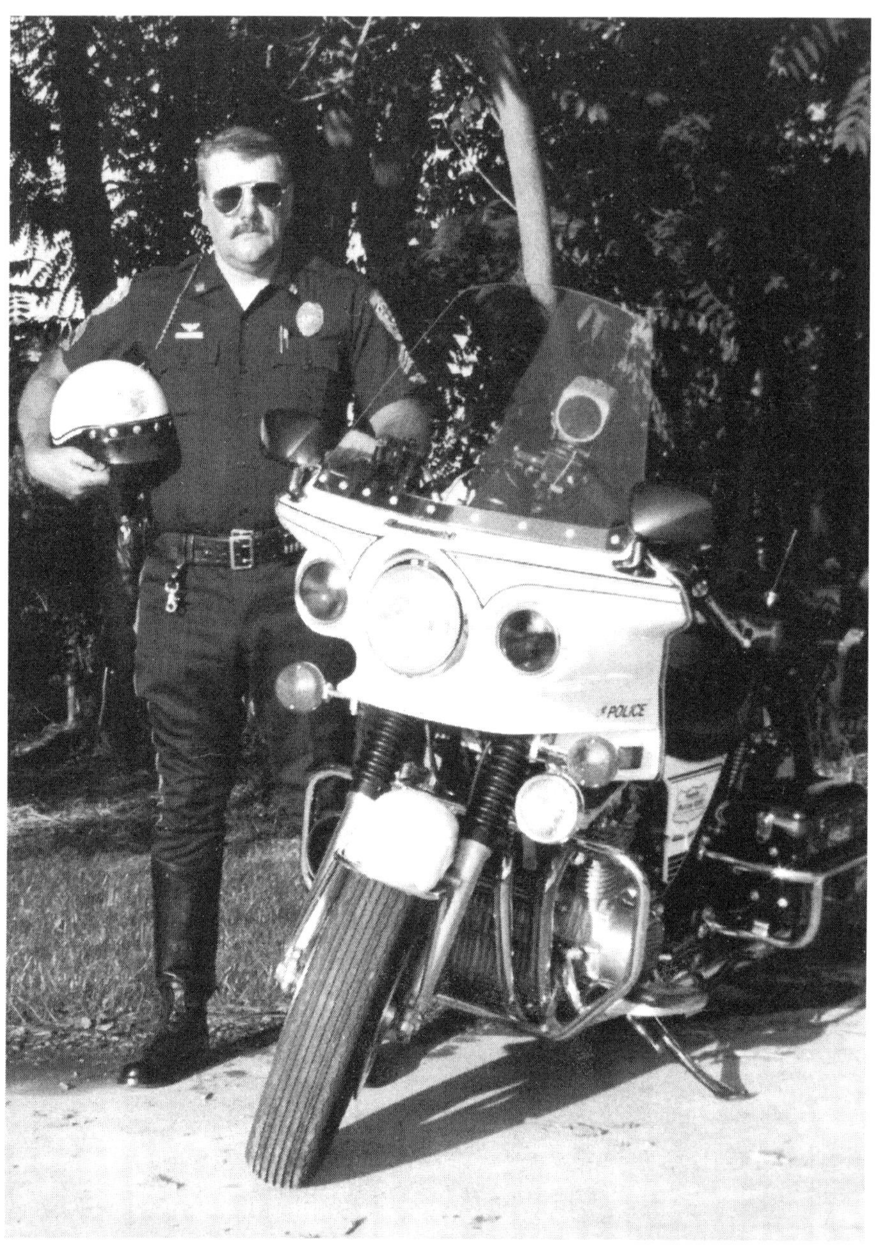

Visalia Police Department Sgt. John Vaughan, 1985
Photo: Vaughan

The conversation went nowhere. Johnson said that he wouldn't talk about what happened during the Richmond case "without counsel present," and that he would not answer questions without a subpoena because it would put him in "legal jeopardy." Honestly, I expected him to deny knowledge of any wrongdoing, or say he didn't know anything useful, but that didn't happen. He was nervous and looked scared.

Another question I had was exactly *how* things had originally gone so terribly wrong between VPD and the SSD in 1978. The answer was ***hypnosis***.

There is no debate about who popularized the use of hypnosis by the police. It was LAPD psychologist and head of their behavioral-science services, Martin Reiser. He wrote the handbooks and training manuals on the use of hypnosis in criminal investigations. In the early 1970s he started a hypnosis unit that paired medical hypnotists with specially trained LAPD officers, and those two-man teams conducted hypnosis sessions with victims and witnesses. The media called them the "Svengali Squad." There was no end to the hype surrounding Reiser's unit, including a glowing article in *Time* magazine. Sgt. Vaughan believed that it was new, cutting edge science, and might help catch the VR. Both Beth Snelling and Agent McGowen were taken to LAPD, and sat for hypnotized interview sessions with the "Squad" team of LAPD Captain Richard Sandstrom and Ira Greenberg, PhD.

As I told Sgt. Vaughan when we first met, this was a huge red flag for me, as it would be for any criminal defense attorney. Reiser's theories and work are now infamous—not just considered useless, but actively dangerous. Reiser's training for law enforcement was based on his belief that human memory is like a video recorder that reliably records and saves every perception experienced by the witness. These memories are stored in the brain at a subconscious level and are accurately replayed, in their original form, when the witness is placed under hypnosis and asked to remember them. To be clear, this was Reiser's theory, not fact. The actual scientific studies on human memory clearly debunked Reiser's idea, yet it persisted because police loved the results. Suddenly, witnesses were "remembering" all kinds of new information that pointed directly to a suspect or aided the ongoing prosecution of a defendant.

In 1982, the California Supreme Court took a hard look at Reiser's theory and the use of it in criminal cases. In *People v. Shirley*, they found that Reiser's work did not meet the *Frye* standard for scientific reliability, and in fact, the actual science disproved it and argued against the admission of hypnotized witness testimony. The court cited several studies on human memory, but focused mainly on specific work done on eyewitnesses by Dr. Elizabeth Loftus' team at the University of Washington:

> During the time between an event and a witness's recollection of that event—a period often called the "retention interval"—the bits and pieces of information that were acquired through perception do not passively reside in memory waiting to be pulled out like fish from water. Rather, they are subject to numerous influences. External information provided from the outside can intrude into the witness' memory, as can his own thoughts, and both can cause dramatic changes in his recollection.
>
> A number of influences can cause a memory to change during the retention interval without the witness' awareness:
>
> - The witness may "compromise" the memory with a subsequently learned, but inconsistent fact;
> - He may "incorporate" into the memory a nonexistent object or event casually mentioned by a third party, e.g., in later questioning;
> - Post-event information may change the way the witness "feels" about the original incident, e.g., may affect his impression of how noisy, or how violent it was;

- Because a witness is under great social pressure to be complete and accurate he may fill gaps in his memory by guessing, and thereafter "recall" those guesses as part of the memory; and,
- If the witness is subjected to repeated questioning, any erroneous statement he made early on may be "frozen into" the memory and reappear later as a fact.

There is no way to tell, moreover, whether any given detail recalled by the witness comes from his original perception, or from external information that he subsequently acquired.

In the stage of the process known as "retrieval," the accuracy of the witness' memory may be adversely affected by outside factors even as he recalls it:

- The witness may subconsciously tailor his recall to conform to expectations implied by the person questioning him;
- Those expectations may be conveyed, intentionally or not, either by such conduct of the questioner as tone of voice, emphasis, pauses, facial expression and other "body language," or by the particular method of interview used or precise form of question asked; and,
- The witness may be more likely to respond to such cues if the questioner is a status figure (e.g., a doctor or a law enforcement official) than if he is merely a passerby inquiring what happened.

There is no clear correlation between the witness' confidence in the accuracy of his recall and its accuracy in fact: indeed, studies have shown that in some circumstances people can be more confident about their wrong answers than their right ones. To be cautious, one should not take high confidence as an absolute guarantee of anything.

Most people, including eyewitnesses, are motivated by a desire to be correct, to be observant, and to avoid looking foolish. People want to give an answer, to be helpful, and many will do this at the risk of being incorrect. People want to see crime solved and justice done, and this desire may motivate them to volunteer more than is warranted by their meager memory. The line between valid retrieval and unconscious fabrication is easily crossed.

The person under hypnosis experiences a compelling desire to please the hypnotist by reacting positively to these suggestions, and hence to produce the particular responses he believes are expected of him. Because of this compulsion, when asked to recall an event while under direct suggestion of heightened memory ("*hypermnesia*"), he is unwilling to admit that he cannot do so or that his recollection is uncertain or incomplete. Instead, he will produce a "memory" of the event that may be compounds of:

- Relevant actual facts;
- Irrelevant actual facts taken from an unrelated prior experience of the subject;
- Fantasized material ("confabulations") unconsciously invented to fill gaps in the story; and,
- Conscious lies—all formulated in as realistic a fashion as he can.

The likelihood of such self-deception is increased by another effect of hypnosis, i.e., that it significantly impairs the subject's critical judgment and causes him to give credence to memories so vague and fragmentary that he would not have relied on them before being hypnotized.

A witness who is uncertain of his recollections before being hypnotized will become convinced by that process that the story he told under hypnosis is true and correct in every respect. This effect is enhanced by two techniques commonly used by lay hypnotists:

- Before being hypnotized the subject is told (or believes) that hypnosis will help him to "remember very clearly everything that happened" in the prior event, and/or,
- During the trance he is given the suggestion that after he awakes he will "be able to remember" that event equally clearly and comprehensively.
- The witness' conviction of the absolute truth of his hypnotically induced recollection grows stronger each time he is asked to repeat the story; by the time of trial, the resulting "memory" may be so fixed in his mind that traditional legal techniques such as cross-examination, may be largely ineffective to expose its unreliability.

In *Shirley*, the court ruled that:

> Any person who has been hypnotized for investigative purposes will not be allowed to testify as a witness to the events that were the subject of the hypnotic session. It would fly in the face of that consensus to allow a witness to be the judge of which portions of his testimony were actually produced by hypnosis. A witness who has been hypnotized for the purpose of improving his memory is so contaminated that he is thereafter incompetent to testify.

What is so stunning about the court's decision is exactly how decisive it was. The LAPD had based its entire hypnosis unit on Reiser's "idea" about how the human brain stores and retrieves information, but there was absolutely no science behind it—at all. Nothing. Not only was his theory now completely debunked by neurobiologists, the actual studies of eyewitnesses proved how imprecise and suggestible they are. If anyone had believed in the potential reliability of the LAPD's hypnotized statements before

Shirley, it clearly should have ended with that decision on March 11, 1982. This court's ruling was not a "*technicality*," it was a ***total ban*** on the testimony of people interviewed by the "Svengali Squad" as incompetent witnesses.

Unfortunately, that included both Beth Snelling and VPD Agent Bill McGowen. After 1982, they were permanently barred from testifying in court about everything related to their encounters with the VR. This included their statements made before they were hypnotized. Therefore, the direct involvement of this LAPD Squad in these sessions made all of their potential testimony *inadmissible*. The court had good reasons for making this rule, and they were apparent in the changes I saw in their descriptions of the VR.

Beth Snelling gave two statements to VPD *before* she was taken to the "Svengali Squad." Her statements described her attacker as being a white male with pale skin, height between 5'8"-5'11", with a stocky build, between 150-175 lbs. Beth felt certain that he was older than high school age. She described her attacker as having very strong hands and arms, with no deformities, rings, or a watch. He was armed with a blue steel snub-nosed revolver, which he drew from his rear pants pocket or waistband with his left hand. His voice had no unusual characteristics, but seemed to be disguised with a growl. She noticed no odors on his breath, body, or hands while they were over her face. Beth had a good opportunity to watch him walk away, and saw only a normal gait. She remembered him being very demanding, deliberate, and in control. Not shaky or nervous. She said he shot her father twice, using his left hand.

Sgt. Vaughan remembered driving Beth and her mother to Los Angeles for the hypnosis session:

> All the way down Beth was down and introverted and didn't talk much. I got the feeling she thought she was at fault for some of this.
>
> As far as the hypnosis, she was a great candidate—calm, everything. And, one of the things that came out of the

> hypnosis, that we always focused on, was that she they asked her to smell the guy and she says he smells clean "I can't smell anything, he's got good hygiene… I couldn't smell smoke, He didn't drink, He wasn't a doper. He wasn't shaking. He was very calm and she said he has a raspy loud whispering voice."
>
> At the end of the hypnosis, the operator told Beth that she had nothing to do with this case she's innocent—her dad would want her to live a good life. And, all the way back to Visalia, she laughed and talked with us. So, that's what we got out of that.

Beth only added three details when she was taken to Los Angeles for hypnosis: she said the attacker had a round face, with a wide jaw, and had "short stubby fingers." She was still uncertain about his age, but was most confident that he was in his 20s.

Debbie Ward had encountered the VR a few months earlier, as he fled from ransacking the apartment above her family's garage. She described him as 5' 10" and 5' 11", muscular, with strong arms. She said he didn't speak, just grabbed her, and tried to knock her down to get away. He was wearing a black ski mask, so she couldn't describe his face or hair. On the night of the McGowen shootout, her father, Willie Ward, saw the VR briefly in his backyard. Ward remembered him as 5' 10", 180 pounds with a stocky build. He placed his age as in his 20s. Mr. Ward did not feel he could identify the VR because he did not get a good look at his face.

Since Agent McGowen had been injured by flashlight glass in his eye, he had a minor surgical procedure and was hospitalized with an eye patch. VPD Hartman took his report of the incident. McGowen's description of the VR was a white male adult, 25-30 years old. He said he was 5' 10" and 180 lbs. McGowen said he had a pale, round face, and was clean shaven, with short light blond hair, parted on the left. He said the VR was wearing brown cotton gloves rolled down to the middle of the back of his hands, a camouflage-type jacket, dark tennis shoes, and a knit ski mask. McGowen said that the VR had taken the gun from his left jacket pocket, and used his left hand to shoot out the flashlight, firing between the fence slats and hitting the light dead center. McGowen also remembered that the VR's voice got very high-pitched, screaming "don't hurt me," and "my hands are up" right before drawing and firing at his flashlight.

On Thursday, December 18, 1975, the *Visalia Times-Delta* published McGowen's composite drawing of the VR on the front page with the following information:

Visalia Police Department Composite of Ransacker
Illustration Credit: VPD

> The suspect is described as being in his 20s, with light blonde [*sic*] hair, pale complection [*sic*], short stubby fingers, 5-feet, 10-inches tall and weighing 180 pounds. He is thought to frequently wear a fatigue type jacket. Police said they believe the man lives… south of Highway 198 between Court Street and Demaree Road. The man may collect stamps and coins, and is thought to live a normal life in the daytime, and is frequently on the street during the early evening and nighttime hours. He is not believed to be a known criminal. Vaughan cautioned citizens not to approach the suspect, who is armed and considered dangerous.

The only addition to McGowen's original description was Beth's hypnosis detail of "short stubby fingers." Based off that composite and description, VPD received a tip from a twenty-two-year-old college student who was home for Christmas break. He reported an encounter with a guy who appeared to be looking in windows at teenage girls, including his girlfriend. The incident had occurred in the fall of 1973 or 1974. The student said that he had chased and confronted the man, and described him to McGowen:

> A white male, 25-35 yrs, 5' 10" and a "chubby" 180-190 lbs. His hair was blond, combed over, and cut close on both sides. He was "somewhat pale," with an expressionless round face—very similar to a "Mongoloid." His skin was very smooth, and it appeared that he could not shave. The student described a very odd body, with stubby, short, fat legs, short arms and hands, short and fleshy ears, and a "button" nose. He also reported that the "Peeper walked in an unusual manner," and had squinty eyes.

Sgt. Vaughan felt that Beth's hypnosis had been helpful to her, and had not compromised her memory in any way, so in January 1976 he arranged for McGowen to meet with the "Svengali Squad." As he recalled in a recent interview:

So, I thought okay… I'm taking Bill McGowen to L.A. for hypnosis. Bill was not a good candidate. Bill was not Beth Snelling. They had to take his gun away from him…. [During hypnosis,] he got sick, and we had to stop and bring him out, and go back later. He kept saying: *"Where's Shipley? Where's Shipley?!"* He just was a nervous wreck.

He described the guy: "I don't think he even shaves. He doesn't come out in the daytime… he's very white. He's very pale, like a baby."

They said: "Have you ever seen him before?" and he said, "Yes." And I'm sitting there—I mean I was present during Beth's, and I now I'm present during McGowen's. So, I had all the those facts. And he just said, "Yes."… They then took Bill McGowen back two years to Merle's Drive-In, and the guy come in, sat at the counter, ate ice cream and had a green army fatigue jacket with black letters over the right breast pocket. And Bill says, "He kept turning around looking at me." And Bill said the guy had his jacket on and he couldn't understand that because it was hot out. That's the only other time that Bill McGowen said he ever saw him.

Vaughan also described the impact on the investigation:

Now… we relied on Bill trying to identify the Ransacker. We had contributions from lieutenants, sheriff's office, everywhere… the crime line was going crazy. The people were still calling, and every time we get a suspect, Bill would say: "No, that's not him." Bill would even look at the composite on the right [second composite], the one under hypnosis, and say "No, that's not him…" But I personally think that's the [picture] closest to Joseph DeAngelo [of] Exeter PD.

It's clear from Sgt. Vaughan's firsthand description, and the results that came of it, that Agent McGowen's hypnosis session in January 1976 was both traumatic and unsuccessful. Suddenly, the VR had a military haircut with no sideburns, and a soft, round baby face—"he doesn't even shave." He told the hypnotist that the VR had large hips, a large rump, fat thighs, fat calves, fat short feet and hands, short fat ears, and a "ski slope" nose. McGowen also said that the VR ran in a funny manner with his knees together, and squinted when he shot his gun.

McGowen did not suddenly remember a dozen new specific details about the VR's appearance during hypnosis—his memory was *compromised*—he simply "incorporated" the description of the Peeper given by the college student. McGowen was being questioned by a LAPD Captain who told him that he had hidden memories of the VR. That put McGowen under enormous pressure to come up with new information. The descriptors were bizarre because they didn't match the known facts. Debbie Ward, her father, and Beth Snelling had all seen the VR's build, and none of them described a fat guy with a funny walk or run—just the opposite, he was "stocky," but had an extremely strong upper body and muscular arms, and effortlessly leapt over fences and hedges. His known shoe size was a nine medium—the average for an American man in 1975 (and the same as the EAR).

VPD had a suspect for the student's "Peeper," and Sgt. Vaughan was positive that he wasn't the VR. That guy was described as a chain smoker with poor hygiene, and a very pronounced Oklahoma accent. He weighed two hundred pounds. There was no way that Beth Snelling could have put him at 150-170 pounds with no smell or accent to his voice. The college student, his former girlfriend, and a neighbor who had seen the Peeper all identified both the photo and the voice of the suspect. There was no doubt that their Peeper was the suspect, and he didn't deny it. He hadn't committed a crime, except maybe a mild trespass years earlier, and said he liked to go out walking in the evening. His alibi was checked. He was working or out of town during many of the ransacking burglaries, as well as the Snelling homicide. He also took a polygraph exam and was found to be truthful. The chubby Peeper was identified and cleared. He was not the VR. *Simple enough, right?*

It sounds melodramatic, maybe even hysterical to say that McGowen's session with the "Svengali Squad" directly led to at least twelve homicides, but the truth might be that simple. When Sgt. Vaughan approached the EAR investigators in late 1976, they agreed to exchange reports. Unfortunately, that included the VPD report that documented McGowen's hypnosis. Detective Richard Shelby was the lead on the EAR case at the time, and he became focused on that physical description of the VR—which was actually the completely unrelated, identified, and already cleared Peeper. Shelby also had McGowen and Beth Snelling's original interviews and descriptions, along with those of Debbie Ward and her father, but it didn't matter.

Shelby, like every other police officer in California in 1976, believed that the hypnosis was cutting edge science, infallible, and **more** reliable and accurate than the other VR descriptions. SSD simply overweighted the least reliable piece of information that Sgt. Vaughan gave them. In general, police enthusiastically embrace "opinion science," because the "opinions" consistently give them the results they want. The expert's "opinion" says that the hairs, tire tracks, or bite marks match the suspect, and help the prosecution. Suddenly, the witness "recovers" new details under hypnosis, and points right to the defendant, or his license plate. Admitting that it was junk science means overturning convictions and reinvestigating cases, and nobody in law enforcement has any interest in adding cases to the unsolved column, or creating more work for themselves.

In Sgt. Vaughan's mind, the discrepancy had all been resolved for McGowen after he realized that the student's Peeper was not the VR. Vaughan's team was totally focused on the original incident descriptions, and that was the suspect description that they had uploaded to the CII system. Obviously, it *was* a great match for the physical profile Shelby had for the EAR, since CII found the match. After Shelby was taken off the case, the SSD cut off all communication with VPD, and Vaughan's team had absolutely no idea what had happened.

Looking back on it now, Sgt. Vaughan still can't believe that the details added by McGowen during his hypnosis session derailed both the VR and EAR cases. He says that Agent McGowen stood right in front of the Sacramento investigators and told them that the VR and EAR descriptions matched, and he never wavered on that. He didn't internalize the wrong description, he simply felt compelled to say something new and helpful during the hypnosis. To this day, Sgt. Vaughan cannot understand why Sacramento would trust the hypnosis report more than what McGowen told them in person.

After over a year of the Sacramento Sheriff refusing to discuss it, in July 1978 McGowen told *The Sacramento Union*: "I am convinced they're the same guy. We will never stop trying to find and convict him."

Bill Miller, Sacramento Sheriff's spokesman responded in *The Sacramento Bee*:

> There are so many discrepancies between the physical descriptions… it is unlikely they are the same. Visalia police reports said that he had a "baby face, large hips, large rump, fat thighs, fat legs and fat, short feet." McGowen also said the man who shot at him "ran funny with his knees knocking together."—"None of this," said Miller, "fits our man."

There it is… *in black and white*. After this terse exchange in mid-1977, Sacramento Sheriff Duane Lowe cut off all contact with VPD and steadfastly refused to consider the VR as a lead in the EAR case, based *solely* on the physical description details added by McGowen during hypnosis—information he appears to have "incorporated" from the unrelated Peeper. If McGowen had not been hypnotized, or if VPD had not given that one report to Sacramento, there would have been no discrepancy in the physical descriptions, and they would have worked together to identify and lay a trap for a law enforcement officer who had moved from Tulare County in the summer of 1976.

Could Sheriff Lowe have had a reasonable, good faith conversation with McGowen, and asked about the discrepancy? *Of course.* Could the investigators have discovered the error just by looking at all of the witness statements, and the positive identification of the Peeper? *Also yes.* Instead, Sheriff Lowe called VPD, had Sgt. Vaughan and his team removed from the VR investigation, and threatened them with termination if they ever contacted Sacramento again, or made public statements connecting the VR and EAR. Publicly humiliating them with false accusations of incompetence and publicity-seeking wasn't enough, Lowe went after their careers too. This deeply affected Sgt. Vaughan. He knew he was correct, but he was completely powerless to stop the EAR's rampage.

Sheriff Lowe and his investigator, Lt. Ray Root, were terrible at weighing evidence, and obsessed with downplaying the dangerousness of the EAR. It started with the first attacks in 1976, which they tried to hide from the community. After Brian and Katie Maggiore were murdered while walking their dog in 1978, the Sheriff continued to insist—for years—that the EAR was not "a killer." In fact, they were *still* claiming that he had never killed anyone in February 1980 when Santa Barbara Sheriff's investigators were looking at the possibility that the EAR had killed Drs. Offerman and Manning in Goleta, two months earlier.

The *Sacramento Bee* documented the possible EAR/Goleta connection, and quoted detectives as saying only two EAR victims had been injured, which was not remotely true, and they made no mention of the Maggiore homicides. In the end, the Sheriff said that there was no connection, citing his assertion that the EAR was not a killer and the fact that Dr. Manning had not been raped. Lt. Root said that the factor that convinced him was the apparent ineptitude exhibited by the killer in Goleta:

> "It is obvious that the guy lost control of the situation, lost control of the people, and eventually had to kill somebody." Root said that scenario does not fit the East Area Rapist, who never lost control of a situation.

There had also been a matching EAR attack in Goleta just two months before the homicides. The victims had escaped, and the EAR was chased and nearly caught by their FBI agent neighbor. That came just a few months after the last known EAR attack in Danville, where the couple fought back, and the attacker ran—leaving behind some pre-tied shoelaces, just like the ones found at the Maggiore scene. The third EAR attack, back in 1976, had also ended in the EAR running away, naked from the waist down, after a mother fought back to protect her teen daughter.

Lt. Root was almost comically wrong. It was as if he didn't know anything about the offender he was supposed to catch. Reading case files and knowing details is difficult, but come on. It was as if he was looking for any excuse not to find a connection, no matter how ridiculous. Lt. Root was spectacularly wrong, and the EAR definitely wanted him to know it. On March 13, 1980, Root's quotes appeared in *The Sacramento Bee*, and late that night, the EAR killed Lyman and Charlene Smith in their home in Ventura. Another "call and response."

Much later, in a 2003 *Sacramento Magazine* article, an original SSD detective spoke about what he believed happened in the first three years of the EAR investigation:

> "[SSD] was more concerned about who was going to catch him than how. Everybody wanted the glory of catching him, so nobody talked to each other. There was no sharing of information or coordination going on. He wasn't smart; the department just let egos get in the way. It was disgusting, and it still infuriates me when I think about it. Had we caught him, a lot of people would still probably be alive today." In this same article Detective Carol Daly agreed, adding: "There was so much pressure on us from the community to catch him that it caused a tremendous amount of competition within the various jurisdictions. Information wasn't shared. The investigation never came together."

The total ban on discussing a possible VR/EAR connection was still apparent at the ten-year anniversary of Claude Snelling's homicide. New investigators were by then working the case for VPD, and when they were interviewed by the newspaper for an update on the case, there was no mention of Sacramento or the EAR as a possible lead. Sgt. Vaughan was quoted:

> That period was the most frustrating of my career… I thought for a while he could get up and fly. The Ransacker was no ordinary burglar. Even now when my wife and I go out to dinner, if I see someone who fits the description, I just look at him, and she knows what I'm doing. I still look for him every day.

The myth of the EAR that ***never*** injured or killed anyone was maintained for over a decade. In point of fact, the very first public connection between the EAR and Maggiore homicide was a brief mention in a 1990 *Sacramento Bee* article, but it was dismissed as "some investigators have theorized"—nothing more. There wasn't another mention until 2001, when the EAR was finally connected to the Southern California homicides through DNA.

One person who put it all together years before the DNA match was Russ Whitmeyer, a private investigator from Ojai. Whitmeyer had become involved in the case after his friend from high school, Charlene Smith, was killed in the Ventura attack. He explained his conclusions to the *Visalia Times-Delta* in a front page story on March 22, 2008: "As far as I know, it's the largest unsolved serial murder and rape case in California history."

Whitmeyer described the suspect as: five foot, ten inches tall,180 pounds, stocky, with brown hair, and wore a men's size 9 shoe. He said that the knots used in the EAR cases indicated to him someone who had been in the Navy or Air Force, adding: "I believe that, without any doubt, the killer rapist started as the Visalia Ransacker…" As the paper explained, Whitmeyer's belief was shared by Detective Larry Pool of the Orange County Sheriff's Department. Pool had originally connected his cold case in Dana Point with two homicides in Irvine, the one in Ventura, two more in Goleta, and then to DNA from the EAR. Although Orange County had closed his cold case unit, Detective Pool had continued to work the case due to the nature of the offender: "He puts himself at risk time and time again. This guy is so brazen, and he likes terrorizing so much. I think it's that extra quality that haunts you." In 2008, Whitmeyer was offering a reward of $100,000 for any tip leading to the killer. He and Pool both believed that Visalia was the key to the case.

In August 2010, Larry Crompton, the original EAR investigator from Contra Costa County, published a book on the cases, and *The Sacramento Bee* wrote an update story that quoted SSD Detective Ken Clark. The statute of limitations had long expired on the rape cases, but Clark was assigned to the murders of the Maggiores. Clark asked for new tips, and gave the following description:

> The East Area Rapist has blue or hazel eyes, and is between 5 feet 8 and 5 feet 11 inches tall. At the time, he was physically fit, with a muscular chest. He wears a size 9 shoe, and has type A blood. His voice is higher-pitched than average for men, but he often disguised it with a gruff or husky whisper.

Of course, there was not *one word* about Visalia in the story—the town that shall not be named. Had Clark read any of the VPD reports? Beth Snelling's attacker with the strong "arms and hands" and a "growl" disguising his voice; Debbie Ward's "muscular" prowler with strong arms; McGowen's panicked "high-pitched" suspect, who left size 9 footprints at the scene; and, each and every one of them describing the man as 5 feet 10 inches tall. Russ Whitmeyer and Larry Pool tried to tell Ken Clark about the VR, but it didn't matter.

Perhaps Clark was still focused on the details from McGowen's hypnosis report, thirty years after the method and the LAPD team had been thoroughly discredited as garbage. However, I believe at some point the Sacramento Sheriff's Office decided to ignore, and then actively cover up, any VR/EAR connection because their original 1977-78 decision to eviscerate Sgt. Vaughan's team made them look responsible for the later EAR rapes and homicides. Sacramento's bad police work and giant egos caused them to make a critical mistake. The EAR could have been stopped and they let him go. *It really was that simple.*

Russ Whitmeyer died in 2014, but I was able to contact Larry Pool. It was clear from him that he had untangled the problem with McGowen's hypnosis. Pool had even gone so far as to verify the identity of the college student's Peeper, confirmed that he was cleared in 1976, and spoke with VPD and the Peeper's brother, who provided details of the alibi, and how it was proven. Whitmeyer and Pool had simply disregarded the bad information that was irrelevant to the VR, and looked to the original physical descriptions from the Wards, Beth Snelling, and Agent McGowen. *Easy enough.* Pool firmly believed that his suspect had been offending in Tulare County between 1974-76, and he was very interested to hear what Vaughan and I had put together that connected the VR to Jennifer, Donna, and Exeter.

By the summer of 2016, when I reached out to discuss the case, Investigator Pool was working in the private sector. While the EAR episode on A&E's *Cold Case Files* had forever tied him to the case, he still found himself regularly working on it in his "spare" time. He agreed that Donna and Jennifer's homicides should be given another look, and that it would be worth eliminating our top Exeter suspects through DNA. To those ends, he forwarded the information to a current member of the EAR Task Force, Paul Holes. As Pool later confirmed, he had badly misjudged Hole's opinion of a possible VR/EAR connection. Holes didn't just ignore the Exeter information, he decided to attempt to discredit it.

Suddenly, forty years after the original conflict, Vaughan, VPD, and I all found ourselves in the middle of a brand new disinformation campaign. First, I was told, in no uncertain terms, that the Peeper identified by the college student had, in fact, been the VR, but that

VPD had screwed up the investigation, hadn't been able to charge him, and were trying to cover up their mistakes by pointing to the EAR. This assertion was not only disproven by the documented facts, it sounded a bit deranged. The Peeper had been positively identified, confessed to the incident, and cleared of any possible involvement in the ransacking burglaries, the Snelling homicide, and the McGowen shooting forty years earlier.

However, according to Holes, the college student must have seen the VR, and McGowen's ***hypnosis*** description was more accurate and reliable than his original statement. This all meant that the "weird, stubby, fat, stumble walker" was the VR, and could not, *under any circumstances*, be the EAR. What I felt that I was hearing from Holes is something called "*belief persistence*." This occurs when an investigator continues to believe something even after they have seen evidence that contradicts that belief. It's related to "tunnel vision," which occurs when an investigator focuses only on evidence that supports their conclusion (often a suspect), and simultaneously ignores all evidence that points away from it.

In this case, Holes was convinced of four things: the "Peeper" was the VR; McGowen's ***hypnosis*** account was *more accurate* than all of the other VR descriptions; the VR wasn't violent or dangerous; and, that the VR was a terrible, incompetent burglar.

Holes had seemingly focused solely on four pages out of hundreds of VPD reports. If information in a report contradicted his idea of the physical description or behavior of the VR, he simply disregarded it. This is all classic "*confirmation bias*," another common investigative trap.

Holes could only see the page that described the 1973 Peeper incident, the page that described McGowen's hypnosis, the page that described the VR screaming "Don't hurt me," and a page that included the detail that "scratch marks" were found on some homes that did not suffer burglaries. He clung to those four pages as the only evidence about the VR in existence.

Since this "analysis" was happening in 2016, Holes should have known that McGowen's hypnosis session was completely discredited and banned from court after the 1982 *Shirley* opinion. He should have read the other reports about the "Peeper"—where the suspect was both identified and conclusively eliminated as being the VR. If he had read the EAR reports, he should have known that the "scratch marks" weren't signs of failed burglaries, but rather a code that the VR was using to categorize homes and victims that he prowled. The EAR reports and SSD profile also clearly stated that the EAR's natural voice was unusually high for a man, and he disguised it with a growl or whisper.

Holes could not see any report that described the kidnapping of Beth Snelling, her father's murder, or Beth's physical description of the VR. He could not see the 150 successful burglaries that all involved locked homes, rarely being seen, and never being caught inside by a homeowner. Those were just the ones where there was ransacking and stolen items—presumably there were hundreds more that were just prowling and stalking. Was this intentionally dishonest, or the worst case of tunnel vision, confirmation bias, and belief persistence in the history of criminal investigations? I cannot say.

When Holes and I first spoke, it was clear that we were not going to find many areas of agreement. I was focused on observable facts, and Holes believed in his own profile of the EAR. Nothing I said fit his theories. He told me that the VR couldn't be the EAR because killers don't go back to being burglars and rapists, citing "*escalation theory*." That area within the study of criminal offenders is actually called "Acceleration, Deceleration, Escalation, and De-escalation," and should be understood with other concepts like "Specialization and Versatility in Offending," "Trajectories of Criminal Behavior Across the Life Course," "Persistence and Desistance," and "Life Transitions and Turning Points." In other words, the study of criminals across their lives and criminal careers is complicated and variable, and can't be reduced to a simplistic soundbite that defines it as a one-way ladder of increasing severity.

I wasn't interested in getting inside the EAR's head and guessing about his psychological motivations, childhood traumas, or the source of his anger. I knew details of his crimes, his documented interactions with the police, where he had offended, and his general age, race, and physicality. That information pointed to a pool of possible suspects, and eliminated others. Some of the evidence was circumstantial, but it was still evidence—not mere speculation or guesses.

Holes had developed an entire career history for the EAR based upon some school papers dropped on a bike path in Danville in 1978. He was searching for a planful professional who traveled from project to project, committing attacks at each new housing development. On the other hand, I believed that the EAR/ONS scenes were staged, and evidence was planted to misdirect detectives about his motivations, career, and where he lived. Holes told me that he "knew" the VR was not the EAR, and any investigation of suspects in Exeter was a waste of the EAR Task Force's valuable time and resources. There was no common ground or basis of understanding between us.

About one month after that exchange with Holes, the Sacramento FBI held a press conference on June 15, 2016, announcing a new fifty-thousand-dollar reward for information leading to the arrest and conviction of the EAR. Not only were the words "Visalia," "Tulare," "Ransacker," "Snelling," and "McGowen" not mentioned, there were no representatives from Southern California present to give information and answer questions about the ten homicides they had connected to the EAR through DNA. The FBI made a huge show of asking for tips, but gave only a tiny portion of the relevant information that might lead to a break in the case. It was very offbeat, and felt strangely useless.

Unfortunately, the FBI announcement took a dark turn for journalist Michael Bowker, who had written about the EAR for *Sacramento Magazine* in 2003. In September 2018, Bowker wrote a follow-up piece on DeAngelo's identification and arrest. At the end, he shared his personal experience with some "*citizen detectives*":

> Although East Area Rapist victims consistently said the man who assaulted them had dark hair and broad features, the sketch [released by the FBI in 2016] is of a blond, Nordic-looking "surfer boy." Social media trolls, aided by a tabloid television show, soon picked up on the ubiquitous sketch and paired it with the picture of me they found on the back jacket of a book I wrote…on how some international companies knowingly poisoned hundreds of workers with asbestos. It has nothing whatsoever to do with the East Area Rapist case. Suddenly, though, my distant resemblance to the blond-haired "killer" in the sketch, my connections to the case and my having lived in two of the more than one dozen cities where he struck in California (including Santa Barbara) gave the bumbling internet sleuths all the clues they needed.
>
> For the next two years, I received a number of disturbing and threatening anonymous phone calls, and the online libel grew like poisonous mushrooms. It was upsetting to my friends and family. Some of the phone calls weren't so funny, but others were like scripts from bad sitcoms. One woman called and wondered if I could just "confess" to her so she wouldn't have to come all the way to California to "get" me. "All I want is the $50,000 FBI reward," she said."

Bowker's description perfectly captures the extremely angry and unreasonable atmosphere that permeated the investigation in the two years prior to DeAngelo's arrest. Investigation Discovery aired a series that followed Paul Holes around California, offering his opinion about the offender's mindset and occupation. Towards the end, he made his argument that Visalia was not a lead to be followed because he had eliminated a connection. Holes also answered questions from discussion board users that included information he had provided to the case "work group." He was also making presentations to other members of law enforcement, instructing them to ignore the VR as a possible lead. The Australian podcast *Casefiles* Case 53, had a "bonus" interview with him on the topic:

> There are two very credible witnesses that saw, or face to face with him, in decent lighting, saw his face. Saw [his] entire physique, his entire build. And they both consistently describe him as: He had this, you know, round face, with pug nose and funny looking ears, and kind of a hunk neck. And just rounded shoulders, and fat through the hips, and fat through the thighs, and fat butt and short, fat fingers.
>
> One of the witnesses was Officer McGowen gets shot by the Visalia Ransacker, and the other was a 22-year-old Anthropology student. You know someone who at least has some training in taking a look at humans, right? More so than the a… (trails off) And this person, this anthropology student, he says that he looks kind of "*mongoloid*" to him. He had mongoloid-type features, and his behaviors were weird, and he's acting… he's talking in a high woman's voice… and, he's acting kind of scared, and "Don't hurt me. Don't hurt me," and screaming like a woman when he's being confronted. That is not who the East Area Rapist is… The East Area Rapist is a dominant personality. Once he gets the women and men under control, he is dominating them.

One thing had become very, very clear. In the world of Paul Holes, Claude Snelling had never been shot dead trying to stop the VR from taking his 16-year-old daughter. It was always the same story on an endless loop—the student's Peeper was really the VR, and he was a stumbling, terrified idiot, incapable of real violence.

The statement that the EAR was a dominant personality, and that the VR was not, was offered as additional "proof" that the VR was not the EAR—that they were not the same type of offender. Holes made the same argument when answering questions on the discussion board: "The EAR was also a very dominant personality while the VR lacked this characteristic in these interactions."

Compare that to Beth Snelling's description of her attack by the VR:

> He stated: "Don't scream or I'll stab you." As Beth was pulled out of her bed, the suspect stated, "You're coming with me, don't scream or I'll shoot you." Beth recalled that this was the last time the suspect spoke. She kept asking the suspect, "Why are you doing this" and "where are you taking me," but the suspect remained silent.
>
> She stated further that the voice was very demanding and deliberate and it was not wavering, or shaky, or nervous. She had a feeling the suspect was in command of the situation, and did not appear to be undecided on any of his moves.
>
> They heard her father call out from inside the house, "Hey, what are you doing? Where are you taking my daughter?" Beth stated that the suspect made no attempt to run at this time, but stood there and pointed the gun at the back door, waiting for her father to come outside.
>
> Beth went on to relate that as her father ran back into the house, the suspect pointed the gun at her head, then dropped it to his side and kicked her three times in the face.

Paul Holes also seemed to be *completely* unaware of the details of the third EAR attack on August 29, 1976. (*NOTE: This was two days before DeAngelo began working at Auburn PD.*) His intended target was a teenaged girl, but her mother wasn't having any of it:

> The suspect appeared from the kitchen area, pointed a gun at the victim telling her to "freeze," and had her hang up the phone. As the suspect got closer she remembered grabbing the suspect by the wrist to turn his gun hand away. The suspect responded by beating the victim about the head and upper body with a club which he was carrying in his opposite hand. He tried to tie her hands behind her back, but she actively

> resisted, finally breaking loose and struggling toward the front door. She finally got the door open and started screaming. The suspect also fled out the door toward the sidewalk area. The suspect was not wearing any pants, and he had a high kind of voice with no accent. As he got more nervous however, his voice had a "shaky," breaking quality. He held the gun in his left hand and the club in his right.

The victim described the club as small, light-colored wood, covered with leather. This description exactly matched the club stolen by the VR in 1975. That incident was eight months after the McGowen shootout. The EAR didn't win when he was confronted by the husband in his last Danville attack, or when the female victim fought back and escaped in Goleta. The EAR's command of his victims relied upon surprising them in their sleep, threatening them with a gun and/or knife, promising he just wanted money to keep down their panic, keeping them tightly restrained with dishes on their backs and, if confronted with real force, he ran and/or shot the threat. In fact, the EAR had expressed fear, panic, and loss of control at multiple scenes.

Additionally, there were actually *four* credible Visalia witnesses (Willie and Debbie Ward, Beth Snelling, and Bill McGowen) who saw the VR's "entire physique, his entire build," and this "anthropology" student was ***not*** one of them (NOTE: he was a *biology* undergrad, so hardly a trained "expert" in the human form. Such facts do matter, *especially* when they are asserted to ***exclude*** a homicide suspect). The EAR Task Force was actively spreading misinformation, and the media could not get enough of it. Between 2016-18 there was a flood of TV shows, podcasts, blogs, and top selling books that loudly and forcefully argued that they had researched the VR and concluded he could not be the EAR. They cited psychology, "escalation theory," the Peeper, and their personal expertise. All of them were certain—*and 100% wrong*—totally incorrect.

Starting in late 2017, after a lot of pushing from Sgt. Vaughan, Visalia Violent Crimes investigators reestablished contact with SSD EAR investigators, and tried to clear up some of the old misunderstandings. Sgt. Vaughan worked on retired Detective Shelby, asking him to look at Jennifer and Donna's murders as part of the EAR series, and to consider suspects from Exeter. Sgt. Vaughan walked through the physical description problems again, and assured Shelby that the "Peeper" had been cleared, and was not the VR. They also discussed the changes that occurred during Agent McGowen's hypnosis session and the unreliability of that information. We all agreed to go back to McGowen and Beth Snelling's original physical descriptions, and work forward from there.

Detective Shelby took this information to SSD Detective Sgt. Ken Clark, who was investigating the Maggiore homicides. Clark and Shelby were working on something else together, and it fit with the VR. Back in the early 1970s, Shelby was a patrol sergeant in Rancho Cordova, and he dealt with a serial burglar in the same neighborhoods that the EAR hit a few years later. Clark went back and retrieved the case files for those burglaries from microfilm, and found another series of interest. In February, 2018, on the 40th anniversary of the Maggiore homicides, Clark publicly released what he had found:

> A cat burglar operated in the Rancho Cordova, and eastern Sacramento County during 1972 and 1973, striking over 30 times during that period. His crimes were linked by MO, and it was recognized by detectives of that time that the crimes were the work of one man. His method of operation was to enter a home quietly after the occupants were asleep. The burglar typically exited out a different pre-opened door from his point of entry, and evidence indicated the door was likely opened immediately upon entering the home as an escape route. A commonly hit area was between Dolecetto Drive and Malaga Way, and near Coloma Road with over a dozen strikes. He was known in the reports as "The cat burglar that strikes the Rancho Cordova, and East Areas of Sacramento."
>
> Once inside, the burglar went throughout the home as the occupants slept, and took purses and wallets belonging to the

victims. Victims included families with children, couples, and single women. Evidence from many of the scenes indicated the burglar had spent extensive time searching the residence, but most of the items of value outside of the purses and wallets were disregarded. However, the burglar would sometimes take coin collections, silver, or other items including food and alcohol. The burglar also spent considerable time in the bedrooms of the victim(s) as they slept, without disturbing them. The purses/wallets were typically found nearby in an adjacent yard, or on the sidewalk of the residence. Occasionally they were left elsewhere in groups with other victims' property from the same night. The only item usually taken from the purse was money, but occasionally small items or identification was also missing. The suspect would frequently strike multiple houses in a single night.

The areas targeted included Rancho Cordova, Carmichael, Whitney/Mission area, and Citrus Heights. Three of the Citrus Heights cat burglaries were each within a block of one of the two East Area Rapist strikes four years later. The Rancho Cordova burglaries were within blocks of the Rancho Cordova EAR attacks. It was also believed the suspect had extensive knowledge of the drainage canals, and of the American River Parkway.

Cordova Meadows Burglar (1973)

A burglar operated in the Cordova Meadows subdivision, and nearby area in 1973. He struck at all times of the day and night, including when people were home. These burglaries were occurring at their heaviest in the first half of 1973, and included over 20 burglaries by mid-March. Some of the items taken included coins, piggy banks, jewelry, binoculars, hunting knives (some in scabbards), photographic cameras and movie cameras, two-dollar bills (numerous), Blue Chip Stamps, handguns, food, alcohol, and prescription medication. Larger items, most electronics, and other items of value were noted to be disregarded by the suspect.

The burglar exhibited numerous quirks both in his behaviors as well as the things he chose to steal. Stolen during some of the burglaries were photos of female occupants. Additionally, single earrings were taken from pairs.

Some of the MO factors (some quite rare) that frequently cropped up in this series included the following:

- Entry through a kitchen, or sliding glass door;
- Opening of a window in a back bedroom, and placing of the screen on the bed or inside. Deputies processing the scenes noted that, in these instances, the window was being used as an emergency escape only, and was not the point of entry or preferred exit. This escape exit was used on two occasions where the homeowner interrupted the burglary;
- Unplugging of forced air furnace;
- Secondary securing of front door by chair, security chain, or other blocking item;
- Heavy ransacking of bedrooms, and scattering of clothing articles on floor;
- Women's undergarments stacked in other rooms; and
- Ransacking of kitchens.

In addition, this burglar was responsible for other burglaries of the same type as that suffered by the family of a future EAR victim. The burglary to her home in March, 1973, was one of three MO-linked burglaries that happened the same day, including one at the residence next door.

In the burglary of the home next door to the future EAR victim, the suspect stole a movie camera, other related equipment, and money from a piggy bank (bank broken by suspect). The burglary to the future victim was believed to have been a "no loss" burglary, and it occurred at the same residence where she would later be assaulted early in the East Area Rapist series, three years later. This victim also had single earrings stolen from her during the sexual assault incident (1976)."

[*NOTE: The information in the paragraph above refers to the EAR attack on October 9, 1976, where the victim was led to believe she was attacked by her neighbor, Dority, after the EAR had broken into Dority's house and planted stolen items to frame him. This report confirms that the EAR also previously broke into Dority's house in 1973, and he could have been planning to frame him years before he actually carried out the attack.*]

In another suspected related burglary two days prior in Rancho Cordova, entry was made through a side kitchen door. The suspect blocked the front door with a barstool, and ransacked the bedrooms heavily with drawers open and clothing scattered on the floor. The suspect took a Ruger, 7 shot .22 caliber revolver, watches, three rings, old silver coins and bills, a left handled hunting knife in a scabbard, a single earring, Avon "Model A" yellow after shave lotion, and a broken lamp. Other items of value were left behind.

Hang-up phone calls, and odd communications were also present in this series, and were reported by victims in the area. One particular victim, a 17-year-old girl, was living on La Alegria Drive. She received a suspicious unsigned letter stating: "I love you."

She then received numerous hang-up phone calls, and a final call where a subject with a low, adult male voice, stated: "I love you, this is your last night to live."

This victim lived next door to the home where Brian and Katie Maggiore were killed, five years later.

There it was, *for the first time ever*, the Sacramento Sheriff's Department clearly admitted that the EAR had committed odd, "rare," burglaries in 1972-73, and the MO exactly matched the VR and Tulare Cat Burglar. For forty years, they had specifically denied that the VR/EAR MOs matched and said that they had never had a similar burglary series, and yet there it was—it had been right in front of them the entire time. Detective Clark truly wanted to find justice for Katie and Brian Maggiore, and although his information never mentioned Visalia, Tulare County, or the Ransacker, he knew that he was admitting a connection, and offering a clue to the killer's past location.

I had to wonder if Clark had a strong suspect in mind. If that person had been in Visalia or Exeter in 1974-76, it would be smart to publicly imply a possible VR/EAR connection, and it couldn't cause any harm. If the EAR did turn out to be the Ransacker, it would look like SSD got it right, and if not, it was a lead that didn't pan out.

My correspondence with Detective Shelby made it clear that he had changed his mind, and now believed that the EAR could have been in Exeter during the VR years. We agreed to focus solely on suspects who lived, worked, and/or went to school in the East Sacramento area from 1972 to spring 1973, then moved to Exeter. Figuring out exactly where a young man may have been in 1972 was much harder than it sounded. If he didn't appear in a yearbook, newspaper story, or online phone directory, how would you know?

It seems that, after being contacted by VPD and SSD Detective Clark for information on Jennifer Armour's unsolved murder, TCSO Johnson and Dempsie panicked, and decided that they had to act to cut off all further inquiries. On November 16, 2017, my phone suddenly exploded with messages from Visalia. TCSO Dempsie and Johnson had issued a press release and given a TV interview claiming that they "had reason to believe" that Oscar Clifton had killed Jennifer. Sgt. Vaughan and I both knew immediately that this was nothing more than an attempt to intimidate us into stopping our investigation. TCSO also started harassing Oscar's wife and children, showing up unannounced and demanding that they submit to "questioning," and reaching across the country with menacing letters.

Dempsie and Johnson knew that they had no evidence tying Oscar to Jennifer's homicide—just the opposite. He had been fully investigated and cleared in 1975. It was abuse of power—punishment for pushing them to reopen Jennifer's case. The "evidence" they cited was Sgt. Vaughan's own arguments, made in our meeting, that the same person clearly killed Jennifer and Donna, and it was the VR. Dempsie and Johnson were trying to pressure witnesses into implicating Oscar as the VR, which gave Sgt. Vaughan a good laugh. Who knows how far they would have taken their harassment campaign. Luckily, I never had to find out.

In early 2018, the EAR Task Force had secretly created a DNA sample for the EAR and uploaded it to a consumer DNA site designed to create family trees. The EAR was identified, arrested, and charged. He was Joseph James DeAngelo, Jr., AKA Exeter PD Sgt. DeAngelo, 1973-76.

Chapter Nine Sources

1. Vaughan Interview

2. Time Magazine, "The Svengali Squad," September 13, 1976

3. Los Angeles Times - February 2, 1975

4. People v. Shirley, Supreme Court of CA, March 11, 1982; and, California Evidence Code - EVID § 795

5. VPD Report - Gomes September 11, 1975

6. VPD Report - Calhoun September 18, 1975

7. VPD Report - McGowen October 15, 1975

8. VPD Report - Vaughan October 27, 1975

9. VPD Report - McGowen October 2, 1975

10. VPD Report - Hartman December 13, 1975

11. Visalia Times-Delta December 18, 1975

12. VR Composites

13. VPD Report - McGowen January 23, 1976

14. VPD Report - Vaughan January 15, 1976
15. VPD Report - McGowen October 1, 1976
16. VPD Report - McGowen October 5, 1976
17. Sacramento Union - July 22, 1978
18. Sacramento Bee - July 23, 1978
19. Santa Maria Times - January 30, 1980
20. Sacramento Bee - February 26, 1980
21. Santa Maria Times - February 28, 1980
22. Sacramento Bee - March 13, 1980
23. Sacramento Magazine "Unsolved Mystery" - September 2003
24. Sacramento Bee - March 25, 1990
25. Sacramento Bee - April 5, 2001
26. Visalia Times-Delta - March 22-23, 2008
27. Sacramento Bee - August 7, 2010
28. Sacramento Magazine "Unsolved Mystery?" - September 28, 2018
29. Casefiles Case 53
30. Proboard "OriginalNightStalker" Holes Statements
31. "Criminology" Roots in Visalia March 24, 2018
32. Quester Files
33. Investigation Discovery - The Golden State Killer: It's Not Over
34. Case Files of the East Area Rapist - Winters
35. SSD EAR Report - August 29, 1976
36. VPD Report - Vaughan December 2, 1975
37. Sacramento Sheriff Cold Case Investigative Unit February 2, 2018
38. TCSO Cold Case Press Release - November 16, 2017
39. ABC 30 November 16, 2017

CHAPTER TEN

"Sciency"

Back in the summer of 1976, Oscar was still on trial for his life. He had no idea that the man who was wanted for burglary, assault, kidnapping, murder, and attempted murder of a police officer in Visalia was still wearing a badge and uniform, and investigating major crimes in Exeter. As Sgt. Bob Byrd took the stand to tell the jury about what he saw on Neel Ranch, the VR was living just two doors down, and sharing an office with him. The same man had likely been standing in the courtroom, "guarding" with the other Exeter PD officers during Oscar's preliminary hearing.

Joseph ("Joe") James DeAngelo, Jr. had moved to Exeter in May 1973, when he joined Exeter PD as a patrol officer. It was his first real job in law enforcement. DeAngelo was born in upstate New York on November 8, 1945. He had an older sister, a younger sister, and a brother. His father was a decorated Air Force turret gunner, who flew critical World War II missions over targets in Europe and the Pacific in B-24 and B-25 bombers. After the war, the family moved to different air bases, including Germany. In 1956, DeAngelo Sr. was stationed at Hamilton Air Force Base, just west of Vallejo, California. He was briefly assigned to Van Nuys in 1958, and then back to Hamilton until June of 1959, when the family bought a house in Rancho Cordova, a suburb of Sacramento. DeAngelo Sr. was stationed at nearby Mather Air Force Base, but when he was transferred to Florida, Mrs. DeAngelo and the kids stayed behind, and they divorced in September 1964.

Joe DeAngelo Jr. was remarkably unremarkable. He attended Mills Middle School in Rancho Cordova and Folsom High School, graduating in June 1964. He was accepted into the Navy on September 11th, and received his recruit training in San Diego. He hoped to be a naval aviator, but ended up being a repair mechanic on the USS Canberra and USS Piedmont. He served in Vietnam, but never off the ship. He later told stories about losing part of his finger during the war, but friends said that it was really a fireworks accident in Sacramento. He told some people that it had been shot off in combat, and others that he was hurt by a gun recoil, or a rolling barrel on the Navy ship. Looking through the deck logs, there is no mention of an injury onboard, so I tend to believe that the fireworks story is the truth. He was discharged from active duty on August 9, 1968 at Treasure Island, San Francisco, with the note "not interested in Naval Reserve Training Program."

DeAngelo's mother, Kay, married Jack Bosanko in Exeter, California in 1965, just a few months after her oldest daughter and family had moved there for her husband's job as a telephone lineman. The Bosankos purchased five acres in Auburn, CA, and built their dream home. The property had been divided by Jack's employer, Sierra Crane and Hoist, and the other parcels were mainly owned by members of that family, the Burgards. Eventually, both Joe and his younger brother John also worked for Sierra Crane. During the late 1960s the family continued to live in Auburn. Joe worked for Sierra Crane and as a commercial scuba diver while he attended nearby Sierra College, then Sacramento State. He earned an AA in Police Science and a BA in Criminal Justice. He also completed an internship with Roseville PD before moving to Exeter. Joe's hobbies of fishing, hunting, boating, and riding motorcycles made him a favorite with his nephews, who were 12 and 14 years old when Joe moved to town.

In November 1973, DeAngelo married Sharon Huddle, and she moved from Citrus Heights into his rental duplex on Emperor Street. Sharon's time in Exeter is a complete mystery. The neighbor on the other side of the duplex doesn't remember her, and Joe's closest friends at the police station didn't even know that he was married. Sharon pursued her BA in Fresno and worked in Visalia, but didn't involve herself in the fabric of Exeter.

Joe's career advanced quickly. He was uncommonly successful at solving burglary cases, and that earned him a promotion to Sergeant in the fall of 1975 and assignment to the Joint Attack on Burglary (JAB) team, working with neighboring jurisdictions to investigate cases.

Although a lot of people have said that DeAngelo left Exeter quickly after the McGowen shooting, he didn't. Sharon was still finishing her degree, and Joe was investigating major crimes in Exeter—such as they were. In the summer of 1976, DeAngelo's Sergeant salary and JAB position were renewed for another year, and there was no sign that he planned to leave. Yet, he gave his notice in mid-August, then took a backwards step in his career to patrol officer with Auburn PD.

How much of Oscar's trial did DeAngelo attend? Nobody remembers, but with the constant heavy police presence, there was no reason for anyone to notice. Newspaper stories about the trial described a fully packed courtroom with crowds often spilling out into the hallways.

On June 29, 1976, Byrd was back on the witness stand, and he summarized the homicide scene in well-rehearsed patter with DA Powell. He focused mainly on seeing a heel print from a cowboy boot, and tire tracks heading north out of the grove. He also attempted to bolster the claim that Donna had been the victim of a sexual assault: "There appeared to be mud and fluid in the crevice of the buttocks."

When I first read that, I had a lot of questions. Mainly, how could there be visible "fluid" from the murder twenty-four hours later? For instance, the blood was completely dried. Byrd was trying to make the jury believe that it was ejaculate from the killer, and setting up later testimony to support an attempted rape charge. Since I had just read the testimony of Jesus Renteria Lara, it didn't feel like much of a mystery. He said that he had sprayed Donna's body, and continued on to the next row until the tank was empty. It was an odd response to finding a dead girl, but he was very specific about it. Was the tree spray white? *Yes*. And the crime scene photos clearly show it covering Donna's body, including the clump of mud on her backside. The spray can be seen pooled in the leaves above the body, and still dripping down at least ninety minutes after the rig passed by.

Tree Spray on Leaves, Homicide Scene
Neel Ranch—December 27, 1975
Photo: TCSO

On cross-examination, Donahue asked Byrd about the conditions around Donna's body:

Byrd: It's a dark black soil, has a lot of citrus leaves, and citrus stems from the citrus trees matted into it. The soil is heavy, thick soil.

Donahue: Was it dry or wet?

A: Moist.

Q: Now, around that multi-colored knit cap, did you find, or were there any footprints found?

A: There were ladder marks and footprints in the dirt where it appeared that they had been picking oranges.

Q: How about back were the victim was found?

A: Down and south I believe that there was some people working in there, as I recall.

There was not a speck of that thick, black, moist soil, or bits of leaves, stems, or citrus peel in or on Oscar's truck or clothing. Nothing. Donna's hair, clothing, and body was covered with mud, blood, and citrus debris. There were trucks, spray rigs, TCSO officers, and grove workers everywhere, and they left tire tracks and footprints—none of which were documented, compared, or eliminated. There were no interviews with the workers Byrd mentioned. Had they been there the day before? Did they see or hear anything? Had there been *any* unknown people or vehicles in the grove? Nobody knows, because Byrd and his men never asked… not one person. Not one question.

TCSO Hensley took the stand again to discuss tire tracks he photographed on Road 176. Donahue objected, and the jury was excused:

> My objection to the question is that it's not relevant and I don't see that it's even competent. This is all very enlightening, but there hasn't been anything, to this day at least, to indicate that these tire marks were made by the wheels of Mr. Clifton's car, or vehicle. We have sat here for a day or two listening to various tire marks being brought in. Unless there is something brought forth to perhaps an offer of proof to tie all this together. I don't believe at this time that this testimony is relevant.

Judge Bradley overruled the objection, saying that the jury could weigh it for themselves. Bradley was wrong; irrelevant information only confuses the jury, and encourages them to see proof where none exists.

The next person to testify was a local farm advisor named Jim Pehrson. Powell asked him to offer his opinion about a dried-up bit of brown leaf in a jar, and photos of two leaves from Neel Ranch. Pehrson told the jury that in his "opinion" they were orange leaves. Donahue questioned the basis for his statement:

Donahue: What about the sample in the little bottle there?

Pehrson: This is a—at this point somewhat dried up.

Q: When did you first observe it, sir?

A: Last week.

Q: Could it be another type of citrus leaf?

A: The opinion it's an orange leaf is based on its color, the nature of the margins **that show on the photograph** and they sort of eliminate other citrus varieties. [*emphasis added*]

Donahue seemed to miss it, but it was right there: Pehrson made the identification of "orange" based on the photo of the leaves from Neel Ranch, not the dried up bit of leaf from Oscar's truck mirror. Jim Pehrson had no idea what kind of leaf was in the bottle. DA Powell put up an "expert" to give his opinion that known orange leaves, from orange trees at Neel Ranch, were, in fact, orange. From that point on, Powell referred to the leaf from Oscar's truck as orange, and told the jury it proved that Oscar had been on Neel Ranch.

Donahue had absolutely no idea that Criminalist Morton had hired John Strother, an actual expert botanist, to examine the mirror leaf when it was fresh, and he could not identify it as orange. His written report was given to DA Powell, who did not disclose it to the defense. Instead he brought up a local to say that leaves from an orange tree were from an orange tree. The exculpatory evidence was hidden, while misleading and confusing opinion testimony was offered in its place.

TCSO Hensley was brought back to offer more opinions about the tire tracks at Road 176 on cross-examination by Donahue:

Donahue: This is a footprint in that tire?

Hensley: It's what appeared to be a footprint, yes.

Q: Made before or after the car moved in or out of there?

A: Before—pardon me—it was made after the vehicle tire track was made.

Q: Did you tell me a while ago when we were talking about this scene on Road 176, that you didn't find any footprints up there around where the tires were?

A: There were numerous officers at the scene.

Q: Look at this picture. Tell me which officer or officers' shoe print that is?

A: I have no idea.

Q: You don't even know if it is an officer's shoe print, do you?

A: No, I do not.

Q: Well, then what about all the rest of them out there, how did you determine they were all made by the Sheriff's Office; you didn't, did you?

A: I found no foot tracks that appeared to be connected, nor was I instructed to photograph any.

Q: Here is a footprint that you cannot identify, correct?

A: That is correct.

Q: On what basis did you determine this footprint was not connected with this particular crime; did you just guess?

A: I used my judgment at the time, yes, sir.

Q: Based upon what did you make the judgment? You guessed, Mr. Hensley, isn't that correct?

A: All I can say, counsel, is to reiterate that there were no footprints that appeared to be connected with this case, that numerous officers and other people were at the scene, and I was not instructed by the investigating officers to photograph any foot tracks at the scene.

Q: Did Sgt. Byrd see this footprint out there, or do you know?

A: Sgt. Byrd was the primary investigating officer at the scene. I can not recall, or do not know, what he saw or what he took as important at the time.

Q: Isn't he the one that told you to take these photographs?

A: Between him and Detective McKinney, yes, sir.

Q: Isn't it a fact, Sgt. Hensley, you did the same thing at the other scene as far as taking pictures were concerned? Isn't it a fact that you just picked and chose what you thought was important in the case?

A: My own judgment, as well as the other investigating officers.

DA Powell tried to get Hensley's testimony back to matching the tire tracks to Oscar's truck:

Powell: Did you measure the wheel widths and wheel base of the defendant, Oscar Archie Clifton's pickup?

Hensley: Yes, I did.

Q: And what were those measurements, do you have those in your report?

A: Yes, I do. May I check it please?

Q: Please.

A: The measurement on the defendant's vehicle were: rear width 60 3/4 inches; front 64 1/2 inches; wheel base 152 inches.

Q: The wheel base was 152?

A: Yes, sir.

Q: Now comparing those with the measurements you made at the scene… the wheel base you're two inches off?

A: Yes, sir.

This wasn't just perjury by Vern Hensley, it was suborned by DA Powell. Although Hensley made a huge theatrical show of reading from his report to convey accuracy and authenticity, the written report *actually* said that the wheelbase of Oscar's truck (measured by TCSO Johnson in the impound yard at 3:30 pm on December 31, 1975) was ***132 inches***. Hensley lied, and made the wheelbase of Oscar's truck 20 inches longer. *Why?* To match the wheelbase measurement of the tracks on Road 176, which was 150 inches. Powell had read the report, and knew the real measurements, yet he was ready to say that it was only a two-inch difference. This was planned ahead of time and executed in front of the jury, and Donahue either missed it, or just let it go. TCSO Johnson had done a good job with his measurements—because, according to Ford *technical specifications*, the wheelbase of Oscar's truck was 131 inches.

IFS was given about one hundred items of evidence for examination and testing; from those, they obtained hairs and fibers for further examination. On direct examination DA Powell asked Criminalist Morton about four photos of tire tracks, one photo of a partial heel print, one pair of cowboy boots, and the tires from Oscar's truck. Nothing else. ***All*** of the scientific forensic results were entirely exculpatory; they either pointed to someone else who wasn't Oscar (unidentified hairs, fibers, and with blood type A)—***or*** didn't have evidence that *should have* been on the killer and his truck (blood, mud, hairs, fibers, fingerprints).

Powell went with the tire tracks and heel print as purely opinion testimony. There was no scientific method offered. The logic was that Morton was a criminalist and an expert in forensics, so his opinion was more valuable than a layperson's. That is not how expert testimony is supposed to work. The opinion must be based on an accepted scientific method, the *Frye* standard. The first modern book on forensics was

An Introduction to Criminalistics by Charles E. O'Hara and James W. Osterburg, first published in 1949, and republished in 1972. For three decades, this work was the standard guide for all criminalists and police forensic officers across the nation. It set out the procedure to be followed for documenting and comparing tire and foot impressions in soil:

> By far the best means of studying an impression is that of the plaster cast. A photograph of the shoe or tire impression should always be made before a cast is attempted. The impression should be carefully measured with compasses and ruler before it is touched.

O'Hara and Osterburg then delve into *exactly* how to mix and use the plaster of Paris to make accurate casts of the impressions in the soil. It's a detailed set of instructions, meant to be followed point by point. Even if you had never made casts before, the book would walk you through the process:

> The greatest obstacle to the analysis of foot impressions is the confusion contributed to the original situation: relatives and neighbors of the victim, and even police officers. The importance of an impression as evidence lies in its uniqueness. It can be established, however, only if there are a sufficient number of characteristic marks discernible.

There was a very specific, well-established scientific procedure for documenting and collecting tire and foot impressions from crime scenes. These methods were taught to every forensics officer and criminalist after 1949, and had just been republished three years before Donna was killed. TCSO Brian Johnson was only about two years out of his college training, and Morton was a Senior Criminalist at IFS. There is no way that Johnson did not know that he needed to take specific photos, with exact measurements, and then make plaster casts for every single tire or shoe print he collected into evidence. Morton *should have* explained that he didn't have the information he needed to identify the make of the tires or footwear from the photos, and that the lack of individual characteristics meant he could not offer a scientific opinion. Instead, he muddled along through Powell's questioning:

> *Morton:* The pattern is comparable, but there's no way of telling whether it's from the one or the other, these or any other similar tires. Appears to be more comparable to the right rear, although this may be due to some surface effects or lighting.
>
> *Powell:* Would you tell us what a "specific individual characteristic" is?
>
> A: Yes. Those are the kind of things that occur due to wear, damage of an object such as… a tire or a shoe in which it develops characteristics that allow you to uniquely identify that print as having come from that particular shoe, or that particular tire track. In this case, the character of the photographs and the condition at which I saw it did not allow me to make any determinations along those lines.
>
> Q: So, if I understand it, there were no specific individual characteristics by which you could say that these four tires made those particular tracks as opposed to any other tire in the world.
>
> A: That's correct.

That was not expert, scientific, or even a vague opinion that the tracks matched Oscar's tires. However, Morton's testimony about the "boot print" was criminal. There were eight footprint photos taken near Donna's body, and seven of them were immediately excluded as matching Oscar's shoes and boots. They were exculpatory evidence that pointed to the shoes of the real killer, and they were completely ignored as "irrelevant." Morton was left with the partial heel print that

DA Powell had spent thousands of dollars to have evaluated by photo enhancement expert James Harris in San Diego. Not only did Powell ***not*** call Harris to the witness stand, he then hid the exculpatory report from the defense (once again, *another Brady* violation). Morton and Powell knew for certain that Harris had determined that the heel print did not match Oscar's boots, and they intentionally tried to mislead the jury with some "*maybe*" testimony:

> *Morton:* There is, within the center of the impression, a line that corresponds to a depressed area in the soil, and this corresponds ***fairly favorably in a general way***. That is, rather than being an individual characteristic is due to a design pattern in the heel itself, and that… [*emphasis added*]

Donahue immediately objected, and the jury was taken out:

> *Donahue:* I do not believe this evidence is competent. Morton is qualified as an expert, but what he's doing now, he's not giving us any opinion whatsoever. That is not the testimony of an expert. Mr. Morton is saying, "*in these particular exhibits we really don't have anything that we can say yes or no—it is or it isn't. We're just saying, well, we have something favorable in general.*"
>
> *Judge Bradley:* Well, that goes to weight.

Again, Judge Bradley could not have been more wrong. He knew that the jurors would incorrectly believe that Morton was giving scientific testimony, and they would give irrelevant information the same weight as real evidence. This didn't even rise to the level of junk science. Worse yet, it was a known lie, couched as a "possibility." Because Morton knew that it wasn't really a match, it may even have risen to the level of perjury. He was fully aware that he and DA Powell were trying to trick the jury into believing something that wasn't true.

Powell was allowed to finish questioning Morton about the print:

Powell: Is there any specific, I believe you called it, specific individual characteristics about his boots and the heel mark that would say that his pair of boots and no other pair of boots in the world could have made the print?

Morton: No, there is not.

That is ***not*** evidence, or expert opinion, or even science… and the jury *never* should have heard it. At least Donahue objected, preserving the issue for appeal. He also made a lot of good points on his cross-examination of Morton. He asked about the unidentified prints near the body, and the fact that Morton wasn't given any other footwear or tires for comparison or elimination—despite the evidence of dozens of people and vehicles present at the scenes. He also got Morton to admit that there was no blood, mud, or anything else incriminating found on Oscar's cowboy boots (from his bedroom closet).

Donahue: One of your problems in trying to identify this boot print, because there was, as I believe you testified, there was very limited detail because of the focus and that lighting.

Morton: That's correct.

Q: You couldn't tell us how long that shoe or boot was; is that correct?

A: That's correct.

Q: And it is correct that you can't tell us ***whether this was a boot or a shoe***?

A: That's correct. [*emphasis added*]

That was shameful and unprofessional testimony. I still can't believe that it came from a trained Criminalist. It also explains why paid experts for hire are terrible for criminal trials, and it made me lose all respect for, and trust in, Charles Morton. He was working for his client, not justice—as if Donna's brutal murder and Oscar's freedom were just a game, to be won or lost.

DA Powell had very carefully avoided mentioning the fact that Morton had also taken plaster casts of the tire tracks on Road 176, and didn't ask him about his findings. Donahue knew about the casts from TCSO Johnson's report, and asked Morton if they matched Oscar's truck:

> *Donahue:* As a result of taking the plaster casts, and as a result of the photos that were taken, it's your testimony that there were no specific individual characteristics found to, by which you can say the tires on Mr. Clifton's truck are the tires that made these tracks at these various locations?
>
> *Morton:* That's correct.

Donahue *then* asked Morton if he had been able to identify or match the single tire print near Donna's bike, or the ones going north at Neel Ranch:

> *Morton:* I have not, as I've said before, I have ***not*** been able to identify specifically any of these tires. [*emphasis added*]

So exactly what was Morton saying? That "part of" the tread design on "one or more" of the track photos "may" (or may not) have been similar to Oscar's tires, but he couldn't be certain? It is clear that he couldn't identify the actual tire make/model from the photos, and he definitely couldn't match them to Oscar's tires through individual characteristics. Every word of Morton's tire- and foot-print testimony was unscientific, irrelevant, incompetent, and intended to confuse the jury—*which it did.* Mission accomplished.

Since ADA Bleier had successfully argued to the court that Donahue was not entitled to any written forensic reports, findings, or lab notes, Donahue went into his questioning flying nearly blind. His expert, Parker, had been allowed to question Morton, and Donahue had some notes from that conversation. He also had a list of the evidence sent to IFS. After he finished asking Morton about his tire and heel testimony, Donahue went down that list, trying to show the jury that the evidence actually proved Oscar's innocence. He covered the clothing, fingernail scrapings, the unidentified fibers from Donna's clothing, and the soil in and under Oscar's truck. It was all going well until he got to the blond hair collected from Oscar's white sweater. Totally unexpectedly, Morton said that it was "Not similar to any of them except the victim, and Oscar's daughter."

Donahue seemed surprised, but didn't question the conclusion. Not only had Powell hidden the exculpatory ABO testing on the hair completed just days before, Morton clearly knew that Donahue hadn't been told, and that his lie would go unchallenged. This is unforgivable, and I would argue that every single case involving Criminalist Charles Morton should be reviewed for junk science, suppressed exculpatory forensic findings, and perjury. There is no doubt whatsoever that the hair on Oscar's sweater was blood type O, not Donna's type A. Donna Jo Richmond was excluded, positively, with all scientific certainty. Charles Morton lied to the jury, and they believed him.

Donahue then asked about the multi-colored ski cap/mask that Johnson collected at Neel Ranch. Morton said that they had recovered three hairs, but they were not a match to Oscar or Donna. He said that he also found hairs and fibers on Donna's clothing that did not come from Oscar's clothing, truck, or house.

> *Donahue:* Mr. Morton, how do they remove the hairs for this particular test?
>
> *Morton:* These can just be taken off with forceps, or fingers if someone sees a hair located on the surface, if it looks like it may get lost they may just pick it off and place it in an envelope.

I've never been clear why Donahue asked that question, but the answer was *chilling*. Touching evidence with your bare hands was not acceptable forensic practice in 1976, and indicated real carelessness. It immediately made me concerned for all of the DNA testing done on evidence that Morton handled, and I made a note to go back through those bench notes.

Donahue confirmed with Morton that the rape kit slides, and everything he examined, were negative for spermatozoa. He asked about the results on the examination and testing of Donna's pants, only to discover that they were never sent to IFS. Further investigation showed that Sgt. Byrd had them in his custody, at an unknown location, until January 8, 1976, two days after the rest of the evidence was transported to Oakland. Presumably that was intentional, and Byrd had a specific reason for not wanting the criminalists to see them—and they hadn't.

At the end of Donahue's cross-examination of Morton, he asked that the court admit into evidence the list of items examined by IFS. Powell objected, and the judge kept it out. So, in the official trial record, there are no forensic reports, lab notes, or any written document that details the evidence tested, or the results. Looking at Powell's argument to the court, he was demanding that the jury rely on their memory of Morton's testimony and not have a list of all of the items that should have had evidence, but didn't. On Powell's redirect questioning of Morton, he was only interested in one thing:

Powell: When Mr. Donahue asked you, you talked about finding a hair in that white sweater. How did you examine that hair?

Morton: It was examined microscopically.

Q: And visually?

A: Yes.

Q: With regard to that hair, then, did you compare it with a known sample from Donna Jo Richmond's head?

A: Yes, I did.

Q: I also understand you compared it with a known sample of hair from the children of Mr. Clifton?

A: That's correct.

Q: As I understand your testimony then, the hair could have been either from the head of Donna Jo Richmond or Relinda Clifton?

A: That's correct.

There is no question DA Powell was surprised by Morton's testimony about the sweater hair. He would have raised it as a major point during his direct examination of Morton if he had any idea that he was going to say it could have belonged to Donna. Powell had already been given the ABO testing results that proved that it could ***not*** have been Donna's hair on the sweater. Powell did not want the jury to hear that exculpatory evidence, and he wasn't planning to ask Morton to flat out perjure himself. What a huge gift it was for him when Morton offered up the perjury with no prompting.

On top of that lie, Morton's "possible" match relied upon microscopic hair analysis. That is some of the most thoroughly debunked junk science of the last forty years. It was nothing more than subjective, random opinion made to sound "*sciency*" by adding the word microscope. It led to dozens of documented wrongful murder convictions. DA Powell knew, for certain, that the hair did not come from Donna, yet he gleefully jumped on it. Morton had just given him the only piece of physical evidence connecting Oscar to Donna. Because Judge Bradley had blocked Donahue from being given any forensic results, the defense was completely in the dark. For some reason, Donahue still didn't understand that Powell was willing to do anything, no matter how criminal, unconstitutional, or immoral, to win the conviction. His political life depended on it.

Like Morton, Criminalist Grubb had examined and tested dozens of items of evidence in the case, but DA Powell only asked him if it was possible to wash blood off a knife, therefore insinuating to the jury that was the reason no blood was found on Oscar's pocketknife. Grubb said it was possible. Although Grubb had testified at Grand Jury that he had conducted ABO testing on the sample Blake claimed was "semen," and found only blood type A, Powell didn't ask him about any of that. Donahue had been given the Grand Jury transcript, but he didn't seem to understand it—if he read it at all. The lab notes were not turned over to the defense, and Morton didn't tell Donahue's expert Parker about the ABO testing, so Donahue had no idea he should ask Grubb about it on the witness stand.

Donahue did try to fix the knife testimony, and Grubb admitted that Oscar's pocketknife had not been dismantled, had no signs of being cleaned, and debris found at the base of the blade was checked against Donna's clothing, and there was no match. The knife was free of blood, skin, mud, hair, and fibers. Beyond that, Donahue had no idea which items on the evidence list had been handled by Grubb, so the questioning was haphazard at best. However, Grubb confirmed that nothing he examined had hairs or fibers that connected Oscar to Donna, or the scenes. Grubb found no semen on any item, and no blood or mud on anything associated with Oscar—nothing. When Donahue asked about the blue pants Oscar had been wearing on the day of the murder, Grubb said that Hensley had called him and told him not to look at them... *so he didn't.* For some unexplained reason, TCSO hadn't wanted them tested.

At the end of that day in court, Judge Bradley made a ruling on Powell's request to have Oscar's one prior criminal conviction admitted into evidence at trial. It was a 1965 conviction for attempted rape. Powell argued that it showed a unique MO, but Bradley did not agree. He said it wasn't like Donna's kidnapping and homicide, and ruled it irrelevant and inadmissible. It didn't matter... the *Visalia Times-Delta* published the details in the paper, tainting the jurors with inadmissible evidence in the middle of the trial. Since there is no actual evidence tying Oscar to Donna's murder, Tulare DAs past and present have relied heavily on the 1965 conviction to "prove" Oscar's guilt. Because Oscar had maintained his innocence, refused to take a plea deal, and appealed the conviction, I felt I needed to get to the bottom of it.

The first thing I noticed was a gap the size of the Grand Canyon between the police reports and the prosecutor's narrative of the case.

The story went that 19-year-old Susan (a pseudonym) was sunning on the beach at the St. John's River, when she was approached by Oscar wearing blue swim trunks and a nylon stocking over his head. He jumped on her, held her down, and told her to go under a nearby bridge. Susan agreed, he let her up, and she ran to a truck parked on the nearby bank. Her face was bruised and bleeding. The driver, Stanley Miller, used his radiophone to call TCSO. They responded to the scene, found Oscar swimming in the river, and he let them search his car. Susan wanted to press charges, and gave a statement. Oscar was arrested and charged. Some time after, another woman came forward and said that earlier that same afternoon Oscar had come by her house and asked a sexual question. This led to the DA's narrative that Oscar had been on the prowl for a victim. He was convicted, given a few months in jail, appealed, lost, and moved away for a decade.

Nothing about that story matched the documents I had in the defense file. I decided to call Susan and ask her to tell me what happened. She didn't want to talk; she was terrified. I gave her my number in case she changed her mind. Later that night, she called me back. The first thing she told me was "nothing much happened," then she asked if there was any way that Bob Byrd, the DA, or TCSO could come after her. I didn't really understand why they would try. Susan told me that she had been on the beach, and as she started up the bank to leave, she was startled by Oscar walking towards her. She slipped and fell, and as she got up she heard Mr. Miller calling out to her to come to his truck, which she did. Susan was unclear about whether she remembered seeing a nylon mask, or if that came from Mr. Miller. She said Oscar hadn't said anything, jumped on her, or held her down. She hadn't suffered any injuries, and she wasn't bleeding. Susan said TCSO came and talked to her, asked her if Oscar was the man she saw, she said yes, and then she rode her bike home.

Susan said that her mom and Oscar's mom talked about it on the phone that night since they were friends and co-workers at the packing house. Nobody was upset, and that was the end of it. Several days later, Susan was home alone in the morning when a group of TCSO deputies, and Bob Byrd, who was then a Farmersville PD Officer, showed up at her house. They told her that she needed to make a statement and press charges against Oscar. Susan said she didn't want to—that nothing happened. They demanded to speak to her mother, who was at the home of her married sister. They transported Susan there, in a police vehicle. Her mother told the police to leave, and they threatened to charge her with obstruction and being intoxicated. Susan's sister then told Susan that she should just do what Byrd wanted or the entire family was going to be in trouble. Her sister rode along as TCSO and Byrd transported Susan to the DA's office in Visalia. Susan was presented with a pre-typed statement, and felt Byrd forced her to sign it. She said that Byrd told her that Oscar had killed a girl earlier that day, and he "was going to do you like he done her."

Susan said that she was terrified of Byrd, and was extremely upset at being forced to tell his version of the story on the witness stand. She immediately left Tulare County, and never returned. She said that in early 1976, Byrd found her, and threatened her on the phone. He told her that if she did not come back to testify against Oscar, he would have her arrested and transported to Visalia against her will. Susan said that she told him if he did that, she would tell the truth about what really happened on the beach, the threats Byrd made, and her fear of him that led to the signed statement.

Susan's story was completely believable because it matched the police reports I had, and answered a lot of questions about things that didn't add up in the DA's version. The biggest disconnect in his story was the fact that Oscar had not been arrested by TCSO on the scene. If deputies came upon a hysterical, injured, bleeding teen, and Stanley Miller said he saw her being attacked, why hadn't they arrested and charged Oscar right then and there? I also couldn't understand why Susan wasn't taken to the hospital if she had injuries, or even given a ride home. Both Oscar and the woman left the scene on their own. Wouldn't TCSO have worried that he would just grab her again? Also, why didn't they find a nylon mask or a package for one in his car? Why would Oscar have stayed on the scene? There were way too many holes in the story.

Those problems paled in comparison to the strangest fact of all: The night before TCSO showed up at Susan's house, Bob Byrd and a TCSO Officer named Buford had gone to Oscar's house. Oscar's wife says that when Byrd walked into the house, he said, "I told you I would get you." They searched the house and arrested Oscar, despite having no warrants. There was no reason for a Farmersville PD Officer to be making an arrest in a TCSO case. The next morning, Oscar's attorney made it clear that they would be suing for false arrest, and the DA ordered Oscar's release from jail. Bob Byrd was livid, and apparently that led to the events the woman described later that morning. The arrest report was signed by Byrd. I also have a TCSO report that documents the same deputies going to Susan's house, her refusal, taking her to her mother, and threatening to arrest her mother, then transporting Susan to the DA's office. It's all there, in black and white, exactly as she told me. I was even able to find a record of the phone call that Byrd made to her on February 19, 1976. It says: "Witness is reluctant to testify but gave the impression that she would. Case closed pending court action."

So I'm in the position of either believing Susan, the 1965 police reports, and Oscar's wife—or to believe Sgt. Byrd and the Tulare DA's office. I had never heard of threatening witnesses with arrest, and forcing them to testify, but it appears that it was common practice in Tulare County at that time. Consider this 1977 case from Lindsay (six miles south of Exeter), which had a particularly tragic outcome: 25-year-old Chester Cathey sought revenge against his 19-year-old wife, Florene, who had just offered testimony in a domestic violence charge against him. He was released on bail and went to the home of his in-laws, where he shot and killed his wife, her father, her 16-year-old brother, and a neighbor. Chester also shot the neighbor's wife in the back as she fled, then killed himself. Powell blamed the judge who set the bail, and the court blamed Powell for failing to keep the witness safe. The local newspaper accounts filled in many of the facts:

- Powell claims his deputies told him Judge Patrick J. Sullivan threw a temper tantrum when Cathey's wife, Florene, did not show up for a preliminary hearing on November 10. Sullivan then issued an arrest warrant for her, set bail at $20,000, and threatened to throw her in jail for a year.
- Lindsay Police Chief John Beene said the reason Florene did not testify earlier was that she had "left the state because she was afraid of Chester, and she [had to be] brought back by the district attorney's office to testify." Sullivan was asked to withdraw the arrest warrant, which he did, but only after he was assured by the district attorney's staff that Mrs. Cathey would be kept under protective custody. Sullivan said he still was not keen on recalling the bench warrant because he did not want the woman running away again before her husband's trial.
- The district attorney's office found Florene in Oklahoma. They convinced her to return to California and provided protection for her under guard in motel rooms.

Reading through the details of the Cathey case and subsequent grand jury investigation, it is clear that in Susan's case, fears of being arrested, returned to Tulare County, and forced to testify were reasonable—and it's highly likely that her claims of threats from Byrd were true as well. I also believe that the only reason that Byrd and Powell didn't carry out their threats was because Susan said that she would tell the truth on the stand; Oscar did not attack her on the beach in 1965, and Byrd forced her to lie to protect himself from charges of false arrest.

Susan was extremely reluctant to tell her story, and it matched documents she had never seen or read. Oscar's wife also didn't want to talk, and feared more present-day harassment from TCSO. However, they both wanted me to know what Bob Byrd had done, and what they felt he was capable of doing, especially when it came to going after Oscar.

I tried to speak with the other woman who was a witness in the 1965 case, but she had died in 1968 when her father blew up their kitchen while cleaning paint brushes with gasoline. She and her mother were killed, and her daughter was badly injured. I had no police reports with her story, but the newspaper covering the trial said that the incident had happened sometime in the past, not the same day. I also had to consider the fact the Charles Buford had been forced to resign as a DA Investigator in 1970, after covering up for another investigator who had crashed a county car. He seemed to be the type to help Byrd do something illegal.

Chapter Ten Sources

1. Exeter Sun - May 23, 1973
2. Exeter Sun - August 22, 1973
3. Military Record, Joseph James DeAngelo Sr.
4. Sacramento County Property Records
5. Military Record Joseph James DeAngelo Jr.
6. Navy Deck Logs, USS Canberra and USS Piedmont 1964-68
7. Exeter Sun - January 14, 1965
8. Placer/Tulare County Marriage Records
9. Placer County Property Records
10. Roseville Press-Tribune - May 14, 1970
11. Auburn Journal - May 14, 1970
12. DeAngelo/Huddle Marriage License
13. Sacramento Bee - November 22, 1973
14. Exeter Sun - November 12, 1975
15. Visalia Times-Delta - May 11, 1976
16. Exeter Sun - August 4, 1976
17. Exeter Sun - August 25, 1976
18. Testimony of Bob Byrd, June 29, 1976
19. Testimony of Vern Hensley, June 29, 1976
20. Testimony of John Pehrson, June 29, 1976
21. Report of John Strother - April 6, 1976

22. TCSO Report - Hensley January 2, 1976
23. 1967 F-100 Specification Sheet, Ford Motor Company
24. IFS Evidence Receipt January 6, 1976
25. An Introduction To Criminalistics, ©1949, and reprinted in 1972 by Charles E. O'Hara and James W. Osterburg
26. Testimony of Charles Morton, June 29, 1976
27. Testimony of Mike Grubb, June 29, 1976
28. Hearing on Admissibility, People v. Clifton June 29, 1976
29. Visalia Times-Delta - July 1, 1976
30. TCSO Report - Byrd/Buford July 1, 1965
31. TCSO Report - Farris/Barnes/Thatcher/Matherly July 2, 1965
32. Stmt of "Susan," July 2, 1965
33. California DOJ Arrest Disposition Report July 24, 1966
34. TCSO Report - Byrd February 19, 1976
35. Tulare Advance-Register - December 12 & December 14, 1977; Fresno Bee & L.A. Times, both December 11, 1977
35. Tulare Advance-Register - August 18, 1970

CHAPTER ELEVEN

"Shut your damn mouth."

To say that Ed Blake's testimony was a disaster for the defense would be a colossal understatement. Looking at Donahue's trial preparation notes and the correspondence from his expert, Kenneth Parker (who was allowed to talk to Morton, but not see any lab results), it's clear that they both believed that no sperm cells, spermatozoa, or "semen" had been found. They were correct. Parker had told Donahue that the acid phosphatase identified by Blake was a "presumptive" test for seminal fluid, but since there were no sperm cells, it had to have come from another source (female urine, citrus, menstrual blood, nematodes, or the tree spray), and was not semen. Also correct.

One of the biggest mysteries is why Donahue didn't object to Blake as an expert. This was the extent of his qualifications at the time:

Blake: I'm a graduate student at the University of California at Berkeley… working on my dissertation. I have published one paper.

Blake was not an expert. If Donahue had objected, at least he would have saved the issue for appeal, but he didn't. Needless to say, DA Powell got right to the point:

Powell: Did you examine the pubic hair material of Donna Jo Richmond for human semen?

Blake: Yes, I did.

Q: And what was your conclusion?

A: My conclusion was that human semen was contained on those pubic hairs.

Powell: No further questions.

Again, Donahue had been told multiple times by Parker, Grubb, and Morton that there was no semen found on any item. He had no game plan for his cross-examination of Blake:

Donahue: Is it true that there isn't any way at the present time, of distinguishing as to who the donor of human semen might be?

Blake: It's not possible to, what we call "individualize" semen, but there are genetic factors in semen that can be typed.

Q: You can exclude semen; is that correct, of a certain type?

A: That's also possible, yes.

Q: Did you find that the extract was uninformative with regard to the type of semen?

A: I, I attempted to—or, well, let me, let me backtrack just a second… Would you repeat the question? (read back by Court Reporter)

A: That's essentially correct, yes.

Q: Now, if you have something further you wish to add to it.

A: Okay, the reason for that statement was that there was a particular genetic marker, that was typed in that extract and that genetic marker is called PGM. It's not related at all to the ABO genetic markers that most people are familiar with. For this particular marker, Donna Richmond and Oscar Clifton were the same type…

Powell: Pardon me. Objection. I'm not sure if this is responsive.

Discussion held at the bench.

Donahue: I have no other questions.

Donahue was clearly asking Blake about ABO typing of semen, which Blake knew showed that his sample was type A, ***not*** Oscar's O. He did not want to answer that question, so he pretended that he didn't understand, then stalled by rambling about PGM typing. The reason PGM typing was "*uninformative*" is because Donna and Oscar had the same PGM type. Powell jumped in and stopped that line of questioning right before it came back around to ABO.

Donahue should have asked Blake about the basis of his conclusion, especially in light of the lack of sperm cells. Donahue didn't because he was unprepared for the testimony, which is exactly why ADA Bleier had worked so hard to make sure that the court denied the defense forensic discovery requests. If Donahue had been able to give all of the testing and lab notes to Parker, along with Grubb's exculpatory ABO results, they would have been able to make Blake admit that he found only a slow, weak positive AP reaction, ***not*** semen. He also would have had to admit that the sample was previously identified as type A, thereby fully exonerating Oscar.

Donahue also had no plan for cross-examination of the state's next witness. DA Powell wanted the coroner, Dr. Miller, to convince the jury of three things: Donna had died of manual strangulation, Oscar's pocketknife was used to stab Donna, and Dr. Miller collected something that could have been ejaculate from her pubic hair. The only reason I can think of for Powell to want a finding of murder by strangulation, rather than from the obvious penetrating chest wounds, is because Oscar's folding pocketknife could not have made those deep wounds, and Powell knew that was a weakness in his case.

Dr. Miller took the stand and completely dismantled his own argument for manual strangulation. He stated that the only discoloration was to the front of the neck, which he offered may have been lividity from laying on the irrigation furrow. There was no bruising on the sides or back of Donna's neck. There was no damage or fracturing of the cartilage in her trachea and larynx. Most telling of all, the hyoid bone in the front of the neck was not displaced or broken. Donna was not strangled, and the evidence in the autopsy results and testimony of Dr. Miller conclusively proved it.

It was extremely odd that Powell wanted the jury to believe that manual strangulation was the cause of death. It had to be because the knife was so implausible:

> *Powell:* This appears to be a bone handled pocket knife. Is it possible that a knife similar to that, could cause stab wounds such as those?
>
> *Miller:* Yes, entirely compatible.
>
> Q: And by "compatible," I assume you mean that it could have been made by them but you don't know?
>
> A: That's correct.

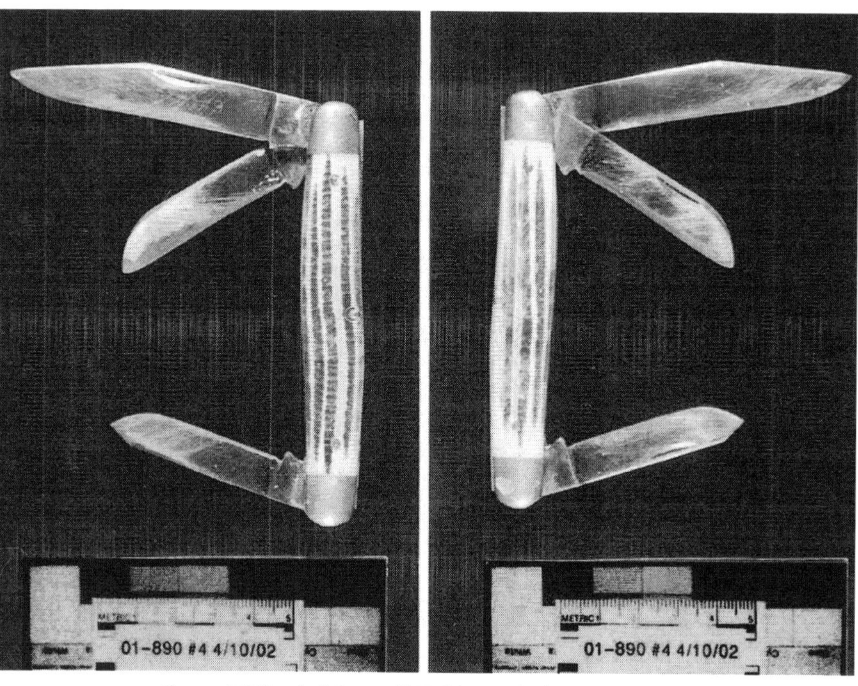

Oscar Clifton's "Queen" Folding Blade Pocketknife
Exhibit Q (Scale in Centimeters)
Photo: FSA

That's it—that is ***all*** of the testimony that makes Oscar's knife the murder weapon. Not an expert opinion, nothing about the character, depth, or width of the wounds that matched. As Grubb testified, there was no blood, skin, hair, or fibers on the knife. The truth was that even the largest of the three small folding blades (2.5 inches x 0.5 inches) could not possibly have made the penetrating chest wounds that actually killed Donna. There is no doubt from the autopsy report: both of her lungs were collapsed, her chest had filled with blood, and she died from lack of oxygen and blood loss. *Where was the actual murder weapon?*

Dr. Miller also testified that he found no sign of physical sexual assault, and Donna was still a virgin. That left only Blake's assertion that the "crusted dirt" from her pubic hair contained "semen." However, it was clear from Sgt. Byrd's report and testimony, the autopsy report, and Dr. Miller's Grand Jury testimony that the "crusted dirt" was the clump of mud covered in white tree spray. It can be seen in the crime scene photos on her backside, and that's exactly where Byrd described it. Donna was face down, and this "white fluid" or "crust" was never anywhere near Donna's pubic hair. Dr. Miller clarified this at Grand Jury:

Powell: Did you examine the victim's pubic hair?

Miller: Yes, I did.

Q: And what did you find with regard to the pubic hair of the victim?

A: The pubic hair was crusted with dirt and there was gray-white material mixed with the dirt, all of this was ***adhered to the skin rather than to the pubic hair.***

Q: Did you take any samples of that hair together with the dirt and gray and white matter that was encrusted.

A: Yes, I did.

Q: And what did you do to that sample of pubic hair?

A: This material was given to Brian Johnson of the crime laboratory. [*emphasis added*]

Looking at the autopsy report, Dr. Miller collected the pubic hair cutting and the "crusted dirt" separately, but either he or TCSO Johnson combined them into one envelope, item of evidence #2.

At trial, DA Powell had carefully coached Dr. Miller not to make the same statement again:

Powell: Did you remove a sample of pubic hair?

Miller: Yes, I did.

Q: And your report indicated it was crusted with something; what was that?

A: This was with dirt, soil, and gray-white material.

Q: And did you—what did you do with this sample of this pubic hair, dirt, and gray-white material?

A: This material was given to Brian Johnson of the crime laboratory.

Q: And by "pubic hair," is that the hair around the vagina?

A: Yes, that's correct.

At autopsy and Grand Jury, Dr. Miller went out of his way to be clear, and stated that the "gray-white" dirt material was ***not*** removed from Donna's pubic hair, but rather from her skin. Sgt. Byrd, the autopsy report, and the crime scene photos all confirm that this was on her buttocks. DA Powell told Dr. Miller not to mention that at trial, and asked a leading question to change it to the front pubic hair area. Dr. Miller told the truth at Grand Jury, then lied at trial. It is really that simple.

For the end of his case to the jury, Powell tried to get ahead of Oscar's alibi by bringing Rick Carter to the stand. Carter's testimony was obviously coached. Under direct examination, he gave clearly rehearsed answers, right down the line. However, during cross-examination, when pressed on his prior inconsistent statements, Carter said either that he "*didn't remember*" or "*didn't know,*" a total of ***forty-two times***. Although Powell had told the jury that Carter's statements proved Oscar didn't get home until 4:45 pm, that wasn't his actual testimony during Donahue's cross-examination:

Donahue: Mr. Carter, you have difficulty in reading?

Carter: Yes.

Donahue: With the Court's permission, then, I will read these few questions to you.

"Okay, did anyone come home after you got there?

"Yes, Oscar did."

"Do you remember about what time that was?"

"About four fifteen."

Q: Is that what you told Detective Chamberlain?

A: I can't remember.

Q: All right, I'll read this to you. See if you recall it.

"*Okay. So you returned at approximately three thirty pm on Friday the twenty-sixth to the Clifton residence. Was there anything special that you were waiting for?*

"*No*"

"*Okay. What time did you note Oscar Clifton come through the living room door?*"

"*Four fifteen. I mean four forty to four forty-five, at that time.*"

Q: Is that the answer that you gave?

A; Yes.

Q: Mrs. Clifton was there sometime that afternoon; is that correct?

A: Yes.

Q: Was Mrs. Clifton there when you arrived?

A: I can't remember.

Q: Do you know whether it was around four fifteen?

A: It was before Oscar got home.

Q: What time was it when Mr. Clifton got home?

A: I don't know. I didn't look at the clock.

Q: Well, Mr. Carter, do you remember or don't you remember whether Mr. Clifton was wearing the brace when he came in somewhere between four fifteen and four forty-five p.m. on December the 26th, 1975?

Powell: Objection, it calls for something not in evidence. This witness testified he came in at four forty-five and Counsel keeps trying to push it back to four fifteen.

Judge Bradley: Well, I think he put it in a span area. *Overruled.*

Powell needed Oscar's time of arrival back home to be 4:45 pm, not a minute earlier, but Judge Bradley clearly ruled that it was a span between 4:15-4:45 pm. It *should have* been a big win for Donahue, but he never got around to telling the jury exactly why it mattered.

Donahue started the defense's case to the jury with a short, rambling, incoherent statement that led nowhere. He then brought up Oscar to recount his activities on December 26, 1975. Oscar was detailed without sounding rehearsed, and very matter-of-fact. He may have seemed detached and unemotional, which he was. He didn't live in Exeter or know the Richmonds. He didn't feel guilty or apologetic; there was no crying or begging the jury to believe him. He thought he had the facts and truth on his side, and wasn't really concerned about being likable or sympathetic.

During the lunch break, DA Powell *personally* got in his car and drove Oscar's blue pants to the DOJ crime lab in Fresno to have them examined. After lunch, Powell produced the one-page report from the criminalist indicating that he found no blood or anything else of evidentiary value on the pants. There was no explanation for TCSO

Hensley calling Criminalist Grubb and telling him not to test the pants at IFS.

Powell's cross-examination of Oscar was almost boring. Oscar said that he had never seen Donna, had not been in Exeter on the 26th, and confirmed the clothing he had been wearing that day.

On re-direct, Donahue asked Oscar if he had ever seen Beth Brumley or Gloria Mascorro, and he said he had not, nor had he been in Woodlake that day. He also said that he didn't know the Richmond family, and had no idea where they even lived. He denied leaving the trail of Donna's clothing leading to his house. He confirmed that the notepad found by the bike did not belong to him, and he had never seen it before. He said that he had absolutely no idea how his invoice book got to the bike scene. He last remembered having it on December 23, 1975 when he used it for two invoices that he hand-delivered to Bill Rose at his office. Oscar and his wife then took the check from Rose to the bank and went Christmas shopping at K-Mart. Oscar didn't remember if the book was last seen on the dash of his truck or in the family sedan.

Oscar believed that when Sgt. Byrd heard that Donna was missing, he went out to the Clifton house (while they were out to dinner), took the invoice book from Oscar's unlocked truck, and placed it by Donna's bike before TCSO Johnson arrived to process the scene. I've always kept an open mind about that scenario because I couldn't disprove it. Looking through the reports, Byrd had plenty of time to do that. The original missing person report and statements from Don and David Richmond made no mention of the invoice book, and their prints weren't on it. Additionally, Byrd made up a convoluted, unbelievable narrative about how hard it was to find out where Oscar lived. If he hadn't known already, he just needed to call the phone company—or radio in from the scene to have it done. There was no big mystery.

Pettyjohn and Donahue should have fully investigated the possibility that TCSO planted the invoice book and the clothing trail, but they didn't. Oscar's family was willing to pay anything to get him the best defense, but sometimes it's not about money. In 1975, there were a few really outstanding public defenders working in Tulare County—they were doing incredible work for their clients, and they fully understood what DA Powell and ADA Bleier were capable of doing to "bend the rules" and get the win.

Pettyjohn was a disaster for Oscar. He was competent and experienced, but totally blinded by his years as an FBI agent. In his world, law enforcement were the good guys, and workers from Oklahoma were Communists and criminals. Over and over again, Pettyjohn took TCSO at their word, and didn't investigate witnesses and evidence for himself. The fact that he completely missed Laverne Lamb's direct family connection to Don Lee was a shameful lapse. Not questioning any of the workers at Neel Ranch or the neighbors around the Lee residence, was another.

In 1975, when he took this case, Donahue's law practice was handling civil matters like estate planning, probates, real estate, and small business issues. That was completely incompatible with criminal defense work. Prominent people in the community wanted to see Oscar convicted, and they would have ruined Donahue's law practice if he got Oscar "off." There was absolutely no thought, at all, that Oscar might be innocent—if Donahue won, it would only be through some legal trick, and justice would not be served. Quietly letting Oscar slip under the bus and into prison would let Donahue save his social life and his law practice. Since he didn't want to represent more criminal defendants, there was absolutely no benefit to winning an acquittal. Add those pressures to the actual threats and vandalism he and his wife endured, and Donahue's inaction makes a lot of sense. It's not right, but it is logical.

DA Powell's re-cross-examination of Oscar was more confrontational, but still Oscar seemed completely unconcerned and calm. There is no question he believed that if he just told the truth, he could not be convicted. Powell tried to tell Oscar that he hadn't been wearing his brace, that he was capable of running, and that he was wearing cowboy boots. Oscar repeated he had on his brace with the built-in black shoes all day, and he couldn't run, with or without it—especially since he'd had a procedure done to have his kneecap removed to relieve pressure and swelling.

Oscar never wavered on the story of his activities on the 26th, and he just kept calmly repeating the same facts. It was a painfully mundane and detailed account of his day. He said when he called the gas company at lunch, they told him what needed to be done for the meter the following Monday—putting on a cap and blowing out the gas line. That's exactly what he did. Reading every statement from Oscar, and the people who saw him that day, I'm repeatedly struck by how focused he was on doing a good job for Bill Rose. He took everything very seriously, including his nice outfit for the building inspection; the visits to Rose's office; the calls to Rose, the inspector, and the utilities; and the pricing of different materials for the job.

Oscar spent part of his lunch break helping his brother-in-law, and later drove well out of his way to help his wife's niece with her dryer. Those were just kindnesses. He was excited about the property he had just bought and was developing with real estate broker Bill Jordan. He was actively working with his attorney in Nevada to collect his $123,000 judgment against the drunk driver who ruined his knee. Oscar was completely devoted to his family and children. He didn't go out at night without his wife—ever. He didn't drink or use drugs, and there were no unresolved frustrations or life problems.

His daughters say that he was never creepy, in any way, with them or their friends, and everyone agreed that he didn't use sexual language, or even tell off-color jokes. I read forty years of psychological evaluations, and he didn't suffer from addiction, depression, anxiety, bipolar disorder, or have any diagnosed personality disorder. He had no history of lying or dishonesty. He was repeatedly examined for psycho-sexual disorders, and there was nothing at all. However, Oscar was known to be quite stubborn, and he reduced things to right or wrong, with no shades of gray. It was easy to understand how he was unwilling to back down from a conflict with Bob Byrd during the Teamsters Union trucking strike in the early 1960s.

Beyond questions about the case evidence, I truly couldn't grasp the state's reasoning in the case against Oscar. What was the trigger? Why wouldn't he have tried to lure or kidnap Beth Brumley or Gloria Mascorro? If rape was the motive, why wasn't it completed? The killer took the time to drag Donna under a tree before he left Neel Ranch. Why would someone kill Donna, but leave the other two witnesses alive? Donna didn't know Oscar or his family, so she wasn't a particular identity risk for him. Also, following the state's theory—let's say that he grabbed Donna, put her in his truck, had her take off her clothes, then changed his mind about assaulting her—why not just leave her at Neel Ranch? Make her walk in the grove a ways so she couldn't see the license plate. If Donna had somehow identified him, the most he would be looking at is a couple of years in prison. It's not really much different than the potential Brumley and Mascorro charges. This narrative makes no sense.

Why didn't Beth Brumley mention Oscar's Okie accent? By everyone's account, it was *unmistakable*. Why hadn't the Mascorros seen the large Ford lettering on the back of his truck? How had Oscar been in N. Visalia and Woodlake, then Woodlake and Exeter at the exact same times? How had Donna been kidnapped at 3:40 pm where her bike was found, and left Don Lee's house over four miles away at 3:45 pm? Why had Brumley and Mascorro been the only people who claimed that they saw Oscar's truck in Woodlake or Exeter? Why hadn't he been seen in or around Neel Ranch, or as he got back on the main road? Why hadn't anyone seen him throwing clothing or placing the shoes next to the road? Nobody saw him driving all over the county for miles and miles, except those two witnesses? I couldn't understand the theory that Oscar was so dumb, and yet so clever. He managed to leave a trail of witnesses and clothing, but didn't get one speck of blood or mud on himself? A very crippled man who weighed 150 pounds and couldn't run overpowered and controlled a fit fourteen-year-old girl, yet had not one scratch or bruise on him? And she didn't leave a trace of herself in his truck? Why weren't her footprints found at the bike scene? Why was her bike wheel turned around, with white car paint transferred onto it? How had he committed the murder and clean-up in zero minutes? Where was the weapon used to stab Donna? None of this adds up, which suggests that the actual evidence was either overlooked or ignored—*or both*.

There was also an odd conflict between the narrative that Oscar had been in a panicked rush and the idea that he would have driven almost 30 minutes from the Roberts house in N. Visalia over to Woodlake. There were plenty of girls and women out walking and working in the fields all around him. Woodlake makes absolutely no sense, especially to drive right into the middle of town. Dozens of people could have seen him, and his truck was highly distinctive. There was no reason to expect to find a girl walking alone there; it wasn't a school day. Same with Exeter and Neel Ranch. There were many more secluded groves with plenty of girls and women picking oranges.

DA Powell couldn't decide if Oscar had grabbed Donna as he made his escape from the Mascorros at 3:40 pm, or laid in wait for her to ride by sometime after 4:00 pm—he told the jury both versions were true. The spot where Donna's bike was found is literally one of the last places in Exeter you would expect a lone girl to ride randomly by around 4:00 pm on the day after Christmas. Maybe a few locals would know that the kids rode there, but even Donna's parents didn't, *which is why* they didn't check there. So was Donna actually kidnapped before she left Don Lee's, or did Oscar just guess that he should sit there and wait for 30 minutes in case a female wandered by? If Oscar stopped and hid there while Mr. Mascorro was chasing him, why would he stay for 30 minutes? Wouldn't he think that TCSO deputies were on their way, and would quickly find him right where he was last seen?

It was up to DA Powell to prove his case and fully answer all of these questions, but he didn't. Whenever he couldn't make facts and times fit together, he would just turn to the jury and say, "We all know what happened." *No, they didn't know*. What Powell was really saying was that facts, evidence, and proof didn't matter, and the jury should replace those with their own feelings. He played to the jurors' emotions. Although the defense has no duty to prove innocence, that's never how juries really operate. They expect a solid alibi, an explanation for the state's evidence, and preferably some idea who really committed the crime.

DA Powell tried a few different arguments to the jury to neutralize Oscar's alibi. The first was that Pettyjohn had found out about the freezer loading on Garden Street from Frank Thomas, and fed the details to Oscar. There were three problems with that theory: the event is documented in Donahue's intake notes—days before Pettyjohn was on the case; Sgt. Byrd specifically suggested that notion to Thomas in his interview on June 22nd, and Thomas was adamant that Pettyjohn knew about the event and the comment before he arrived; and Pettyjohn didn't canvass Garden Street looking for possible witnesses (which he absolutely should have done), he only went to the Thomas house. Donahue had that information in front of him, but didn't tell the jury any of it. Instead, Powell accused Oscar of lying:

Powell: Now, isn't it true that those words are what someone who investigated this case for you told you?

Oscar: No sir, I know they're not.

Q: This is nothing you're making up?

A: This is nothing I'm making up.

Q: In other words, you knew this before someone told you they had found someone who talked about that incident; is that right?

A: I gave them the very words to ask the people.

Q: I see. Okay. And isn't it true that you had contacted the people before?

A: I had?

Q: Yes, sir.

A: No sir, I have never talked to them.

Q: Isn't it true that you had someone do it for you, sir?

A: Mr. Pettyjohn.

Q: No, I mean before that?

A: No, sir.

This was the lowest form of questioning, and Donahue should have objected because it assumed facts not in evidence. Powell was trying to testify to the jury that Oscar, or someone he "sent," had talked to Frank Thomas before Pettyjohn, and fed the information back to Oscar. Powell knew for certain that it never happened. Thomas had been asked, and said no. He didn't know Oscar or his family—he had never met anyone involved in the case. Also, if Powell really believed it, he would have just asked Frank Thomas and Pettyjohn about it on the witness stand so the jury could hear their answers—but he didn't. He knew it was a lie, but he got the jury to believe it because Donahue never objected or disproved it. Powell hadn't hit bottom yet:

Powell: Nobody saw you there, did they?

Oscar: I don't know whether they saw me or not.

I got to that line in the transcript and stopped dead. Something was very, very wrong. That testimony was on July 6th, and on June 23rd, TCSO Chamberlain had given Sgt. Byrd two taped interviews with eyewitnesses who had seen and/or spoken to Oscar during the freezer loading—and a photo lineup with Oscar's number four photo identified. Powell taunted Oscar about not being seen, right in front of the jury, and Oscar didn't correct him. Why didn't he know about the alibi witnesses, and how could Powell say that in open court with no objection from Donahue? The answer was horrific. Sgt. Byrd had taken the tapes and hidden them in his office, then destroyed the six pages of Chamberlain's report that recounted the statements from ***both*** Brent Trueblood and Johnny Guerber. The tapes were not transcribed, and the defense was never told what they said.

I have never seen nor heard about a more clear-cut, intentional, and blatant case of police and prosecutorial misconduct. It is the very definition of a *Brady* violation—hiding exculpatory evidence from the defense. Sgt. Byrd and DA Powell knew, for a fact, that Oscar was innocent, and if the jury heard from Trueblood and Guerber, they would never convict him. They took the U.S. Constitution, put it in the office shredder, and carried on with the trial like nothing had happened. Powell knew about the witnesses, looked Oscar in the eye, and taunted him about how he "hadn't been seen." What kind of person, let alone a District Attorney, behaves like that? No amount of disdain for Oscar or desire to get a conviction makes sense. What about the man who brutally killed Donna, how could he just let him go free?

The defense then continued with Gene Owens, who repeated his original statement. According to one of the TCSO reports, Owens also gave a taped statement to TCSO at their headquarters, but either Sgt. Byrd or DA Powell hid it, and it was never given to Donahue. Clearly, Owens didn't change his story, and placed Oscar driving by his home at 3:00 pm on December 26th. Powell didn't even try to impeach Owens on cross-examination, and in his closing Powell conceded that Oscar was, in fact, in N. Visalia at 3:00 pm.

Frank Thomas was up next, and he was positive about the time that the freezer loading guys arrived and that he spoke the words that Oscar heard ("*It's about time you got here*"). Powell made absolutely no attempt to impeach Thomas' credibility or testimony, and he didn't try to get him to say he'd given the details to Pettyjohn first, or been contacted by some other person representing Oscar. Powell knew that was all a lie, but it was an effective trick. He could always hope that jurors would forget that he hadn't actually proven it, just stated it as truth. It was prosecutorial misconduct, and Donahue should have objected, but once again let it go.

Donahue brought on Danny Boland next. He was the concrete contractor who had been working on Garden Street on the 26th, and had talked to Oscar about re-doing the front walkway at the Rose house. Boland had been interviewed by Pettyjohn early in 1976:

> Boland stated that when Clifton contacted him the two occasions on 12/26/75 he was wearing a heavy knit pullover type long sleeve sweater, white or off white in color, a pair of dark double knit slacks, and black oxford type shoes. He stated Clifton was not wearing his leg brace and told him so. He stated he was positive about his wearing black shoes with a moccasin type toe and positive he was not then wearing cowboy boots. He did not recall his wearing glasses at either time.
>
> Boland stated he does not know Clifton's present address. The last he knew, he was living in a two-story house in Farmersville. He stated he has known Clifton by sight for some time but never talked to him other than to say hello when they chanced to meet, until Clifton contacted him on 12/26/75.

Due to his two prior statements to Pettyjohn, Donahue felt that he knew what to expect from Boland's testimony:

Donahue: Are you acquainted with Oscar Clifton, Mr. Boland?

Boland: I know who he is, yes, sir.

Q: How long have you known him?

A: He and my father were friends. I, I guess probably ten years, I guess, off and on.

Q: Mr. Boland, are you acquainted with the Richmond family that's involved in this particular case?

A: Yes, sir.

Q: And they live in Exeter, also?

A; Yes, sir.

Q: And about how long have you known them?

A: Quite awhile. Probably six, seven, eight years.

Q: And you knew their daughter, Donna Jo?

A: Yes, sir.

Donahue asked about the time Boland had seen Oscar on the 26th, which wasn't really in dispute. It was a big nothing.

Powell wanted to show that Oscar wasn't wearing his brace because that narrative made him seem more able-bodied, and that also allowed him to have been wearing cowboy boots, which Powell tried to match to the heel print from Neel Ranch. Oscar's family, including his in-laws, swore that Oscar was wearing his black shoes with the integrated leg brace—and each saw him at multiple points during the day and evening. That left Danny Boland in the extremely uncomfortable position of being forced to prove Powell's case:

Powell: Mr. Boland, how was Mr. Clifton dressed that day?

Boland: He had on a white sweater and dark, kind of double knit pants.

Q: What kind of shoes did he have on?

A: Kind of shoes?

Q: Yes, sir.

A: I think they were, I think they were black shoes.

Q: Did he have his brace on?

A: No, sir.

Q: And how do you remember that?

A: We talked about it.

Q: And he did not have his brace on?

A: No, sir.

Q: Were those dark shoes he had on, could they have been a dark brown?

A: They could have been.

Donahue had a defense witness that only seemed to help Powell, and he was in the position of trying to fix the damaging testimony:

Donahue: Now, as a matter of fact, Mr. Boland; didn't you expressly tell Mr. Pettyjohn that you were positive that Mr. Clifton was wearing black shoes?

Boland: Yeah. I thought he was wearing black shoes. Yes.

Q: As a matter of fact, you described them as a moccasin-type shoe, didn't you?

A: Well, they were black. It seems like they were black flat shoes with a little seam.

Q: Like an oxford?

A: Yeah, I guess so.

Q: Mr. Boland I'll show you cowboy boots which have been introduced into evidence. When you saw Mr. Clifton on December the twenty-sixth you observed the shoes he had on; is that correct?

A: In all fairness, sir, when I, when I was—when I found out who had done this, you know, supposedly was arrested for the, the thing, what I did—people calling me—I tried to remember certain things. I didn't try to remember everything just the things that I, you know, like time and all that stuff. Now, I can't tell you exactly what he had on. In all fairness, I can't. I can tell you what I remember, but I can't tell you if he had those on or didn't have them on. That wouldn't be fair.

Q: Do you remember whether he was wearing these cowboy boots or something similar to these?

A: No.

Right there on the stand, in front of the jury, *within 30 seconds*, Boland moved from "Well, they were black. It seems like they were black flat shoes with a little seam…" to "I don't remember." Between those two answers he explained the pressure that he'd felt with "people calling him," and how he didn't think it would be "fair" for him to say one way or another. Boland was trying to be truthful without appearing to help the defense. It is obvious that he was coached to say that he couldn't remember, or wasn't certain, as a way to avoid possible perjury charges, while still letting Powell use him to make vague statements about the possibility of boots.

There is no doubt that Boland saw Oscar wearing his black shoes—that was what he said in his March statement and his July testimony. I don't believe that he had a sudden memory lapse on the stand, but I do think he was afraid of going against Powell and Byrd.

This was a real lost opportunity for Donahue because Powell wanted the jury to believe that Oscar was not disabled, and had been wearing his cowboy boots. Donahue clearly knew the details, because he asked Oscar about it when he was on the witness stand:

> *Donahue:* When you were over and saw Mr. Boland, you didn't have your brace then, did you?
>
> *Oscar:* Yes, I did.
>
> Q: Oh, you did?
>
> A: Yes.
>
> Q: Okay. And the only pair of shoes that you can wear with your brace is the pair of shoes you have on now; is that right?
>
> A: That's true.

Donahue should have found a way to make sure the jury understood that when Boland said he saw the black shoes, that indicated that the brace was on, and Oscar *couldn't even* wear the cowboy boots with the brace. The black shoes meant that Oscar was disabled, and couldn't have left the heel print at Neel Ranch. Powell kept winning the game of confusing the jury.

Why would Danny Boland make up a story about the brace, and try to back out of his own statements about the black shoes? My thoughts on that are based on other information I have about Boland. He admitted to both Pettyjohn and Donahue that he was close to the Richmonds, and he testified that he specifically knew Donna. In fact, I've been told by a reliable source that Donna babysat for the Bolands' twins in the year leading up to her murder. Boland did not want to assist Oscar's defense in any way or give the appearance of helping, even indirectly. He was under tremendous community pressure. The Richmonds were counting on him to help secure a conviction, and he had a business that relied on referrals and reputation. It's fairly easy to understand how his memory about the shoes suddenly grew foggy, and he seemed to remember a comment about the brace while they were just "passing conversation."

That's my optimistic view of Boland's testimony. My other thoughts end up back at Sgt. Byrd and the stick used on uncooperative witnesses. Danny Boland could have been a really good suspect in Donna's homicide. Oscar stopped by Danny's job site and asked for a bid on the walkway at the nearby Bill Rose house. According to Oscar, Boland went over and looked at the work, and then gave Oscar a bid later that day, when they talked a second time, after lunch. So, Oscar's truck, with the invoice book possibly still on the dash, was at Boland's job site, and Boland was at Oscar's job site on the 26th. Boland admitted to Pettyjohn that he was aware of Oscar's 1965 conviction, which makes sense since his father had been the pastor at the Cliftons' church.

Additionally, when asked about his alibi, Boland said that he went for a beer after work, dropped his worker at home in Farmersville around 3:00 pm, then drove home. By his own words, he directly placed himself *driving east* on Visalia Road (in Exeter) at the ***exact*** same time Donna, Carol, and Judy were heading west, on their way to Don Lee's house. That statement also placed him at home, at E Street and Firebaugh, at the time Donna would have ridden by that location on her way home. Donna knew him, trusted him, and would have gone into his house or accepted a ride home from him. Boland knew where Donna lived, and about the grove road that ran behind her house. He had access to Oscar's unlocked truck that day, and specifically knew that Oscar would be a believable person to frame.

What else do I know about what Boland did after he got home around 3:00 pm? He told Pettyjohn that he "cleaned up and then went to town." Could Byrd have made it clear to Boland that he looked like a good suspect, and that it would be in his best interest to make sure Oscar was convicted? Given the false murder charges filed against Carter to make him change his statement, and Lamb's relationship with the Lees, I believe any level of witness intimidation was possible.

Another witness that seemed susceptible to Sgt. Byrd's intimidation tactics was Bud Brumley. Donahue called him for the defense, which was really odd. The purpose was to point out that the physical description he gave when he reported Beth's "incident," didn't match Oscar. It didn't lead anywhere, but two different stories in *The Exeter Sun* provide a possible reason why Brumley could have been pressured into making up the story about Beth that Donahue didn't probe:

> Brumley named assistant Principal at Exeter High: Weldon (Bud) Brumley has been named assistant principal at Exeter Union High School. Brumley came to Exeter in 1974 after serving at Woodlake high school the last seven years. [August 7, 1974]

> Manuel Kouklis has accepted the position of Dean of boys at the Exeter Union High School following the resignation last week by Weldon "Bud" Brumley for personal reasons. Brumley's resignation was accepted by the trustees during a special board meeting on March 1. The teaching portions of the position which were handled by Brumley are being handled by various teachers. A decision will be made during the summer as to how the position will be handled next year. [March 9, 1977]

According to correspondence between Oscar and Donahue, the "personal reason" was Bud Brumley's inappropriate relationship with a female student at Exeter High. I have spoken with former students who describe Brumley being "caught" at school with the girl. He was described as acting like he was a student, and being overly friendly and handsy. It is so typical for the 1970s that Exeter pushed him out in a panic, mid-year, instead of seeing that he was prosecuted or had his teaching license revoked. They let him quietly go away, and he ended up at a neighboring school district for several years. I don't believe that Brumley's inappropriate behavior suddenly started at Exeter High, and his immaturity provided another motive for him to have inserted himself into Donna's homicide case.

Oscar's daughters were next up on the witness stand, and they both confirmed seeing him in the house just before 4:30 pm. They recounted his clothing, including the brace and black shoes. Neither of them noticed anything unusual about his appearance or behavior when he got home. On cross-examination Powell accused them of lying to protect their father. In speaking with Oscar's older daughter during the research I did on this case, Powell caused an enormous amount of psychological damage, and really magnified the hurt, loss, and confusion she was already suffering. DA Powell made her feel dishonest and insignificant, not worthy of the jury's consideration.

Jeanie Esajian from the *Visalia Times-Delta* was called to authenticate the photo she took of Sheriff Wiley showing Oscar's booking photo to the Mascorros. She went over her interview with Gloria, and the fact that Gloria made several statements that confirmed she had been shown Oscar's photo. Powell did not cross-examine Ms. Esajian. Although Powell told the jury that the story was wrong—Sheriff Wiley had really been showing Gloria a photo of Donna—he did not want the jury to hear Esajian's denials and certainty.

I've spoken to Jeanie several times over the years, and she remembers the events like it was yesterday. *There was no mistake.* Two external factors confirm that: First, neither Sheriff Wiley nor Powell asked the paper's editor to correct or retract the photo caption and story; second, there was no thought that Donna made it all of the way home on the 26th, thus no reason to show her photo—especially to people who worked for her family and were standing next to Donna's house. They knew Donna. There is no question, whatsoever, that if Sheriff Wiley had really shown Donna's photo, ***not*** Oscar's, Powell would have called Wiley to the witness stand to tell that to the jury. That didn't happen. Instead, Powell pressured a twenty-year-old farm worker to commit perjury.

This may all seem like a minor point, but it was incredibly important to the jury. The ***only*** testimony they asked to have read back to them during deliberations were the portions from Jeanie Esajian and Gloria Mascorro. Only one of them was telling the truth, and clearly the jurors chose to believe Gloria. The crimes of perjury and suborning perjury (getting someone to lie under oath) are felonies that can be charged up to three years after being "discovered." This is one of the reasons Tulare DA Tim Ward does not want an outside investigation or court hearing on Oscar's conviction—or even a question of DeAngelo's guilt. Several critical witnesses are still alive, and could face prison for their lies about central issues in dispute during the trial. If Criminalist Morton, and multiple TCSO officers like Byrd, Johnson, Hensley, and Logan, were convicted of perjury, that would destroy hundreds of criminal convictions in Tulare County from 1964-2003.

Harry Moyer testified next. He managed the BF Goodrich store in Visalia. He said that there were five or six other tire stores in Tulare County that sold the tires that were on Oscar's truck. They were very popular, standard truck tires. Although Donahue didn't explain it to the jury, the point was that even if Criminalist Morton had found treads similar to Oscar's, it was meaningless since they were so common, especially on work trucks in orange groves.

Kenneth Parker was the criminalist hired by Donahue. Oscar and his family thought that he was going to conduct his own examination and testing of the evidence, but he didn't. Parker was expecting to review the Morton, Blake, and Grubb lab notes and reports, and then decide what items needed further exploration. Presumably, those would be items that appeared to implicate Oscar in the homicide. However, after Bleier objected to producing any written forensic findings, and the court agreed, Parker was reduced to a verbal meeting and discussion with Morton at the IFS lab. Right there, things had gone well off the rails for the defense. Not only was Parker taking Morton's word for the results of the scientific testing, he was then transmitting it to Donahue, so it was really third-hand knowledge.

Unlike Donahue, Powell played hardball, and demanded a full hearing into Parker's qualifications as an expert prior to his testimony. Powell had done his research, and he ripped Parker to shreds in front of the jury. He brought up a trial where the defense attorney had asked for Parker's entire testimony to be stricken from the record after the jury started laughing at him. It can only be described as an unmitigated *disaster* for Oscar's defense.

Parker had simply taken Charles Morton at his word—that none of the forensic science found semen or implicated Oscar. Blake's testimony about the pubic hair and Morton's about the hair on Oscar's sweater had both hidden the ABO testing that exculpated Oscar, and Parker hadn't known about *any* of it. Maybe if he had, he would have tested the evidence himself. When he tried to explain to the jury that there were marks and defects on Oscar's tires that should have been seen in the tracks but weren't, Powell just mocked him.

Donahue then called Sgt. Byrd back to the witness stand to explain why he had ordered TCSO Hensley to call IFS, and tell them not to examine or test the blue pants Oscar wore on the day of the homicide. No surprise, Byrd lied:

Donahue: Would you tell me, sir, what your reason—if you were the person who advised the Institute, or had the Institute advised that they were not to run any tests on this pair of blue pants?

Byrd: My instructions were that every piece of evidence was to be analyzed.

Q: Did you, sir, tell Sgt. Hensley to tell the Institute not to analyze these various pieces of evidence that had been sent to them?

A: No, sir, I did not.

Q: Who in the Sheriff's Office, if you know, advised Mr. Grubb not to analyze that pair of pants?

A: To my knowledge, no one.

One of the items I found in the defense file was Byrd's "to do list." It was created on (or about) January 8, 1976, and it covered all of the things Byrd personally wanted documented on the case *before* he handed it over to the DA's office. It covers things like the missing TCSO reports that Byrd needed officers to "create" and backdate to support the clothing trail and forensic findings. It's a shockingly dishonest document. Back to the issue of the pants, item number 10 says: "Have lab in Oakland check tan shirt and dark brown trousers for blood stains. This assigned to Sgt. Hensley 1-8-76 at 0755 hours."

TCSO Hensley placed that call to Grubb on January 8—just two days after he personally delivered all of the evidence to IFS in Oakland. On January 8, 1976, Morton wrote in his notes: "Call from Sgt. Hensley. Clothing suspect was wearing on date of crime: 'dark brown pants, light tan or cream colored shirt, white high neck sweater (one of 2 in evidence).' This info from Det. Byrd >Sgt. Hensley>Mike Grubb"

Unfortunately, due to DA Powell's intentional evidence suppression, Donahue didn't have Byrd's list or Morton's notes. Those were both turned over when Tulare Superior Court Judge Sevier *finally* entered a new discovery order in 2002. Because he didn't have the documents, Donahue missed his chance to ask Byrd why he had suddenly wanted a tan shirt and dark brown pants tested, instead of the pants and shirt that everyone agreed that Oscar was wearing on December 26th.

Looking back at the chain of custody cards, the tan shirt and brown pants were collected from Oscar's house during the second search, on December 29th. They were trying to find some kind of footwear to match to the heel print at Neel Ranch. During that second search, they took three of Oscar's sweaters, a pair of coveralls, one short sleeve tan shirt, and a pair of dark brown slacks. Only the sweaters and coveralls match what I know Oscar wore that day, and make total sense.

Reviewing all of the witnesses: Gene Owens didn't see Oscar's clothing as he drove by; Beth Brumley and Mr. Mascorro didn't see the truck man's clothing; Gloria Mascorro described a white turtleneck sweater and very light pants, possibly tan or gray; and Danny Boland remembered dark blue pants and plaid shirt, with the white sweater. I dug through Bill Rose's interviews and testimony, and nobody seems to have ever asked him what Oscar was wearing. Ben Owens, the City Building Inspector, wasn't asked until the trial, and he remembered Oscar wearing blue jeans and nothing about his shirt or a sweater. TCSO didn't interview Oscar's daughters, and Rick Carter said that he didn't remember what Oscar was wearing.

At some point, Byrd became convinced that Oscar had ***not*** been wearing the shirt and pants taken from him at the jail, but rather a tan shirt and dark brown slacks—and he directed TCSO King to look for and collect matching items from Oscar's house. Why? I don't know. My best guess is that there is a missing witness—someone who wasn't documented in any report or interview turned over to the defense. That witness, or witnesses must have described seeing a man at a critical time and location wearing the tan and brown outfit. The obvious choices are along Marinette, at Neel Ranch, or near the bike scene. It could also be someone seen by Carol or Judy as they rode away from Don Lee's house.

The strangest thing about this entire episode is that Byrd's order to Hensley, and the call to Grubb, were totally unnecessary. If the goal was to make sure the tan and brown items were examined and tested for blood, all they needed to do was... ***absolutely nothing***. Hensley had already delivered them to Morton on January 6th—they are items #17 and #22 on the custody receipt. What happened between Jan 6th and the 8th to make Byrd so incredibly certain that Oscar had been wearing that outfit? Who was it who was seen wearing a tan shirt and brown pants, and why was Byrd positive that the person in *that outfit* was Donna's killer? I have to conclude that it was some statement that Byrd heard from a witness, but never disclosed to the defense.

That was the end of the main defense case. It was a shambles. Donahue never laid out the distances involved, the drive times, the timeline of events in the alibi, the credibility and lack of bias of the defense witnesses, and the pre-identification tainting of Brumley and Mascorro. His expert, Parker, had offered nothing scientific or of substance, and was openly mocked by Powell in front of the jury. Powell had dismissed the alibi testimony of Oscar's daughters as lies, and taunted Oscar with "nobody saw you there, did they?" The jury wanted an explanation for the invoice book, or perhaps forensics pointing to a different suspect, and an alternate story of who else may have kidnapped and killed Donna. They got nothing.

There was an interesting exchange, one that happened when Donahue asked the court to admit the tires from Oscar's truck into evidence. Because he had objected, twice, to the tire testimony, it was preserved on appeal. Donahue wanted to make sure that the tires would be kept for later examination. Powell objected to it:

> *Powell:* The problem is that as the court and counsel knows, the clerk has to keep the evidence, and under certain circumstances has to be kept basically forever, and I'm sure the court and counsel know the problem with that size of an exhibit.

Donahue won, and the tires were admitted into evidence as Defense Exhibit V.

Powell then started calling his witnesses to rebut Oscar's alibi. Again, this was an alibi that TCSO had not checked, at all, until jury selection was already underway on June 22, 1976. Powell wanted to sell the jury on the idea that Oscar had seen the freezer loading, and heard Thomas make the "late" comment, but that it had really happened an hour earlier, at 2:15 pm—***before*** Oscar went to the Roberts' house. It still didn't fix the problem of Oscar still being in both N. Visalia and Woodlake at the same time, but it gave the jury a way to explain how Oscar and Pettyjohn had known everything that happened before talking to Frank Thomas.

First up for Powell was Rose Cowles. She was the Director of Medical Records at the Tulare District Hospital. She testified that Bill Irwin's wife Iverna arrived at the ER at 1:55 pm on December 26, 1975.

Bill Irwin was called to change his story a third time, carefully coached by Powell. His first statement to Pettyjohn, in early January, had placed his arrival at the Thomas house sometime after 3:00 pm, and he said he was there for about 30 minutes. He said that he was "quite late" and was supposed to arrive between 1:00-2:00 pm. When TCSO Chamberlain interviewed him after the start of the trial, Irwin said that he arrived at the Thomas house between 1:30-2:00 pm, but admitted that his memory of events was better when he spoke to Pettyjohn, and said he made "a couple of stops" after dropping his wife at the hospital—before going to the Thomas house.

On the witness stand, Irwin's story had been "fixed" by Powell. Now he said that he drove straight from the hospital to the Thomas house, as fast as possible, even with the second truck following him. They jumped out, grabbed the freezer, and rushed off. He omitted the stop to buy the Kelley freezer and the other "stops" he mentioned to TCSO Chamberlain a few days earlier. On cross-examination, Irwin lied about everything. It was just blatant perjury. He said that he told Pettyjohn that he was supposed to be at the Thomas house between 11:00 am-12:00 pm, and denied telling him that he arrived after 3:00 pm. When Donahue confronted Irwin with his former statement that he was at the Thomas house for thirty minutes, Irwin said:

> *Irwin:* Well, twenty minutes, fifteen, fifteen to twenty minutes would be approximately half an hour I would say.
>
> *Donahue:* Well, was it—could it have been a half an hour?
>
> A: I don't really think so.
>
> Q: All right.

At that point, if I had been on the jury, I would just yell "liar," and walked out of the courtroom in disgust. Obviously, this is why defense attorneys don't sit on juries. How could *anyone* give this any credibility? Bill Irwin was literally making it up on the witness stand, in real time, right in front of the jury. It is mind-numbing.

Donahue asked Irwin how long the drive from the hospital takes. Why hadn't Pettyjohn driven the entire route back in January? Irwin said that he did it in ten minutes, but in reality it would take more like twenty. Somehow that also didn't need to include driving to the Kelley house first, loading that freezer, making "other stops," and *then* getting to Garden Street. Even after all these years, I still have no idea what other "stops" Irwin and the other truck made between the hospital and the Thomas house. Donahue didn't know either. In the end, the jury seems to have believed Powell's alternate timeline—that Irwin arrived at the Thomas house at 2:10 pm, and was gone before Bill Rose and his investor arrived at 2:30 pm.

Bill Irwin changed his story *three* times, under obvious pressure from TCSO and DA Powell, and his final version left out a known stop. This timeline also had the trucks driving 60 mph on city streets. The jury chose to believe that over Frank Thomas who told the exact same story three times, had no bias or reason to lie, and agreed with Irwin's first statement to Pettyjohn.

I don't understand exactly why Powell called Iverna Irwin to the stand. In my mind, she put the final nail in her husband's lies. She testified that she was released from the hospital at 3:10 pm, but Bill was not there to drive her home. She said that he did not return to the hospital until 4:15 pm. Bill Irwin claimed in front of the jury that it took him only 10 minutes to get from the hospital to the Thomas house, but an hour and forty-five minutes to make the drive back. Coincidentally, the actual, known drive time of twenty minutes matches leaving the Thomas house at 3:55 pm—the estimate given by both Frank Thomas and Bill Irwin himself in his original statement. Again, how is it possible that Donahue couldn't find a way to make the jury see this, and why didn't they figure it out for themselves?

In order to rebut the defense's testimony that Oscar had been wearing his knee brace with his black shoes—implying that he was disabled and could not have been wearing the cowboy boots—Powell called a guy named Charles Manning. Oscar had applied spray stucco to his house about three months before the murder, and Manning testified that Oscar lifted up his pants to show him (a random stranger) that he was not wearing his knee brace. Manning was a card dealer and a professional gambler. He had a long history of being a DA witness in exchange for having pending charges dropped. He had zero credibility, but Donahue didn't investigate him, and the jury had no idea.

Finally, on July 8th, the last day of trial testimony, Sgt. Byrd was called to testify about the distances and drive times between the various locations at issue. He had just completed the drive that ***same*** day. It had been more than six months since the homicide, and neither TCSO (nor the defense) had *ever* checked to see if it was possible to drive between the sites in the state's allotted time, or how long each interval would take. Well, it turned out that nothing asserted in the state's case was even remotely possible. This should have been the centerpiece of Donahue's opening argument. Instead, Donahue had no idea what to do with the new information. Surprisingly, Byrd didn't lie, his times and distances were accurate:

- 14.4 miles from Roberts house to Brumley - 23 minutes;
- 11 miles from Brumley to Mascorro - 15 minutes;
- 0.7 mile from Mascorro to bike scene - 1 minute;
- 3.4 miles from bike scene to Neel Ranch - 8 minutes;
- 7.7 miles from Neel Ranch to Road 176 - 12 minutes;
- 1/2 mile from Road 176 to Pants - 1 minute;
- 0.3 mile from Pants to First Shoe - 1 minute;
- 2 miles from First Shoe to Second Shoe - 3 minutes
- 1.6 miles from Second Shoe to home - 3 minutes

[*NOTE: The distance from Neel Ranch to Clifton residence was stipulated at 12.1 miles; and a travel time of* ***twenty minutes***]

Powell argued that Oscar arrived home at 4:45 pm, putting the departure from Neel Ranch at 4:25 pm. Generally, Powell's argument to the jury was that the "extra" forty minutes was the time Oscar had available to commit the murder and clean up before walking into his house. Presumably, because Donahue didn't do his job, that's the story the jury chose to believe.

The biggest problem with Powell's narrative is that Donna ***did not*** leave Don Lee's house any earlier than 3:45 pm, and needed twenty-five minutes to ride to the bike scene. That places the arrival time at 4:10 pm. The drive from there to Neel Ranch and then the Clifton residence is twenty-eight minutes, so now it is 4:38 pm, giving Oscar exactly seven minutes to kidnap Donna at the bike scene, murder her on Neel Ranch, and clean up. At this point, it should be obvious why TCSO tried to force Rick Carter to change his statement on Oscar's arrival home from 4:15 to 4:45 pm. The state's very best, most optimistic version of the case relied upon giving Oscar a seven minute window. In his closing statement, Powell estimated about five minutes for the kidnapping, taking the time for the homicide and clean up down to two minutes. But again, that absolutely relied upon 4:45 pm, a time even the judge agreed wasn't really Carter's actual statement. Something Carter wasn't too sure of either.

Donahue had no ability to think on his feet. He should have immediately figured out a way to show the jury the conflicts in the state's own timeline, starting with Powell's agreement that Oscar was at the Roberts' residence at 3:00 pm:

- Oscar was ***not*** in Woodlake at 3:00 pm. Beth Brumley and her mother either lied or Beth saw a different man, in a different truck, at 3:00 pm;
- Gloria Mascorro testified that she first saw the man in the white truck at least five minutes before the flashing incident, which she placed firmly at 3:30 pm based on the radio. Driving from Woodlake, Oscar could not have arrived before 3:38 pm (and that assumed no random driving around Woodlake looking for a girl or the time

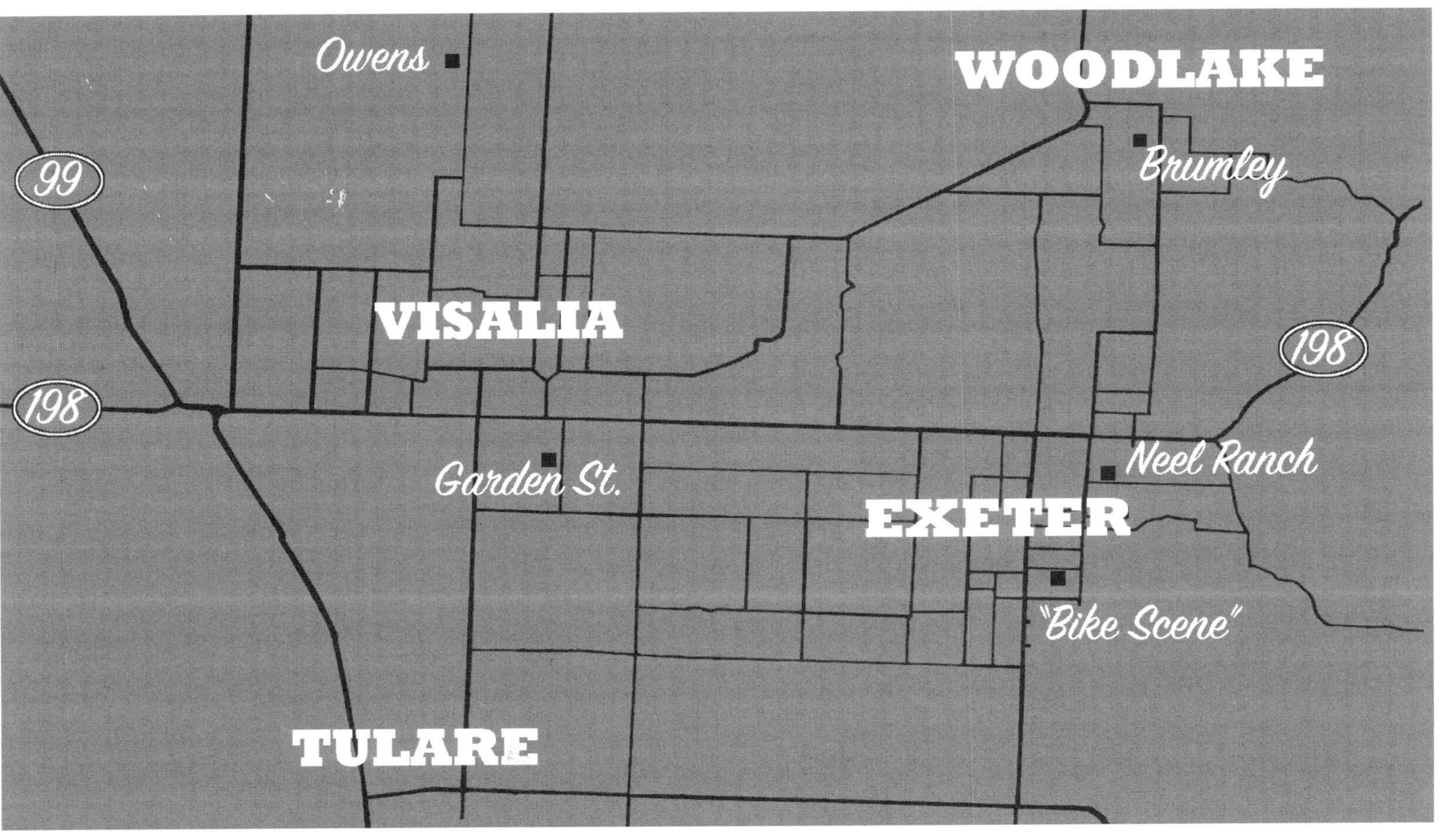
Owens
WOODLAKE
Brumley
99
VISALIA
198
198
Garden St.
Neel Ranch
EXETER
"Bike Scene"
TULARE

State's Timeline "A"

- 3:00—Woodlake Incident
  [Beth Brumley]
- ***3:14–Donna Departed Lee Home on Bike, NW Exeter***
- 3:30—List & Spruce, Incident, SE Exeter
  [Gloria Mascorro]
- 3:39—Donna Kidnapped, Bike Scene, SE Exeter,
  [D.A. Powell]
- 3:47—Donna & Killer Arrive Neel Ranch, NE Exeter
  [D.A. Powell]
- **4:25—Killer Departs Neel Ranch, NE Exeter**
  [D.A. Powell]
- 4:45—Clifton Arrives Home
  [D.A. Powell]

Defense's Timeline

- 3:00—Oscar Arrives Roberts home, N. Visalia
  [Owens, Oscar, D.A Powell]
- 3:15—Oscar Arrives Garden St., E. Visalia
  [Oscar, Thomas, Trueblood, Guerber]
- 3:45—Donna Departed Lee Home on Bike, NW Exeter
  [Don Lee]
- 3:50—Oscar Departs Garden St., E. Visalia
  [Oscar, Trueblood]
- 4:15—Oscar Arrives home, Rural Visalia
  [Oscar, Family]
- 4:45—Oscar Departs home in family sedan, Rural Visalia
  [Oscar, Family]

Using this timeline, Powell told the jury that Oscar had a window of opportunity of 38 minutes to kill Donna, hide her body, and clean up all evidence of the crime. That window relies on Donna's time of departure from the Lee residence.

State's Timeline "B"

- 3:00—Woodlake Incident
  [Beth Brumley]
- 3:30—List & Spruce, Incident, SE Exeter
  [Gloria Mascorro]
- **3:45—Donna Departed Lee Home on Bike, NW Exeter**
  [Don Lee]
- 4:10–Donna Kidnapped, Bike Scene, SE Exeter,
  [D.A. Powell]
- 4:15–Donna & Killer Depart Bike Scene, SE Exeter,
  [D.A. Powell]
- 4:23—Donna & Killer Arrive
  Neel Ranch, NE Exeter
  [D.A. Powell]
- ***4:23—Killer Departs***
  Neel Ranch, NE Exeter
  [D.A. Powell]
- 4:45—Clifton Arrives Home
  [D.A. Powell]

Defense's Timeline

- 3:00—Oscar Arrives Roberts home, N. Visalia
  [Owens, Oscar, D.A Powell]
- 3:15—Oscar Arrives Garden St., E. Visalia
  [Oscar, Thomas, Trueblood, Guerber]
- 3:45—Donna Departed Lee Home on Bike, NW Exeter
  [Don Lee]
- 3:50—Oscar Departs Garden St., E. Visalia
  [Oscar, Trueblood]
- 4:15—Oscar Arrives home, Rural Visalia
  [Oscar, Family]
- 4:45—Oscar Departs home in family sedan, Rural Visalia
  [Oscar, Family]

However, Don Lee disagreed with the time of departure, and stated that Donna left his house at 3:45 pm. The bike ride was timed by TCSO at 25 minutes, putting Donna at the bike scene at 4:10 pm. Powell offered *this* version of the timeline to account for that discrepancy.

talking to Beth). Five minutes after that now placed the flashing at 3:43 pm. *Again*, either Gloria made up the incident or she saw another man and another truck between 3:25-3:30 pm; and

- Powell told the jury that as Oscar was fleeing with Mr. Mascorro chasing him, he turned right down the grove road, Donna swerved and fell off her bike. Oscar supposedly used that opportunity to grab her, dropping his invoice book in the process. The chase immediately followed the 3:30 pm flashing, and it was less than a mile. How late could it have been? 3:40 pm, maybe. At that moment in time, Donna was still at Don Lee's house, *over* four miles away.

Sgt. Byrd's testimony and Powell's narrative of the case clearly prove that it was impossible for Oscar to have been the man seen by Beth Brumley and/or Gloria Mascorro. In order for Oscar to have kidnapped Donna at the bike scene at 3:40 pm, there would need to be clones or time travel involved. The judge never should have allowed Powell to make any of these arguments to the jury because his own evidence disproved them. Donahue didn't object or fight, and Judge Bradley would have allowed it all anyway, but at least the prosecutorial misconduct would have been on the record and preserved for appeal.

Instead of doing any of that, Donahue recalled Oscar to the stand to refute Charles Manning's testimony that he had allegedly been working without his brace. It was useless—the jury either believed Manning's story or they didn't, and Oscar denying it wasn't going to change their minds. However, describing his clothing covering the brace during the Manning job, Oscar mentioned wearing a pair of white painters pants sold at the hardware storofferinge. They're meant to be worn a few times, then thrown away. Powell immediately seized on the pants during his cross-examination:

Powell: Mr. Clifton, those white painter's [*sic*] pants that you can take off and then throw away, are those the ones you were wearing the day you killed Donna Jo Richmond?

Oscar: Sir, I stated I did not do what you've claimed. I had nothing to do with it.

Powell: No further questions.

Donahue: That's all, Mr. Clifton.

Judge Bradley: You may step down.

I read that, and couldn't stop screaming "mistrial, mistrial, mistrial!" Donahue didn't even object. In California, prosecutorial misconduct is defined as "the use of deceptive or reprehensible methods to persuade the court or the jury." It is misconduct for the prosecutor to state facts not in evidence, and a violation of the confrontation clause when the DA effectively becomes his own "unsworn witness."

There was ***no*** evidence, at all, that Oscar wore the painters pants on the 26th, or that they had been "thrown away." Not only was Powell offering testimony as his own witness, he was committing perjury.

It turns out that DA Powell was one of the few people who knew *exactly* where the painters pants were—they were sitting in evidence at TCSO. He was present when Oscar's truck was searched, and TCSO Johnson photographed the pants on the passenger floor next to his evidence stand. DA Powell knew that the pants had not received an evidence tag and number, or been logged in on a chain of custody card—presumably at Powell's own direction. Powell had a photo of the pants, in TCSO custody, but had not turned it over to the defense, entered it into evidence, or shown it to the jury.

Looking at Donahue's notes and closing statement, he knew how devastating the "missing" pants were. Powell had offered the jury a full explanation for the lack of blood and mud on Oscar's clothing. In reality, the pants were clean, other than some stucco on them. Donahue scoured the lists of evidence, TCSO reports, search warrant receipts, and photographs, but could not figure out where the pants

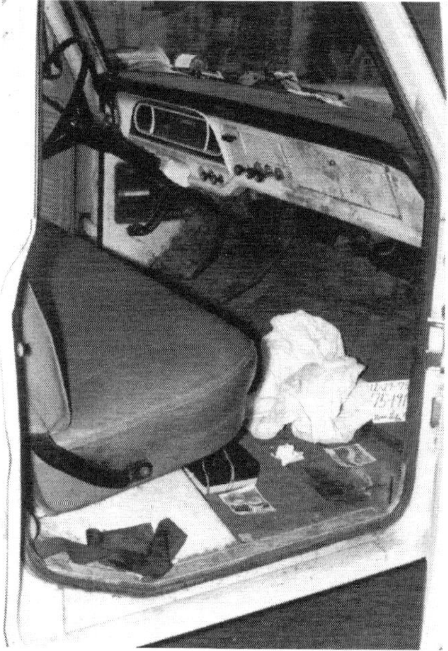

Evidence Photos Truck Interior with Painters Pants
December 27, 1975
Photo: TCSO

were. Oscar didn't remember taking them out of his truck. Nobody on the defense ever imagined, not even for one second, that TCSO forensic deputies Johnson and Hensley and the District Attorney would intentionally hide evidence and then lie about it. However, Donahue should have taken a hard look at the Borbon case overturned just a month earlier for prosecutorial misconduct—the warning was right there.

Powell's closing arguments were a textbook example of every single thing a prosecutor is not allowed to say: he made misleading statements to the jury; he repeatedly referred to inadmissible evidence; he gave the jury the impression that the defense was hiding evidence; he suppressed testimony about key alibi witnesses; he failed to disclose information that impeached the credibility of his witnesses, including tainted identifications and prior inconsistent statements; and he did not disclose the DUI dismissal given to Rick Carter in exchange for his changed testimony. It was an endless litany of bad faith. Donahue didn't object to any of it.

The defense's closing can honestly be described as the ramblings of a very drunk or hung over person. There was no structure, form, or points made. The general tone was that it wasn't Donahue's job to prove Oscar's innocence, or even raise reasonable doubt, but that Powell was required to prove his guilt. It was a disaster, and it took the jury fourteen hours to bring back a guilty verdict. Oscar was stunned. Donahue had told him that they didn't need a strong defense because there was no evidence against him. Oscar could not figure out what had happened. As he waited by the courthouse elevator on his way back to jail, TCSO Brian Johnson approached Oscar and gave him the surprise of his life. Johnson said, "Don't worry, someday the truth will come out." Before Oscar could reply, Sgt. Byrd walked up and yelled at Johnson, "Shut your damn mouth."

Chapter Eleven Sources

1. **Donahue - Trial Preparation Notes**
2. **Parker/Donahue Correspondence**
3. **Testimony of Edward T. Blake, June 29, 1976**
4. **Ed Blake Report, February 3, 1976**
5. **Testimony of Leonard Miller, July 6, 1976**
6. **Tulare County Coroner Autopsy Report, January 16, 1976**
7. **Testimony of Leonard Miller, Grand Jury, February 5, 1976**
8. **TCSO Chain of Custody Cards**
9. **TCSO Report - Johnson December 26, 1975**
10. **Crime Scene Photos**
11. **Testimony of Rick Carter, July 6, 1976**
12. **Testimony of Oscar Clifton, July 6, 1976**
13. **Cal DOJ Lab Report, July 6, 1976**
14. **Clifton/Jordan Property Deed**
15. **Clark County District Court Judgment December 5, 1973**
16. **Prison Psychology Evaluations**
17. **Testimony of Gene Owens, July 7, 1976**

18. TCSO Report - Holguin December 29, 1975
19. Testimony of Frank Thomas, July 7, 1976
20. Testimony of Danny Boland, July 7, 1976
21. Testimony of Bud Brumley, July 7, 1976
22. Exeter Sun - August 7, 1974
23. Exeter Sun - March 9, 1977
24. Correspondence Oscar/Donahue September 1, 1977
25. Testimony of Relinda Clifton, July 7, 1976
26. Testimony of Annette Clifton, July 7, 1976
27. Testimony of Jeanie Esajian, July 7, 1976
28. Stmt to Pettyjohn of Jeanie Esajian January 5, 1976
29. Interviews with Jeanie Esajian
30. Testimony of Harry Moyer, July 8, 1976
31. Testimony of Kenneth Parker, July 8, 1976
32. Testimony of Bob Byrd, July 8, 1976
33. Bob Byrd's "To Do" List, January 8, 1976
34. Charles Morton's Notes re: Instructions on Tan//Brown Outfit
35. Search Warrant Receipt - King/Clifton December 29, 1975
36. Testimony of Rose Cowles, July 8, 1976
37. Testimony of Bill Irwin, July 8, 1976
38. Testimony of Iverna Irwin, July 8, 1976
39. Testimony of Charles Manning, July 8, 1976
40. Testimony of Bob Byrd, July 8, 1976
41. Tulare Sheriff Report - Byrd July 8, 1976
42. Testimony of Oscar Clifton, July 8, 1976
43. TCSO - Chamberlain December 27, 1975
44. Evidence Photos Clifton Truck December 27, 1975
45. Oscar Letter to Donahue, September 24, 1976
46. Oscar Letter to Brian Johnson, April 16, 2001

CHAPTER TWELVE

"Word for word—for the world to read"

It was no surprise that it took the jurors only fifty-four minutes to bring in a death sentence; DA Powell had told them that they had no choice. According to Judge Bradley's instructions, since the jurors had convicted Oscar of murder in the first degree, and with the "special circumstances" of attempted rape and kidnapping, that was an "automatic" death sentence. However, attempted rape was not a "special circumstance" under the law, and the kidnapping should have merged into the homicide, so in reality it was not a death penalty case. However, this was Powell's strategy from the beginning. When the false rape and sodomy charges were quietly dropped before Grand Jury, Donahue should have made a motion to remove the death penalty enhancement, but he didn't.

Lying on the witness stand, or encouraging/forcing another person to testify falsely is a serious felony, and I've documented dozens of instances of this during Oscar's prosecution. Reasonable people cannot imagine a DA, ADA, or police officer sending a man to death row when they know that he is actually innocent, but the pervasive suppression of exculpatory evidence and witnesses proves that is exactly what Jay Powell, Brenton Bleier, Bob Byrd, Vernon Hensley, and Brian Johnson did to Oscar. If you think this sounds like a serious crime, the California legislature agrees. In 1976 California Penal Code §128 said: "***Every person who, by willful perjury or subornation of perjury, procures the conviction and execution of any innocent person, is punishable by death.***" [*emphasis added*]

If Oscar had been executed but later found innocent, multiple people could have been charged with capital murder and sentenced to death ("***or*** life imprisonment without possibility of parole" was added to §128 in 1977). In 1976, Oscar's innocence could have been proven through a fingerprint match, the killer's blood type/secretor status/PGM type combination found on the evidence, new eyewitness testimony, or the identification and conviction of the man who really murdered Donna. Did Byrd tell Lavern Lamb that she could be executed for lying about finding Donna's pants? Of course not. Only the police and prosecutors understood the real consequences of the perjury.

Immediately after the death penalty was handed down, Powell started giving newspaper interviews predicting that Oscar's death sentence would be overturned, and making it sound like a larger constitutional issue. However, when the California Supreme Court struck down the state death penalty statute later in 1976, Oscar's case was not directly covered (his jury held the required separate deliberations), so he had to appeal his sentence based on the lack of "special circumstances."

It might have been helpful for Donahue or Oscar's family to read the *Exeter Sun*, because a week after the conviction, this statement from Powell was on the front page:

> A problem which arose at the time of the investigation of Donna Richmond's death has resulted in the addition of new equipment in the Sheriff's Department. The special camera with a fixed focus that was then used to photograph footprints and tire tracks was ***found to be defective.*** Two separate cameras are now used, and solid castings are made of tire tracks. [*emphasis added*]

Every word of Criminalist Morton's testimony about the possible tire track and heel print "similarities" to Oscar's tires and boots was based exclusively upon photos taken by that ***same*** defective camera.

I found probably a hundred newspaper clippings in the defense file, and that story was not among them. I couldn't see any mention of it in Oscar's correspondence or his appeal briefs over the years. Morton's testimony was riddled with qualifiers and suggestions about the poor quality and distortion in the track and print photos, but at no point was it disclosed to the defense, court, or jury that the camera was malfunctioning and taking inaccurate images. The *entire* basis for Morton's "expert" testimony was an instrument giving bad readings and information. This fact alone should have been grounds for a new trial. Considering how Morton's tire and heel print testimony was critical to the conviction, and Donahue had preserved the issue by objecting to the testimony on the record.

Before Oscar was formally sentenced in September, Donahue made a motion for a new trial based on two pieces of information that had come to light. The first was the testimony of Charles Manning, who had said Oscar hadn't been wearing his brace during the stucco job. Someone had seen Manning in the courtroom listening to testimony for several days prior to taking the witness stand. DA Powell disputed that, and used Sgt. Byrd as his proof:

> *Powell:* Mr. Byrd, who is the investigating officer in this case, knows Charlie Manning and tells me that Mr. Manning was never present before he testified in the court. Byrd called him to come down and testify the night before.

That testimony summed up what I had already figured out about Manning, and the way that Byrd "found" witnesses when he needed them. When it looked like the defense had done a good job showing just how disabled Oscar was due to his knee injury, Sgt. Byrd was sent out to get a witness to rebut it. It also explains why there were no prior statements from Manning or TCSO reports showing that Manning had ever been questioned. Byrd literally called someone he "knew," and told him that he needed to come to court the next day and say that Oscar had shown him that he wasn't wearing his knee brace. Just like the "call" Danny Boland said that he got. Byrd had known Laverne Lamb for at least a decade before he called her and asked her to say that she had found Donna's pants. Did he call Bud Brumley too? *Probably.*

If TCSO Sgt. Bob Byrd had a *Modus Operandi*, this was it: He used people he knew to fill in case gaps that needed witnesses. He needed their "help" so the bad guy wouldn't get off. If they didn't testify they might find themselves or someone they loved charged instead, he could make life "hard" for them at work or school. The alternative was that he could see to it that pending criminal charges were dismissed. Carrot or stick; whatever worked. DA Powell had what he called a witness "slush fund" that he used for cash payments to witnesses. In the Borbon case it came out that witnesses were offered sex with women in the DA's office or in TCSO vehicles, and heroin in the county jail. It is all on the court record.

Judge Bradley took Byrd at his word, of course, and found that Manning had not been in the courtroom prior to his testimony, and even if he had, it wouldn't have affected the trial. The other issue raised by Donahue was a sworn statement by Hershall Joslin. He was a member of the Golden Valley Search and Rescue Party, and they were called in to assist with the search for Donna on December 26th. Joslin responded directly to the bike scene at about 8:00 pm that night, and TCSO instructed him to guard the area around Donna's bike. Joslin said that he watched a deputy (presumably Brian Johnson) take photographs and measurements of tire tracks and footprints by the bike, and then make at least two plaster casts. Joslin testified that he saw the casts put into a bag, and then loaded into the back of the TCSO forensics truck.

This information also matched up with something I had seen in a letter from Oscar to Donahue:

> I know that they had a shoe print the first night, for they also took my shoe print. John Deathriage is the one that took the plaster casts of my shoes, so he should have made a report. This was just before daylight, the 27th of December. Ask about his report. They should have given it to you long ago.

Obviously, they did take plaster casts at the bike scene, and they didn't match Oscar's tires or shoes, so they hid that exculpatory evidence from the defense. Another constitutional due process violation under *Brady*, and Judge Bradley said it was fine and that it wouldn't have had any impact on the jury. Was this part of the "truth" that TCSO Johnson told Oscar "would come out someday?" I'm sure it was. Hershall Joslin worked for the county road department, and thought of himself as a very pro law enforcement person. He was positive about what he saw, and I believe him. I think everyone knew he was telling the truth. But Judge Bradley had no intention of ordering a new trial; he would leave that question to the appellate court.

Oscar was formally sentenced in September 1976, and it was done very strategically. He was given the death penalty for the homicide, but his additional sentences for Brumley, Mascorro, and the attempted rape charge were *permanently stayed*—meaning that he would never have to serve that time, no matter what happened with his appeals. It seems like a minor, inconsequential point, but it was huge and very telling. The stays meant that Oscar wasn't in "legal jeopardy" for either of those convictions, so he ***could not*** appeal them, because they were moot in the eyes of the court.

Normally, Judge Bradley would have just given Oscar standard sentences, to run concurrently with the murder, but that's not what DA Powell asked for—he wanted those two sentences stayed. That immediately told me (and should have told Donahue) that Powell knew the eyewitness identifications in Brumley and Mascorro were fatally tainted, *and* that Criminalist Grubb's ABO typing disproved the attempted rape conviction and pointed to a different suspect. If any of those three convictions were overturned on appeal, the entire homicide case would fall apart. It was a genius move by DA Powell and Judge Bradley.

Beth Brumley had never herself given any description of the man in the truck or his clothing; only her father had. The Woodlake PD and TCSO reports documented her prior viewing of Oscar as "murder suspect" on the front of the paper, and being shown a photo of Oscar's truck. There was no investigation into the scene, or attempt to find other witnesses. Finally, Powell himself impeached her testimony when he told the jury that Oscar had been in N. Visalia at 3:00 pm, not in Woodlake as Beth and her mother said. Even in the 1970s this appeal would have been a slam dunk. Powell had literally no arguments on his side.

Mascorro was also an easy win. Jeanie Esajian firmly stood by her photo of Sheriff Wiley and interview with Gloria saying she was being shown Oscar's mugshot. Wiley did not ask the paper for a retraction or correction, and he did not testify at the trial and tell the jury that it was Donna's photo, because that would have been perjury. Gloria also saw that same "murder suspect" photo of Oscar on the front page of the newspaper on the evening of her lineup ID. The lineup itself was also a constitutional violation since the other men were police officers and didn't resemble Oscar. She described a plain white truck, and a man wearing different clothing, and wearing glasses. The Mascorros were biased, and possibly coerced, as employees of Donna's family. If TCSO had believed Gloria's story they would have examined the "flashing" scene for foot and tire prints, but they didn't.

Also, the attempted rape conviction should have merged into the murder, and was not supported as a separate charge. The only evidence offered for this particular crime was the removed clothing (which was staged) and Blake's supposed positive acid phosphatase reaction. Again, Criminalist Grubb's finding of no blood type O in the sample conclusively eliminated Oscar.

Overturning that charge would have been almost automatic, but it couldn't be attacked as its own appeal because there was no prison time to serve. Instead, Oscar could only attack the evidence from Brumley, Mascorro, and the attempted rape as part of the overall murder case, and *only* if he could persuade his appellate attorney to do so.

There was one more missed opportunity for Oscar that came immediately after his conviction. During jury selection, one of the jurors from Porterville, Betty Lou Galloway, was asked: "Now, do you have any members of your family, or close personal friends who have been charged with a crime of assault or a sex crime such as charged in this case?"

Mrs. Galloway answered "no," which was technically correct in late June. However, she did not disclose that, during the course of the trial, her nephew, Bennies Galloway, had been questioned and was a prime suspect in a series of violent rapes committed by a man dubbed the "*Porterville Rapist*" by the local media. Five days after Mrs. Galloway voted to send Oscar to death row, her nephew was arrested and charged with thirteen rapes. The warrant was served by Sheriff Bob Wiley, Capt. Ollie Farris, and Sgt. Bob Byrd.

When I saw Betty Galloway's name on Oscar's jury, I fell right into a rabbit hole. As far as I could tell, this issue had never been noticed or raised on appeal. Since Mrs. Galloway knew that her nephew was a rape and assault suspect, she could have wanted to see Oscar convicted to take suspicion off of Bennies, or in the hope that they would drop him and go after Oscar for the Porterville rapes. She shouldn't have been on the jury. The first attack had been in the summer of 1974, when Galloway, wearing a stocking mask, raped two teen girls at gunpoint on the banks of the Tule River. Who was the investigating officer? *Sgt. Byrd.* I suddenly realized exactly how Byrd had known that Oscar was living in Las Vegas when Jennifer Armour was killed a few months later—he had looked at Oscar as a suspect in the Tule rape case.

The detailed information about the Galloway case was contained in the *Porterville Recorder*, which could only be read on microfilm at the Porterville Library. When I started rolling through the pages I found something that made me stop cold:

> Sacramento law enforcement authorities also are investigating the possibility of Galloway's involvement in several rapes in that area, officials said. They placed a "hold" on Galloway pending investigation, Sheriff Wiley said.

The similarities in the MO of the Porterville Rapist and East Area Rapist were so strong, Sacramento had blocked Galloway's release from jail while they investigated him. As Captain Farris told the *Advance-Register* on July 20, 1976: "Authorities in Sacramento County have been investigating rapes with a similar method of operation and have shown interest in questioning Galloway." So Sheriff Wiley, Capt. Farris, and Sgt. Byrd all knew about the East Area Rapist in July 1976—four months before the press or citizens of Sacramento found out. Who was handling Galloway's case in court? Judge Bradley and ADA Bleier. Apparently, nobody thought, "*Hey*… I wonder if this violent, armed serial rapist of teen girls might have killed Donna Richmond." *Apparently not.*

Galloway was indicted on a total of 35 counts of rape, attempted rape, sex perversion, burglary, and false imprisonment involving attacks between July 8, 1974-July 14, 1976. By November that year, when the plea deal was entered, the sentencing tally was reduced to 19: nine counts of rape, nine counts of sex perversion, and one attempted rape. TCSO Richard McGowen noted that the "Secret Witness" had made payment to the informant leading to the arrest of Galloway, which left only two cases on the list—*Armour and Snelling*. It's easy to see why Sacramento was interested in Galloway, his MO was unique, specific, and matched the EAR:

> He wore a mask over his face, and was waiting for the victims in their homes. He told them not to scream or he would kill them. He blindfolded them and tied their hands behind their backs. At least one victim was struck in the head with the attacker's gun. He removed window screens, and entered through sliding windows. The victims were stalked, and he knew their routines. He often stayed in the victims' homes for hours.

VPD had eliminated the Porterville Rapist before Galloway's arrest mainly because the suspect described was a much shorter (5'

4") and thinner man than the VR. However, the EAR seemed to have lifted Galloway's MO almost exactly, and even learned to disguise his voice and wear gloves, since those mistakes got Galloway caught.

In a 1977 interview, Sacramento Sheriff Lowe confirmed that he was aware of Galloway, and the similarities to the EAR, while ranting about pornography:

> It happened in Tulare County this past year where a rapist similar to The East Area Rapist was apprehended. He admitted that, prior to each of the rapes which he committed, he had attended a hardcore movie.

When Galloway entered a guilty plea, he blamed pornography, which was much more comfortable for the community than trying to figure out how a good Mormon, with a wife, kids, and a thriving small business, chose to hurt so many girls and women.

In June 1976, the EAR started attacking in Rancho Cordova using a combination of the VR and the Porterville Rapist MOs. In July, Sheriff Lowe made the connection between the EAR and Tulare County, and told TCSO. Ten months later, VPD traveled to Sacramento, and told Lowe that the VR and the EAR were the same offender. Sgt. Vaughan also told the *Visalia Times-Delta*, and the story that the VR had started offending in Sacramento in the summer of 1976 was carried in papers throughout Tulare County. Clearly, Sheriff Lowe, Sheriff Wiley, Capt. Farris, and Sgt. Byrd now knew, for certain, that the EAR had been living in Tulare County between the spring of 1974 and the summer of 1976, then moved to the Sacramento area.

After reading all of the Galloway information, I was really shaken, and had so many more questions than answers. Had Sheriff Wiley, Capt. Farris, and Sgt. Byrd held off on arresting Galloway until after Oscar's trial so that he wouldn't be raised as an obvious alternate suspect? Had any of them applied pressure to Betty Galloway while she was a juror? *What did it mean* that Sgt. Byrd had actual knowledge that the VR had copied Galloway's MO and taken it to Sacramento?

Why didn't Donahue tell the jury that a serial rapist of teens was on the loose in Porterville, and that the VR had murdered Jennifer Armour, kidnapped Beth Snelling, and was stalking Debbie Ward just days before Donna was killed?

The question about Donahue's failure to bring up Jennifer's homicide, in an orange grove, on the Friant-Kern Canal, within eyesight of Neel Ranch *really* bothered me. Oscar's alibi for that crime had already been fully investigated, and there was no danger that he would be accused of killing Jennifer. Also, why avoid discussing the Ransacker? Beth Snelling and Debbie Ward were about the same age and physical type as Donna and Jennifer. It's not as if white, middle-class teenagers were routinely being kidnapped and murdered in Tulare County—this was an unheard of spree. Donahue and Pettyjohn each had six VR burglaries within a block of their homes, so they were fully aware of the MO and targeted stalking victims.

As usual, Margie had the answer. Ray Donahue's son, Tim, had been a VR suspect. I looked back at Sgt. Vaughan's suspect list, and realized that she was right:

> *November 20, 1975.* "The following list of names are being mentioned at this point in an effort to centralize the subjects who have entered into the course of this investigation as possible suspects. These persons are to be considered as subject, and will be given a number at this time which will stay with the name throughout this investigation from henceforth.
>
> (25.) *Timothy Joseph Donahue*: Lives in the area of the homicide, usually wears tennis shoes, prints to be sent to the lab."

I feel confident that if someone—anyone—had told Oscar, or any member of the Clifton family, that Ray Donahue's son had been added to Sgt. Vaughan's murder suspect list one month *before* Donna was killed, he would have hired a different defense attorney. Since VPD had collected Tim Donahue's fingerprints, it seems highly likely that Tim would have asked his father for legal advice. Not only was Ray Donahue ***not*** going to point the finger at the VR in Donna's homicide, but this gave him another possible motive to see Oscar convicted.

Unbelievably, I found *another* conflict of interest for Donahue that explained his failure to raise Galloway's arrest in his motion for a new trial. It was in a written exchange between Oscar and Donahue in October 1976:

> *Oscar:* I'd like to know if you have seen what the man said he had done—and to who—the one that had 37 charges of rape and made a deal of a lesser charge. I think he said he had killed some. I'd like to know if he did what I am here for.
>
> *Donahue:* You have asked concerning a case involving a man by the name of Galloway, who was charged with some 30 counts of rape, or attempted rape. Mr. Galloway pled guilty to approximately 20 some counts of rape, or attempted rape, and was given six 3-to-life consecutive sentences, and three concurrent sentences. My partner, Mr. Heusdens, represented Mr. Galloway, and so far as we can ascertain, there isn't any connection between Mr. Galloway and the victim in your case.

It turned out that while Donahue was representing Oscar, he had opened a second law office, in Porterville, in partnership with Jim Heusdens—so Donahue's firm was representing Oscar and Galloway at the same time, and for some reason Oscar took Donahue's word that Galloway hadn't killed Donna. Just *nope, he didn't do it.* Not that Galloway had an alibi, or something else excluded him. Galloway didn't serve life, and by 1990 he was living back in Tulare and facing charges for stealing an "adult" video from a local store. At the time of this writing, he is 83 years old, and remains on the sex offender registry for life.

The best documentation of Oscar's feelings after his conviction, and his mindset for his appeal, exist in his correspondence with

Donahue and, later, his appellate attorney, Ted Isles. At first, Oscar was focused on trying to understand how he had been convicted, and what he needed to do for the truth to prevail:

> If you only knew how it hurts for them to say I did these things. I couldn't hurt any one, or any thing, but to prove it to some is hard. If they only had to go through this then maybe they would not be so quick to judge. You never know, but a man like myself dies just a little each day from heartache and hurt, knowing that it is wrong to be here. I don't like to lay here for someone else, or die for them. I know they are still free. I love my family and they do mean so much to me. I know I didn't have a trial like I should have.
>
> They told me here to not tell anyone why I was here, because they will kill someone that did those things, but I told them I wouldn't lie no matter if it did end my life. They let me help out where the office is after three or four days. I like to do things to help. The time goes by so much better, and I don't worry so much.
>
> They do have the wrong one. So help me, if you can, to prove this. I still say Johnson would too. At least he did part at first from what he said to me that day. I feel he would. He knew I was framed more by cops. That I feel hurt me more than the man who did put my book there.
>
> This place is hell on earth. I'd like for Powell to spend a little time in here, and then maybe him and them wouldn't lie so… then maybe they could see just what it is like. I'll never understand how they could lie. They knew the girl wasn't raped, but they charged me anyway to make it look bad on me. I know I am here with lies from Powell and cops, to get those girls to lie, and the newspaper running me down. I was framed as much by the Sheriffs as the one that murdered that girl. And before it's over, I'll prove that. Someday I know the truth will come out, and Powell will be right in on it.

I still say if the FBI had been called they would have been the right ones. Then all wouldn't been covered up that could have helped me. I received some more statements tonight as to what Powell tried at my trial with my witnesses. He tried to get them to go against me. Thank God they will not, even though they do not know me that well. But they know I'd never do what he said.

I hope to see the day that the people that sat on the jury wake up to the law, and see that some are innocent. They don't realize that a man can be. I need all of the help that I can get now to prove this. If we didn't have people in the Sheriff's office that lied, maybe they could have come out with the truth. I still feel that the boyfriend had something to do with it, but I cannot prove it. I still cannot understand why semen cannot be typed for blood type.

Send me anything so I can go over it. I do not want to be in the dark this time. This is my life, and I shouldn't be here. I wish I did know who did it. Whoever killed her got away free for what they did, and cops just wanted to close the case. There are more bad cops than bad men on the street it seems.

I was setup, it's plain to see, but I guarantee one thing, I will try til the day I die to prove I am innocent, and if I don't get a trial, the world will be able to read and hear all through the TV Reporter that comes here. Powell and the others that did this will be here before this is over. Too much is coming out. Somehow I hope to find out the truth. If I don't I will put all of these transcripts together, word for word for the world to read. Then, they can see how the lie was. Maybe this will help someone else to see how easy it is to be framed.

You may not believe me—you're the only one that knows that—but I didn't lie, I was in Visalia. I know what I said and I know that two men wouldn't ask the same question I did in the same afternoon. I only wish I had gone and talked to them the four hours I was out. If I had known that was the time I needed, I may have, but I told my wife that the girl had just run off, and they would find her at someone's house. I just went to sleep, but I should have used those few hours for my life.

I do believe in you as an attorney, but one other thing I can't understand is why you never answer my question that I ask you. I've asked you more than one time how you feel. If you feel I'm innocent or not. I know I can say I am, over and over, but only God knows I am for sure. But, I would truly like to know how you feel. I hope you do help, so I can prove how wrong they were.

Donahue:

In answer to your question, as to whether I believe that you are innocent, the answer is "yes." I have never felt otherwise. However, I am just like you are, for in your last letter you state that you do not know how your invoice book got to the location of the bicycle. If I had the answer to that question, then perhaps I would know, for sure, as to who the third party may have been.

Oscar:

I know you keep saying "the girl and the book"—the book was took, I don't know where last that book was. As you remember, I said I did not know if the book was in my pickup or car.

I hope you keep your eyes open and try to see some of these men who are still doing things. I pray they get him before he murders someone again. I hope the people around Exeter open their eyes now, and think.

Donahue:

In regard to the various crimes which have occurred in Tulare County since your conviction, I do not have the manpower to make an investigation of each of them.

Oscar:

Please get me the things I asked for soon. They should give you all. I have got to work some for myself now, I have my wife and kids to think of. I will try to make sure Powell will not get away with what he did, and it's not right that he should.

These next items I need so I can read them to see just what was said:

- Copies of Charles Morton's reports, all of them
- Copies of Edward T. Blake reports
- Copies of the lab reports of the man you had to do them
- Copies of Michael James Grubb reports
- Could you look at the bike and see if any paint is off it where the white was, or how the bike looks? It says here the bike was root beer brown. I wish they had brought it to court too. I wish we had some of the white paint to see if it came off the cop's car. I would like to have a supply of the paint and the one on the bike, taken through a lab test. We have to now prove that the paint did come from someone that did that terrible thing, and I would like to know
- Was there ever any answer why Carol and Judy did not come to the trial? Also the boy that was with the Richmond boy when they found the bike
- Can you tell me how far it is from Judy Stewart's house to Don Lee's home, in miles. How long does it take to ride a bike to his home? So, I'd like to know how long it would take to ride - it had to be well after 3:00 when they left Judy's home
- Why did you not push the fingerprints in my pickup? They were unknown. At my trial, Powell tried to make it look like someone had tried to take all of the prints out of my pickup. Showing there were prints in my pickup could have proven that Powell was lying

- Why did DA Powell ask you to ask me to take 2nd Degree if he didn't know they had framed me as much as the man that murdered the girl. Maybe he felt that he did not have a case. Why?
- Why was the ski cap not tested or shown at my trial? It belonged to someone
- Why did you not make them show the footprints at the bike? I know they said one was the brother of the girl, but what did we have to prove that? Plus, there was more than one kind
- Why were the photos from 34-40 not shown? They were footprints at the body
- Dr. Miller's report
- Mike King reports. The first night, and all
- Pages of the invoice book that were in evidence, numbers 7116 and 7125
- I'd like copies of the San Diego Lab Reports.

Please get me these things right away, I'd like to get back to court soon. Thank you for your time.

Donahue:

I do not have any report from a lab in San Diego, photos number 34 to 40, Mike Grubb reports, nor any reports from Charles Morton.

I do not know the distance from Judy Stewart's home to Don Lee's home.

I do not know why Carol and Judy were not called as witnesses by the prosecution. I would assume that they were not called simply for the reason that the girls could not present any evidence other than perhaps the time they left the victim at the Lee home.

[NOTE: *The girls should have been asked if they saw a man or vehicle near the Lee home, and testified about* ***exactly*** *what time they arrived* *and departed, if they spoke to anyone while out riding, and if they had been followed.*]

Donahue:

The ski cap in question was found approximately 50 to 100 yards from where the body was found, and it was determined that there was no connection between the cap and this crime. That is my opinion of why the cap was not tested.

Oscar:

The ski cap was there. They went miles to put tire prints against me, so this cap should have been given to the lab, it did have hair in it [NOTE: *This is according to Parker's report*], they looked at the hair. I say anything there should have been at my trial, you didn't see them not showing the invoice book.

Also, they did not even have Mr. Morton look at the tennis shoe impressions tracks, and photos at the various locations. He said he knew nothing about them.

About the San Diego report I've asked for. I'm asking because you should have received it for sure. I'd like to see what they said about the shoe or boot impressions found at the scene near the body.

This is right from Hensley's report: "*The immediate area of the scene of the body was then examined, and several footprints were photographed next to the body, evidence stands number 34-40 were utilized to show locations for these footprints.*" That is ***not*** just one print, so I'd like a copy of them.

Donahue:

All the exhibits that are in evidence will be available to you on appeal, and your attorney may obtain such copies as he may wish. Going back once more to stands 34-40, these exhibits were put in evidence, and will be available to you. I do not have any copies of the same.

Again, I have not received any San Diego reports. The information I received was that the lab in San Diego could not make an identification of the print of the boot.

Oscar:

Mr. Donahue, you have never said why Bob Wiley did not show in my trial. I'd like this answered. Then, as I've said before, Byrd was in on that 1965 charge. Plus Farris at that time. Farris said some day he'd get me, and see that I went to prison.

Can you tell me just who found the shoe? This was just before they found a body and they knew anything about where to look. This was also before the woman called them, the one that found the pair of lady's capris, a day before.

Donahue:

Evidently, the reason Mr. Wiley was not called as a witness was that he had no testimony to give.

In regard to the finding of the shoe, I presume that the Sheriff's Office simply started looking for any possible clues they could find, and happened to locate the shoe.

Mrs. Lamb found the green capri pants about 5:45 pm on December 26th. She found them on Ave 264. The next day she called the Sheriff's office (I do not know what time it was that she called, but it is in the transcript) and reported finding the pants. I assume that when she told them where the pants had been found that the Sheriff's office took the brother and his friend to Ave 264 to look for anything else that might have belonged to Donna Jo.

Oscar:

I'd also like to add this about the boys who found the shoe. They found this at 0940 12/27/75, **before** the woman called the Sheriff's office. On 12.28.75 at 0730 hrs officer received a call advising that a Lavern Lamb had found a pair of dark green ladies capris in the road on Ave 264 - this was a day **after**, look at Byrd's report. I hope you note that the shoe was found one day before the woman called the Sheriff's office.

Please send me copies of the white notepad with the numbers.

Donahue:

Enclosed please find a sheet of paper from a notepad I purchased during the course of the trial. The notepad was similar in size and color.

You have asked me to furnish you copies of the various items placed into evidence. All of the items of evidence will be maintained, and your counsel may examine any or all of them.

Oscar:

Thank you for what you have sent. At least it helped put a little light on the picture. It is very plain to see they wanted to put me here right from the first. If they had tried, maybe they would have the right one. I wish I had seen these papers before my trial. Write me back soon and send the paper and pictures so I can go through all. I've got to find out how they made the lie up.

The white note pad I asked for was the one that had all the numbers on it. You showed me in jail. I'd like copies of those, not the size.

Donahue:

I am enclosing a copy of the pages from the tablet. Also enclosed are copies of the pages of the invoice book. I do not have copies of invoice numbers 7116 and 7125.

Oscar asked for the used pages from the notepad found by Donna's bike about a dozen times over six months, and Donahue kept ignoring it. Eventually, he sent Oscar a blank page from a random notepad that he had purchased, which I found incredibly weird and suspicious. After Oscar pushed him again, Donahue *finally* sent copies of the three pages from the actual notepad, with the columns of handwritten numbers. *Did he contact Sgt. Byrd or DA Powell to get those?*

> *Donahue:*
>
> Mrs. Clifton picked up all of your clothing, and the guns that were seized. The remaining clothing, which is in evidence, will remain in evidence until the appeal is completed.

I personally have a copy of the receipt for those items, which were given to Mrs. Clifton on February 7, 1977. Donahue was correct. None of the seventeen items returned to her was admitted into evidence at trial. This was Donahue's second, specific written promise to Oscar that the evidence and exhibits were being held and would be available for future examination and testing which could be used to impeach the test results and trial testimony of Blake, Morton, and Grubb.

> *Oscar:*
>
> I am writing this letter tonight to see if you can find any error that might help to get me a new trial when you went through the reports and transcripts. If so, would you let me know what you found as soon as you receive this. Can you tell me what you objected to at my trial? I can remember part, but if you will let me know all you can. My opening brief has to be filed by 30 days from February 15, and that's not long. So, please help if you will. They've tried to get me to go to the hospital, but I've just got too much to do. For I do want to prove that I am innocent before I die.
>
> A person does not know how easy it is for the Sheriff's officers to lie just to keep from looking. I saw if they had used what they had in their reports, they would have had the right

> man. I wish I could have read some of these statements before, and Sheriff's reports. They just added whatever they like to put me here.
>
> There were good latent prints in my pickup. At my trial Powell said there were none in my pickup whatsoever. Now I'd like to know if these prints could be matched to this man, John Scheuren.

Based on the timeline of prior correspondence, I believe this last request was received by Donahue on Thursday, February 25, 1977 or possibly on Friday the 26th—Oscar wrote on Sunday, and Monday was President's Day, so no mail went out until that Tuesday.

On February 28, 1977 at 2:30 pm, TCSO Sgt. Lovett destroyed ***every single item*** of Richmond case evidence in his custody. He noted that he disposed of each piece of evidence on the chain of custody cards in the case, *and* that he did so upon the direct order of Sgt. Bob Byrd. On April 8, 1977 at an unknown time, TCSO Brian Johnson destroyed the four items of evidence stored in the crime lab refrigerator: a vial of Donna's blood, a vial of Oscar's blood, the envelope containing Donna's pubic hair sample and crusted dirt removed from her skin at autopsy, and a sample of Donna's stomach contents. Again, Johnson made two notes that he did this under the direct order of Sgt. Byrd. The only items that survived were Donna's pants, her underpants, and Clifton's pocket knife—which were found in a box at the courthouse in 2001.

It wasn't an accident or mistake—it was an intentional, highly illegal order. In 1977, CA Penal Code 135 stated:

> Every person who, knowing that any book, paper, record, instrument in writing, or other matter or thing, is about to be produced in evidence upon any trial, inquiry, or investigation whatever, authorized by law, willfully destroys or conceals the same, with intent thereby to prevent it from being produced, is guilty of a misdemeanor.

The purpose of PC 135 is to prevent obstruction of justice. Sgt. Byrd, Sgt. Lovett, and Deputy Brian Johnson each committed a crime, and faced up to six months in jail. They were also implicated in a criminal conspiracy under PC §182.1—a separate criminal charge. The evidence and exhibits could not be destroyed, legally, until one year ***after*** Oscar was no longer in prison, or was on probation.

In early 1977, Oscar was in San Quentin, on Death Row. He was sentenced on September 16, 1976, and Sgt. Byrd ordered the destruction a mere five months later. In addition to the general rules and laws that required TCSO to properly maintain the evidence in their custody, there were also two notices to preserve evidence filed in Tulare County Superior Court and in effect at the time of the destruction. All evidence, whether used during the trial or not, was deemed material, and necessary to the appeal, and TCSO had a duty to maintain the evidence. Obviously, Sgt. Byrd was aware of the appeal and orders, and knew he could be held in contempt of court. Not only was he willing to face jail and the loss of his job, but he also risked letting Oscar go free if he won his appeal and got a new trial.

Even back in 1976, California law said that destruction of evidence violated a defendant's due process rights if the evidence was important to the case, and the police intentionally destroyed it or failed to follow "rigorous and systematic" procedures to preserve it. Just having the test results from the evidence wasn't enough, because further testing of the items could get different results, or point to another suspect. Outside testing could impeach the state criminalist's results or testimony. For instance, the pubic hair sample and Blake's slides could be retested for AP, found to be negative, and Blake's lab findings and testimony about "semen" proven to be false. The California Supreme Court had found that the only remedy for evidence destroyed by the police was the total suppression of all test results and testimony that followed from that evidence.

The Tulare DA would have needed to have each actual item for a new trial. Without Oscar's tires, boots, and invoice book, about half of the trial testimony instantly disappears. There is no "semen" on the pubic hair or blond hair from Oscar's sweater. Sgt. Byrd knew for certain that the moment he destroyed the evidence Oscar could never, under any circumstance, be retried for Donna's murder. Sgt. Byrd, Sgt. Lovett, and Deputy Johnson risked being fired, having all of their prior cases overturned, going to jail for a year, and letting Oscar go free. *For what?* There really is only one possible answer: They had actual knowledge of Oscar's innocence and they feared that one or more items of evidence would prove the identity of the real killer. Additionally, Sgt. Byrd must have believed that the threat of discovery was imminent, and he had to act right away.

The timing here feels too spot-on to be a mere coincidence. If Donahue contacted TCSO on Thursday, and asked that the fingerprints from Oscar's truck be compared to a suspect in custody for a different crime, would that have been enough for Byrd to panic and have the case evidence destroyed on Monday? Possibly, especially if he had been told that Sacramento had just identified the EAR's blood type as "A," the same type Grubb found. Could it have been the notepad that appeared to belong to an Exeter PD Officer—someone who had moved to Sacramento just six months earlier?

The evidence destruction happened behind the scenes. Neither Donahue nor Oscar had any idea. More than a month after Oscar asked to have the fingerprints in his truck checked against a known sex offender in the area, Donahue finally responded:

> I had asked the Sheriff's office to compare the fingerprints found in your pickup with those of John Scheuren. I have been waiting for a reply from the Sheriff's Office to these inquiries before sending this letter to you, but to date I have not had a response. I will let you know as soon as I hear about the fingerprints.

> *Oscar:*
>
> Now can you say why the fibers found on the girl that was murdered were not pursued, and why that was not said in my trial? This may prove something.

I'm still looking for the lab test on the paint, what date it was done, and by who. That is one thing that should have been tested first, but it's not even on the list of the things that went to IFS. Why?

Donahue:

You have copies of every report that I received.

I also requested the Sheriff's Office to compare the fingerprints found in your pickup with those of John Scheuren, and it was found that the fingerprints in your pickup were not John Scheuren's.

In reference to the paint sample, I was told that it did not come from your truck. I do not recall receiving a written report on the same. Again, I suggest that your letters to me should be directed to your court-appointed counsel.

I've done my best to piece together the events around the time that Sgt. Byrd destroyed the evidence. I've read through Oscar's correspondence, the EAR Sheriff's files, the newspapers, VPD reports, and talked with Sgt. Vaughan and Detective Shelby. There were several things converging in February 1977. The most glaring to me now is the discovery of the EAR's blood type, which was found to be "A," and given to Detective Shelby on February 8, 1977. This matched the type A that Grubb developed from Blake's supposed "semen" crusted dirt (NOTE: assuming the sample was semen). *The only possible blood type that had been developed for Donna's killer now matched the EAR.* This information would have been added to California CII immediately, so that other police jurisdictions could try to match their cases and offenders to the EAR.

Additionally, on *the same day* that Sgt. Byrd ordered the evidence destroyed, a new reward was announced in the *Tulare Advance Register* for the murders of Claude Snelling and Jennifer Armour:

The Tulare County Secret Witness program has grown by another $750 with donations from the Tulare County Deputy Sheriff's Association, Visalia Police Association, and county Peace Officers Association.

The groups combined to donate the $750 bringing the total Secret Witness fund to more than $6,000.

Begun last June, the Secret Witness program has accumulated valuable leads in several serious unsolved county crimes, according to Sgt. Richard McGowen of the Tulare County Sheriff's Office. So far, the Secret Witness panel has authorized payment for the solution of one series of crimes—a spate of rapes in the Porterville area.

"Rewards will be paid for information on two cases included on the Tulare County Secret Witness list:

Reward $4,000
Homicide
Claude Ray Snelling, 45
532 Whitney Lane, Visalia

Reward $1,500
Homicide
Jennifer Lynn Armour, 15

It seems likely that the growing reward, and the focus on Beth and Jennifer's cases together, increased the pressure on Sgt. Byrd. The girls were the same age and physical type, and were kidnapped a few blocks apart from each other. They were in the same class at Mt. Whitney, and VPD was aware that the VR targeted homes of the school's female students and teachers. Additionally, the VR had been active in the area around Jennifer's kidnapping in the weeks leading up to it. There were no other girls killed in orange groves along the Friant-Kern Canal in rural Exeter—just Jennifer and Donna.

Secret Witness had just paid out the offered reward in the Ben Galloway case, as Byrd would have been well aware. Was TCSO Richard

McGowen wondering if the man who almost killed his brother, and was responsible for Snelling the same offender who also attacked his next door neighbor and possibly killed Jennifer? How could he ***not*** have put all of that information together and then wondered about Donna too? Byrd was likely under an enormous amount of pressure to hide any connection between Donna's murder, the VR, the EAR, and Jennifer. Inquiries were coming in from the Sacramento Sheriff, VPD, Ray Donahue, and now reporters. If Oscar was executed, but then the truth of his innocence came out from a witness, arrest, or the evidence, everyone who committed or suborned perjury would also then be facing their own murder charges.

The request to have the fingerprints from Oscar's truck compared against suspects, the match of the EAR's blood type to Grubb's findings, and the Secret Witness reward all converged on Byrd at exactly the same moment. His reaction made it clear that he knew that the evidence would prove who really killed Donna, and it wasn't Oscar Clifton.

Chapter Twelve Sources

1. Special Circumstances Death Penalty Verdict, July 15, 1976

2. Exeter Sun - July 21, 1976

3. Motion for New Trial, July 15, 1976

4. Hearing on Motion New Trial, August 31, 1976

5. Oscar/Donahue Correspondence

6. Clifton Sentencing Hearing, September 16, 1976

7. Voir Dire Jury Selection Testimony, June 23, 1976

8. Porterville Recorder - July 20, 1976

9. Visalia Times-Delta - September 28, 1976

10. SSO Lowe Interview w/ Mike Boyd KCRA, February 1977

11. VPD Report - Vaughan November 20, 1975

12. TCSO Evidence Receipt, February 7, 1977

13. TCSO Chain of Custody Cards #1-14

14. TCSO Report - Lovett February 28, 1977

15. **TCSO Report - Johnson April 9, 1977**
16. **TCSO Receipt - Lovett February 7, 1977**
17. **California Penal Code, §135**
18. **Sacramento Crime Lab Report, February 11, 1977**
19. **Tulare Advance-Register, February 28, 1977**

CHAPTER THIRTEEN

"Sure loser"

Oscar to Ray Donahue, ***May 30, 1977***:

I hope you've seen that the Visalia Police think that the Sacramento Rapist is the one that murdered Claude Snelling, plus some other cases. Note if that's so, he was there in December of 1975, by what the Police say. Note that the Sacramento Rapist uses a ski cap or a ski mask. Plus he always leaves something of someone else at the places that he does these things. The attorneys and the newsman that are trying to help me, found this out. This Sacramento Rapist carries a knife and gun, so the Police say. Will you ask the Visalia Police what the other cases are? What kind of cases? Please do this before the Sheriff's Office covers it up. I know they are not telling all that is still going on, but I have people writing me that I don't know, and telling me.

Now, you may not have received them, but you should have received copies of all tests run. That's the only way you could have proved that I was innocent. Now, since you didn't, the appeal attorney can't see them. I paid you to get all that would help, so ask for these things. I need all of them to show to people who are trying to help, so that they can go over everything. They've been here two times, and they're coming back again this week. I told them that I haven't been able to get those lab reports or my trial transcript yet, so please get these things so they can help. Some officers may see you about my case. They may bring out the truth.

I know the truth that can help is in the lab reports. We should have had those before my trial. The rape charge should have been dismissed on December 27, 1975, when Dr. Miller made his report. They just used that to run me down with. I hope the day comes that they will have to go through what I have. Then they will understand just how it feels to be framed.

I can tell you this much, by looking at the picture with the bike in them… I have looked at these pictures and reports almost every day trying to understand what went on there. You can look straight across the bike in more than one tire track picture, how did the car go right across the bike? It had to be dumped there.

Would you please go talk to the man, Wayne Matheney, that went back out to the body with Renteria, and ask him if he looked at the body, or went up to it[?] Ask him what kind of boots, or shoes he had. Please go get a picture of the spray rig, take it yourself, and the tires also.

"Would you please get a court order to keep them from doing away with the two so called rags, that is a shirt, and a sleeve of that shirt. They were near the shoe. The ski cap also.

I just wish you had the time to sit down and talk with me, then I could show you a few things in these photos and reports that do not make sense. Most of all, in the reports, one cop's report is not like his statement at my trial, plus one of the other cop's reports proves he lied to the Grand Jury. You may not want to help me, for you keep saying "ask my appeal attorneys"—but they were not my trial attorney, and they don't know since they weren't there. So, please answer my questions. Thank you for your time, and please come here if you will.

Donahue:

I have received several letters from you over the past few weeks. I have forwarded to you all the reports that I have, or have available to me. I've also received a copy of the appeal brief filed by your attorney in the appeal. His appeal is not upon any of the items that you are requesting, and I do not therefore understand your repeated requests for items which I do not have in my possession. Accordingly, I do not feel that there is anything more that I can do to be of assistance.

Oscar:

You have said that the things I am asking for are not part of the appeal. I understand this, but the lab reports were part of my case, and they should have been given to you. They could have helped at my trial. They should have been available to you in January, 1976. There is no way you should not have asked for them long ago.

Oscar was correct, about *everything*. He had a TV reporter and volunteer attorneys who believed that the VR/EAR had killed Donna, and they were trying to prove it. Their efforts had reached members of law enforcement, and Oscar really believed that Donahue would tell the officers that he agreed that Oscar was innocent, and that the VR/EAR was the real murderer. That was not going to happen. Oscar also accurately described exactly what had happened when Sgt. Byrd was confronted with the fact that the VR killed Donna, and used the specific MO of planting evidence to frame innocent men: "Please do this before the Sheriff's Office covers it up."

By the time the new information reached Oscar in San Quentin, the evidence was gone. Sgt. Byrd had a head start, and his cover-up was complete before Oscar even got in the race. Soon, Sacramento Sheriff Lowe told the press that the VR was not the EAR, and he called VPD and had Sgt. Vaughan's team taken off the case. That convinced the Sacramento TV reporter and the volunteers helping Oscar that the EAR had not killed Donna, and they drifted away. Sheriff Lowe not only gave Joe DeAngelo forty years of undeserved freedom, costing at least a dozen future lives, but these actions also helped hide the truth of Donna and Jennifer's murders, and the "new suspect" that should have freed Oscar from prison.

This last batch of letters to Donahue are hard to read. I hear a man screaming his innocence from death row, and a grossly overpaid defense attorney expressing nothing more than impatience for being mildly bothered. Oscar was not citing feelings or theories, he was pointing to facts and evidence that proved constitutional errors at his trial, and he had even identified the real killer. One thing Donahue tried to point out, that Oscar didn't really understand, was that his appeal was over. The brief had been filed, and it didn't contain any of the issues Oscar had raised. It was too late—again.

The State Public Defender's office had submitted a brief that was Oscar's *one and only* chance to argue ***all*** of the legal errors in the investigation, Grand Jury, and trial. Oscar had not been given the trial transcript, and Donahue completely ignored the request for his list of appealable errors and issues preserved through objections. Only two issues were appealed: the death sentence and the Miranda violations on the night of Oscar's arrest.

The brief was only about twenty pages of arguments, and looks like a poorly written and researched fifth grade book report. Inexplicably, the arguments seem as if they were written by the prosecutor; they assert that Oscar was 100% guilty, but the death penalty should be overturned because of sentencing errors. His appellate attorney, Ted Isles, even argued against Oscar getting a new sentencing hearing. Isles clearly hated Oscar, believed that he was guilty, and committed gross legal malpractice in his representation.

If Isles had taken the time to listen to Oscar, read the documents, and pay attention, he would have easily seen an avalanche of suppressed evidence, tainted and coerced witnesses, shocking police and prosecutorial misconduct, and the real killer. Henry Borbon's attorneys had just argued the **exact** same issues and won a new trial. Isles could have obtained a copy of that brief, and just replaced a few names and dates.

I had to ask, who was Ted Isles, and why did he seem to want to keep Oscar in prison? Looking at Isles' history felt too much like a repeat of Jay Powell. They both really wanted to be judges, more than anything. Isles ran for Municipal Court Judge in Chico in 1970, and was asked about his views on public defense work for an article published on Tuesday, May 26, 1970 in the *Chico Enterprise-Record*:

> There are attorneys in the state of California who are ready to challenge the constitutionality of the public defender system on the grounds that it is discriminatory against the middle class who pay for it, and who can't use it.
>
> When asked why he was running for the court post, Isles gave four reasons:
>
> I am eminently qualified, I want to live here, I want to get back where the action is, and it pays well.

Isles lost that election, with only 26% of the vote. In 1975, Isles sought appointment from Governor Brown to be Superior Court Judge in Placer County. He was not appointed, and another disappointed candidate said of Brown: "The appointments appear to be from the minorities, women, people who are involved in legal aid, ACLU… totally different from the usual appointment."

Isles ran against an incumbent for Sacramento Superior Court Judge in 1976; he got only 34% of the votes that year. That led him to take a position with the newly formed State Public Defender's Office. His sudden interest in public defense work appeared to be wholly motivated by his desire to win favor with Governor Brown, and a future judicial appointment.

As terrible as Donahue's defense was, he did at least attempt to preserve a couple of key critical issues for appeal. Perhaps the strongest, and most important, was his objection to Morton's testimony about the tire and heel print evidence as being non-expert, unscientific, and prejudicial. That objection, coupled with the suppressed expert opinion from the San Diego lab that the heel print was ***not*** a match to Oscar's, *and* the post-conviction disclosure that the photos Morton relied upon for his opinion had been taken with a defective camera that distorted the images, should have been enough to overturn the conviction and get Oscar a new trial. Those were blatant constitutional due process violations. Instead, Ted Isles told Oscar that the issues weren't appealable:

> The photographs of foot prints which were exhibits at your trial will be available to you, or your trial attorney if you win your appeal and have a new trial. At that time, you can obtain discovery of the San Diego laboratory report concerning the footprints, if such a report exists. Mr. Donahue's letter to you of May 6, 1977 states that he did not receive such a report, and that his information was that the San Diego laboratory could not identify the footprints. Even assuming that the San Diego report exists, it has no relevance to your appeal; and because of the other evidence received at your trial, your conviction could not be successfully attacked in habeas corpus proceedings even if we speculate that the San Diego laboratory positively identified the footprints as being someone else's.
>
> It is a mistake to water down a brief with arguments which are sure losers. I would be doing you a disservice if I let you be the one who decided what goes in your briefs. If you win your appeal, your trial attorney will decide whether to use the new evidence at your second trial.

Isles was *one hundred percent wrong*, and his decision blocked Oscar from later raising the foot and tire prints on appeal.

Another issue that Isles rejected was the judge's decision not to move the trial to another county due to extreme pre-trial press coverage. Oscar argued with Isles, and pointed out the stories about the charges against him for rape and sodomy, which were quickly dropped (because the crimes literally didn't happen)—Powell had intentionally, in bad faith, corrupted the local jury pool with highly prejudicial false information. Isles said that it didn't matter:

> The venue point was not raised because it has no merit. Adverse publicity is not enough in itself to require a change of venue.
>
> Regardless of your willingness to pay for copies of the transcripts, please understand that this office cannot ask its secretaries to spend their time photocopying records as long as yours.

This is particularly frustrating. Denial of a change of venue motion was an easy issue to win on appeal, and I have never seen a more clear-cut case of a tainted jury pool and biased, inaccurate information released to the media. This is another example of an argument that Isles could have cut and pasted from Henry Borbon's brief. After Borbon's conviction was overturned, his attorney won a change of venue for his second trial, and there was nothing nearly as inflammatory as fake rape and sodomy charges. Again, that was Oscar's one and only chance to make that argument, and Isles ignored it.

Some of Isles' letters to Oscar were not only condescending, but almost comically incorrect:

> You must leave strategy decisions to us. Nothing you have sent us, and nothing you have described in your letters would have any effect on your appeal; nor would it provide you with any basis to successfully petition for habeas corpus. What your trial judge previously ordered to be given to Mr. Donahue is of no importance now, since no claim was made at trial that the discovery order was violated. The record does not show that the district attorney acted in bad faith. The record does not show that law enforcement officers were in the lineup.

Donahue had filed several motions that argued that DA Powell and ADA Bleier were violating the discovery order. That led to the hearings where Bleier argued that he was not required to give the defense any of the written forensic findings. That issue, in and of itself, was proof of "bad faith" from the DA's office—what possible "good faith" reason would they have for preventing the defense from seeing the forensic testing? Isles' last response in that letter was just gaslighting. Not only were ***all*** of the other men in the lineup TCSO deputies, their names and ranks are *clearly listed* in Detective McKinney's report of December 30, 1975:

1. Det. Sgt. McCoy - TCSO
2. Cadet Gordon - TCSO
3. Oscar Archie Clifton - Suspect this Case
4. Dep. Harris - TCSO
5. Dep. Johnson - TCSO
6. Dep. Franzen - TCSO

The record of Gloria Mascorro's identification of Oscar was riddled with constitutional violations.

Isles kept making references to "new evidence," and then saying that it didn't matter. Again, this was an element of Henry Borbon's conviction reversal—DA Powell had intentionally hidden critical exculpatory evidence about the potential murder weapon—yet another paragraph that could have been lifted straight from that brief. Oscar had a "new" suspect, the VR/EAR, and he had evidence that was "new" because Powell had intentionally hidden it from the defense. Both of those are appealable issues. Of course, Isles was full of praise for both Donahue and Powell:

> To spare you future disappointment, regardless of whether you would have liked to see other investigations made, or

other facts placed in evidence, the appellate court would certainly say that Mr. Donahue represented you diligently. We have to work with the record we already have—not with some different record that you would like us to assemble using new evidence. When your appeal is over, we can better advise you to the time which you must serve if you do not win a new trial.

You must accept the fact that it is an uphill battle. Based on the prosecutor's evidence the appellate court is not going to look kindly on your case. I cannot guarantee that my approach will win—but I can guarantee that your approach would certainly lose.

Reading this from Isles is very much like reading his brief; he could not stop arguing that Oscar was guilty, and there were no grounds to overturn his conviction—only his death sentence:

Your unending discussions of the evidence have forced me to conclude that either you do not read my letters, or else you do not understand them. I have no reason to think that a personal interview with you would be any different.

Because of the shocking nature of the crime charged, and because the jury believed the DA's evidence, the appellate court will be very reluctant to accept the Miranda argument I have raised. However, you can be sure that you would have no chance of winning with any of the points of law you have raised (or with any of the other points that I examined and found to have no merit).

The only good news in Isles' last letter to Oscar was that he wasn't going to be representing him in the future:

My secretary mailed all of the transcripts to you yesterday. Insofar as my legal research is concerned, you will have to settle for what is in the filed briefs. Your appeal in the state courts is over. If you yourself personally wish to file a petition for cert with the US Supreme Court, it must be done within 90 days after May 18, 1978.

Generally speaking, issues which were, or could have been raised on appeal will not be considered on a petition for writ of habeas corpus. However, my advice is that you raise them anyway just to be on the safe side—and let the court say "no." Contrary to what many jail house lawyers and members of the public think, appellate courts do not reverse murder convictions on "technicalities" where the DA introduced substantial evidence of guilt (which the jury believed).

From this time on, you will have to rely on legal sources other than the State Public Defender, since our role in your case is finished. I have always felt that the evidence against you was "too pat" to be true. Good luck to you.

Isles had the power to kill Oscar's chance for a new trial, and he did. You can't win an appeal if you don't even ask the court to consider the issues, and Isles plainly refused to do so. The circular argument is mind-numbing. Oscar was barred from raising every one of the constitutional violations he had asked Isles to include in his brief—and then Isles says Oscar's choices are "limited." *Whose fault was that?* This was truly a no-win situation for Oscar.

Isles' advice that Oscar raise the issues anyway, and "let the court say no," after arguing he wasn't going to "water down" his brief with issues that were "sure losers," is insufferable. I've talked with people who worked with Isles at that time, and they described him as a forced hire, someone who was pro police and prosecution, but was brought in to make the public defender's office look balanced—not too liberal. Isles was rude, incompetent, and completely wasted Oscar's direct appeal and his best chance at overturning his conviction. There is no way to justify his dismissive and condescending tone, or how shockingly wrong his legal opinions were.

Imagine sitting on death row and finding out that your trial attorney never received ***any*** reports from the forensic lab that tested the evidence, and that the experts hired to examine the heel print and the leaf from your truck told the DA that they *didn't* match you. Then, when confronted, your trial attorney just shrugs, and your appeal counsel berates you for wasting his valuable time.

Under our legal system, Oscar had two choices for his state appeals:

- He could argue that TCSO and DA Powell had violated his due process rights by hiding, planting, and lying about evidence; pressuring witnesses to make false identifications; presenting incorrect, misleading, and non-expert forensic testimony; and tainting the jury with knowingly false statements *or*
- He could claim ineffective assistance of counsel based on the threats Donahue received, the lack of proper diligence on the case, and failure to preserve the due process violations through proper objections on the record.

Ted Isles refused ***both*** options and instead tried to gaslight Oscar. The real truth of our justice system is that trials are meant to find the defendant guilty and generate headlines for the DA's re-election, and appeals are designed to make sure those convictions are maintained even in light of evidence that proves actual innocence.

In the end, DA Powell admitted to the appeals court that there were no "special circumstances" to support the death penalty. The attempted rape was not a separate crime, just the supposed motive for the murder, and it could not be used for the death penalty enhancement. Although Judge Bradley had found that Donna's kidnapping had a purpose separate from just facilitating the homicide, the appeals court did not agree. The attempted rape and kidnapping charges merged into the homicide, and there were no separate felonies to qualify for the death penalty, so Oscar's sentence was commuted to life in prison with the possibility of parole on May 22, 1978.

Two weeks later, Jay Powell faced his first re-election primary, and he came in *third place* of four contenders. With just over 20% of the vote, he failed to advance to the general election—a shocking, yet fitting, outcome for the incumbent district attorney.

By September 12, 1978, Oscar was representing himself again, and turned back to Donahue for help:

> Now what I need from you is some advice as to how I can obtain all lab reports so that I can have a lab run tests on them. I'm talking about all—the shirt with blood, and hair, and foot prints. Tire prints, and then everything that was put in as evidence.
>
> I also would like a report about the paint test that was run on my pickup with the bike. The court had ordered them to give you all reports. Also one from San Diego by Mr. Harris, of the shoes, or boot or what ever it was. This report had to [have] been helpful to me or they would have given you a copy, and had him in the trial.
>
> There was a report by Dr. John Strother, of the University of California. He compared the leaf on the mirror with some from the grove where the body was found. These reports should have been given to you before my trial.
>
> Now Mr. Donahue, you could help me to get a new trial if you would. You know more about my case than anyone else. I know a lot was left out, some that you did not see. I hope you understand, and if you know any way that might help, let me know. As soon as I receive these things I'll have a lab go over them. Can you tell me one that will not lie about their tests, no matter if it is good for me or bad, all I ask for is what is true.
>
> Please help me get these reports so that I can file a writ to prove that they did withhold evidence that could have helped me.
>
> Thank you for your time.

All of the evidence that Oscar wanted to have tested had already been destroyed *more than a year earlier*. What he was suggesting was impeaching the state's lab results through independent testing—something that he had paid for during the trial, and believed was being done. The fact that the evidence was intentionally destroyed and could not be impeached or challenged was a clear due process violation, and should have prevented the Tulare DA's office from using any of the destroyed evidence or testing results in their arguments against Oscar on appeal. That clearly would have overturned the conviction with no chance of a retrial. Of course, subsequent Tulare DAs just hid the evidence destruction, then lied about it.

On September 21, 1980, Oscar wrote his last letter to Donahue:

> Just a line to inform you that after almost five years, I now have the eyewitnesses that did, in fact, place me on Garden Street at 3:30 pm on December 26, 1975. They even gave statements to the Sheriff's officers. Why were their statements withheld from my trial? You know as well as I do that the prosecution did in fact know about them. One of these witnesses even went to the trial courtroom to testify on my behalf, but was told that they did not need them.
>
> I am filing a motion for a new trial on the grounds of withheld evidence known to the prosecution, but not made available to me. Everyone may have given up, but I'll never give up until I find out just who set me up. I now have nine new statements that will help me get a new trial. I also have evidence that should have come out at my trial. If you know of any way that you can help me to get a new trial due to the fact that the prosecution withheld these eyewitnesses, please let me know since I have got the hearing without the help of any attorney.

Donahue:

Thank you for your letter. I am happy to hear that you state you are making some progress in your appeal motions. I do not know of any witnesses withheld by the prosecution during your trial. Good luck to you in the future.

For the first time in the case, Oscar had something go right. It came to him in the form of the aunt of Johnny Guerber, the boy who had talked to Oscar on Garden Street. Guerber's aunt contacted Oscar's family, and told them that not only had TCSO Chamberlain interviewed Johnny, but also that his mother had taken him to the courthouse to testify, and someone had sent them away. Johnny no longer had any memory of the interview, but his mother, Laverne Easley, had been present, and she remembered what his statement had been. Oscar was able to use her statement to get a hearing in Federal Court based on a *Brady* violation—the state had intentionally suppressed and hidden an exculpatory witness.

Once he had the hearing, Oscar got new attorneys, and they reached out to both Pettyjohn and Donahue to confirm, for certain, that neither of them had any knowledge of Johnny Guerber during the trial. That affidavit was filed with the court on March 2, 1981. TCSO flatly denied that any of their deputies had interviewed Guerber, and said it must have been Pettyjohn. I had to roll my eyes at that, since Mrs. Easley had described a red-headed deputy, with a badge and police car, which *had to be* "Rusty" Chamberlain.

However, a few months later, on April 29th, right before the scheduled hearing, Oscar's attorneys received a new letter from Pettyjohn, saying that he had found a scrap of paper with the name Guerber on it, but he couldn't remember why he had the note, or what it meant. In the defense file, I found the original, hand-written draft of Pettyjohn's letter, with Donahue's corrections on it. The final letter was typed by Donahue's secretary. Why did Donahue ask Pettyjohn to change his story, and try to kill Oscar's appeal hearing? Pettyjohn tried to offer an explanation in a deposition before the hearing:

Pettyjohn: I looked through my entire file because it took me twice going through my notes and file to find it.

Bernstein: Did you go through it once and come to the conclusion that you had never talked to this boy?

A: Well, I didn't find it where I had talked to him, no. So I went through it again.

Q: Did Mr. Donahue ever ask you to look through your file?

A: Yes, because he had talked to you first; told me you had called.

He said that he had nothing in his file regarding a Guerber boy. At that time, I couldn't find anything in my file. So we are still very much in doubt and can't recall how we came to get that information… As I said before, I went through them once and didn't find 'em. And when I looked again, I came across those, which is the only notes I could find or that are in my file referring to Guerber.

Q: Looking at those notes now today, are you—is the most that you're able to say is that based on these notes, that you may have talked to those boys?

A: Yes—or for some reason or the other I didn't talk to them—I have a cross mark there indicating that I either was not going to contact them, or had already contacted them. I don't know which.

As an attorney, the first thing I saw there was that Pettyjohn was being very careful not to commit perjury, while still trying to help the DA's office and TCSO. He refused to give any meaning to the note, and was just trying to create enough doubt for the court to maintain Oscar's conviction. The idea that both Pettyjohn and Donahue would totally forget about a potential witness on Garden Street is not believable. If the witness said that he saw the freezer loading, but didn't see Oscar, that would be damaging, and they would worry about that witness. If he said yes, I saw and talked to Oscar, they would have transported him to the trial in a limousine with a security escort. This is the worst lying and cover-up ever. Someone had applied pressure to Donahue to make him change his story, and it felt like they had used the stick, not the carrot.

Oscar's appeal hearing was set to start in Visalia at 9:00 am on May 15, 1981, and Ray Donahue was the only witness who mattered. If he took the witness stand and said that DA Powell had not told him about Guerber during the trial, it would be a clear *Brady* violation, and the court would have no choice but to order a new trial. DA Powell's statement that "nobody saw you there" was the crux of his case against Oscar's alibi, and the fact that he knew it was a lie and his bad faith would just be further reason to overturn Oscar's conviction.

Donahue had two choices: he could tell the truth, be blamed for overturning Oscar's conviction, and accept the consequences of publicly accusing TCSO and the DA's office of misconduct; or he could commit perjury, and say that he had known about Guerber during the trial, but decided not to call him as a witness. The truth would make him and his family outcasts in the community, but the lie would open him up to charges of ineffective assistance of counsel, a civil suit for malpractice, and possible sanctions.

On the night before the hearing, Donahue attended the annual County Bar Association dinner at the Tulare Golf Club. Most of the local attorneys were at the event, and Donahue spoke with Superior Court Judge Ballantyne and spent time chatting with people at different tables. He told the other attorneys that his son, Tim, was getting ready to leave the DA's office and join his firm. Donahue left the dinner around midnight for the twenty-minute drive north to his home in Visalia. Two hours later, Kings County Sheriffs received a call to respond to the scene of a fatal crash on Boswell Cotton Company property. Ray Donahue was dead, and there would be no hearing that morning.

Donahue's car hit the south bank of the canal after driving straight at a hairpin turn in the road. Newspaper reports stated that the car flew 60 feet across the canal, but the distance is more like 100 feet. The physics of the crash as described are impossible. Accident consultants

I've asked say that Donahue's car could not have reached the south bank of the canal. However, the bigger question is why Donahue drove forty minutes to the southwest, past endless cotton fields, instead of north to his home. That was not a wrong turn or mistake. If he drove there alone to meet someone in a secluded spot along the canal after midnight, I have a lot of other questions.

Site of Ray Donahue's Fatal Car Crash
Credit: Reid

I've never seen photos of the accident itself, so I don't know the condition of the car or exactly how it was positioned. I have two different descriptions from the Kings County Coroner's Office: Coroner Moore said that Donahue's body showed "no obvious external injuries," but later, the office's spokesman stated that "there were visible chest injuries." Donahue's death certificate lists "multiple injuries due to trauma," with no further details. His body was cremated, there was no coroner's inquest, and the manner of death was listed as accidental. Oscar believed that Donahue had been murdered to prevent him from testifying at the hearing. I can't disprove that, but I tend to lean more towards suicide.

Murder makes sense if you believe that the topic of Oscar's hearing came up at the Bar Meeting, and Donahue mentioned that he was going to tell the truth and say that he hadn't known about Guerber. If Donahue said that he expected Oscar to get a new trial, any of the men who knew about the destroyed evidence could have panicked. I can't imagine that Sgt. Byrd, Sgt. Lovett, or Deputy Johnson were at the dinner, but someone could have called them, or there could have been a person from the DA's office who had participated in the decision to destroy the evidence, and heard Donahue. If Donahue didn't testify, Oscar wouldn't win his appeal, the conviction would stand, there would be no new trial, nobody would know the evidence was gone, and there was no risk of their getting fired or going to jail. That is a motive for murder, and exactly what Oscar believed. I can't disprove it, but I haven't been able to find any evidence to support it.

The same scenario also supports suicide. If Donahue said he expected a new trial, someone at the dinner could have told him that the evidence was gone, that Oscar would walk free, and Byrd, Lovett, and Johnson would go to jail instead—and it would all be Donahue's fault for telling the truth. If he lied and said he knew about Guerber and did not call him to testify, that would be perjury, and Oscar would not have rested until he saw Donahue disbarred and broke for being so negligent, as well as being sent to prison. Add some drinks to that mix, and I can see Donahue feeling despondent, going for a country drive to think, and letting himself go straight at the hairpin curve.

Oscar's hearing was rescheduled for July, and the judge ordered TCSO to make a new search for reports or interview tapes that mentioned Johnny Guerber. The deputy assigned to the task didn't find those, but he located the tape of Chamberlain's interview with Brent Trueblood. It was found in a box of things that had been cleared out of Sgt. Byrd's filing cabinet when Major Crimes moved to a new office. The tape was quickly transcribed, and Oscar's defense team scrambled to use it with only a couple days until the hearing.

Tim Donahue had taken control of his father's law office, and had firmly refused to turn over the defense file to Oscar or his attorneys. Brent Trueblood said that he no longer remembered December 26, 1975, or the details of his interview, so they were going to need to rely on the tape. Suddenly, Rusty Chamberlain thought to check his old briefcase, and magically found the photos that had Trueblood's identification of Oscar that he had "forgotten" to turn over to the defense.

The Trueblood tape all but assured Oscar would win and get a new trial. There was no question that Trueblood saw Oscar at the Rose house during the freezer loading, and coupled with Guerber's prior statement that he spoke to Oscar, just as Trueblood had told Chamberlain, it was a slam dunk—until it wasn't. Tim Donahue was working for the DA's office, and said that he invited their investigator, TCSO Deathriage, to look through Oscar's defense file and take whatever he wanted, after denying the defense access to the same file. Yes, that violated attorney-client privilege, and probably ten other rules of professional conduct for attorneys. Tim should have been disbarred immediately.

Deathriage walked into the hearing with an item that he said he took out of Donahue's file—an invoice from Pettyjohn that had time billed for interviews with Guerber, Trueblood, their friend Tracy Artley, and a man named Jim Erwin. The defense objected to the "invoice" being admitted to evidence for a number of good reasons. Donahue was dead, and Pettyjohn was too ill to attend the hearing. They were literally the only two people who could possibly authenticate the invoice as being a true and original document. That is the bare minimum for having a document admitted into evidence in court—it has to be both reliable and relevant. It took only a glance to know it was probably fake. Pettyjohn had just testified in his deposition that he and Donahue had gone through their files twice, and failed to find any document with the name Guerber on it.

Instead, the judge allowed Tim Donahue to verify the invoice. Not only was he not working in his father's office in 1976, he hadn't even gone to law school yet. Tim had no direct knowledge upon which to base his statement. Additionally, he worked as a prosecutor for the Tulare DA's Office. The judge should have been ashamed of himself for even considering a document sprung on the defense in open court, let alone one that couldn't be authenticated. The "invoice" changed everything. It raised the possibility that Pettyjohn and Donahue had known about the witnesses, but had not told Oscar or called the boys to testify. That was allowed under the broad discretion given to defense attorneys.

TCSO Rusty Chamberlain testified that he gave his report and interview tapes to Sgt. Byrd, who said he didn't remember any of it, but he would have told DA Powell and Donahue about any witnesses. Powell said he didn't remember hearing the names Guerber and Trueblood until the hearing, but he would have told Donahue. They were all careful to say they "would" have told Donahue, but never that they actually "did," because that would have been perjury. It was all a lot of "maybe," but it raised enough doubt. Donahue wasn't there to tell his story; the fake invoice told it for him. The judge said he was disturbed by the events surrounding the witnesses, but Donahue likely knew, so it wasn't a *Brady* violation.

Oscar's attorneys got to work immediately after the hearing. Brent Trueblood signed a statement saying that he never spoke to Pettyjohn, or anyone other than Rusty Chamberlain. Guerber's and Artley's mothers said the same: They never met with, or spoke with, Pettyjohn—the invoice was a lie. The addition of Jim Erwin was a huge mistake made by the person who created the fake invoice. Bill Rose had hired Jim Erwin to finish the work on the Garden Street house after Oscar was in jail, awaiting trial. That was in March 1976, a month after Oscar had been indicted by the Grand Jury. Jim Erwin knew nothing about December 26, 1975, there would have been no reason for Pettyjohn to interview him about Oscar's alibi, and Jim Erwin swore, under penalty of perjury, that it never happened. The invoice was a complete fraud.

Oscar's attorney won a new Federal hearing, but suffered an immediate setback when the Tulare DA changed his strategy. He admitted that Guerber and Trueblood had not been disclosed as witnesses to the defense (Byrd and Powell had been "mistaken" at the 1981 hearing), but it wasn't a *Brady* violation because Donahue's discovery request had only asked for tapes of "prosecution witnesses," and since the boys were ***defense*** witnesses, TCSO and DA Powell had no duty to disclose them. The judge agreed. That changed the standard for the hearing. The judge would have to find that if the witnesses had been disclosed, the jury would have, *for certain*, voted to acquit Oscar. The defense team was crushed. It was an impossible standard to meet, and they warned Oscar.

The hearing went as well as it could have for Oscar. Pettyjohn had died a few days before, but everyone testified that they had never met or spoken to him. Trueblood said that he didn't remember the day or his statement in any detail, so his interview tape stood on its own. The judge ruled that the trial jury could have found that Trueblood was mistaken about the day, time, or person he saw, and he upheld Oscar's conviction. TCSO Chamberlain, Sgt. Byrd, and DA Jay Powell intentionally hid two critical alibi witnesses, and got away with it. If the boys' testimony didn't prove Oscar's innocence, why did they hide them? If they proved his guilt, why didn't Powell call them as witnesses for the state? It's all very depressing, even forty-five years later.

In 1993, the Innocence Project agreed to represent Oscar in his attempts to have the case evidence tested for male DNA. Instead of opposing the testing, the Tulare DA should have immediately disclosed the evidence destruction, and told the judge that testing was impossible. Instead, the DA stalled—for years. Finally, in September 1997, the DA stated that the evidence was "*gone*." The court simply denied Oscar's request for DNA testing with *no inquiry* into the illegal destruction.

Oscar's attorney then fought for another four years to get any kind of explanation, which came in the form of a report from the DA's investigator in September 2001. The report confirmed that Sgt.

Byrd had personally ordered the evidence destroyed in 1977, but the investigator said he had located Donna's pants, her underwear, and Oscar's pocketknife in a box at the court clerk's office, and those items were available for DNA testing.

The items were sent to none other than Ed Blake, who at that point had a successful DNA testing lab. I have a lot of thoughts about the Innocence Project trusting Blake and agreeing to use his lab. Although it could have been worse, he did manage to find a way to harm Oscar, and his attorneys didn't seem to notice it—at all. The underpants were examined for sperm cells, and when none were found, they were put aside. Blake sampled some spots on Donna's pants which appeared to be menstrual blood and collected some pet hairs, but did not find any sperm cells or male DNA.

Blake took apart Oscar's knife, and used swabs on surfaces inside it. They were negative for the presumptive test for blood. He then took a test strip and directly rubbed it on a rusty spring inside the knife, got a positive reading for oxide (rust is iron oxide, and the test is not to be used on rusted surfaces), and reported that he had found a positive *presumptive* reaction for blood on Oscar's knife. He refused to run the test for human blood, a required confirmation, or do ABO typing on it.

This all sounded very, very familiar. This was Blake's MO: throw the testing protocols like dilution rates, development times, and surface preparation in the garbage; refuse to conduct the necessary confirmatory tests for human blood or sperm cells; and then draw incorrect and overstated scientific conclusions from the results. Blake did not find human blood; he did not even test for it. He found oxide on a sample of iron oxide, and only when he directly rubbed it on the testing strip, yet he reported finding blood. It was a repeat of his false positive for AP, which he then called "semen." It's infuriating, and all too common in wrongful conviction cases. Forensic "opinions" for sale.

The only good news for Oscar Clifton was that the "material" inside the knife did not contain Donna's DNA or any female DNA, but Blake found a way to turn this into a negative for Oscar too. He stated that the amount of "blood" was too small to obtain a reliable DNA result. Suddenly, the absence of Donna's DNA was made to sound like it was really present—there just wasn't enough to find with testing. Personally, I believe that every single case that involved Ed Blake is suspect, and the presumption should be that he used faulty methods and overstated results in his reports and testimony.

The Innocence Project attorneys didn't seem to take Blake at his word, and asked for the forensic analytical bench notes, which he was required to provide when asked. He didn't. The defense got a court order, and Blake still refused. They got another order, and he stalled, but eventually turned over the notes. Oscar's attorneys gave it to their DNA expert for review—they were certain that the killer's DNA should have been on Donna's pants and underwear, but they completely ignored the knife testing. The information about the rust, test strip, missing human blood, and ABO test was all right there, if anyone had bothered to read it. Instead, Oscar's attorneys just accepted that there was blood on the spring inside Oscar's knife, and repeated it as fact in later briefs.

Immediately after that DNA testing was finished, Charles Morton told the Tulare DA that he had suddenly found some items in storage, but none were case evidence. They were mostly the hairs and fibers removed from Donna's and Oscar's clothing that Morton had mounted to slides on March 25, 1976. Oscar wanted every one of the items held by Morton sent for DNA testing, but the DA objected, saying that they weren't *made or held as evidence*. The judge seemed to be frustrated, and ordered that TCSO, Morton, Grubb, and Blake all search their files and storage, and turn over everything they had on the case to the defense. Grubb and Blake said they didn't have notes, reports, or items. But, in May 2002, Morton finally turned over hundreds of pages of lab reports. Oscar finally had the details from all of the forensic documents that ADA Bleier had fought so hard to hide from the defense in 1976.

That was the very first time that Oscar or his attorneys ever received *anything* that documented the original evidence examinations used at trial. The ABO testing of the sweater hair, the results of which excluded Donna, and the Type A on the pubic hair sample, which excluded Oscar, were both right there. There was also other information, like notes written by Morton during a 1985 phone call with Tulare ADA Couillard that said both: "pubic hair sample destroyed by B. Johnson," *and* "M. Grubb indicated type A." Couillard knew right then and there that the evidence had been destroyed by TCSO, but did not disclose it to the defense. He then actively pretended not to know anything about it for at least sixteen years. Worse, by far, was the fact that he also knew Oscar's blood type O had been excluded from the pubic hair sample. According to Morton's notes, Couillard specifically asked him to *leave out* the exculpatory blood typing finding from his report—and Morton complied.

Couillard was a prosecutor and judge in Tulare County from 1980 until he retired in 2007. How many times did he see police and DA misconduct, and just looked the other way? How many of these cases did he go ahead and prosecute, argue on appeal, or adjudicate from the bench? He knew that TCSO forensics officer Brian Johnson had intentionally destroyed critical biological evidence in his custody and control, yet Ronn Couillard did nothing. He didn't have Johnson fired or have his cases thrown out; he just sat silent.

As is their sole focus, the Innocence Project attorneys were still looking for the DNA of Donna's killer, and they saw potential in a slide on Morton's list. It was the one labeled "Victim's Pubic Hair" (VPH). Oscar's attorneys wrote for clarification, and Morton's response was clear: Slide VPH was not an item of evidence and slide VPH did not have semen on it.

Based on Morton's written assurances, the Innocence Project attorneys determined that there were no items remaining that could possibly contain the DNA of Donna's killer, and they withdrew from their representation of Oscar. A huge pile of exculpatory forensic findings that had been intentionally withheld by DA Powell, ADA Bleirer, and ADA Couillard had just been turned over to the defense, and the attorneys merely walked away and left Oscar to represent himself. I understand that the Innocence Project only handles cases that have DNA evidence, but really, come on now. Oscar was still actually innocent, and wrongfully convicted, and they had more than enough to win a Federal Civil Rights case. They didn't even find him another attorney willing to file on the newly discovered *Brady* violations. To me, and to Oscar and his family, this was unforgivably cruel.

Oscar tried to have slide VPH sent for DNA testing, but the California Attorney General's Office sent a team of attorneys to argue against it, and they won. The court found that VPH was not an item of evidence, did not contain semen that could identify the killer, and under no circumstance could the slide be used to exculpate any suspect. Oscar then filed a Federal Civil Rights suit, claiming that Sgt. Byrd, Jay Powell, and other members of TCSO and the DA's office violated his civil rights when they intentionally withheld exculpatory lab findings and alibi witnesses, intentionally destroyed the physical evidence, and put perjured and/or coerced witnesses on the stand. Oscar asked the court to have the hairs and fibers sent for DNA testing. The court said it would consider the testing issue separately, and gave Oscar time to find an attorney to file a proper brief on the issue.

Eventually, years later, in 2010, Oscar's attorney reached a confidential settlement of the case. Oscar agreed to drop his lawsuit against Tulare County, and in return the DA would agree to have a few of the items sent for DNA testing. The court signed an order granting DNA testing of several hairs and fibers, including slide VPH. The hairs on the slide were further examined using "Christmas Tree Stain," a pair of chemicals that specifically stains sperm cells for analysis, and the results were crystal clear: "***no cellular material of any kind was found.***" The hairs were then washed, and that fluid subjected to testing for male DNA. Three very weak alleles were found, but further control testing showed that the wash fluid (reagent blank) had been contaminated with unidentified male DNA, so the testing was invalid, and could not be redone.

I also noticed an entry from the criminalist documenting that he had cut through a piece of tape to remove the slide cover from VPH, so I went back to look at the evidence photo taken when it reached DOJ. Yes, there was a piece of *regular Scotch Tape* on the photograph of this slide—yet another source of possible DNA contamination. I went back further, to handwritten notes from Charles Morton dated June 12, 2002, which stated that when he opened the package of forty-five slides for the first time since 1976, he found the slide covers loose or missing, put them back "in place," and taped them down. So there is no way to know which hairs from the packet were really on Slide VPH by the time it reached DOJ in 2011. It was unthinkable evidence handling—beyond negligent. Those slides belonged in a garbage can, not the DNA lab.

DOJ's report to the DA said that no interpretation of the alleles could be made (could be used to inculpate or exculpate any suspect), and that the court-ordered "semen check" was negative. Oscar's deal with the DA meant that none of the civil rights violations would be heard or decided.

Oscar had one last chance at freedom: his next parole hearing. He had been trying to get parole for thirty years. Every single time he would be recommended based on his lack of "dangerousness" and likelihood to re-offend, and every time he was denied. The parole board always cited the same three factors: Oscar refused to express remorse, the brutal "rape and sodomy" of Donna, and the fact that she had been "run down" on her bike. Why would the parole board think that Donna had been raped, sodomized, and run down when they had the conviction information right in front of them? Because Sgt. Byrd kept writing letters telling the board that was what happened. Later, after Byrd retired, the same letters and in-person testimony to the board continued to be sent by the Tulare DA's Office.

Oscar and his attorneys repeatedly went to the Attorney General, and obtained orders to have the letters with the false facts removed from his file. Not only did they remain, but more and more were added every year. The prison psychologists tried to explain to the parole board that it was unreasonable to ask someone who maintained his innocence to express remorse. How could he feel bad about something that he didn't do? Oscar was told, repeatedly, that if he just admitted guilt and expressed sorrow to the board he could easily win parole, but he refused.

Oscar's 2006 hearing was a perfect example of what had been happening for twenty-five years. Deputy Tulare DA Ruth McKee made her case to the parole board:

> *What Donna Jo does have is something that no fourteen year old should have—and that's a headstone. Donna Jo was bludgeoned over the head with a tire iron, or a crowbar. She was raped... there's evidence that she may even have been sodomized. She was strangled, and she was stabbed seventeen times, and left to claw her way out of the dirt.*

At this point, the Tulare DA's office was just adding random, made-up details, but the "tire iron, or a crowbar" was still shocking. There was no evidence that Donna was hit on the head with any such object, and nothing like that was said in any report or in any testimony at Grand Jury or at trial. It was completely bizarre. Again, Donna wasn't ever raped or sodomized, and all of the evidence proved that it ***didn't happen,*** which is exactly why those charges were dropped, and never even given to the Grand Jury for consideration. It was blatant prosecutorial and attorney misconduct right out in the open, and McKee knew that she would never face any consequences. In fact, her behavior would probably be rewarded. This was, and is, the Tulare DA's Office motto: The ends justify the means. The goal is never truth, it's to win, and to maintain convictions at any cost.

It's impossible to know how Oscar's appeals would have progressed had the evidence been available for DNA testing back in 1993. Donna's fingernail scrapings could have identified her killer, or maybe he cut himself during the murder and left his own blood on her clothing. Oscar could have proven that there was no semen, which would have given him a re-sentencing, and a real chance at parole. Later, after "touch" DNA testing was possible, they could have tested all of Donna's clothing and jewelry. The notepad had possibly usable fingerprints, handwriting, and DNA. Profiles could have been developed from the hairs. Bob Byrd and Brian Johnson committed a crime, and walked away scot free.

As Oscar developed more and more health problems, and was losing his fight with cancer, he was suddenly transferred to a prison hospital far away from his wife and siblings.

He was able to send his wife one last card:

> My Dearest Wife,
>
> I have been missing you pretty lady. I love you so much. Sorry sweetheart, I know you are worried sick. They send me from one end of the state to the other, so it is too many miles for you to drive. Now no phone calls.
>
> I hope you are doing ok. No one seems to understand that just because we are older, we are still very much in love. We have strong ties, and need to be together. I should stop, and mail this now, so it might go out tomorrow.
>
> Oscar xoxo hugs - S.W.A.K.

Oscar Clifton died on February 18, 2013 without seeing his family again. His wife is still hoping that one day Oscar's ashes can be interred at the Veterans Cemetery, per his wishes. 38 US Code § 2411 bars a person with a standing capital murder conviction from such honors, "other than a person whose sentence was commuted by the Governor of a State." Without an official exoneration in court or a commutation by the California Governor, there is nothing that Oscar's wife can do.

Oscar Clifton with Daughters.
Source: Clifton Family.

Chapter 13 Sources

1. Oscar/Donahue Correspondence
2. Appellant's Opening Brief, Fifth Appellate District, June 17, 1977
3. Chico Enterprise-Record - May 26, 1970
4. Sacramento Bee - April 4, 1976
5. Isles Correspondence to Oscar
6. TCSO Report - McKinney December 30, 1975
7. Remittitur May 24, 1978
8. Affidavit of Bernstein, March 5, 1981
9. Pettyjohn Letter to Bernstein, April 29, 1981
10. Transcript of Habeas Hearing July 16, 1981
11. Declaration of Brent Trueblood, September 19, 1981
12. Declaration of Jim Irwin, May 20, 1983
13. Transcript of Habeas Hearing June 1-2, 1983
14. Tulare Advance-Register - May 8, 1981
15. Visalia Times-Delta - May 15, 1981
16. Tulare Advance-Register - May 16, 1981
17. Hanford Sentinel - May 15, 1981
18. Donahue's Death Certificate, May 18, 1981
19. Hearing Invoice Exhibit, July 16, 1981
20. Tulare Advance-Register, August 15, 1980
21. Tulare DA Case Report - Smythe September 27, 2001
22. Letter of Public Defender, Michael Sheltzer September 18, 1997
23. Blake Report November 15, 2002
24. Forensic Analytical Discovery Materials, June 27, 2002
25. TCSO Report - Kyke October 3, 2001
26. Letter N CA Innocence Project - Linda Starr February 14, 2003
27. Declaration to Tulare Superior Court - TCSO Logue April 2, 2003
28. Memorandum from DA Howard to Judge Sevier October 2, 2001

29. Criminalist Morton's notes of ADA Couillard call - July, 1985
30. NCIP Letter to Howard, January 16, 2003
31. Tulare Superior Court Order, Judge Moran, February 26, 2003
32. NCIP Letter to Blake with Court Order, March 6, 2003
33. Blake Letter, March 7, 2003
34. NCIP Letter to Blake with Court Order, March 12, 2003
35. Grubb Letter, March 24, 2003
36. Blake Forensic Bench Notes 2002 Testing
37. Letter from Forensic Analytical to NCIP, April 3, 2003
38. Blake to Couillard with Notes, July 29, 1985
39. Letter from Forensic Analytical to NCIP June 23, 2003
40. NCIP Withdrawal, June 25, 2003
41. Ruling Re: Nature of Slide VPH, June 22, 2004
42. Confidential Settlement Agreement, November 13, 2008
43. Ruling on DNA Testing, Judge Sevier, October 4, 2010
44. Reports and Bench Notes of DOJ Senior Criminalist Scott Lewis 2011-12
45. Byrd Letters to Parole Board
46. Letter from AG to CDC, October 7, 1987
47. Parole Hearing, October 30, 2006

CHAPTER FOURTEEN

"You're just a patrol cop"

On April 25, 2018, I was up at 4:30 am drinking coffee and catching up on the news. I got an alert on my phone, and saw an out-of-context newspaper clipping about a 1979 shoplifting case posted by the comedian Patton Oswalt. He was on a book tour for his deceased wife, Michelle McNamara, who had been writing a book about the East Area Rapist, whom she dubbed "The Golden State Killer." I knew the name in the shoplifting story. I put down my coffee, reached for my laptop, and opened my folder of suspect clippings from the *Exeter Sun*. I opened the first one, dated August 22, 1973, exactly six years before the shoplifting article, and there he was in his Exeter PD uniform, staring right at me. Joseph James DeAngelo, Jr. It was over. Sgt. Vaughan and I were right, the VR and EAR *were* the same person, and he had been living in Exeter from May 1973 to August 1976.

I immediately checked the jail records in Sacramento to see if he was under arrest. He was indeed in custody. I reviewed his date of birth to confirm. It matched. The man who had tried to kill VPD agent McGowen was a fellow police officer, serving only a few miles away. I looked at my list of Exeter suspects for sneaky DNA grabs—there he was, I had added him as a "person of interest" on February 28, 2017, just days after I first started going through the *Exeter Sun* pages. I went back to Patton's feed and found more details. They had a confirmed DNA match to the profile from the homicides and rapes. I started posting the information I had, and contacting the journalists that I knew would be heading for the press conference in Sacramento later that day. I called Sgt. Vaughan, Margie, and Oscar's daughter. For a few hours, it felt like a celebration.

By that same evening it was over. I knew, for certain, that there would be no justice for Donna or Oscar. The first troubling indicator came early in the morning, when I saw the press release issued by the District Attorney:

> After terrorizing communities throughout California between 1976 and 1986, Joseph James DeAngelo, 72, alleged to be the perpetrator of twelve murders, 45 rapes, and 120 residential burglaries, was arrested in Sacramento.
>
> DeAngelo, who is reported to be a former Auburn, California police officer was fired may years ago for shoplifting. He allegedly began this crimc spree in 1976 in Rancho Cordova, a suburb of Sacramento.

I confirmed with three different journalists that the information they had been given did not mention Visalia, the Ransacker, Exeter, Exeter PD, Snelling, McGowen, or any crimes prior to June 1976. I sent them what I had on DeAngelo in Exeter so that they could follow up later with authorities at the press conference. Everyone told me not to worry, it couldn't have been intentional, authorities probably just didn't know everything yet. Although I heard (and later confirmed) that DeAngelo had quickly confessed to being the VR, to killing Claude Snelling, and to shooting at Agent McGowen, the Sacramento DA, Anne Marie Schubert, opened her statements to the press with a completely different narrative:

> Let me first by saying this the answer has always been in Sacramento… It became personal for many of us, for me, here. In Sacramento County, in June of 1976. I grew up in the East area of Sacramento near the cluster where these crimes began. Today, we found the needle in the haystack, and it was right here in Sacramento.

Clearly, the press release had not been an oversight; Schubert appeared to be trying to minimize or hide DeAngelo's history in

Visalia and Exeter—I had to assume because the Sacramento Sheriff, FBI, and EAR Task Force had all gotten it so terribly, terribly wrong. When I read the search and arrest warrant affidavits signed on April 24, 2018 by Sacramento Sheriff's Detective Robert Peters and Detective Sergeant Kenneth Clark, I found confirmation:

> Between April 1974 and May, 1986 an unidentified white male hereafter referred to as the East Area Rapist (EAR) committed no less than 57 attacks that included sexual assaults and an additional 13 homicides throughout California. He was responsible for hundreds of sexually motivated burglaries, prowling events, and hang up/lewd phone calls. The suspect in this series has now been identified by DNA as Joseph James DeAngelo.
>
> DeAngelo's connection to these crimes has been established through his geographic ties to the locations where the attacks occurred, numerous circumstantial links, and a *Modus Operandi*. The geographic connections include his presence in Tulare County, CA as an Exeter Police Officer during the MO linked VR series. Visalia is less than 20 minutes away from DeAngelo's residence at the time. The College of the Sequoias campus is the epicenter of VR crimes and it was a professor at this college that was murdered in September of 1975 following an attempted abduction of the professor's daughter in the middle of the night.
>
> A brief summary of a pre-EAR burglary and sexual assault series known as the VR series is included (1974-75). This series culminated in the attempted abduction of a young woman from her bedroom, and the murder of her father, Claude Snelling. A couple months later, the offender was confronted while prowling by an on-duty undercover Visalia Police Officer, William McGowen. The offender shot at Officer McGowen, wounding him with glass debris prior to escaping.

[NOTE: *A full description of the kidnapping and homicide at the Snelling house, and McGowen shooting followed.*]

There was no doubt that both the press release and DA Schubert's statement had changed the facts as stated in their own warrants—which said that the crimes started in April 1974 (not June 1976) and included thirteen (not twelve) homicides. That was not a mistake or an oversight, it was an intentional effort to shift the narrative, and eliminate public inquiry into Visalia and Exeter. It worked. By the end of the day, I had already read a story in the New York Times that followed Schubert's "revised" statement of the facts. Claude Snelling's murder had disappeared, like it never really happened.

The only thing the warrants included that tied DeAngelo to the Ransacker at all was the fact that he lived and worked in Exeter. The Sacramento Sheriff's Office and EAR Task Force *relied upon Exeter* to get the court's permission to arrest DeAngelo and search his house—after spending two solid years publicly and actively trying to discredit an Exeter connection to the EAR. The details in the warrant actually became even worse when discussing the MO in the killing of Katie and Brian Maggiore in Rancho Cordova in February 1978:

> The [VR] EAR had demonstrated in the Snelling and Officer McGowen incidents that he would resort to explosive violence if met with resistance from a male. This pattern continued during the later cases. It is the opinion of your affiant that Brian Maggiore became involved in a close quarters confrontation with the EAR as he was involved in stalking, prowling, or burglarizing behavior. I believe the EAR shot Brian Maggiore, pursued Katie on foot and shot her.

Less than a year earlier, on May 2, 2017, EAR Task Force member Paul Holes had written: "The EAR was also a very dominant personality while the VR lacked this characteristic in these interactions."

The "explosive violence" was always the truth. In addition to the actual shootings, I always focused on Beth Snelling's description of her attacker:

> The voice was very demanding and deliberate and it was not wavering or shaky or nervous. She had a feeling the suspect was in command of the situation and did not appear to be undecided in any of his moves.

Then, after DeAngelo's arrest, one newspaper reported: "Holes helped write DeAngelo's arrest warrant, finally bringing some measure of closure to a case that had haunted him for decades."

It was an intentional choice for the EAR Task Force to have previously ignored Beth Snelling's kidnapping, her father's homicide, and the attempted murder of Agent McGowen, and focus obsessively on the physical description of a completely unrelated and eliminated "Peeper" for forty-one years. Some screaming meant to distract the policer officer who had him at gunpoint didn't erase or change the VR's cold-blooded nature—he tried to kill McGowen a few seconds later. I suppose if I had gone on television, podcasts, and discussion boards to make statements that were aggressively wrong, I might be embarrassed too. However, I would never try to hide my mistake, or erase the people that DeAngelo killed in Visalia and Exeter. It turns out that some people will never admit an error.

Sacramento's reliance on the VR and Exeter may seem like a minor point, but the *only* case that Sacramento could still prosecute was the Maggiores. The statute of limitations had long expired on the rapes and burglaries. Sacramento was using the MO of the Snelling and McGowen shootings to prove Maggiore, and the only thing that connected DeAngelo to being the VR was Exeter. Without the VR connection to the Maggiore case—the "explosive violence"—Schubert would have had to give the prosecution to Orange, Santa Barbara, or Ventura County since they had the homicides with DNA matches.

DA Schubert wanted the homicide cases tried together in Sacramento County, under her supervision. None of the Sacramento rapes were connected by DNA because the Sacramento Sheriff's Office had (lawfully) discarded the rape kits. However, Maggiore rested entirely on the match to the EAR zone in Rancho Cordova and the shootings in Visalia. Behind the scenes Schubert was relying on the VR and Exeter, yet to the TV cameras and newspapers, she tried to eliminate their existence completely.

I assumed, like the judge who signed the warrants, the DNA match had come through CODIS, the DNA database available to law enforcement. The U.S. Supreme Court has found that we have a privacy interest in our genetic code under the Fourth Amendment to the Constitution. The basis for this is the fact that, unlike fingerprints, our genetic code discloses personal information, such as familial connections, ethnic heritage, and propensity for disease. This is information that we have a right to keep private from the police and government—even if we voluntarily choose to disclose it to others.

The courts have carved out an exception for people who have been convicted of serious crimes. The reasoning is that they have lost many of their privacy rights at the point of conviction. The same is true of people who leave their DNA at the scene of a crime; they have no expectation of privacy, and that profile can also be uploaded to CODIS.

This rule becomes complicated when you consider "familial searches." Some states allow the police to ask for a list of close matches to the sample from their crime. These searches are generally limited to possible parent/child or sibling level relationships. A few states have completely banned familial DNA searches. California has strict rules: Members of law enforcement are not allowed to access the identity of potential family members, and familial searches are only allowed within the state—not in the national database. Almost immediately, Paul Holes started giving interviews explaining that he hadn't used CODIS at all; he had asked the lab to take the known EAR DNA profile and create a GEDCOM file that could be uploaded to a site called GEDmatch.

Holes then got help from a person who could build a family tree based on the DNA matches he obtained from the GEDmatch search. That tree eventually led to Joseph DeAngelo. This was not a new idea, it had been discussed for years as a possible way for law enforcement to solve cold cases, but every District Attorney turned it down as a privacy violation and warrantless search and seizure—violations of the Fourth Amendment. The danger was unacceptable: If a court later ruled that the search was illegal, the now identified killer would walk free, totally untouchable forever. Even if the killer confessed, and they found evidence in his house, it wouldn't matter, it would all be fruit of the poisonous tree—and inadmissible in court.

There is no scientific standard or professional accreditation for the people who do the familial research, and then hand over suspects to law enforcement. What if they make a mistake, and an innocent person is harassed, embarrassed, or falsely arrested? It turns out that Holes did exactly that before identifying DeAngelo. The "research" initially identified the wrong man as the EAR, and Holes obtained a search warrant for a man in a care center in Oregon, and law enforcement went into his room and took a swab of his DNA from him. It wasn't a match; it was all a mistake.

How would you feel if your friends, family, neighbors, or co-workers heard about that? Would anyone really look at you the same way again? This is exactly why we have such strict rules for police intrusions into our privacy, and it shouldn't be guesses about who might be in our family tree. What about sperm and egg donation, bone marrow/stem cell transplants, adoption, extramarital affairs, and people just lying about who they are on GEDmatch? This is not science, and it shouldn't be the basis for probable cause for a warrant. These are just some of the reasons that DAs had rejected exactly this type of search in cold cases. The risks of something going wrong were too high. Innocent people could be hurt, and the guilty could go free.

However, Holes had found an ally at the Los Angeles FBI office, Steve Kramer. He told Holes that the search was legal under the theory of "third party doctrine"—the information wasn't private (requiring a warrant) because GEDmatch users had shared their DNA profiles with the site. This seemed way beyond a legal stretch since that theory only applied to general business records held by a third party, not something that we generally have strong privacy interest, like our genetic code. It turned out that the Supreme Court struck a huge blow to Kramer's argument in *Carpenter v. United States*, issued on June 22, 2018, just two months *after* DeAngelo's arrest.

> The location information obtained from Carpenter's wireless carriers was the product of a search. As with GPS information, the time-stamped data provides an intimate window into a person's life, revealing not only his particular movements, but through them his familial, political, professional, religious, and sexual associations. These location records hold for many Americans the "privacies of life."
>
> The Government's primary contention to the contrary is that the third-party doctrine governs this case. In its view, cell-site records are fair game because they are "business records" created and maintained by the wireless carriers.
>
> The third-party doctrine partly stems from the notion that an individual has a reduced expectation of privacy in information knowingly shared with another. But the fact of diminished privacy interests does not mean that the Fourth Amendment falls out of the picture entirely. Instead, we consider the nature of the particular documents sought to determine whether "there is a legitimate 'expectation of privacy' concerning their contents."
>
> Having found that the acquisition of Carpenter's CSLI was a search, we also conclude that the Government must generally obtain a warrant supported by probable cause before acquiring such records. Although the ultimate measure of the constitutionality of a governmental search is reasonableness, our cases establish that warrantless searches are typically unreasonable where a search is undertaken by law enforcement officials to discover evidence of criminal wrongdoing.

If you have a privacy interest in your cell phone location records because they reveal your "familial, religious, and sexual associations" then you most definitely, without *any* doubt, have a privacy interest in your genetic code, and the personal information it reveals. There was one other flaw in the logic with Kramer's reasoning—DeAngelo didn't upload his profile to GEDmatch, some distant cousin did. He didn't "knowingly share" his genetic code with the database. It is highly unusual that one investigator and an FBI attorney alone made such a monumental decision about the constitutionality of evidence handling, and a search, in such an important case, but that's exactly what happened:

> Holes, who worked on a task force reporting to the Sacramento County DA's office, said an FBI agent who's also a lawyer [Kramer] had told him it was OK to submit the crime-scene DNA data to GEDmatch. "We just went ahead and did it. It's an open-source site and a public database. We likened it to Facebook." Holes said.

GEDmatch is nothing like Facebook, where you can look at the friends, family members, photos, and personal information of complete strangers. On GEDmatch, you can only see your *own* genetic matches—your blood relatives. In order to search for matches to the DNA of the EAR, Holes and Kramer checked a box that said:

Please acknowledge that any sample you submit is either your DNA or the DNA of a person for whom you are a legal guardian or have obtained authorization to upload their DNA to GEDmatch: (You will not be able to make comparisons if you do not answer yes)

○ Yes
○ No

Governmental police authority was used to obtain a DNA file from a crime scene sample in Ventura, and gain access to the private search and familial matching section of GEDmatch. While DeAngelo had no privacy interest in the DNA he left at the scene, the members of GEDmatch, including DeAngelo's extended family, had a right to be free of warrantless government searches into their private matters. There was nothing "public" about the matches, or the user's DNA data, and Holes was clearly searching for proof of criminal wrongdoing. Today, GEDmatch informs members that police use the database, and each user must "opt-in" to allow police searches for criminals and matches to unidentified human remains, or else choose no law enforcement searches at all.

Although DeAngelo didn't contest his warrants based on the GEDmatch search, his case led to dozens of other matches and arrests. Some of the men identified through forensic genetic genealogy are appealing their convictions based upon right-to-privacy violations and warrantless searching by police in GEDmatch and Family Tree DNA. This includes the "NorCal Rapist," Roy Waller as well as Gary Hartman in Tacoma, Washington who was convicted of the brutal rape and murder of 12-year-old Michella Welch in 1986. The first forensic genetic genealogy case conviction has already been overturned on appeal due to jury bias. William Talbott was convicted of killing a young Canadian couple in 1987 in Snohomish County, Washington. His case will continue to be argued on appeal, and in a possible retrial. This story is being repeated all over the United States, and it remains to be seen what the courts will do when faced with these possible state and federal violations. If the GEDmatch searches are struck down as unconstitutional, a lot of brutal killers could completely escape justice.

Two states, Montana and Maryland, have already passed laws specifically restricting unwarranted law enforcement searches of consumer genetic databases. Several other states, including California, Florida, Utah, and Arizona, have passed new genetic privacy acts that will limit law enforcement access without specific, affirmative permission from the actual subject of the search, not just their distant relatives. Additionally, Maryland's law requires that the genealogists who assist police in identifying suspects must be certified—a qualification that doesn't exist, or even have an agreed upon outline of training, experience, and testing standards yet.

Kramer recently left the FBI to form a private company to "automate" the forensic genealogy search process. In a recent interview, he told the New York Times: "I don't consider genetic genealogy for just cold cases. We've solved active homicides within weeks."

The current US Supreme Court rulings only allow law enforcement to search the DNA of felony arrestees and convicted criminals, so there are no rules, or even vague guidelines, that cover what Kramer is doing. In *Maryland v. King*, Justice Scalia rejected Kramer's plan:

> The Court repeatedly says that DNA testing, and entry into a national DNA registry, will not befall thee and me, dear reader, but only those arrested for serious offense[s]. Today's judgment will, to be sure, have the beneficial effect of solving more crimes; then again, so would the taking of DNA samples from anyone who flies on an airplane, applies for a driver's license, or attends a public school. Perhaps the construction of such a genetic panopticon is wise. But I doubt that the proud men who wrote the charter of our liberties would have been so eager to open their mouths for royal inspection.

Many GEDmatch users felt the same way, and the site was forced to add the "opt-in" feature after members got upset at the way law enforcement was accessing their DNA. The police searches had quickly drifted from cold case murders to simple assaults. The San Francisco police crime lab also decided there were no more rules, laws, or restrictions on their powers, and started entering the DNA of rape victims into their criminal offender database. That led to the charging of a rape victim in a later shoplifting case. The DA dropped the charges, calling it a violation of the Fourth Amendment.

Restricting government intrusion into our private matters is a fundamental right. Requiring that police investigate, and develop, probable cause before searching the genetic material of random citizens isn't setting the bar too high. According to Holes, the DAs in Orange and Contra Costa counties told him the exact same thing, and banned him from accessing the EAR/ONS DNA evidence in their labs for upload to GEDmatch. Holes' response: "Attorneys don't dictate investigations. They only get in the way."

Holes offered more explanation for his actions:

> Recently retired detective Paul Holes had been on the case since the late 1990s, when he was a newly minted deputy sheriff in California's Contra Costa County. "I started working on this case as a hobby," he says. "Nobody ever assigned this case to me; I just decided, 'I'm going to take this and run with it.' It just snowballed over the years until I was obsessed, to be frank, with getting this solved.
>
> "This has always been my one big case that I was spending most of my time on. It was maybe a year ago when I realized that all the investigative strategies that I and others had employed just wasn't cutting it, and trying to figure out how can we leverage the DNA technology." Just a month ago, Holes was sitting in his car outside DeAngelo's house in Citrus Heights, trying to decide what to do. Holes' retirement was the next day.
>
> [DeAngelo] had become interesting to me to a point where I felt I needed to go see where he lived, and I even considered, I should just knock on his door. I'm here, I drove all this way. Just talk to him, get a quick interview, ask if you'd give a consent DNA sample, and say 'Thank you very much, sir' and leave. And I just don't know enough about him, and that's when I decided, I gotta drive away and we need to find out more.

A "knock and talk" is a great way to get your suspect to destroy any and all evidence, set his house on fire, and shoot himself in the head—at least that's what happened when the FBI did it in another case I investigated. I cannot imagine even one good reason to consider doing that, and to me it just highlighted the impatience of the investigators leading up to DeAngelo's arrest. There have been numerous statements by detectives and prosecutors indicating that DeAngelo committed many unidentified and uncharged crimes, and "*we'll just never know.*" They could have known. Using undercover agents to gain the trust of DeAngelo, his family, and his friends could have provided more information about his jobs, locations, recreation, vacations, friends, and activities over the years. Did anyone help him, or cover for him? Where are all of the stolen items? The only rush seemed to be Holes' pending retirement, and his desire to solve the "mystery."

DA Schubert's assertion that Sacramento was the proper venue for DeAngelo's prosecution felt nonsensical, and like an insult to the other jurisdictions that had tried to stop DeAngelo, only to have the Sacramento Sheriff's Department insist that the EAR was not a murderer. Sacramento dismissed every lead brought to them, including the VR in 1977, and the Goleta homicides in 1980. The CII system that connected these series was designed to assist identification of offenders who might be operating statewide. Rather than focus on why CII had matched the MO moving into and away from Sacramento County, SSD spokesman Bill Miller politely explained the cases in Goleta: "Some officers say no, others say yes.... Anything is possible, but let's just say, we are not adding the murders to our list."

The news wasn't much better in Tulare County. Exeter PD tried to say that DeAngelo had never worked for them. They stated that they could not find any records, and then, when confronted with the newspaper stories from the *Exeter Sun*, attempted to minimize: "DeAngelo was, for a short period of time, a police officer with the Exeter Police Department."

May 1973-August 1976, doesn't seem short to me, especially at the rate that Exeter PD burned through officers during those years. He was a veteran and senior investigating Sergeant when he left Exeter. As for the lack of records, Exeter PD had "yearbooks," and DeAngelo was in three or four of them. None of it was a big mystery. In a post-arrest interview, one of DeAngelo's fellow officers, Farrel Ward, had no problem remembering him:

> "I liked him, but he's not the type of guy that I'd have over for a barbecue. He's just… stand-offish. Too serious. Seems like he's always thinking," Ward said.
>
> "He was just over-educated for the small department of Exeter. He just knew anything you wanted to talk about," said Farrel Ward, who worked in the department for 30 years. "I think he had a bachelor's degree, all kinds of training. He didn't fit in with the other guys. We liked to joke and screw around and take the stress off of what we were doing. He was always serious.
>
> "He was an educated idiot and he kind of laughed about it and I said, 'you should be in the FBI,' because he knew everything about everything," said Ward.
>
> Ward said DeAngelo was one of the many officers around the county who worked the Snelling case as part of search parties and canvassing. Officers with Exeter PD were also given a lot of autonomy at the time as the department patrolled in one-man shifts:
>
> "It was common for our officers to back up Farmersville PD or the Sheriff's Department and even the Visalia Police Department," Ward said, recalling that he himself was often called up by other agencies as one of the few K9 units in the county at the time. "I wouldn't be surprised if after killing the guy, he'd changed his clothes and came in to join the search," Ward said in hindsight.

> Ward said DeAngelo was the lead detective in the department which meant he could have collaborated with the Tulare County Sheriff's Office (the agency that investigated the Donna Jo Richmond murder). "He could cover up anything you wanted—if you're an investigator. Oh, you know, because they talk all the time about you know different cases—what's going on. Police, once they share with each other information, and that's how we catch the guys… so, him as an Exeter police officer, he could have had all the information."

Seven months earlier, I had believed that it was so obvious that DeAngelo had killed Donna, I met with TCSO cold case investigator Chris Dempsie. During our meeting, he told me that TCSO had destroyed the entire case file for Donna's homicide. I offered him the defense file, and the information I had on DeAngelo in Exeter. He never took me up on it. I soon heard that the Richmond family had been contacted, told that TCSO was sure that Oscar had killed Donna, and DeAngelo's arrest was just a strange coincidence. This information was later confirmed by an interview with Donna's sister published in *The Fresno Bee*:

> Debra Richmond, Donna's sister, said investigators had additional evidence against Clifton that wasn't shared at trial, and she believes the right man was put in prison. "Even though it wasn't legal evidence in court, they did double check just to make sure," she said. "They knew he had done it."

The only "evidence" that DA Powell tried to have admitted, that Judge Bradley denied, was Oscar's 1965 conviction. It didn't hurt Powell's case at all, since the *Visalia Times-Delta* let Powell tell his version of that case on the front page of the newspaper on the long Fourth of July weekend leading into the jury's deliberations. Of course even the worst-case version of the 1965 story paled in comparison to any of DeAngelo's admitted attacks. There was no secret evidence of Oscar's guilt—it was just more lies.

One of the most pressing questions on the day of the arrest was whether or not DeAngelo had ever appeared on any of the VPD's official or unofficial suspect lists. I hadn't remembered seeing his name there, and a quick check confirmed that. However, it does seem that Agent McGowen got very close to finding him. Sgt. Vaughan's team had looked at several suspects with law enforcement training, including at least one who had served with Exeter PD in 1971. Agent McGowen had made notes about his efforts to track down the "yearbook" with photos of the officers. He was so close…

DeAngelo's arrest also caused me to revisit other attacks that Sgt. Vaughan and I had considered possibles for the VR. When I first looked at Donna and Jennifer's homicides, I could not understand why the cases weren't immediately connected to each other. Maybe young teen girls were so regularly kidnapped and murdered in Exeter that it didn't seem unusual enough to draw attention. Of course that wasn't the case. Exeter has never had any other similar murders, before or since. Most homicides in Tulare County in the 1970s were related to domestic violence, drug deals, drunken fights, or a combination of all three. Pretty standard stuff, and arresting the killer didn't involve solving a mystery, just tracking down the known suspect.

Did DeAngelo commit the two unsolved random stranger attacks that Sgt. Vaughan believed should have been matched to the VR/EAR MO—Mary Murphy and Kay Nieman in October 1974? Any argument that DeAngelo's crimes were limited to the known Ransacker cases in Visalia is not credible. Miller, Nieman, Armour, and Donna matched each other and DeAngelo's known MO, and he seemed to be taunting and challenging Sgt. Bob Byrd and other members of TCSO directly.

In July 2018, TCSO cold case investigators Dempsie and Johnson announced that they were investigating DeAngelo as a suspect in Jennifer's homicide. Just nine months earlier they had publicly argued that the evidence showed that the same person killed Jennifer and Donna, trying to point to Oscar; now they were arguing that it was obvious that the VR had killed Jennifer. The community and the press immediately noticed that TCSO arguments meant that Donna was killed by DeAngelo, not Oscar. That seemed to be the end of Dempsie and Johnson on the case. Future media inquiries into Jennifer's case went unanswered.

The Tulare DA's office also made it perfectly clear that they "had no questions" about Oscar's conviction, and would not be looking at DeAngelo as a suspect in Donna's homicide. Since there was a new suspect that cast credible doubt on the conviction, Tulare DA Tim Ward had a duty to conduct a complete investigation of the original case evidence and DeAngelo's availability to commit the murder. He didn't. In September, 2018, I asked the California Attorney General to conduct an independent investigation into DeAngelo as a suspect in Jennifer's and Donna's murders, and the question of Oscar's actual innocence. It did not go well. It was assigned to a Deputy AG named Clifford Zall. His father had been a criminal prosecutor in Tulare County from 1974-77, working for DA Powell and ADA Bleier. Clifford had been in the same class at school with Brent Trueblood, and lived in the VR zone. He knew the kids and families who had been victims of DeAngelo, as well as Oscar's most critical suppressed alibi witness.

The Attorney General's only interest was to maintain Oscar's conviction at any cost, and they assigned the perfect person to make sure all of the prior police and DA misconduct was covered up. Eventually Ward issued a report confirming Oscar's conviction. One-third of the "evidence" was the 1965 conviction, another third was Morton's tire and footprint testimony based on the broken camera, and the rest was from Brumley and Mascorro.

Ward's report omitted much of the discredited evidence originally heard by the jury, like the hair on Oscar's sweater, the white painters pants, and his pocketknife as the murder weapon. The Attorney General had no way to know that the jury's decision was based upon long-ago discredited "evidence." What Ward did include in his report were mainly outright lies like Blake's sample hadn't been ABO typed, and that Oscar wasn't seen on Garden Street. All exculpatory evidence was omitted. In Ward's version of the case, Trueblood and Guerber didn't exist. DA Ward's actions weren't just "legal maneuvering"—he committed a felony under California Penal Code §141(c):

> A prosecuting attorney who intentionally and in bad faith alters, modifies, or withholds… relevant exculpatory material or information, knowing that it is relevant and material to the outcome of the case, with the specific intent that the… relevant exculpatory material or information will be concealed or destroyed, or fraudulently represented as the original evidence upon a trial, proceeding, or inquiry, is guilty of a felony punishable by imprisonment… for 16 months, or two or three years.

Not only did Ward conceal the exculpatory evidence that was suppressed by DA Powell at trial, he added his own intentional bad faith lies about it. Blake's sample matched DeAngelo's blood type, not Oscar's. At least six different credible witnesses confirmed Oscar's alibi. There was no mention of the notepad found with Donna's bike, or the unreliability of the Mascorro and Brumley identifications. DA Ward relied on Lavern Lamb's testimony, but failed to tell the AG that she was Don Lee's "aunt," and that TCSO had planted the trail of Donna's clothing. Ward relied upon TCSO Hensley's known perjury about the wheelbase of Oscar's truck, and he withheld the exculpatory fact that it was actually nineteen inches shorter than the tire tracks. Ward repeated Morton's junk, vague opinion about the heel print and tire tracks without mentioning the broken camera, or Harris' report that the heel didn't match Oscar's boots. The 1965 case was not only ruled inadmissible at trial, and could never be used to support the murder conviction, but Ward included several factual lies, and hid Byrd's inappropriate involvement in a case outside his jurisdiction.

Ward's biggest, boldest lie was that the DNA testing on one of Morton's hair comparison slides back in 2011 had eliminated DeAngelo as Donna's killer. The lie in the report was very specific:

"In 2011, a partial Y-STR DNA profile was developed from semen attached to one of Donna's pubic hairs."

This is the exact language from the CalDOJ criminalist. He described the evidence examination as: "Slide VPH (victim's pubic hair) was "examined microscopically for spermatozoa, with negative results." That 2011 report was signed by Senior Criminalist Scott D. Lewis, who had conducted the examination and testing himself. His lab bench notes on that microscopic examination of slide VPH were equally clear: "no cellular material seen; debris only; no sperm."

The Tulare DA's Office had been told, specifically, in writing, that there *absolutely, positively, unequivocally* was no "semen" on Slide VPH. Although three male alleles were identified, they were presumed to be random contamination since the cellular source could not be found, and there was documented, unidentified male DNA contamination in the reagent blank. The DNA was also very "low level" which pointed away from body fluid (a rich source of DNA) and towards skin cells, or secondary transfer from another object. None of this was a surprise. Morton's lab had told Oscar's attorney and the Tulare DA the exact same thing in a letter on June 23, 2003:

> Our laboratory is in receipt of your request to locate and identify the photocopies of the slides contained in the discovery materials on page "00033 through 00037." Mr. Morton located the slides. These slides remain in our custody. Our laboratory does not have slides of the victim's hair containing semen.

Slide VPH was on page 00035. That was consistent with Morton's testimony that he had found no sperm cells, spermatozoa, or any component of semen on any item of evidence in the case, including Donna's pubic hair. These slides were also the subject of a Tulare County Superior Court Ruling:

> Although it does appear that some other hairs gathered during the investigation remained in the custody of Forensic Analytical, their letter also makes clear that these are not the pubic hairs containing the perpetrator's semen. Rather, the hairs still in their custody are reference samples from known donors, or samples taken from the clothing of the victim, or clothing from petitioner. Clearly, testing the reference samples would accomplish nothing. There is no basis upon which it can be assumed that there would be any means by which exculpatory evidence could be found by further DNA testing.

Although the Tulare DA agreed to allow the testing in exchange for Oscar dropping his civil rights violation lawsuit against the county, the outcome of the testing was exactly as expected. There was no "semen" on the pubic hair slide, and no way to exculpate any suspect in the case. Without a known cellular source there was no way to guess if the alleles were from one, two, or three men. This was exactly the same situation addressed in the Kevin Duane Galik case—the alleles didn't implicate (or exculpate) any suspect—they were presumed to be transfer contamination, unrelated to the crime. This was the conclusion of Criminalist Lewis' report as well:

> The Y-STR typing result from the washing from the victim's pubic hair (item VPH) consist of only three alleles, and ***no interpretation of these alleles is being made***. [*emphasis added*]

It probably goes without saying that District Attorneys in California are not allowed to lie about the evidence in reports to the Attorney General, yet that's exactly what DA Tim Ward did. He made up false, fake, and phony forensic results in an official review of a murder conviction. He lied about what the examination and testing of slide VPH found, what the report of Criminalist Lewis said, and the conclusions drawn. He not only sent that to the Attorney General, but he issued it as a national press release. He violated about ten different rules of professional conduct with that single act. DA Ward and his ADA, David Alavezos, then used that lie to remove DeAngelo as a suspect in Donna's murder—and apparently Jennifer Armour's as well. Ward's entire report was the most shameful criminal behavior I can possibly imagine from a modern prosecutor in California.

If semen had been recovered, and by some miracle had survived Sgt. Byrd's destruction orders, it would have been great evidence in the case that could have proven once and for all who killed Donna. The sperm cells would have contained the murderer's DNA, and a profile could have been developed at the lab—but none of that ever happened. The closest the evidence ever got was the finding of blood type A on the pubic hair samples. That only points directly back to DeAngelo, not Oscar.

However, this entire line of thought defies science and logic. You cannot have semen without sperm cells, and nobody has ***ever*** asserted they were found on any item of evidence in the case. There was no physical sexual assault—that was the finding at autopsy and the testimony at Grand Jury and trial. It wasn't a maybe or inconclusive, it was a NO—Donna was not sexually assaulted. The state's criminalists, Morton, Grubb, and Lewis, confirmed, in writing, that there was no semen or any biological component of semen (pre-ejaculation seminal fluid) found on any item of evidence, at any time.

The fact that Donna's killer intentionally staged the scene to point away from his true motive should have been a *huge* investigative clue. Staging, evidence planting, and framing comprise a very specific *Modus Operandi*, and it belongs to Joseph DeAngelo. He had motive, means, and the opportunity to kidnap and kill Donna, frame Oscar, and direct the investigation away from himself behind the scenes.

Was the killer's DNA under Donna's fingernails? We'll never know. What about "touch" DNA on her clothing where the murderer dragged her under the orange trees? Possibly. The same could have been true for the notepad by the bike, or even Donna's bike itself, but Sgt. Byrd destroyed those items to cover up the truth, and DA Ward lied about the testing and evidence to escape blame for what TCSO and DA Powell had done to help DeAngelo stay free to continue to rape and kill. DeAngelo never could have eluded capture without their help, inadvertent or not.

Although TCSO and Exeter PD intentionally avoided conducting any investigation into DeAngelo, after his arrest, Sgt. Vaughan and I heard from three former Tulare County residents who had very specific encounters with DeAngelo and his Exeter PD authority.

The first person to come forward publicly and accuse DeAngelo of an uncharged crime was Liz Silva. She had been kidnapped and raped by DeAngelo on about March 13, 1974, just shy of her thirteenth birthday. Liz's stepfather was Joe Collins, a community policing officer with VPD. He was tasked with issues like youth bike safety, and did not carry a gun. Collins is black, and Visalia was the home of the Ku Klux Klan in California during the mid-twentieth century. Newell Bringhurst wrote the definitive history of the Klan in Tulare County, and it is well worth a read. James Ward and Calley Cederlof updated that story in 2019 for the *Visalia Times-Delta*, when local black students were still regularly being harassed and called the "*n-word*." In 2018, the ACLU filed a federal civil rights violation suit against the Visalia School District: "Peers joked about hanging black students from trees, promoted "white power" messages, referred to black students as "slaves," and wore Confederate symbols to school."

This came after the school district had already settled a 2006 lawsuit based on the same type of allegations targeting one particular black student. This was nothing new. During the Civil War, Union troops had to be stationed in Visalia because there was so much pro-Confederacy activity. This eventually spilled onto the people who made their way to Tulare County from Oklahoma ("Okies," the "*o-word*") during the Dust Bowl, including Oscar's family. Hate and discrimination had been woven into the fabric of the community, and in 1974 almost nobody welcomed the idea of seeing Joe Collins in a police uniform.

I've interviewed Liz and read her writings about DeAngelo's attack on her. I believe her completely. She suffered greatly from the trauma of the attack, but her memory is clear. I was able to verify each of the details she gave me, and everything she told me is consistent with the known facts, dates, and places. Liz said that she was supposed to be at school, but instead she was hanging out at Jefferson Park, near Mt. Whitney High, in Visalia. She was approached by Joseph DeAngelo, in his police uniform, and told that she was under arrest for truancy. DeAngelo handcuffed her and placed her in the back of his marked police car. Liz says that she did not notice the police agency; she assumed that it was VPD.

Liz said she immediately knew something was very wrong, because just about a block from the park, DeAngelo entered the freeway heading east. She asked DeAngelo why they weren't going to the police station, and he said that her father was doing target practice by the river, and he was taking her to him there. She knew that was a lie, since Collins did not carry a gun, and wouldn't have been at the river during the work day—it made no sense.

DeAngelo exited the freeway at Road 140, and drove north to St. John's River. The area has a recreational trail, houses, and a middle school now, but in 1974 it was undeveloped, and just outside the city limits. DeAngelo parked in a dry drainage area and removed Liz from the back of the police car, still handcuffed. While he raped her, Liz said that he made comments about her mother being a "n-word lover," and said that her stepfather had no business being a police officer. DeAngelo described the inside of her home, including items in her brother's bedroom, and said that he would come back to her house and kill her entire family in their sleep if she told anyone.

DeAngelo also made it clear that nobody would believe her, especially since she was a school-skipping delinquent. Liz said that being blamed for her own attack took an especially devastating toll, and contributed to her 44 years of silence. It's very easy to convince a 12-year-old child that something is her fault, and that she'll get in more trouble if she tells on an adult. Eventually, DeAngelo removed the handcuffs. Then he picked up the buttons from her Levi's, which he had forcibly pulled off her jeans, and put them in his pocket. He drove off, leaving her to walk home. It was seven miles, and took her over two hours. Liz remembers the walk vividly, especially having to hold her pants closed with her hand the entire way.

Liz lived two blocks from Jennifer Armour, and she was kidnapped in the VR "hot zone." The kidnapping was in Visalia, but the assault occurred in TCSO jurisdiction. Liz says that the attack completely changed her life, and keeping the secret nearly destroyed her. She was filled with both anger and terror, with no place to direct it except towards herself. This was confirmed by her stepfather in a post-arrest interview:

> Collins says Silva's behavior changed dramatically around that time: "She got wild, she totally became a different person. We didn't know what the reason was behind the behavior change. She totally changed into another person." Collins says Exeter police officers were often in Visalia because it is the site of the Tulare County Jail.

The first suspected VR burglary occurred a week after Liz was attacked, about a mile northeast of her home. There is no doubt that DeAngelo was violent and extremely dangerous ***before*** any of the ransacking burglaries started. How many other victims did he "arrest"? There are many more questions than answers about DeAngelo's criminal history before he arrived in Exeter in 1973, but there is no reason to believe that he started offending when he was 28 years old. This includes his internship with Roseville PD. What police resources did he use then as the "Cordova Cat Burglar"? *Nobody seems to care.* In fact, shortly after the arrest in 2018, SSD intentionally removed all of the information Detective Clark posted about both the Cordova Cat Burglar and Cordova Meadows Burglar—made it disappear as if it had never happened. It had to be covered up because it was impossible to explain how SSD had failed to match that offender to the VR. It was easier to delete it than to apologize to John Vaughan and his team for the public attacks and discrediting of their work.

A few weeks after Beth Snelling was attacked, in late September 1975, a 13-year-old girl, Marsha (a pseudonym), who lived near the VR zone, was walking alone from her home to a store in downtown Visalia. As she walked near Jefferson Park, on a residential street, a police car driven by a uniformed officer pulled up next to her and offered her a ride. He stated that it was too hot for her to be walking, but she declined the offer, did not approach the car, and continued on the sidewalk. The car drove off quickly in her direction of travel. However, after walking a couple more blocks, the car circled back around behind her again. While still seated in his car, the officer ordered Marsha into the car, and threatened to "report" her if she did not comply.

Marsha was scared, and felt that something was wrong. Instead of complying, she turned and ran in the opposite direction. She cut through a yard and then into an alley, which she often used as a shortcut. She made her way home going through yards and staying off the sidewalk. Marsha immediately told her parents what had happened. Later that night, her siblings observed a police car parked down the block from their house. Her parents, believing that she was in some kind of trouble for eluding a police officer, contacted VPD —the correct jurisdiction for the events. It was soon confirmed that the officer who approached Marsha was not with VPD, although it is unknown if he was identified that night. VPD took a report of the kidnapping attempt, but it never led to an arrest. In 2018, Marsha positively identified Joseph DeAngelo as the officer who had threatened her, and referred VPD back to her original report from 1975.

Hearing the stories from Liz and Marsha solidified what Sgt. Vaughan and I had long suspected: Neither Jennifer Armor nor Donna Richmond were kidnapped by force. We had determined that long before DeAngelo's arrest. The evidence pointed to each girl getting into a car with someone they trusted. That meant either a friend or someone in a position of authority. That was the commonality in both kidnappings that always pointed to a member of law enforcement.

Why would Jennifer accept a ride when she was only a block or two from where her friends were waiting for her? If it was a different friend, how would it also be someone that Donna trusted? Jennifer had only lived in the area for about a year, and there were no known connections between the girls.

Since Donna wasn't seen riding through Exeter, she had to have been kidnapped near Don Lee's house. There was no way to imagine that a stranger could have controlled Donna and gotten her bike in his vehicle—or why he would have even tried on a busy road in full daylight. In order for Donna to think everything was normal, her bike had to be going with her. Absent any evidence of there being a trusted friend they could have had in common (*and none were ever discovered*), it suggested that the perpetrator was an adult authority figure, likely law enforcement using his car, uniform, and badge. It makes sense that DeAngelo falsely arrested Jennifer for hitchhiking or something similar, and Donna for some minor bike infraction, like riding on the wrong side of the road or a missing reflector. Both girls would have complied, and been in the car and gone within a minute. One thing that's easy to see in police questioning sheets from the time is that they always asked witnesses if they saw anything "unusual" or "suspicious." That kind of questioning would never result in the reporting of a police car or officer in the area.

On Thursday, December 18, 1975, the *Visalia Times-Delta* had the Ransacker on the front page. It was a large composite drawing from Agent McGowen, and a description of the man, including possible habits. A few hours after the paper hit the newsstands and front porches, the Bardone family was burglarized. Gary Bardone got off work at Lonnie's Auto Parts in Exeter, stopped by his house to pick up his wife and infant son, and they proceeded to Visalia for dinner with family. The Bardones left Exeter at about 6:00 pm and returned at 9:00 pm. Their house was at 209 S. Belmont, near the intersection of Ave 277—the street where Donna's friend Judy lived.

It is well-documented that DeAngelo responded to the press coverage of his crimes and statements by law enforcement with direct and immediate action. That led me to wonder exactly how the VR reacted on the night that the McGowen composite and description first appeared in the *Visalia Times-Delta*. The Bardone burglary was interesting due to the timing, location, and the fact that Gary looked a lot like DeAngelo. I assumed that the VR had some immediate concern when he saw some version of his face on the front page of the newspaper. I had wondered for years if the Bardone burglary was the VR's reaction to that story, and if so, why?

When I reached out to him, Gary was initially not interested in talking about it. He had remarried, moved out of state, and did not want to revisit that time in his life. However, a friend of his convinced him that his story was worth telling, especially since Gary was facing a cancer recurrence and didn't have long to live. It was now or never, and Gary decided that he didn't want his story about DeAngelo to die with him. My taped interview started with Gary's description of his returning home to the burglary:

> When I got there I opened the garage door, drove in, and turned the car off. I just looked up at the door and I noticed that the door wasn't closed. It was just left open. I always locked the doors, it was something my parents told us to do when we were young, and living on the ranch. So, I told my wife to stay in the car. I opened the door and yelled out something like, "Hey, is there anybody here?" I went into the kitchen, which is right there, and I turned the kitchen lights on and looked around. I noticed the stereo was gone, and as I was going back out to the garage to tell my wife what's going on, I noticed that our Mr. Coffee was gone. I told my wife to bring our son inside—we've been robbed. My wife put our son to bed because by then it's about 9:30 pm, and he was a little cranky and tired, and he went right to sleep.
>
> My wife didn't have a lot of jewelry, and she kept it in a small box on the nightstand. It was strange that it was still there, but of course it wasn't real valuable. I went to the spare

bedroom, that was our little storage room. That's where I had my rifle, and had a few small tools. They were all individually laid out, but they didn't take any of those. This musket rifle that was stolen was a muzzle loading rifle. I bought it as a kit that you assembled. I had an interest in those types of guns, and I thought that would be kind of neat to horse around with. The stereo was a small little unit, with two speakers that would have been easy to carry, you could tuck it under your arm. The dresser drawers were pulled out, but they were shoved back in part way because we had a large bed in there. To be able to really get around in there, you'd have to shut it six inches or so.

I walked out to the garage and that's when I noticed the side door on the garage was askew, it was still locked. What they did was somehow jimmy the lock that went to the outside, and used like a small screwdriver, or a real thin sharp knife, and just kind [of] kept prying and prying. It was scratched up, and so was the striker plate, and the trim board around. It was messed up pretty good. Then I went and looked at the door from the garage to the kitchen, and the same thing on that door as well.

It was rather quick when the Exeter PD got there, two officers responded. I knew one of them, his name was Robert Matthews. I went to high school with him. The other officer that showed up was Joseph DeAngelo. They came in, and introduced themselves, and then DeAngelo went straight into my house, and I stayed out in the garage for a few minutes talking to Matthews. DeAngelo just walked right on in there, he just took it upon himself. He didn't even say "I'm gonna go inside the house and check it out." He just walked right on in.

Matthews said, "I'm gonna go talk to some neighbors." Matthews came back, and he said, "Well I spoke to your neighbor just right next door. He said that he heard some noise coming from your house and your garage, and then he looked up again, and he saw a silhouette of a guy running from the corner of the garage diagonally across your backyard." I didn't have a fence up yet because we just moved in not that long before all this happened, so he just disappeared into the darkness.

DeAngelo said, "Well, we could take fingerprints, but it's already been contaminated. I mean you've used it yourself, and you might have touched the doorknob. The chances of getting fingerprints is minimal to none." It's my house, of course my fingerprints are going to be all over the place anyway. That seemed like an odd thing to say. DeAngelo is the one that said that, and Matthews was just kind of like "okay, yeah, all right, yeah" he ran along with it.

Matthews suggested that I just turn it over to my homeowners. He said, "Gary you know as well as I do you're not going to get that stuff back. That's what happens in these type of burglaries. They go for small easy to sell quick stuff, and they're out of there. You probably need our report for the insurance."

DeAngelo stayed mainly in the house and for that time he was alone in the house. No, I take that back, he wasn't alone in the house. My wife had put our son down, and she stayed inside the house. It was chilly outside, so she stayed there with my son.

The officers were at my house 45 minutes to an hour. They left me their business cards. I kept those for a while, and they ended up being tossed because of where I worked. The police department was right behind Lonnie's, you just walked across the alley, and there you were in the police department. The police chief, I knew him, it was more of an acquaintance type thing because he would come over to the store and have a cup of coffee and talk to Lonnie, or to Jerry Dutch, the co-owner. I called him Chief Henry and he said, "oh, just call me Hank." Nice small town, and real nice guy—all business, but I mean he's just a real, real nice person.

I wasn't expecting to hear anything more from Exeter PD at that point because of the way we left it—"you're not going to see that stuff again, you got homeowners," yeah, I'll turn that over to them. I knew that the police department wasn't gonna drop everything and go try and chase down a coffee maker, a stereo, and a musket loader.

DeAngelo came back, I don't really recall how long it was, it was late at night, around nine o'clock. [Gary placed it on a weeknight before Christmas Eve, so Monday the 22nd or Tuesday the 23rd.] He knocked on the door, and I answered, and lo and behold there's DeAngelo there, but he wasn't in uniform. He was dressed in a cheap, navy blue, JC Penny suit. He said he was there to follow up on the investigation of the burglary, and I said, "okay," so he came in. My wife was sitting down on the couch, and we had been watching TV.

He said, "I just need to ask you a few questions, if you'll have a seat." So, I sat down on the couch by my wife. He says "we think that it was somebody you know who broke into your house." I said, "What? I don't know or hang around any riff raff like that. I work in a parts store here in town, everybody knows me. I hang around decent people." He goes, "well we think it's somebody you know, but either that, or it was you."

I said, "whoa, whoa, whoa, whoa, wait a minute, what are you talking about? Who is this "we" that you keep bringing up?" DeAngelo says, "well it's not really "we," it's me. You know I'm a detective. This is what I think happened." I said, "I don't really care what you think," and he said, "well I need to talk to you and your wife separate, so I want your wife to go into the back bedroom, the master bedroom, and you stay here and I'll question you first, and then I'll go in there." I said, "oh no, no, no, no, no, we're not going to do that—that's not going to happen."

Then he came forward towards me a little bit more, and started trying to act like he was a detective, a police officer, "you will do what I say." I said, "well no, you're not a detective, you're just a patrol cop. So unless you're here to write me a ticket for speeding, or running a red light or something, I suggest that you leave." He says, "Nope, I am the police here, now you go to the back bedroom." I turned to my wife and I said, "you stay right there, you stay right there." He got in between me and my wife, and was being very bossy like.

It's just running through my mind—wait a minute this isn't right, something is wrong here. Here it is around nine o'clock at night, he's a police officer, and now he's calling himself a detective, and he's coming up with this foolish idea. Something's wrong. So, I got in between him and the hallway, and I had my wife go down to the end of the hallway, to my son's room, and pick him up. She brought him into the living room. I didn't like it. I didn't like what was going on, something was not right. You could feel it in the air—you could almost smell it. He just kept pushing the fact that he wanted my wife to go down to the master bedroom, and I stay there. I said, "No, you're not, it's not gonna happen—who is this "we" you keep referring to?" He says, "well me, I do, that's what I think. I said, "well, your thinking is wrong mister."

When I first answered the door, and he was standing there, he was somewhat his normal casual self. He was able to gain entrance. I mean had he started ranting and raving right at the doorstep, the door would have been slammed, and I would have called the police. But he was somewhat casual, until he got to the point where he was accusing me, and then told my wife to go to the master bedroom down the hall. In fact he had taken like a step back, and with his left arm kind of pointed in a motion to go down the hallway to the master bedroom. That's when I told my wife, "nope you stay right there, stay right there, you're not going anywhere." That's when he went from somewhat his cordial demeanor, the expression on his face just turned completely different, and his voice got a little louder, and his eyes were getting upset looking because I wasn't following orders, or whatever. I was getting in his way, of what his purpose really was—I don't know, but his voice had gone up quite a few octaves, and his eyes…

The more I said "no," the more upset he got—his mouth was almost like a pucker, he was straining to keep his mouth quiet. It was upsetting him, because the longer he stayed, the more it seemed that something is not right here. Police officers don't do this, especially at nine o'clock at night, they just don't. I said, "I suggest you leave, and leave right now." He said, I am the police here." I said, "no you're not, you're just a cop but, I know the police. If I have to, I'll call Henry Fry. I know Hank, I know him very well. If that's what you want me to do that's what I'll do. I'll call him right now. It's time to go. I'll be there first thing in the morning, I'll answer any and all questions."

DeAngelo had backed himself up to the front door, and opened the door with his hand behind him. He said, "I'll be seeing you then." I said, "well fine, sure, okay, whatever, yes," and then he went out. I got to the door and I locked it, locked it quick. Right after, I was just somewhat shocked. I go, "what in the world was that all about?" My wife said, "what happened to him?" I said, "I don't know, something's not right here, something is not right. He is a weird duck." She said, "heHe doesn't act right, Gary."

A short while later he would drive by, and slow down. I could recognize that it was DeAngelo because of the street light, it's one of those big mercury street lamps. It was on the corner, and I was the second house in. It was dangerous, he would drive real, real, real slow—just a crawl, and then slowly speed up, and keep going down Belmont. On the shoulder of the road where the sidewalk would have been. They hadn't installed the sidewalks at that time. He did that a good four, five, maybe half a dozen times over a period of a month or so. He was leaning towards the passenger door, looking out the passenger door window. No doubt in my mind—he was in an Exeter police car. I think one time he was in a dark brown, or a dark blue car—no insignias.

He was looking through two windows, the kitchen window, and the master bedroom. The first time, I just happened to be in the kitchen and getting a glass of water. I saw some headlights out there, and lo and behold, there it is, Exeter Police Department, and it slowed way down, I mean it was a crawl, and I was leaning over the sink looking through the window, and I looked and said, "That's DeAngelo, what in the world?"

Later, I was waiting on the counter at Lonnie's and Joe came in, and he acted like we've never met, and he was a real soft demeanor. He said that he was going to restore a vintage Chevrolet, somewhere around the 1950s, and he wanted to know how much this would cost. I had to explain to him two or three times—I can't quote you a price right now, those are specialty items, you have to go through specialty warehouses that have accumulated all these old parts. You have to pay that day's going rate. It's not a set price like the stuff we stock there on the shelf. He was absolutely an entirely different person. I mean that's a little bit strange. He seemed kind of, lacking a better term, almost like a coward, cowardice. He was asking questions politely.

The last time that he came in the store it was all a pre-rehearsed routine, you know his "still looking at restoring this Chevy of mine." Then the co-owner, Jerry, he came over there and he said, "Excuse me, Gary has some stuff in the back he has to do. So, unless you're here to buy something we can't do anything for you. If you want to buy some parts for that Chevrolet, then you bring some money in, and put it down, so we can get the ball rolling. Other than that, we can't help you, have a good day." So, he brushed him off is what he did, and Joe didn't come back ever again after that. Like I said, he was a completely different person from the night of the visit at the home, and then to come into the parts store he was very mild, his demeanor was just the complete opposite.

He was alone in my house with my wife the night of the burglary when I was outside in the garage talking to Matthews. I have heard that he would make the husband lay down, and he would put dishes on his back, so if he made a move naturally a dish will slide off and make noise. That ran through my mind, and then I also thought well, what was to keep him from somehow killing me, and then going right back to the master bedroom and do whatever he does. That bothers me. I really look at it as well, I dodged a bullet—literally. Putting all this together he was there for a purpose and it was not police work. He emphasized splitting me and my wife apart. He was more interested in that. We argued about that and I kept telling him it ain't going to happen. I absolutely will not let this happen.

I didn't have a lot of questions for Gary after hearing his story. The rifle caught my attention. DeAngelo made a point of stealing only older or foreign firearms that had no serial numbers, so that fit with his MO. I also wondered if that was the only gun in the house, and Gary confirmed that it was. I knew that DeAngelo had entered the homes of future rape victims ahead of time, and unloaded and/or moved their firearms. This made the burglary look a lot more like preparation for DeAngelo's later visit, knowing that Gary would be unarmed.

I had spent months reading every copy of the *Exeter Sun* from 1973-76 before DeAngelo's arrest, and everything about Gary's burglary was unusual. I had been looking for anything that matched the VR's MO, and Gary's burglary stood out. Dinnertime break-ins were almost unheard of in Exeter, I found only a handful. Most residential burglaries involved people who were out of town, or entry was made through an unlocked door or window—they didn't take a lot of skill or bravery.

I was originally contacted about Gary's encounter with DeAngelo by an Exeter resident, a friend of his who learned about the investigation through the podcast. I expected confirmation of a VR burglary, but never imagined anything that directly involved DeAngelo. Circumstantial evidence clearly pointed to DeAngelo as the original burglar—probably to search for and remove any firearms from the house. The other items were likely taken simply to make sure the gun wasn't the only thing missing. The neighbor was able to confirm that the burglar was a single male, on foot, that exited across the alley into a vacant lot behind Gary's house. Additionally, the entry through the back garage door and then the door into the kitchen is classic VR/EAR entry, especially the chiseling around the striker plate—sometimes he would even take the striker plates with him. It also appeared that Gary's house was targeted. There were plenty of easy houses, with unlocked doors and more valuables than a young couple with a baby had. Also, there were no other consistent burglaries in that area or time frame. It was a lot of effort, in an unlikely location, for not much gain.

Gary noted that his general likeness compared to DeAngelo was striking. Similar age, height, and build; both were Italian, with dark hair and light eyes. Since Gary's workplace backed onto the Exeter PD station, it would be easy to understand how DeAngelo could have decided to target him as a believable VR suspect. It's impossible to hear Gary's story and not think about an EAR attack or ONS homicide—only under color of law, using his badge. If Gary and his wife were going to be killed, it would have been a double homicide. Would it have looked like a murder/suicide, with the Snelling or McGowen gun placed next to Gary? Would the police have found VR loot in the house? I don't know, but clearly, the fear of that night weighed heavily on Gary, even after all of these years.

In some ways none of this is a surprise. Stalking, planning, watching, planting evidence, and framing are all well-known and established DeAngelo behaviors. Complicated, premeditated, and bizarre are a perfect fit for him. Gary's wife was eighteen, a year younger than Debbie Ward, who DeAngelo had been stalking just eight days earlier, so she was a believable victim if the goal was to make it look as if she was attacked or killed by the VR.

I also thought about the fact that DeAngelo loved seeing himself in the newspaper, and it didn't matter if it was for being a hero police officer or clever criminal who outsmarted the cops who were chasing him. Without any doubt, the most important investigation DeAngelo ever worked was the murder of Exeter PD Officer Thomas Schroth, on October 22, 1975. A man shot his wife and then brought her to the hospital. As Officer Schroth arrived to investigate, he encountered the husband in the parking lot. The husband killed Officer Schroth and then himself. I had to wonder if DeAngelo was trying to put himself in the news again by framing Gary as the VR, staging the scene to look like murder/suicide, solving the VR cases, and taking the pressure off himself in the process.

On the surface, it may sound farfetched, but there is no doubt that DeAngelo had been committing burglaries and then arresting men for his crimes since he moved to Exeter. The burglary rate literally doubled when he arrived, and then dropped in half again the year after he left Exeter. He went from a rookie to sergeant to major crimes investigator in about thirty months. He was appointed to the JAB (Joint Attack on Burglary) team to work cases with TCSO and Farmersville PD. He wasn't a great investigator, following leads and solving cases—instead, he planted evidence, framed innocent men, and sent them to jail or prison. Imagine sitting on a jury and hearing that the police found the stolen items in the defendant's car or home, and that his only defense is that the real criminal broke in and planted the items. Nobody would believe that, not in a million years.

Yet, I know for a fact that this exact behavior was one of DeAngelo's most distinctive and consistent MO points, as Sgt. Vaughan tried to argue to Sacramento: "… the 'peculiarity' of taking things, often items of little value, from one house and leaving them in another."

Gary Bardone and I talked on the phone a few more times before his death on November 18, 2019, and he was haunted by the question of exactly what DeAngelo had planned for his family that night. At no point ever was there any actual follow-up on his burglary, nor were there any "questions" for him about his own involvement in the crime from Exeter PD. Gary's thoughts about DeAngelo returning to his home to commit an EAR-style couples attack feels off. DeAngelo had just missed being captured twice when assertive men had stepped in and forced him to shoot and flee. From June 18, 1976-March 18, 1977, DeAngelo committed seventeen EAR attacks, and on March 20, 1977, *The Sacramento Bee* stated: "He has never attacked while there is a man in the home."

On April 2nd, DeAngelo started attacking only couples. It was an MO prompted wholly by what he saw as a challenge issued by the press—a dare, not his own deep-seated need to include men. Given that, it seems likely that DeAngelo's reason for separating Gary and his wife would have been to incapacitate them, and the ruse of "official questioning" was intended to make them comply without the use of force. Presumably, he could have then handcuffed Gary at gunpoint, left him in the living room, and either handcuffed or tied up Gary's wife. At that point, he would have been free to plant VR stolen items in the house and shoot the couple with the Miroku used to kill Claude Snelling—or the Smith & Wesson that shot out McGowen's flashlight.

In that case, Gary and I agreed that DeAngelo would have made it look like a murder/suicide. Exeter PD major crimes investigator DeAngelo would have been called to the scene, maybe by a neighbor hearing the shots, and discovered the VR loot and gun. What would the supposed motive be for Gary to have killed his wife and then himself? We had two guesses: Gary's wife figured out he was the VR from the composite in the newspaper and threatened to go to the police or DeAngelo became suspicious about the burglary, and his questioning prompted Gary to panic, thinking he was close to being identified as the VR and sent to death row.

Even if Gary had an alibi for some of the VR dates, would it have mattered if he had the murder weapon and stolen items in his possession? The case would have been fully within Exeter PD jurisdiction, so DeAngelo could have manipulated the investigation and conclusions from the inside. If the police and DA want to close a case or get a conviction, every alibi witness becomes either mistaken or a liar. Gary was basically a better-looking Joe DeAngelo. Would McGowen have believed it was Gary who shot at him in the dark? Probably. DeAngelo's motive was clear: With the VR identified and dead, he could go on living and working in Exeter, with no worries about accidentally running into McGowen in the future. DeAngelo's wife was still finishing her BA in Fresno, and he had just been promoted. It would have seemed very suspicious for DeAngelo to just pack up and leave Exeter at that point. He had to find a way to stay—at least until his wife finished her degree six months down the road.

The real problem in trying to figure out Gary's story of DeAngelo's visit is finding an innocent explanation. DeAngelo made it clear that he was the only one who was accusing Gary—it didn't come from Exeter PD, and it clearly had no basis in fact. Nine pm is not a reasonable time to visit a family with a sleeping baby or conduct any type of routine investigation. DeAngelo had been alone in the house with Gary's wife for an extended period of time after the burglary, and had every opportunity to question her away from Gary. Also, if DeAngelo had really been on Exeter PD business, he would have welcomed Gary calling Chief Fry, but he didn't. That threat was enough to make him leave the house. There was also no investigatory purpose for driving by Gary's house at night, basically stalking him, and watching his nightly habits. Was he checking on the Bardones when he encountered Donna riding home alone on Belmont later that week, and decided she would make a believable VR victim, and rather than framing Gary, he went with Oscar?

Chapter 14 Sources

1. Auburn Journal - August 22, 1979
2. Exeter Sun - August 22, 1973
3. DA Press release, April 25, 2018
4. Transcript of Schubert Press Conference, April 25, 2018
5. SSD Search and Arrest Warrants April 24, 2018
6. New York Times - April 25, 2018
7. "OriginalNightStalker" ProBoard, May 2, 2017
8. VPD Report - McGowen October 15, 1975
9. Mercury News - April 26, 2018
10. San Francisco Chronicle - April 27, 2018
11. KATU - April 30, 2018
12. New York Times - April 27, 2018
13. Sacramento Bee - April 28, 2018
14. Rolling Stone - August 22, 2018
15. KPBS/NPR April 27, 2018
16. Carpenter v. United States, No. 16-402, 585 U.S. (2018)
17. Los Angeles Times - May 1, 2018
18. New York Times - "The True Crime-Obsessed Philanthropists Paying to Catch Killers" - March 27, 2022
19. Visalia Times-Delta - April 27, 2018
20. FOX 40 - April 27, 2018
21. Exeter Sun-Gazette - January 2, 2019
22. Our Valley Voice - April 25, 2018
23. ABC 10 - "Framed By the Golden State Killer?"
24. Interview with Farrell Ward
25. Sacramento Bee - July 22, 2018
26. Handwritten Suspect List - Agent McGowen
27. Exeter Sun-Gazette - July 11, 2018
28. Buzzfeed News - July 25, 2018
29. CA State Bar Court #89-O-11273-JG, IN RE Harvey Zall
30. Visalia Times-Delta - June 9, 1977
31. DA Ward's Report to Attorney General, January 7, 2019

32. Reports and Bench Notes of DOJ Senior Criminalist Scott Lewis 2011-12
33. Letter from Forensic Analytical to NCIP June 23, 2003
34. Ruling Re: Nature of Slide VPH, June 22, 2004
35. Interview with Liz Silva
36. Bringhurst, "*The Ku Klux Klan in a Central California Community: Tulare County During the 1920s and 1930s.*" Southern California Quarterly, vol. 82, no. 4
37. Visalia Times-Delta - February 23, 2019
38. CAP Radio - April 30, 2018
39. Interview with Gary Bardone
40. Tulare Advance-Register - October 23, 1975
41. Exeter Sun - March 20, 1974
42. Exeter Sun - January 18. 1978

CHAPTER FIFTEEN

"Two sides of the same coin"

In September 2020, Joseph DeAngelo entered a guilty plea to the thirteen murders in the original charges. He also admitted responsibility for the EAR rapes, kidnapping Beth Snelling, the VR burglaries, and the attempted murder of VPD Agent Bill McGowen. The victims and their families were allowed to make statements prior to sentencing, and he was given life in prison with no parole. Margie called Tulare ADA Alavezos to learn if he had asked DeAngelo to confess to the murder of Jennifer Armour, and Alavezos said that he had not. His reason was simple, and ridiculous: TCSO had never referred the case to him for prosecution. DeAngelo has never denied killing Jennifer or Donna, and he has been clear that he will never speak about any of his crimes, including those that are uncharged. Personally, I was surprised that he didn't want to brag about how easily he fooled his fellow police officers who had been hunting him. It seems that he feels that not talking infuriates his perceived enemies and gives him more power.

I came to believe in Oscar's innocence not because I knew who killed Donna, but simply because of the impossibility of his guilt. No matter how many times Rick Carter was asked, he kept saying that Oscar really got home at 4:15 pm, and he passed a polygraph on that statement. I also don't believe that Oscar's daughters lied on the witness stand, or are lying today when they confirm that time. I believe Frank Thomas made the late comment at 3:15 pm; he was one of the only people to look at their watch the entire day, and he had no reason to lie. If you believe either Carter or Thomas, then Oscar is innocent; there is no scenario where he could have killed Donna, let alone approached Brumley or Mascorro. Even Powell agreed that Oscar was in N. Visalia at 3:00 pm. I don't know if Beth Brumley talked to a man, but if she did, it couldn't have been Oscar. Just like the Mascorros definitely did not see Oscar's distinctive ***F O R D*** tailgate on his truck.

Why was Oscar's invoice book by Donna's bike? Because it was planted there. I tend to think that Donna's killer put it there, but Oscar may have been correct, it could have been Bob Byrd. Why Oscar? If it were DeAngelo, it could have been because he knew that Oscar was discussed among law enforcement, likely by Byrd, as a VR and/or Porterville Rapist suspect. DeAngelo also sought out random confrontations, and he could have gotten into a "thing" with Oscar at the hardware store or at K-Mart. He was extremely vengeful, and a couple of his EAR attacks were known to be directed at the husbands, not the wives. However, I do know that Oscar didn't wipe his prints off the invoice book or Donna's bike, and I know that the notepad didn't belong to him.

I wasn't the first one to be suspicious that the notepad belonged to an Exeter PD Officer. PI Pettyjohn thought so too, and he met with Chief Hank Fry to discuss it. The notes I have also show that he was looking for someone who was left-handed. He had already cleared the Cliftons from consideration. It didn't take an expert to see that Oscar's numbers could not have been a match since he closed his "4s," crossed his "7s," and put curls on his "3s" and "5s."

There really wouldn't have been any reason for Clifton to admit ownership of the invoice book, but then randomly deny the notepad. Pettyjohn didn't make a report of his meeting with Fry— I just have his notes and time billing. Before DeAngelo was identified, I wondered if this all meant that the notepad was accidentally dropped by one of the officers searching that night, and it contaminated the crime scene. That would explain Byrd and Powell trying to hide it from the jury.

After DeAngelo's arrest, I wanted to know if the handwriting in the notepad was consistent with DeAngelo's numbers, and luckily I was able to obtain all of his handwritten Auburn PD reports from

August 1976-July 1979. The numbers are all consistently formed, and are as much of a confirmatory match as the limited information in the notepad allows. Why would DeAngelo's pocket notepad be with Oscar's invoice book, next to Donna's bike? He either dropped it in the dark and didn't notice, or accidentally picked it up with the invoice book, and set it down underneath it—the way it was photographed. I can see from the copies that there were unidentified fingerprints on it, which points to another possible reason for Sgt. Byrd to order the evidence destroyed.

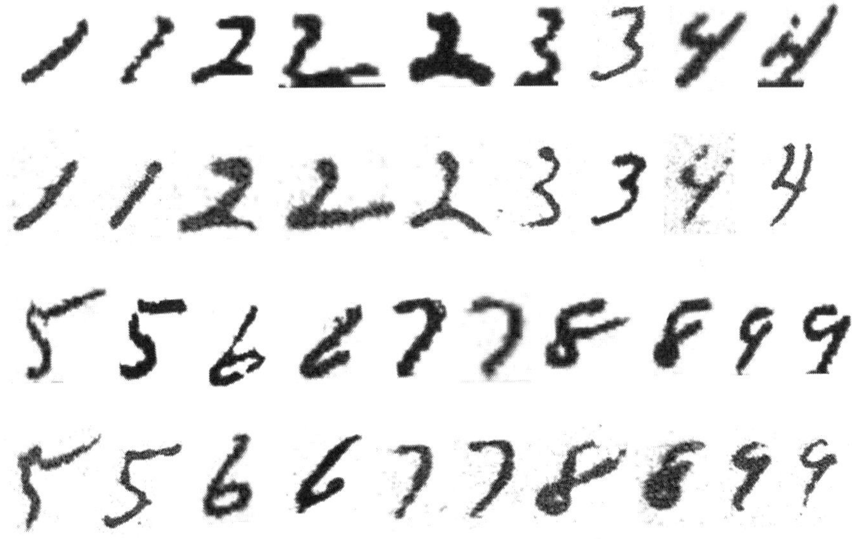

ROWS 1 & 3: DeAngelo APD Reports
ROWS 2 & 4: Notepad at Bike Scene

Since there is nothing left of the physical evidence to examine or test, the handwriting match may be the only direct evidence that implicates DeAngelo in Donna's murder. However, there is a mountain of *circumstantial* evidence that ties him to the case through MO, motive, means, and opportunity:

- Donna Richmond was DeAngelo's preferred victim age and physical type. He is an admitted serial rapist and murderer, with dozens of known victims between the ages of 13-18 years, as demonstrated by their photos.

Jennifer, Beth, Debbie, and Donna
Credit: Jennifer, Beth, and Debbie: MWHS Yearbook “Oak” 1974-1975;
Donna, Richmond Family, 1975

- DeAngelo lived and worked along Donna's route home, and less than two miles from Neel Ranch, Don Lee's house, and the bike scene.
- Donna grew up with DeAngelo's nephews. They were the same ages as Donna and her brother. Donna's family was prominent in Exeter, and DeAngelo would have known who she was, where she lived, and the short-cut through the grove where her bike was found. As a police officer he also would have had grounds to ask her that information, or obtain it from the registration displayed on her bike.
- TCSO forensic officers testified at trial that they ignored numerous footprints and tire tracks at the scenes that belonged to law enforcement personnel and vehicles.
- White paint transfer marks found on Donna's bike were identified as likely coming from a law enforcement vehicle.
- TCSO Johnson testified that he did not photograph or document "wavy" tennis shoe prints observed near Donna's bike. The same type of tread design was noted at multiple EAR scenes in 1976-77.
- DeAngelo regularly inflicted knife injuries. EAR victims had knife cuts on their temples, throats, arms, and legs. On October 18, 1976, the EAR pulled a woman from her car, took her to a pre-staged attack site in a nearby yard, jabbed his knife through her clothing into her chest until he drew blood, and then left the scene without raping her. Forensic reports and autopsy photos confirm that Donna was stabbed through her clothing.
- Jennifer Armour was killed 1.5 miles north of Donna. Both locations were orange groves along the Friant-Kern Canal. TCSO named DeAngelo as a suspect in Jennifer's murder in 2018 based upon her kidnapping in the VR zone, proximity to the Snelling homicide, and similarities in physical type, age, and school. In November 2017, TCSO stated that Jennifer and Donna were killed by the same person. TCSO has already publicly argued that

Jennifer was kidnapped and killed by the VR, **and** that she was killed by the same person who killed Donna.

Not only is Jennifer circumstantially tied to the VR's known activities, but also her outside attack location, along a cement-lined canal, and being bound with her own bra connect her to EAR cases. DeAngelo bound at least two of the EAR victims with their own bras, including the very first EAR attack in June 1976:

- There are at least two credible reports of 13-year-old girls being approached by DeAngelo under color of law in Visalia. Both girls have positively identified DeAngelo, and one made a contemporaneous report to Visalia PD in 1975. Given the lack of defensive injuries and witnesses to a struggle, it appears that both Jennifer and Donna got into their killer's car without the need for physical force.
- Exeter PD was conducting a bike "crackdown" targeting young riders. Those who were 14 years and over had to appear before a judge with their parents to answer the citation. This could have been used as grounds to "stop" Donna, and tell her she was being transported home or to the Exeter PD station.
- Beth Snelling described the mask worn by her attacker as having a "multi-colored zig zag design;" the ski mask found at Neel Ranch, apparently dropped by Donna's killer, was described as "multi-colored," and the evidence photo shows a zig zag pattern. During the July 17, 1976 EAR attack, DeAngelo took a "multi-colored" ski or stocking cap from the closet of one sister, wore it while he attacked the second sister, and then placed it in a drawer before he left the home.
- Several empty bottles and cans were found near Donna's bike, including "Pepsi" and "Coors" cans. TCSO Johnson was unable to find fingerprints on any of those containers. This was consistent with the lack of prints

on the invoice book and Donna's bike. This is also a well-documented VR and EAR MO point. Specifically, the EAR favored leaving empty "Coors" and "Pepsi" cans, sometimes brought to the scene. He also left other empty beer bottles and soda cans at numerous EAR attacks, often on the back patio of the victim's home. Additionally, an empty rum bottle was found by Donna's bike and under a bush in the Snelling yard.

- It appears that DeAngelo chose the October 9, 1976 rape victim, and the neighbor, Dority, to frame, as early as 1973, before he moved to Exeter. He broke into both of their homes as part of the 1973 "Cordova Meadows" series. In 1976, DeAngelo entered Dority's house prior to the rape, and planted a bag of EAR stolen jewelry and coins. DeAngelo then made several statements to the victim leading her to believe that he lived nearby.
- DeAngelo created secondary staged scenes by stealing EAR victims' cars, and parking them at specific locations. When the cars were located, deputies spent days canvassing the neighbors for possible sightings, and running them down as potential suspects. Did the EAR live nearby? Had he parked his own car on the block? Did the location indicate he lived in that general direction? The locations meant nothing. These staged clues wasted hundreds of investigative hours, increased the frustration and tension within the Sheriff's office, and distracted from the real evidence in the cases.
- During the early EAR attacks, several victims were punched and kicked. Injuries ranged from a broken nose and loss of consciousness to raised lumps and bruises. A victim who resisted was beaten with a billy club, had a concussion, and needed stitches for multiple head wounds. Beth Snelling was kicked in the face and head while she was sitting on the ground offering no resistance. Donna was hit on the back left side of her head, and kicked in the left kidney area, likely while on the ground.

- Several of DeAngelo's early EAR victims were kidnapped outside, or taken from inside, to an outside attack location. This includes a woman who was punched into unconsciousness as she was loading her car, a woman who was forcibly dragged out of her car at knifepoint after DeAngelo reached in a partially open window, and a couple walking from a house to a car. Several victims were raped in their yards, and one was walked over 1/4 mile to a wooded open space. Sacramento Sheriffs documented the EAR's use of, and preference for, attacks near cement-lined canals and ditches—like the Friant-Kern Canal in Exeter.
- The November 10, 1976 EAR attack has many commonalities with Donna's murder, especially the elaborate scene staging. The 16-year-old girl was kidnapped on DeAngelo's third wedding anniversary. He broke into her house at dinnertime when she was alone, watching TV. Before kidnapping her, DeAngelo staged the house to make it appear that the girl had simply gone out. He walked her over a fence, into the neighbor's yard, into a concrete-lined ditch, under the street, and 1/4 mile between backyards to an open space that he had pre-selected for the attack. He forcibly removed the victim's lower clothing at knifepoint. When she finally made her way home after a couple of hours, she discovered that her parents had no idea that she had been kidnapped, and were annoyed that she had left on too many lights. The story DeAngelo had told through staging had worked perfectly.
- DeAngelo was under enormous pressure from the exhaustive Visalia PD investigation and public focus on the VR, the Snelling murder, and the McGowen shooting. His composite and description was on the front page of the *Visalia Times-Delta* on December 18th. Whatever he had been planning for Gary Bardone and his wife had not worked out. He had a strong and pressing motive to frame Oscar as the VR.

- It is unlikely that sightings of DeAngelo or an Exeter PD car would be reported as "suspicious" by any witness or citizen. Additionally, the Exeter PD firing range was located in a remote area along the Friant-Kern Canal between Neel Ranch and Donna's bike. It was not unusual to see Exeter PD cars using the limited-access roads, including the canal siding road.

In the fall of 2018, Lilia Luciano, a journalist with ABC10 in Sacramento, started working on the story of Oscar's wrongful conviction, and DeAngelo as a suspect in the murders of Jennifer Armour and Donna Richmond. She and her producer, Mike Bunnell, worked on the story for a year, and reached the exact same conclusions Sgt. Vaughan and I had reached. Oscar was factually innocent, all evidence pointed to DeAngelo being responsible for the Exeter homicides, and the actions of TCSO Sgt. Byrd and DA Powell had helped DeAngelo escape suspicion in Tulare County and left him free to kill at least another twelve people.

Lilia left no stone unturned. She conducted multiple hours-long on-camera interviews with DA Ward and ADA Alavezos, and gave them every opportunity to make their case for Oscar's guilt. They had no argument for DeAngelo's innocence because they did not investigate him—at all. Lilia asked them for the supposed report from DOJ that found semen, and DA Ward couldn't give it to her, because it didn't exist. Lilia was given full access to the entire DA's file on Oscar's case, and they had almost nothing. No original witness statements, no Grand Jury or trial transcripts, not even the DOJ bench notes from the DNA testing.

The DA's review of Oscar's conviction was based upon reading their own appeals brief arguing his guilt. Neither Ward nor Alavezos seemed to have any familiarity with DeAngelo's actual crimes or MO, and Ward argued that Oscar's 1965 conviction was worse than anything DeAngelo had done, including the thirteen murders. DeAngelo's last victim, 18-year-old Janelle Cruz, was beaten so badly the coroner had to pick fragments of her teeth out of her hair, but sure, Oscar was the real monster in Exeter. The lies in the interviews were endless and shocking. I was given the opportunity to fact check the DA's false claims, and they were brazen:

- Oscar had not received the death penalty, nor had he ever been on death row
- It was routine, and not illegal, for TCSO to destroy all of the case evidence and trial exhibits months after the conviction
- Oscar had been arrested at the river by the responding TCSO officers in 1965
- Bob Byrd had not been involved, let alone arrested Oscar in 1965
- Showing eyewitnesses a photo of the suspect and telling them who to identify prior to the lineup did not taint them
- There were no coveralls found that matched the ones described by Brent Trueblood
- Donna had been raped
- DeAngelo did not stage scenes, plant evidence, or frame anyone in his other cases
- DeAngelo did not cut anyone with a knife
- DeAngelo did not use his badge or police authority to commit his crimes
- There was no ABO typing of Blake's sample, and no match to DeAngelo's blood type A
- No plaster casts were taken of the tire tracks by Morton
- Oscar was seen by Gene Owens at 1:00 pm, not 3:00 pm.

Obviously, those were all lies, and DA Ward was unable to provide evidence to support anything he told Lilia. When she showed them documents disproving each point, it generally ended with an angry, bullying, off-point tirade by ADA Alavezos. The video is really uncomfortable to watch. Lilia also got a critical phone interview with Bob Byrd in which he lied about arresting Oscar in 1965 and 1975, ordering the evidence destruction, and even knowing DeAngelo—his neighbor and co-worker for three and a half years. The only thing that he admitted to was having a dispute with Oscar prior to 1965, and personal animosity towards him.

Unfortunately, none of it really mattered. Lilia's good work and video series were completely overshadowed by bigger productions like ABC's 20/20, and a HBO "documentary" series based on Michelle McNamara's book. It is difficult to know how McNamara's story would have ended if she hadn't tragically died before she finished writing. The book was completed for publication by her researchers. The project was originally launched from McNamara's piece in *Los Angeles* magazine that examined the EAR and Original Night Stalker cases. She dubbed the offender "The Golden State Killer." I was impressed by that work—especially the inclusion of Investigator Larry Pool and his belief that the VR was the same offender. McNamara included the real story of the VR, including Beth Snelling's description of him. There was nothing about the "Peeper," McGowen's hypnosis, or that long-ago discredited physical description. The story was well-researched and balanced, and it relied upon primary sources and interviews.

In *I'll Be Gone*, the chapter titled "Visalia" starts with a disclaimer:

> EDITOR'S NOTE: The following chapter was pieced together from Michelle's notes and early drafts of "In the Footsteps of a Killer," a piece Michelle wrote for Los Angeles magazine, originally published in February 2013 and later supplemented online.

To be clear, the Visalia chapter wasn't written by McNamara. It solidly argued against a VR/EAR connection based, once again, on the flawed "Peeper" connection and on McGowen's hypnosis information. Having discussed it with Larry Pool, and understanding the direct investigative work he had done to clear the Peeper as the VR, I couldn't understand how the book had veered so far off course. Pool hadn't changed his opinion, and he had been a huge influence on McNamara's original work. Suddenly, the story was Paul Holes' narrative—the exact same arguments he had made to me, in podcasts, and on TV specials. The chapter had a long section on McGowen's session with the "Svengali Squad," and gave it reverential treatment. It was uninformed and troubling. The squad's work had been so thoroughly debunked in 1982 that it caused a ban on hypnotized witnesses. So why was this junk science still peddled in 2018 as being the ***most*** reliable information?

My experience with Paul Holes has been frustrating and circular. There were no documents, assurances from VPD, or discussions with Pool that could change his mind—he was fixated on the Peeper as the VR. I had the impression he was arguing that someone else killed Claude Snelling, and it was wholly unrelated to the other cases, but it was never clearly stated. Since Holes consistently repeated that only the "Peeper" witness and McGowen had ever seen the VR, something was deeply wrong with his understanding of the Snelling case.

There is no question: Paul Holes' reaction to DeAngelo's confession to being the VR was less than gracious. It was in especially stark contrast to SSD Detective Shelby, whose book on the EAR, *Hunting a Psychopath*, had included an entire chapter arguing that there was no way the VR was his offender. After the arrest, Shelby simply stated that he had gotten it wrong, and then spent every interview urging further investigation into DeAngelo's uncharged crimes—especially Jennifer's and Donna's in Exeter. Shelby used his platform as an original investigator to try to help get more answers. Holes used his to bury the truth.

Holes doubled down on the argument that the VR and EAR were nothing alike either physically or criminally—despite his knowledge that they were literally the same person. In Holes' version, DeAngelo was a terrible burglar who couldn't get anything right, and he basically ran around Visalia being terrified and screaming for three years. Holes went on true crime podcast *My Favorite Murder*, and even laughed about the VR: "I would say—Visalia, he was in the minor leagues. The VR was not a very good burglar. He struggled to get inside houses even... [*laughter*]" He and the hosts had a great time joking about what a fat, incompetent doofus he was.

I thought back to the newspaper quotes about the VR from Larry Pool, Russ Whitmeyer, Bill McGowen, and John Vaughan, and the evil "phantom" that had terrorized Visalia just for the thrill of it. I couldn't let go of Beth Snelling's description of her horrific kidnapping, and watching her attacker walk back and wait for the opportunity to shoot her father to death in front of her. When I closed my eyes to sleep, I saw Donna's body, with her face resting on her hand and her hair streaked with blood. Clearly, I have no sense of humor and don't get the joke.

I shouldn't have been surprised by what happened with the HBO series. Both Sgt. Vaughan and Detective Shelby predicted it, and tried to warn me. I was interested to see what the director, Liz Garbus, would bring to the story. I had watched her 2019 documentary *Who Killed Garrett Phillip?* which appeared to be a fact- and evidence-based narrative, and had to completely rethink my opinion about Oral Hillary's innocence and the evidence as presented. Garbus and I clearly have different definitions of "documentary." Since the HBO's *Gone* series was based on McNamara's book, I knew that there wouldn't be any mention of Exeter, Donna, or Jennifer. However, DeAngelo had confessed to the Visalia crimes, so it seemed like the best idea was to tell the story exactly as McNamara had in *Los Angeles* magazine, and not worry about anyone's ego or feelings about getting it "wrong" in the book.

Instead, Garbus completely *erased* the Snellings, and inexplicably included the erroneous statement that DeAngelo first killed in 1978 (and repeated that lie *three times* during the series). These weren't mistakes, they were intentional manipulations of the facts and evidence to make it look reasonable that Holes and the McNamara team had just reached the wrong conclusion about the VR as a lead. Let's be honest, there is no way to hear about what DeAngelo did to Beth and Claude Snelling and not know that he was an extremely violent, dangerous, and capable man. He was never, at any time, a laughing matter. It was exactly as SSD described it in the warrants—"explosive violence"—a *direct* match to the EAR and Maggiore homicides.

Would I say that you had to be a terrible investigator to miss the VR/EAR MO? *Yes, for certain.* I feel that the HBO audience would have agreed had they seen the truth. It was clear that Garbus didn't see a way to portray her team as investigative geniuses with such an obvious clue overlooked or discarded. Apparently, the answer was to change the facts: just delete Claude Snelling, and simply make the shooting of Katie and Brian Maggiore be DeAngelo's "first homicide." Even stranger, Garbus doubled down on the argument that hypnotized statements are ***more*** reliable—a slap in the face to the past forty years of science, objective reality, and the law.

ABC's 20/20 episode on DeAngelo accidentally included the words "Visalia Ransacker" when a clip of the Orange County Prosecutor was played from the day of the arrest—apparently before he got the memo that they were supposed to ignore Tulare County. In the entire two-hour episode on DeAngelo, his family, and his victims, there was *no mention* of any place or person in Tulare County, or an explanation for the reference to the VR. Sgt. Vaughan wasn't asked to explain how his team had caught DeAngelo in their stakeout, or how and why he had been so convinced that the EAR was the same offender. More revisionist history disguised as news and documentary narrative. A neat package that conveniently erased all of the hard truths about how DeAngelo used his badge and training to burglarize, rape, and kill, and how he really escaped capture.

The majority of what has been written and produced since DeAngelo's identification has followed the same narrative: The Sacramento Sheriff, FBI offices, and the EAR Task Force were heroes that valiantly followed every lead, and never stopped trying to catch him, but he slipped through their dragnet. Of course, in order to tell that story you have to erase the VR, Claude Snelling, Sgt. Vaughan,

Agent McGowen, Russ Whitmeyer, Exeter, and Investigator Pool's work that involved the VR linkage. The truth is quite simple: *Tulare County was always the key to finding DeAngelo.*

If major investigative resources and information sharing had been poured into the Tulare County connection as a valuable lead, just as Sgt. Vaughan repeatedly requested, it would have been relatively easy to narrow down the suspects. SSD should have been willing to listen to Vaughan's advice about how to conduct their stakeouts, and tried to push DeAngelo out into the open using statements to the press. Any story, from any source, that says that DeAngelo couldn't be stopped in 1977 is a lie—a tale told to soothe bruised and battered egos incapable of admitting their errors. No lessons have been learned, nothing has changed, and criminal police officers still prey on citizens with protection from their departments, prosecutors, and the Attorney General's office.

Obviously, TCSO Sgt. Bob Byrd and Tulare DA Jay Powell also could have stopped DeAngelo with nothing more than proper police investigations. Asking who could have staged Neel Ranch and the bike scene, and framed Oscar with the invoice book, should have pointed to a limited number of suspects. Calling in VPD and California DOJ investigators to help canvass for witnesses, collect evidence, and share suspects likely could have led to DeAngelo's immediate identification by McGowen as the VR. Even just circling back to VPD when Jennifer's murder stopped being an "accident" could have solved the entire series. Sgt. Vaughan's team contacted TCSO and Exeter PD multiple times to ask for ***any*** crimes they had that could have been related to the VR, and got nothing.

I believe, but cannot prove, that at some point, no later than February 1977, Bob Byrd suspected, or knew, that DeAngelo was the EAR. Not only did he have information on all of the crimes in Tulare County, he knew about the EAR's MO when it was still a secret from people in Sacramento. The great unknown is how much DeAngelo inserted himself into Donna's murder case. If he conducted an "interview" with Don Lee, as I've been told, I have to imagine that Byrd was aware of either direct interference with the investigation and/or sightings of DeAngelo near the scenes.

I cannot imagine Byrd ever arresting a local police officer for killing Donna. His fellow cops would have hated him for breaking the "blue wall," and the citizens would have lost their trust and respect for all officers in the area. I'm not sure DA Powell would have even allowed it. The criminal cases DeAngelo investigated would have had to have been dismissed, and those defendants would have been able to sue the city and county for wrongful arrest and prosecution. I think if Byrd and Powell ever suspected DeAngelo, they would have turned their heads and looked the other way.

It may sound insane to suggest that Byrd would have knowingly let DeAngelo remain free to rape and kill, but Byrd would have lost everything if the truth had come out. How could he have pointed to DeAngelo as the EAR without Oscar immediately going to court and asking for a new trial? Byrd already knew that the EAR's blood type matched Grubb's testing, and VPD said that the EAR had been living in the county when Donna was killed. It would have taken two seconds to understand exactly what had happened to Donna, and who had hidden the evidence. However, incompetent or intentional doesn't really matter; Byrd's actions directly helped DeAngelo escape detection for more than forty years.

There were a couple more good opportunities to catch DeAngelo, especially after his arrest and conviction for shoplifting in Citrus Heights in July 1979. That case was handled by SSD, including the same unit that had investigated the EAR burglaries and rapes in the neighborhood just two years earlier. The feud between VPD and SSD had been on the front pages of both Sacramento newspapers in July 1978, and yet somehow, nobody at SSD wondered if there was a connection when they arrested a former Exeter PD officer stealing a hammer and dog mace in the EAR zone. What about Auburn PD? Did they conduct any kind of investigation into DeAngelo's use of his police authority? Did they inform defendants that their cases had been handled by a dishonest officer who had been convicted of theft and fired? What did Chief Willick tell Exeter PD, and what investigation followed there? There should have been giant red flags waving everywhere, and an easy match to the information Sgt. Vaughan had made so public.

I feel certain about one thing: DeAngelo believed that SSD was on to him after his arrest. It's hard to know if that was just his assumption that they would put it all together, or if an investigator asked him if he was the EAR. My certainty lies in what DeAngelo did next. He was off work on the day of the shoplifting, July 2, 1979. The Pay 'n Save was on Greenback Lane, 1.5 miles from his in-laws' house—an area he knew well. The next day he was back on patrol with Auburn PD as usual. DeAngelo was also acting as a shift supervisor, so clearly Chief Willick had not yet been told of the arrest. The same for the next day, July 4th. DeAngelo's last documented police call was at 10:25 pm, but at 3:50 am on the 5th, he was 111 miles from Auburn, on Sycamore Hill Court in Danville, attempting another EAR attack. The couple had heard about the nearby rapes and practiced their possible escape, and it worked. DeAngelo fled, dropping pre-tied shoelaces, just like at the Maggiore homicide scene.

The entire attack was unusual for DeAngelo. He almost never hit on the second floor, or in a condominium with so many close neighbors. He made a noise that woke the husband, and nearly got caught. It always seemed off, but it makes a lot of sense when you realize that DeAngelo worked a full shift patrolling and supervising in Auburn, then got in his car and drove 90 minutes to Danville with a very short window until daybreak. By 3:00 pm, he was back at work in Auburn. Why take the risk? Because he wanted to make sure that the EAR was seen striking over a hundred miles away while he was going to work as normal. That was the furthest he could reasonably drive and attack, and he hoped that it would be enough to make SSD believe that he could not be the EAR. That same logic also explained the June and July 1976 EAR attacks while he still lived in Exeter. DeAngelo wanted to make sure the series had started ***before*** he moved, so the timing wouldn't point directly towards him. He knew how the investigators would think.

DeAngelo was an active-duty police officer from May 1973-July 1979, and had an internship with Roseville PD before that. How many innocent men did he frame and arrest for his own crimes? How could any criminal case that involved his "investigation" or testimony be trusted? It shouldn't be. Every single person who had an arrest, charge, or conviction touched by DeAngelo should be completely exonerated, receive a public apology, and be compensated for the harm caused to their lives. Are any of these men still in prison? I know of at least one. Making wrongs right again matters to the accused men and their families—no matter how small the actual harm.

There has been no investigation into any of the other rapes and murders that lead back to DeAngelo. Multiple rape victims not included in the original warrants were told that they would be given the opportunity to speak at the sentencing hearing, but were never contacted. The narrative from the Sacramento DA's office, who have controlled the entire case, is that miraculously every single crime that DeAngelo committed was identified by DNA or MO years prior to his arrest. That is not a credible statement, nor is it what the evidence shows. They have refused to go back and look at the old rape case forensic reports for evidence that matches DeAngelo's blood type, secretor status, and PGM type—a combination that is found in less than 1% of males—almost as good as DNA evidence. That forensic evidence exists, but Sacramento will not look because they're afraid that the additional missed cases will make their prior investigations look even worse.

Multiple investigators have stated that DeAngelo "left the area" after the suspect composites in the Maggiore homicide were published. That's just another lie—or wishful thinking. He was with Auburn PD for another eighteen months, and then continued to live in Auburn until he bought his house in Citrus Heights on April 11, 1980. DeAngelo may have wanted investigators to believe that the EAR had moved, and they may have fallen for the ruse, but facts and reality prove that it didn't happen. All evidence shows that DeAngelo continued his pattern of hitting in ***both*** Sacramento and other counties, just like he had been doing since September 1977. I understand why SSD lied and told the public that the EAR was gone—people were mad that he was running circles around the police, and the press was constantly critical of their performance. SSD simply went back to how they started the EAR investigation—hiding his attacks from the press and public, and calling every rape "unrelated." Another illustration can be found in the EAR Task Force memo about an attack in Rancho Cordova in March of 1979:

21 March, 1979

To: Lieutenant B. Pitkin, EAR Task Force Commander
From: Sergeant Rod Carpenter, CCCSO Analyst

I have conducted a preliminary investigation with Sergeants Larry Crompton, CCCSO, and Jim Bevins, SCSO, in regards to Sacramento County's recent burglary/attempt rape/robbery case. The original report lacked several points which we were able to answer.

It is my opinion that this is an EAR case. At present, Sacramento Sheriff's Office administrators would like to keep the possible EAR attack quiet so that the press will not over-react [*sic*] to the case. They are still working the case, and attempting to develop leads and evidence.

The EAR has made six other Tuesday attacks. He has returned within two to 24 days after every Tuesday attack. [*Followed by typed list of 13 prior attacks showing pattern*]

Note that on each Tuesday attack, EAR has switched cities on the next offense. It is unknown why the suspect left in the middle of this attack. Possibly he left because the victim's daughter's alarm clock went off. If the case was considered as an aborted attempt, then the… data can be studied. [*Followed by typed list of seven prior attacks showing pattern*]

Note again that EAR switched cities on each attack. It is unknown if he needs to complete a sexual act to be satisfied. The aborted attempt might be sufficient for his purpose.

It is suggested that this department consider the case of 3-20-79 an EAR attack and prepare for another attack in the near future.

As Sgt. Carpenter predicted, the next EAR case arrived quickly in a different city—on April 5th in Fremont. He was also correct about the EAR's return to Sacramento, it was on a Tuesday; September 25th. That offense is specifically tied to the June 11, 1979 EAR and prowling cases in Danville by the unique Adidas "Tobacco" shoes, and the same size 9.5, worn by the suspect. SSD made sure that *The Sacramento Bee* did not convey any of Sgt. Carpenter's warnings in their story on March 21, 1979:

Masked Man Fails at Rape

A masked man attempted to rape a 38-year-old secretary after tying her up and striking her early Tuesday, Sacramento sheriff's deputies said. The man entered the woman's home in Rancho Cordova about 5a.m. and assaulted her with an object the woman was not able to identify, deputies said. The attacker tied the woman with a cord and attempted to rape her but was unsuccessful. The man wore a stocking mask over his head and talked through clenched teeth during the attack, according to reports. Before leaving, the man took jewelry and money belonging to the woman.

Sheriff's detectives have **ruled out the incident** being related to the work of the East Area Rapist who has recently raped 41 women in the Sacramento area, Davis, Stockton, Modesto and the Bay area. [*emphasis added*]

Unfortunately, someone at SSD decided that keeping the case "quiet" meant lying to the press, and the public. They not only knew that the EAR was alternating attack locations, including Sacramento, but that he was likely to return on a Tuesday. How would *you* feel if you were the woman attacked in her home on September 25, 1979? SSD, and *The Sacramento Bee* had again assured her that the EAR was gone, and if she locked the doors and windows in her new middle-class suburban home, she would be safe. It was all an intentional lie. Larry Crompton's description of the events in *Sudden Terror* are specific and detailed. Lt. Pitkin told investigators Carpenter, Crompton, and Bevins that they were just trying to "convince themselves" that the EAR was still in Sacramento.

These later rape cases exist, as do over a dozen unsolved homicides for which DeAngelo is a strong suspect and has not been eliminated. I get it; these cases are embarrassing. They make a lot of different law enforcement agencies and some specific investigators look terrible. However, these victims and families deserve answers and resolution to their cases, not more cover-ups.

Paul Holes has variously described the research process that went from genetic sequence to identifying DeAngelo, yet stumbled near the goal line. One year before the arrest, Holes wrote about his various working theories on the offender, detailing in particular his most likely occupation: "I believe he was employed in an occupation that would necessitate having had several years of experience… in the development/building/real estate industry." This seemed to provide an explanation for the extensive, crisscross route across California for the attacks. However, even armed with an exact match between the criminal's genetic profile and the name of an actual human being, the incongruity was apparently debilitating. A month after the arrest, he explained: "The thing that really bugged me about DeAngelo, even as a suspect: he's in Auburn.… How is he a full-time law enforcement officer in Auburn and then committing all of these attacks?"

This is opposed to opening his mind to reality that the profile that matched Joseph James DeAngelo, Jr. ***also*** belonged to a powerful predator, one trained to know how the crimes would be investigated. Yes, as Larry Pool properly stated, the EAR actually had driven hundreds of miles for the sole purpose of "misdirection," yet Holes *still* expressed confusion. DeAngelo the offender knew exactly what he was doing. He wanted the investigators to believe that this criminal had a job that took him to these different cities, and law enforcement would follow these clues to reach that conclusion. In the video interview, made one month after the arrest, Holes remained disoriented, stuck in his prior beliefs and personal theories, and still hoping for an answer to his question, even though the answer was right there in the form of a highly trained, intelligent police officer, already matched by a computerized MO system as he moved both to and from the EAR series.

How many times did DeAngelo use his badge, car, uniform, and other direct police resources to commit his crimes? He was one of the officers who Exeter residents were urged to call to evaluate the security of their homes, or report when they were going out of town and wanted "extra patrols." Did he run license plates and driver's licenses of women he saw and wanted to stalk? *Of course he did.* He also inserted himself directly into investigations of his own crimes.

DeAngelo was highly trained, with two degrees in police sciences. He knew how crimes were investigated, and had a deep knowledge of forensic evidence—how not to leave it at a scene, and how to frame someone else with it. At EAR scenes he left cigarette butts, and even a used Band-Aid that did not belong to him, hoping it would confuse SSD about his real blood type. He never left a fingerprint at any scene, ever. *Not one.* The last case connected to him by DNA is from 1986, the same time that DNA from a rape kit was first used as evidence in a criminal trial in the United States. Do I think he stopped killing? No, I believe that he just learned not to leave his DNA.

The only MO I would ever discount for DeAngelo would be luring using charm; he had none. He was too intense, flat, and unsettling.

His possible victims could be almost anyone. He attacked very young teens, single women, mothers with children, and couples. He picked fights with random men, often inciting incidents on the road and taking them into parking lots. He was known to be armed with knives, guns, and clubs. He used a wide variety of bindings, sometimes obtained at the scenes, and often brought with him—pre-cut and pre-tied. He burglarized empty homes, and those with sleeping victims. He stalked certain women for years, both leading up to the attack and then with calls later. In the early 1990s, he started harassing victims from 1976.

When one of his victims moved to a newly built area in Danville in 1976, he chose a house just six blocks away in her neighborhood to commit new attacks in 1978-79. The mother of a thirteen-year-old victim from 1977 decided that she needed a fresh start, and moved them to a gated community in Dana Point in 1980. Weeks later, DeAngelo killed the Harringtons four blocks away, within the same gates. It appears that he chose to terrorize the neighbors where his own friends and family lived, making them secondary victims. Only DeAngelo knows the full extent of his crimes, but clearly the charged cases have only scratched the surface.

Why can't there be an exoneration for Oscar, or a thorough investigation into DeAngelo's crimes? Because police, prosecutors, and judges operate with complete immunity in California. Nothing can or will hold them accountable. We elect sheriffs, district attorneys, and judges, and the way they get elected and re-elected is to be "tough on crime." Voters want safe communities, and they mistakenly believe that arrest numbers and convictions are a measure of that. The Office of Attorney General (AG) is called the "Top Cop," and when it comes to criminal cases, his deputies are always prosecutors. In California, the AG has defied multiple court orders to release police disciplinary records to defendants. If a police officer is caught planting evidence or lying on the witness stand, it is all kept confidential and completely secret. Until the fall of 2021, if an officer was fired for misconduct, they were free to take a job with another department. It remains to be seen if the new decertification process will actually work as designed.

In short, the justice system is a closed circle, made up of police officers, pro-police prosecutors, and former DAs as judges and justices. They agree with each other, protect each other, and serve each other's re-elections. That is how they obtain power, and keep it. The only way any of that will ever change is through the will of the voters; if they decide they want actual justice rather than just tidy crime statistics.

There is also a simple answer for past wrongful convictions. The Governor could appoint an independent commission to review cases where the claim is actual innocence. In California, only 2% of felony cases go to trial. 81% of those result in felony convictions, 4% resolve as misdemeanors, and 15% end in acquittal or dismissal of the charges—the vast majority of criminal cases are settled through guilty pleas. Giving a fair, independent review, investigation, and hearing to those who claim that the DA and jury got it wrong is ***not*** an overwhelming burden on the State of California, especially if it is reserved for defendants who have already exhausted their appeals. A commission of attorneys, investigators, and forensic experts would happily work for a small stipend to cover their expenses, and would have no pressure from the community or an election campaign. There is every reason to do this, and no reason not to, yet it never seems to happen.

Joseph DeAngelo's criminal case is over. The California Attorney General has refused to investigate Oscar's wrongful conviction and the police and prosecutorial misconduct that created it. However, I feel an obligation to tell the truth of Oscar's story, and to correct the record when it comes to the investigative work of Sgt. Vaughan's team, Investigator Larry Pool, and PI Russ Whitmeyer. As Vaughan told ABC 10: "He's the most prolific serial killer rapist in the history of California, and it didn't have to happen… he should have been caught."

In many ways, it's no surprise that Sgt. Vaughan had a completely unique perspective on DeAngelo, and that his insight gave him an advantage. They were both born fifty miles apart in upstate New York and had grandparents from Italy. They both dreamed of riding motorcycles for the California Highway Patrol. They're both left-handed/ambidextrous, with an unusual way of solving problems. It was like two sides of the same coin, as if Vaughan were hunting the evil version of himself. He trapped DeAngelo by shining his light to the left, but looking right.

Chapter 15 Sources

1. PI Pettyjohn Notes and Invoice, February, 1976
2. Auburn Police Department Reports; August, 1976 - July, 1979
3. ABC10's "Framed by the Golden State Killer?" Pt. 4 @ 3:15
4. PaperTrail Podcast Episode #117 "Clifton conviction," 2019
5. Michele McNamara, "In The Footsteps of a Killer," Los Angeles Magazine, February 27, 2013
6. Michele McNamara "I'll Be Gone in the Dark," 2018
7. My Favorite Murder podcast Episode #122 "Surprise! It's Paul Holes," 2018
8. HBO Documentary Films "I'll Be Gone in the Dark," 2020
9. ABC 20/20 "The Monster Among Us," October 31, 2020
10. Sacramento County Recorder Deeds
11. Contra Costa SD Sgt. R. Carpenter, EAR Task Force Memo, March 21, 1979
12. Sacramento Bee - "Masked Man Fails at Rape" March 21, 1979
13. SSD EAR Case File October 18, 1976
14. Dana Point residential and school records
15. Washington Post - March 2, 2019; and, Xavier Becerra v. San Francisco & First Amendment Coalition, January 29, 2020
16. Kenneth Ross Jr. Police Decertification Act, September 30, 2021
17. "California's Criminal Courts" Fact Sheet, published October 2015 https://www.ppic.org/publication/californias-criminal-courts/

Appendix—Timeline

November 8, 1945 - Bath, New York: Joseph James DeAngelo, Jr., born.

August 1, 1956 - February 23, 1958 - Novato, Marin County: Joseph DeAngelo, Sr. stationed with USAF Hamilton Air Force Base.

June 22, 1959 - August 4, 1962 - Sacramento County: DeAngelo, Sr. stationed at Mather Air Force Base.

September 1959 - June 1961 - Rancho Cordova: DeAngelo attended Mills Jr. High, grades 8 and 9.

September 1961 - June 1964 - Folsom: DeAngelo attended Folsom High School, grades 10 through 12.

September 1964 - Florida: - DeAngelo's parents' divorce granted.

September 11, 1964 - San Francisco: DeAngelo accepted into the US Navy, Treasure Island.

September 15, 1964 - November 25, 1964 - San Diego: DeAngelo attended Recruit Training,

December 10, 1964 - San Diego: DeAngelo reported to USS Canberra.

January 5, 1965 - San Diego: USS Canberra departed for service tour.

January 1965 - Exeter: DeAngelo's older sister (Rebecca) moved to Exeter from Los Angeles.

February 4, 1965 - Auburn: Kay DeAngelo and Jack Bosanko's marriage license was issued in Placer County; they married on February 6 in Exeter, Tulare County.

May 7-11, 1965 - Chu Lai, Viet Nam: USS Canberra participated in troop landings.

July 7, 1965 - San Diego: USS Canberra returned to U.S. base.

Mid-February 1966 - San Diego: USS Canberra departed for service tour.

Late June 1966 - San Diego: USS Canberra returned to U.S base.

.

Tuesday, July 26, 1966 - San Diego: DeAngelo reported as AWOL from USS Canberra. *Unknown date of return.*

October 11, 1966 - San Diego: USS Canberra departed for service tour in Vietnam.

June 1, 1967 - San Diego: USS Canberra returned to U.S. base. On the same date, newspaper article in Auburn stated that DeAngelo was expected home on leave "soon."

July 20, 1967 - Long Beach: USS Canberra docked.

November 16, 1967 - San Diego: DeAngelo was reassigned to USS Piedmont.

February 16, 1968 - San Diego: USS Piedmont departed for service tour.

August 9, 1968 - San Francisco: DeAngelo was discharged from U.S. Navy active duty, USN Treasure Island. At this same time, USS Piedmont was moored in Kaoshiung, Taiwan.

September 10, 1968 - Rocklin: DeAngelo started two-year AA program in Police Science at Sierra College, CA.

Thursday, March 1, 1969 7:00 pm - Exeter: An Exeter PD patrol car was stolen from behind the police station. Chief Morehouse, coordinating the search from the station, received an anonymous call that the stolen car could be found at Neel Ranch—next to the Friant-Kern Canal, off Marinette. The car was located there at about 10:00 pm. The car was undamaged, and forensics found no clues to help identify the thief. *(Unsolved)*

Monday, August 25, 1969 4:00 am - Sacramento: A 17-year-old girl woke to a young man shining a flashlight in her eyes. He wrapped his arm around her neck and mouth, threatened to kill her, and forcibly dragged her out of her house. He took her to a nearby yard, raped her, and then left on foot. He had entered the house through an unlocked door and taken money from a wallet and purse before waking the girl. The neighborhood location was described only as "*expensive homes on the east side of Sacramento.*" The girl's parents were asleep in the home at the time of the kidnapping, heard a scream, and found their daughter missing. They immediately called the Sacramento Sheriff's Department (SSD) and were talking with deputies when the girl came running back home. *(Unsolved)*

Tuesday, December 16, 1969 2:25 am - Exeter: A prowler shot at trying to climb in a bedroom window on List Ave. *(Unsolved)*

June 12, 1970 - Rocklin: DeAngelo graduated from Sierra College with an AA Degree in Police Science.

September 10, 1970 - DeAngelo's Navy record stated "*No participation in Reserve Program. Never served or reported.*"

September 21, 1970 - DeAngelo started BA Degree in Criminal Justice program at Sacramento State University.

Friday, Jan 29, 1971 - Exeter: Ransacking burglary. *(Unsolved)*

Monday, Sep 27, 1971 - Exeter: Ransacking burglary. *(Unsolved)*

Fall 1971 - Auburn: DeAngelo's mother, stepfather, and brother (John) moved from Auburn, CA to Whittier, CA.

Tuesday, December 28, 1971 - Exeter: DeAngelo attended his brother-in-law's birthday party in Exeter. He was living in Citrus Heights.

June 10, 1972 - Sacramento: DeAngelo graduated from Sacramento State University with a BA Degree in Criminal Justice.

June 1972 - January 1973 (Total of 32 weeks; dates may have been earlier) - Roseville: DeAngelo's internship with Roseville PD, Identifications and Investigations Division.

Tuesday, July 4, 1972 - Exeter: Ransacking burglary. *(Unsolved)*

Sunday, September 10, 1972 - Exeter: Nazarene Church and Fairway Apt: Multiple units ransacked and burglarized. *(Unsolved)*

Mid-1972 to Mid-1973 - Sacramento County: The "*Cordova Cat Burglar*" committed over 30 burglaries in Rancho Cordova, Carmichael, and Citrus Heights.

Tuesday, January 3, 1973 - Exeter: First Baptist Church and Exeter Library ransacking burglaries. *(Unsolved)*

January-May 1973 - Rancho Cordova: The "*Cordova Meadows Ransacker*" committed at least 20 burglaries (March 3, 1973 being one confirmed date for the series).

May 18, 1973 - Exeter: DeAngelo started his employment at Exeter PD.

May 1973 - April 1976 - Exeter: Over this three-year period, the city experienced a sharp rise in home burglaries, including occupied homes at night and "ransackings" where little of value was stolen. There was also an increase in obscene phone calls, serious arsons, car and bike "borrowing," occupied vandalism (police called), and false alarms, including both fire and police.

Thursday, June 28, 1973 - Exeter: Blue Chip Stamp machine stolen from Jerry's Arco. *(Unsolved)*

Tuesday, September 4, 1973 - Exeter: Ransacking burglary. *(Unsolved)*

November 10, 1973 - Auburn: DeAngelo married Sharon Huddle at the Auburn First Congregational Church. Address on marriage license listed as 601 Emperor Street, Exeter, CA.

March 13, 1974 - Visalia: Liz Silva, nearly 13 years old, was picked up by a uniformed police officer, supposedly for being truant from school. Liz has identified Joseph DeAngelo as her attacker, and stated that he was wearing an Exeter PD uniform at the time of the kidnapping.

Monday, March 18, 1974 - Exeter: Two overnight ransacking burglaries. *(Unsolved)*

Monday, March 18, 1974 - December 10, 1975 - Visalia: Located approximately 11 miles west of Exeter, the city experienced over 150 ransacking burglaries with a very specific MO. DeAngelo committed first attributed "*Visalia Ransacker*" (VR) burglary on 3/18/74, and continued into December 1975. DeAngelo has admitted responsibility for this series of VR burglaries.

Saturday, April 6, 1974 - Visalia: DeAngelo committed three VR burglaries.

Saturday, May 4, 1974 - Visalia: DeAngelo committed one VR burglary.

Sunday, May 5, 1974 - Visalia: DeAngelo committed one VR burglary.

Saturday, May 11, 1974 - Visalia: DeAngelo committed two VR burglaries.

Friday, May 17, 1974 - Visalia: DeAngelo committed two VR burglaries.

Saturday, May 18, 1974 - Visalia: DeAngelo committed three VR burglaries.

Saturday, May 25, 1974 - Visalia: DeAngelo committed three VR burglaries.

Sunday, May 26, 1974 - Visalia: DeAngelo committed three VR burglaries.

Sunday, June 23, 1974 - Visalia: DeAngelo committed one VR burglary.

Saturday, September 14, 1974 - Visalia: DeAngelo committed one VR burglary.

Friday, October 4-5, 1974 - Visalia and Tulare: DeAngelo committed a ransacking burglary in Visalia, and stole a .22 caliber revolver. Later that night, and into Saturday morning, five distinct cat burglaries occurred in Tulare.

Wednesday, October 9, 1974 - Visalia: Caldwell Ave, just outside city limits. Mary Murphy* *(* denotes pseudonym to protect victim's identity)* attacked in her home by a blue-eyed man, wearing a mask with only eye holes, armed with a handgun, who entered through an unlocked kitchen door. *(Unsolved)*

Saturday, October 12, 1974 - Tulare County: TCSO publicly announced the arrest of a suspect, a young neighbor, in the Murphy* attack, "*after investigation by Sheriff's detectives.*" Saturday night into Sunday morning, the "*Tulare Cat Burglar*" hit six houses. Purses, wallets, and cash were taken from bedrooms of sleeping victims.

Sunday, October 13, 1974, 10:00 pm - Tulare County: South of Tulare city limits in TCSO jurisdiction, Kay Nieman* was attacked in bed while asleep. She suffered injuries nearly identical to Mary Murphy* (10/9/74). *(Unsolved)*

Saturday, October 19, 1974 - Visalia: DeAngelo committed three VR burglaries.

Wednesday, October 23, 1974 - Visalia: DeAngelo committed two VR burglaries.

Friday, November 1, 1974 - Visalia: DeAngelo committed five VR burglaries.

Saturday, November 2, 1974 - Visalia: DeAngelo committed four VR burglaries in the NW sector. Two of the burglaries were within three blocks of the last place Jennifer Armour was seen on November 15th *(below)*.

Friday, November 15, 1974, 7:30 pm - Visalia: 15-year-old Mt. Whitney High School sophomore Jennifer Armour vanished while walking from her home to meet friends for a ride to the football game. She was last seen in area of recent VR activity.

Saturday, November 16, 1974 - Visalia: Jennifer's mother reported her as missing, after discovering she had not spent the night with friends as planned. The police treated it as a possible runaway, and no public plea for information was released.

Sunday, November 24, 1974 - Exeter: An orange rancher discovered Jennifer's body in the Friant-Kern Canal on the edge of his grove.

Tuesday, November 26, 1974 - Tulare County: TCSO's Sheriff Bob Wiley issued a statement regarding Jennifer Armour that stated: "There is no reason to believe that the girl may have been murdered."

Friday, November 29, 1974 - Visalia: Between 5:00 pm-11:00 pm, while Jennifer's services were held nearby, DeAngelo committed five ransacking burglaries. Later that same evening, the *Tulare Cat Burglar* hit one house after midnight; entered through garage door into kitchen, and took coins while victim was sleeping.

Saturday, November 30, 1974 - Visalia and Tulare: Between about 5:00 pm-11:00 pm, DeAngelo committed thirteen ransacking burglaries in Visalia. Overnight, the *Tulare Cat Burglar* hit eight houses between roughly midnight Saturday and 6:00 am Sunday morning. In each case, the offender took a purse and/or wallet from the occupied bedroom. One of the victims in the Tulare spree was at the home of TCSO's Rusty Chamberlain, where a gun and coins were also taken.

Saturday, December 14, 1974 - Visalia: DeAngelo committed four VR burglaries.

Monday, December 16, 1974 - Visalia: DeAngelo committed one VR burglary.

Saturday, December 21, 1974 - Visalia: DeAngelo committed four VR burglaries.

Sunday, December 22, 1974 - Visalia: DeAngelo committed four VR burglaries.

Saturday, January 25, 1975 - Visalia: DeAngelo committed two VR burglaries.

Sunday, February 2, 1975 - Visalia: DeAngelo committed three VR burglaries. One homeowner found a bottle of lotion that was not from their house. The item was brought to the scene by the VR.

Wednesday, February 5, 1975 - Visalia: Claude Snelling chased a prowler away from a rear window of his home.

Sunday, February 16, 1975 - Visalia: DeAngelo committed three VR burglaries.

Saturday, February 22, 1975 3:00am - Goleta: 21-year-old Nadine Kopplin was bludgeoned to death in her home at the Sesame Tree Apartments. *(Unsolved)*

Saturday, March 1, 1975 - Visalia: DeAngelo committed one VR burglary.

Monday, April 3, 1975 - Visalia: A 16-year-old girl was offered a ride, and then forced into a car on W. Walnut at Woodland. She was raped in a “rural area,” and dropped back at Chinowth Road and Harvard Ave. The suspect was described as 29-32 years old. *(Unsolved)*

Monday, April 14, 1975 - Visalia: The suspect initially identified as the *Tulare Cat Burglar* entered a guilty plea for only six residential burglaries—however, all those were in the city of Visalia. All of them were unlocked homes, with no physical contact or assault or the residents, and VPD’s Sgt. Vaughan was the arresting officer. The entire balance of crimes, described as roughly 200 burglaries occurring in Tulare, Porterville, and Bakersfield, were unsolved.

Saturday, May 24, 1975 - Visalia: DeAngelo committed four VR burglaries.

Saturday, May 31, 1975 - Visalia: DeAngelo committed one VR burglary.

Wednesday, July 23, 1975 - Exeter: *The Exeter Sun* ran a news story in the “Police Blotter” about DeAngelo investigating and solving a local burglary case.

Thursday July 24, 1975 - Visalia: While returning to her home on W. Kaweah Ave, 18-year-old Debbie Ward surprised DeAngelo during a mid-day burglary. The masked burglar was seen leaving the tenant’s apartment over the garage. After ransacking the unit, he was heading down the outside stairs when he spotted Ward, DeAngelo grabbed her and knocked her down to make his escape.

Friday, July 25, 1975 - Visalia: DeAngelo committed two VR burglaries.

Friday, August 1, 1975 - Visalia: DeAngelo committed one VR burglary.

Saturday, Aug 23, 1975 - Visalia: DeAngelo committed three VR burglaries.

Sunday, August 24, 1975 - Visalia: DeAngelo committed two VR burglaries.

Friday, August 29, 1975 - Visalia: DeAngelo committed one VR burglary.

Saturday, August 30, 1975 - Visalia: DeAngelo committed one VR burglary.

Sunday, August 31, 1975 - Visalia: Between 6:00-10:45 pm, DeAngelo committed a ransacking burglary at a residence on W. Royal Oaks Ave. He stole a .38 caliber Miroku revolver with a 4 1/2" barrel, which was loaded with three steel jacket, hollow point bullets. He also took two boxes of 12-gauge ammunition, three boxes (100 count each) of .38 ammo, a necklace, and one silver dollar. The Miroku was later positively identified as the same weapon used to murder Claude Snelling. *(9/11/75, below)*

Sunday, August 31, 1975 - Visalia: VPD report that both Snelling cars parked in their carport were broken into, and the glove boxes rummaged. Nothing appeared to be missing.

Thursday, September 11, 1975, 2:00 am - Visalia: 16-year-old Mt. Whitney High School junior Beth Snelling was awakened by a masked DeAngelo on top of her in bed, smothering her, and pinning her arms down with his legs. He threatened to stab and shoot her if she made a noise, and he ordered her to go with him. DeAngelo dragged her out of her house through the back door and into the carport. Beth's 45-year-old father, Claude, heard the commotion and yelled from the house. DeAngelo then shot Mr. Snelling twice, kicked Beth several times in the face, and briskly walked away from the scene.

Thursday, September 11, 1975, 12:00 pm - Several of Beth Snelling's close friends pulled into the parking lot at Mt. Whitney High School. They were returning to the same space they had left a short time earlier. As they got out of their vehicle, they noticed that someone had written on the side mirror of the truck next to them, and turned the mirror out so that it was visible. On the mirror was written "*Beth, I'll get the rest.*" It appeared to be written by a finger in the dust on the mirror.

Friday, September 19, 1975 - Tulare County: A citizen reported discovery of a Taurus .38 caliber revolver in a ditch on Ave 256, between Visalia and Exeter. He called VPD directly (instead of TCSO) because he thought it could be the Snelling murder weapon. VPD matched the serial number to one stolen by DeAngelo in a VR burglary on May 24, 1975. It was confirmed not to be the gun that killed Claude Snelling. Employees of a nearby fertilizer plant were checked for possible VR suspects.

Monday, September 22, 1975 - Tulare County: VPD investigators continued searching the ditches between Visalia and Exeter where they found a large flathead screwdriver matching the dimensions noted at several VR scenes and several rounds of .222 caliber ammunition, wrapped in a vinyl raincoat. These items were located on Ave 256, about 500 yards from Hypericum Rd., the location of the home of Oscar Clifton's parents.

Monday, September 22, 1975 - Visalia: DeAngelo committed a VR burglary at the home of Ruth Swanson* with more extreme ransacking than normal, including leaving a cut-up bra and wadded up panties on the pillow of the teen daughter's bed.

September/October 1975 - Visalia: Marsha*, a 13-year-old girl in 8th grade at McCann School was walking alone to a store downtown after school. As she walked on a residential street, a car driven by a uniformed officer pulled up, ordered her into the car, and threatened to "report" her if she did not comply. Marsha felt that something was wrong, and turned and ran in the opposite direction. She has since made a positive identification of DeAngelo as the man who ordered her into his car.

October 21, 1975, 3:00 pm - Visalia: The *Visalia Times-Delta* published an update story on the Snelling Homicide: "Presently, Sgt. John Vaughn and agents William McGowen and Duane Shipley are handling the investigation. All are confident they will succeed. 'We are getting a lot of leads and tips. Lots of things are being worked on,' Vaughn said. 'We'll catch the guy,' McGowan said." That same afternoon, Ruth Swanson* heard someone trying to open her front door. When she looked out the peephole, she saw that the person was holding his hand over it. Shortly after, she received a series of disturbing phone calls that used her name. She immediately called VPD, but the suspect was not located.

October 21-23, 1975 - Exeter: Over a weekend, while the resident was out of town, a home was ransacked. Items stolen were described as watches, mandolins, a Masonic ring, ninety-seven old silver dollars, thirty Kennedy silver half-dollars, $300 in other coins, three boxes of .22 ammunition, a flashlight, and a Roman coin dated 50 BC. *(Unsolved)*

Friday, October 24, 1975 - Visalia: DeAngelo committed four VR burglaries, including one that was just 325 feet from the Snelling home. Sgt. Vaughan noted in his scene report that the only motive for much of the ransacking appeared to be to "*draw attention*" and "*to leave his calling card.*" VPD investigators believed that they were being taunted for their comments in the newspaper.

Wednesday, October 29, 1975 - Visalia: DeAngelo committed one VR burglary.

Sunday, November 2, 1975 - Visalia: DeAngelo committed two VR burglaries.

Thursday, November 6, 1975 - Visalia: DeAngelo committed one VR burglary.

November 12, 1975 - Exeter: DeAngelo was promoted to rank of Sergeant, and named head of Exeter PD's anti-burglary unit and assigned to the multi-jurisdictional "JAB" *(Joint Attack on Burglary)* task force.

Monday, December 1, 1975 - Visalia: DeAngelo committed four VR burglaries.

Monday December 8, 1975 - Visalia: DeAngelo committed one VR burglary.

Fall 1975 - Visalia: DeAngelo continued to commit VR burglaries, but avoided nights when VPD was conducting stakeouts.

Tuesday, December 9, 1975 - Visalia: VPD McGowen responded to Ward residence to investigate footprints under the window of Debbie Ward's room. After suspecting that the VR was somehow aware of their planned activities, VPD arranged a radio-silent, unannounced stakeout at the Ward residence on W. Kaweah.

Wednesday, December 10, 1975, 8:30 pm - Visalia: DeAngelo appeared outside Debbie Ward's window, was held at gunpoint by Agent McGowen, gunfire was exchanged, and DeAngelo escaped. VPD was quickly called to a nearby ransack burglary, and it was determined that items dropped by the VR during the shooting matched those from the earlier burglary.

Thursday, December 18, 1975, 3:00 pm - Visalia: VPD released a composite sketch and description of the VR, which was printed in the *Visalia Times-Delta* in that day's issue.

Thursday, December 18, 1975, 6:00-9:00 pm - Exeter: Gary Bardone's house on S. Belmont in Exeter was burglarized. Exeter PD Sgt. DeAngelo responded to the scene with another EPD officer, and spent an extended period in the house alone with Gary's 18-year-old wife and infant child. 25-year-old Gary was told to wait in the garage. DeAngelo instructed the other EPD officer to canvass the neighbors during that time.

Tuesday, December 23, 1975, 9:00 pm - Exeter: DeAngelo returned to the Bardone home, dressed in plain clothes, and demanded that he interview Gary's wife alone in the bedroom. Gary asked Sgt. DeAngelo to leave, which resulted in a tense confrontation and DeAngelo's eventual exit from the house. Bardone also reported observing multiple drive-bys over the next weeks.

Friday, December 26, 1975 - Exeter: 14-year-old Exeter High School freshman Donna Jo Richmond disappeared while riding her bike home from her boyfriend's house at around 4:00 pm. The ride home was over four miles, but there were no reported sightings of her after she left her boyfriend's house on Marinette.

Saturday, December 27, 1975, 1:30 am - Tulare County: Oscar Clifton was arrested at his rural Visalia home on suspicion of kidnapping Donna Jo Richmond.

December 27, 1975, 1:30 pm - Exeter: The body of Donna Jo Richmond was found on Neel Ranch, an orange grove next to the Friant-Kern canal on Marinette, three miles due east of Donna's boyfriend's house on the same road where she was last seen.

December 27, 1975, 5:00 pm - Exeter: TCSO found a ski cap/ mask on the edge of the grove at Neel Ranch. The unique description appears to match the description of the mask worn during the Snelling homicide three months earlier.

Tuesday, January 6, 1976 - Visalia: The "MO" of the VR, including descriptions of the suspect and stolen property were entered into the California DOJ database, CII.

Sunday, February 15, 1976 - Exeter: Residence of a local dentist ransacked; stolen items included silverware, coins, and stamps. *(Unsolved)*

Monday, March 15, 1976 - Exeter – A pink lunch box filled with old silver coins was stolen in a home burglary. *(Unsolved)*

May 11, 1976 - Exeter: State grant funding announced for DeAngelo's JAB position, slated to cover the period of August 1976 to July 1977.

May 1976 - Exeter: DeAngelo's brother John moved to Exeter with his wife and infant daughter.

June 2, 1976 - Visalia: Sharon DeAngelo's letter to the editor regarding pay increases for state employees is published in the *Visalia Times-Delta.*

June 7, 1976 - Sacramento: Sharon DeAngelo departed with her grandmother for a three-week trip to Canada.

Friday, June 18, 1976, 4:00 am - Rancho Cordova: DeAngelo committed the first EAR attack, on a 23-year-old woman. She was home alone while her father was out of town. Attributed as the first of the East Area Rapist ("EAR") series.

Monday, June 21, 9:55 am - Visalia: Start of jury selection in the trial of Oscar Clifton for the homicide of Donna Jo Richmond.

Monday, June 21, 9:30 pm - Visalia: TCSO's Byrd interviewed Frank Thomas, a Garden St. resident, for information on the sale of a freezer and two bikes on the day of the homicide. Mr. Thomas provided the name of his neighbor, Brent Trueblood, as a possible witness.

Tuesday, June 22, 3:16 pm - Visalia: TCSO's Rusty Chamberlain interviewed Garden St. resident Brent Trueblood regarding the man he saw working at the Bill Rose worksite on the afternoon of the homicide. Trueblood described Oscar Clifton, his truck, then also identified him from a photo lineup. Trueblood gave Chamberlain the name of his friend, Johnny Guerber, as another possible witness.

Tuesday, June 22, 5:00 pm - Visalia: TCSO's Rusty Chamberlain interviewed Johnny Guerber in the presence of his mother, Laverne Easley. Guerber confirmed being at the Thomas house during the freezer loading on the afternoon of the homicide. He said that he rode his bike by the Rose house and spoke with Oscar Clifton.

Thursday, July 15, 1976 - Visalia: Oscar Clifton was convicted for the murder of Donna Jo Richmond, and the jury found special circumstances, recommending the death penalty.

Saturday, July 17, 1976, 2:00 am - Carmichael: DeAngelo attacked 15- and 16-year-old sisters. The girls were home alone while their parents were out of town.

Tuesday, July 20, 1976, 1:26 am - Porterville: Ben Galloway was arrested for multiple rapes between June 1974 and July 1976 *(known as the "Porterville Rapist").*

August 4, 1976 - Exeter: The Exeter City Council approved Sergeant DeAngelo's EPD salary in the City's next fiscal year budget, 1976-77.

Wednesday, August 25, 1976 - Exeter: Sgt. DeAngelo's resignation from Exeter PD was announced.

Sunday, August 29, 1976, 3:20 am - Rancho Cordova: DeAngelo broke into a home and assaulted the 41-year-old female homeowner when she resisted his attempts to bind her and her 12-year-old daughter. The presumed target was the woman's 15-year-old daughter, who escaped out her bedroom window. The antique billy club used in the attack matched one stolen by the VR on October 24, 1975.

August 31, 1976 - Auburn: DeAngelo reports for duty as a patrolman for Auburn PD.

Saturday, September 4, 1976, 11:00 pm - Carmichael: DeAngelo attacked a 29-year-old woman in the driveway at the home of her parents. The woman's parents were out of town, and she was forced back into the house and assaulted.

Sunday, September 5, 1976 - Sacramento: SSD entered the EAR MO and descriptions of the suspect and stolen property into the California CII.

September 16, 1976 - Visalia: Oscar Clifton was formally sentenced to death and sent to San Quentin's Death Row.

Monday, September 27, 1976 - Porterville: Ben Galloway entered a plea of guilty to multiple charges associated with the "Porterville Rapist" attacks.

Tuesday, October 5, 1976, 6:30 am - Citrus Heights: DeAngelo attacked a 30-year-old woman alone in the house with her young son. DeAngelo entered the house immediately after the woman's husband left for work.

Saturday, October 9, 1976, 1:00 am - Rancho Cordova: DeAngelo burglarized the house next door to his attack victim, and planted jewelry and coins stolen from earlier EAR scenes. John Dority was staying alone for the weekend in his parents' house while they were out of town. Dority became the prime suspect in the EAR cases. He was cleared by SSD officers who had him under surveillance during the next EAR attack. *(This same residence was noted in the report as one that had been burglarized on March 7, 1973.)*

Saturday, October 9, 1976, 3:30 am - Rancho Cordova: DeAngelo attacked a 19-year-old who was alone in her home while her father was out of town. Her house had been burglarized on March 7, 1973.

Monday, October 18, 1976 - Carmichael: DeAngelo attacked a 32-year-old woman alone in her home with her two sleeping children.

October 18, 1976 - Rancho Cordova: DeAngelo attacked a 19-year-old as she parked her car in her driveway. After taking her to a neighbor's yard and tying her up, he stole her car. Her car was located about a mile away, with the dog locked in the trunk, unharmed. The car was locked, and the keys with a "ribbit" frog keychain were taken.

Thursday, November 4, 1976 - Sacramento: *The Bee* first reported on a serial rapist attacking lone females in Rancho Cordova, Del Dayo, and Crestview. SSD Shelby said that they had been hoping to catch him in a stakeout. The series had become public at a community meeting at the Del Dayo school.

Wednesday, November 10, 1976 - Sacramento: *The Bee* published its first article on the EAR, titled "*East Area Rapist... Fear Grips Serene Neighborhoods.*" SSD admitted to failing to publicize the rapes and warn the neighborhoods because they feared "widespread panic." Community meetings, guns, locks, alarms, and local patrols were discussed. One woman was quoted: "Maybe when he [the rapist] sees that we're not going to be terrorized, that we are going to get our men organized and face him, by God, he'll think before attacking another woman."

Wednesday, November 10, 1976 - Auburn: DeAngelo's third wedding anniversary.

Wednesday, November 10, 1976, 7:30 pm - Citrus Heights: DeAngelo kidnapped a 16-year-old San Juan High School student in her home while her parents were out to dinner. The girl was watching TV with her dog on the couch when DeAngelo broke in, tied her up, and walked her, at knifepoint, to a pre-selected attack site over a quarter mile from her home. He took her over a fence into a neighbor's yard, into a culvert under the street, and then through a drainage canal that ran behind nearby homes to a clearing. Prior to leaving the house, DeAngelo turned off the television, turned on lights, replaced a window screen, and locked the door. When the victim's parents returned home, they assumed she had left voluntarily, and did not alert the police.

Saturday, December 18, 1976, 6:30 pm - Carmichael: DeAngelo attacked a 15-year-old girl who was alone in her home while her parents attended a holiday party.

December 1976 - Danville: EAR victim from October attack relocated to Leeds Court, Danville. *(See 12/9/78)*

Monday, January 17, 1977 - Auburn: A newspaper story appeared in a local paper detailing the pursuit and capture of some escapees from juvenile hall. DeAngelo and Nick Willick were described as responding officers, giving chase and capturing the offenders.

Wednesday, January 19, 1977, 1:00 am - Sacramento: DeAngelo attacked a 25-year-old pregnant woman just inside Sacramento PD jurisdiction. He cut up a photo of the victim and her husband, and only took the portion with the victim. DeAngelo stole her car, then left it parked approximately one mile away on Folsom Blvd.

Monday, January 24, 1977, 12:15 am- Citrus Heights: DeAngelo attacked a 25-year-old woman alone in her home.

Monday, February 7, 1977, 6:45 am - Carmichael: DeAngelo attacked a 31-year-old woman alone in her home immediately after her husband left for work. She fought DeAngelo, and he cut himself with his knife, leaving blood in the victim's hair. On February 8, forensic testing from this attack confirmed the EAR's blood type, identified as A+.

Wednesday, February 16, 1977 - Sacramento: 18-year-old Rodney Miller was shot chasing a prowler from his yard in Ripon Court; Sacramento PD jurisdiction. *(Unsolved)*

Monday, February 28, 1977 - Visalia: TCSO's Sgt. Byrd ordered the destruction of ***all*** evidence held by TCSO in the Donna Jo Richmond homicide case before an appeals attorney was even appointed.

Wednesday, March 2, 1977, 11:30 am - Granite Bay: PG&E employees, 28-year-old Carla Burkart and 55-year-old Bill Harrington, were shot to death in their truck while delivering work notices to homes on Lone Pine Place. They were shot in front of a home that was burglarized and ransacked—a large TV was placed in front of the main door. *(Unsolved)*

Monday, March 7, 1977 - *The Sacramento Bee* reported that the PG&E investigation had stalled. PSCO said "*the leads are leading nowhere... they're out beating the brush*" but investigators are "*absolutely stalemated.*" A reward of $20,500 was announced.

Tuesday, March 8, 1977, 3:45 am - Sacramento: DeAngelo attacked a 37-year-old lone female in her home in Sacramento PD jurisdiction.

Wednesday, March 16, 1977 - Rancho Cordova: *The Grapevine* newspaper published a story about a community meeting on rape prevention to take place that night at the Mills Station Restaurant on Folsom Blvd.

Friday, March 18, 1977, 4:15-5:00 pm - The PBX board operator at SSD received three phone calls from an unidentified male. The caller disconnected the call each time before the operator was able to switch it to the communications center, where the caller would have been recorded.

1. "*I'm the East Area Rapist*"—the caller then hung up.

2. "*I'm the East Area Rapist*"—followed by laughter and another hang up.

3. "*I am the East Area Rapist and I have my next victim already stalked and you guys can't catch me.*"

Friday, March 18, 1977, 10:45 pm - Rancho Cordova: A 16-year-old Cordova High School student was attacked. This is the only DeAngelo case where it is confirmed that he was already inside the house, and apparently waiting for the specific victim to return home. The girl's parents were out of town, and their packed car had been parked outside the previous night. The girl's brother lived away from home, and her younger sister was spending the night with a friend. She was confronted by DeAngelo in the kitchen as she returned from work at the nearby KFC (across the street from the Mills Station meeting), and had dialed the phone to call the friend with whom she was spending the night. DeAngelo appeared from the master bedroom, holding an axe.

DeAngelo had entered through the garage/kitchen doors by chiseling out the wood around the lock striker plates on three doors, then prying the jams. The house was ransacked to a "significant degree." The victim's canopy bed had been moved to block the door to her room, and the drawers and jewelry boxes had been dumped on the floor. The bed in the master bedroom was broken and the mattresses were "strewn about," and the dresser drawers were emptied onto the floor. One of the end tables in the living room had been placed on a couch, and the other moved the middle of the room. The victim's purse was dumped onto the kitchen floor, and DeAngelo left empty Diet Dr. Pepper bottles at the side of the garage. The victim had been receiving hang up phone calls for about two weeks prior to the attack.

The attack was interrupted by the insistent calling, and eventually knocking, of the friend she had been calling when she arrived home. DeAngelo escaped out of the back sliding door and over the back fence. He left the axe balanced on top of the fence.

March 20, 1977 - Sacramento: *The Bee* published an EAR story covering the recent attack on the 18th, stating: "*He has never attacked while there is a man in the home.*"

March 23, 1977 - Rancho Cordova: *The Grapevine* also reported on the attack on the 18th, but with the headline "*No proof Rancho attacker is East Area Rapist.*" SSD suggested that the girl simply surprised a home burglar, and quoted an unidentified spokesman: "We have absolutely no proof the attack was made by the East Area Rapist." That was not truthful—SSD had already matched footprints from prior attacks, and were 100% confident in the MO and pre-attack phone calls matched the EAR.

Saturday, April 2, 1977, 2:30 am - Orangevale: DeAngelo attacked a 26- and 29-year-old couple in their home.

Friday, April 15, 1977, 2:30 am - Carmichael: DeAngelo attacked a 19- and 24-year-old couple in their home.

Tuesday, May 3, 1977, 2:30 am - Sacramento: DeAngelo attacked a 30- and 36-year-old couple in their home in the Sacramento PD jurisdiction.

Thursday, May 5, 1977, 12:15 am - Orangevale: DeAngelo attacked a 25- and 34-year-old couple in their home.

Saturday, May 14, 1977 4:00 am - Citrus Heights: DeAngelo attacked a 22- and 30-year-old couple in their home.

Monday, May 16-Tuesday, May 17, 1977 - Carmichael: At 11:00 pm, a 27-year-old man was watching television in the family room of his home on Haskell Ave. He looked up to see a man looking in his kitchen window. The man then saw the suspect hop a six-foot fence into the neighbor's yard. He described the suspect as white, athletic, 5'9" - 5"10" tall. SSD deputy Weinberger answered the homeowner's call, and while they were outside talking, they noticed the suspect hiding between two houses. Weinberger gave chase until he lost the suspect at the nearby electrical substation.

Returning to Haskell, Weinberger discovered that the new, unoccupied house next to the homeowner had been broken into via the sliding glass door. Multiple units were called in to hunt for the suspect, and Weinberger was taken up in a helicopter to try to locate a car he had seen leaving the area of the substation.

Tuesday 1:30 am - Carmichael: DeAngelo committed an EAR style attack on a 26- and 31-year-old couple on Sandbar Circle in Del Dayo. The husband in the home was a man who had publicly confronted SSD Richard Shelby at the nearby community meeting at Del Dayo School on November 3, 1976. DeAngelo was particularly threatening during this attack, and made statements directed specifically at SSD:

"I'm going to kill everything in this house if you don't do as I tell you. I'll kill everything in the house and then I'll leave in the night. If I hear these dishes, I'm going to come back and kill for the first time. Those fuckers, those fuckers, those pigs—I've never killed before but I'm going to kill now. I want you to tell those fuckers, those pigs, I have bunches of televisions. I am going to listen to the radio and watch television and if I hear about this, I'm going to go out tomorrow night and kill two people. People are going to die."

Back on Haskell, the homeowner left for work at 7:30 am, and returned home for lunch around noon. Upon his return he found a religious pamphlet tiled "Four Spiritual Laws" shoved in his front door. In perfect ink block lettering, on successive pages, was written:

"*ALLMOST* [*sic*] *HAD ME NEXT TIME YOU DIE*"

Wednesday, May 18, 1977 - Sacramento: Visalia PD officers Vaughan, McGowen, and Shipley traveled up to meet with SSD EAR investigators in an attempt to convince them that the Visalia Ransacker and EAR were the same offender. Their conclusion was based on a review of the EAR description and the related burglaries as well as on a CII MO match. This meeting was reported on the front page of the *Visalia Times-Delta* on the same day.

Sunday, May 22, 1977 5:45-8:50 pm - Carmichael: The homeowners on Haskell, feeling stalked by the EAR, had a home alarm system installed on Saturday the 21st. On Sunday evening they went bowling. Upon their return home they noticed footprints in fresh plaster dust on the washing machine, and the attic hatch had been disturbed. Upon a full search of the house, they discovered that the master bedroom window had been opened, and the window screen was damaged. The footprints appeared to match the herringbone pattern located at several EAR scenes, including the March 18th attack.

Friday, May 27, 1977 - Sacramento: *The Bee* published a story about the new EARS citizen patrol to catch the EAR, titled "*CBers' Night Watch—Rape Patrol Rolls with Cops' Rules.*" The story described 100 volunteers in marked "EARS PATROL" cars patrolling assigned areas previously targeted by the EAR. The organizer said they would patrol until the EAR was stopped: "If he's apprehended or if he's scared off... we win either way."

Saturday, May 28, 1977, 2:30 am - Sacramento: DeAngelo attacked a 28- and 32-year-old couple in their home in Sacramento PD jurisdiction.

Wednesday, July 27, 1977, 12:30 pm - Citrus Heights: A 19-year-old female was kidnapped in her car in the parking lot of Albertsons, at Greenback San Juan Center. The man had a gun, and gave her specific, turn by turn, directions to a location in Granite Bay. After missing a turn, and attempting to turn around, the car got stuck, and the attacker walked her to a nearby wooded drainage area. The victim was then stabbed repeatedly and left for dead in a culvert. Searchers found her the next morning after discovering the nearby vehicle.

Wednesday, August 17, 1977 - Sacramento: *The Bee* published a story from SSD disclosing the receipt of an anonymous, typewritten letter the day before. The letter claimed to have information on the EAR, asked SSD to put a message in the press if they wanted more information, and was signed "Afraid."

Thursday, August 18, 1977 - Sacramento: *The Bee* published an update on the "Afraid" letter, saying that SSD had received several calls claiming authorship of the letter, but that the tips were still being evaluated. SSD spokesman Bill Miller again urged the author of the "Afraid" letter to contact the department directly. The story noted that they EAR had not struck since May 28th.

Thursday, August 18, 1977, 1:00 pm - Rancho Cordova: 15-year-old Linda Sue Kuykendall and 16-year-old Christine Riley left Christine's house to walk across the Sunrise Bridge to Linda's house in Carmichael. The girls disappeared somewhere along the route. Although they had taken nothing with them, and Linda was barefoot, SSD determined they had run away from home. The public was not informed of their disappearance. *(Unsolved)*

Sunday, September 4, 1977 - Sacramento: *The Bee* published a "News Quiz" with the following question: This person was credited with increasing home security in the Sacramento area, thus cutting down on burglaries: (a) The Sacramento police chief; (b) The Sacramento County Sheriff; (c) The East-Area Rapist. [Note: *The correct answer was identified as "c," the EAR.*]

Monday, September 5, 1977 - Davis: 27-year-old Elizabeth Mary Wolf was found stabbed to death in her apartment. Elizabeth was a special education teacher who had just moved into the Sundance Apartments to start her new job teaching at Green Gate Center for the deaf. She was stabbed 12 times in the back, twice in the abdomen, and twice in the hand/arm. She was found in her bedroom, fully clothed, and there was no sign of a sexual assault. She was last known to be alive on Sunday evening at about 10:30 pm. The TV was on and the front door was unlocked when she was found by a friend. There was no evidence of forced entry or burglary. *(Unsolved)*

Tuesday, September 6, 1977, 12:15 am - Stockton: DeAngelo attacked a 29- and 31-year-old couple in their home.

Tuesday, September 20, 1977 - Citrus Heights: The home of Kenneth Lane was burglarized. The break-in was reported to SSD and Lane's insurance company. *(See 10/4/77, below)*

Thursday, September 22, 1977, 12:00-3:00 pm - Granite Bay: The residence of James Williams was burglarized; items reported stolen included a gun and costume jewelry. Chain placed across front door, and a large television console moved in front of the door; a serialized handgun was unloaded and moved from the bedroom to a new position—displayed over the fireplace mantle. Williams was the first person to call 911 after the PG&E murders (3/2/77), lived next door to the homicide scene. He was the uncle of that homeowner, and was quoted in *The Sacramento Bee* on March 4th as saying: "I don't mind telling you that if I got the chance, I'd plug 'em."

Saturday, October 1, 1977, 1:30-2:00 am - Rancho Cordova: DeAngelo attacked a 17- and 21-year-old couple in their home.

Monday, October 3, 1977 - Sacramento: *The Bee* ran a story titled "*Police Believe Rapist Is Toying with Them.*" SSD spokesman Bill Miller said it was believed that the intense investigative pressure and citizen patrols had temporarily pushed the EAR out of Sacramento. Stockton Sgt. Jackson said: "He's playing with us; there's no doubt about that. But anything about him is pure speculation. You try to build a theory about this guy, and he just blows it apart. The only consistent thing about him is that he is inconsistent."

Tuesday, October 4, 1977 - Auburn: Kimberly Best and Paige Sinclair, both 15 years old, were last seen near a freeway on-ramp in Auburn, CA. They were found the next day by deer hunters. Kimberly had been shot in the head, and Paige had been bludgeoned. They were thrown down an embankment on the side of a remote dirt road in the mountains above Auburn. They had run away from their homes in Oregon a few days before, and were on their way to Reno. The girls were not sexually assaulted, and their belongings were found with their bodies; there was no apparent motive for their murders. At the homicide scene, investigators reported finding (but not collecting) several other items, including cigarette papers, a pack of cigarettes, soda and beer cans, a shotgun shell, and a "notebook." *(Unsolved)*

Thursday, October 20, 1977 - Rocklin: The *Placer Herald* carried a front page story on the arrest of Kenneth Lane, including a perp walk photo. The story claimed that a star eyewitness had seen Best and Sinclair get into Lane's truck, and then memorized the license plate and called it in. *(It turned out later that the license plate numbers were fed to her in the second of two sessions of being "hypnotized" by a PSCO deputy. She recalled zero numbers from the plate during her first two interviews.)* The same article and photos had run in the *Auburn Journal* the previous day. The *Roseville Press Tribune* had a front page story that featured photos of PCSO investigators searching Kenneth Lane's home in Citrus Heights. The address of the home was included. The story said that they were searching for the murder weapons and any bloody stained items; nothing was found.

Friday, October 21, 1977, 3:00 am - Sacramento: DeAngelo attacked a 32- and 35-year-old couple in their home in the Foothill neighborhood. He told the female victim to give a message to the police, "*Tell the pigs I'll be back New Year's Eve.*" It was the first attack in the Foothill neighborhood, which was also located about 18 blocks south on Roseville Road from Kenneth Lane's house. *(That attack location was also 900 feet from the home of Jim Huddle's* [*DeAngelo's brother-in-law*] *business partner in Terra Nova Produce.)*

The woman in this attack had been receiving hang up phone calls for several weeks, and a few days prior to the attack she had come home to find the door between the kitchen and garage open. Several months before that, the family had found the sliding glass patio door open.

Friday, October 28, 1977 - Sacramento: *The Bee* reported on a community meeting held at Foothill Junior High School to discuss the EAR. The meeting was attended by 900 residents, and SSD Carol Daly told the audience that they were doing "everything possible" to catch the EAR including consulting a psychic and asking someone to prepare a "biorhythm chart," which was impossible since they didn't know the offender's birthdate.

Saturday, October 29, 1977, 1:45 am - Sacramento: DeAngelo attacked a 22- and 27-year-old couple in their home; Sacramento PD jurisdiction.

Wednesday, November 9, 1977 - Sacramento: *The Bee* reported on a community meeting to discuss the EAR. The meeting was held at Mira Loma High School, and attended by 700 residents. The story was accompanied by a large photo of the crowd, and photos of SSD Carol Daly (photo caption: … he's average) and Gary Iames (caption: … we are ready for him). The officers advised the crowd on deadbolt and sliding glass door locks, and Daly suggested that any homeowner who shot the EAR would "*probably get a commendation or an award.*"

Thursday, November 10, 1977 - Auburn: DeAngelo's fourth wedding anniversary.

Thursday, November 10, 1977, 3:30 am - Sacramento: DeAngelo attacked a 13-year-old girl in her home while her 56-year-old mother was tied up in another room; Sacramento PD jurisdiction.

Thursday, December 1, 1977 - Auburn: The *Placer Herald* and *Roseville Press Tribune* both carried front page stories about the possibility that Kenneth Lane's cancer was terminal, and he might not be able to stand trial. His plea entry was delayed while he was sent to the hospital for evaluation.

Friday, December 2, 1977 - The *Auburn Journal* ran a story about PSCO Lt. Engellenner, who served as jail supervisor. Engellenner, the "*trained hypnotist*," was planning to make a presentation on hypnosis at a convention of homicide and robbery investigators in Oregon. According to the article: "Engellenner reportedly used hypnosis to help a witness remember a license number which led to the arrest of Lane."

Friday, December 2, 1977, 11:00 pm - Sacramento: The operator at the SSD unrecorded complaint line received a call from an unidentified male who whispered "I'll commit another rape tonight," and hung up.

Friday, December 2, 1977, 11:30 pm - Sacramento: DeAngelo broke into the home of a woman in her mid-30s in the Foothill neighborhood. Her husband was at work, and she was alone in the house with her sleeping children. DeAngelo tied her up, but was distracted by a group of noisy kids in the street outside, and left without any further activity.

This was the second attack near Lane's home, and was two blocks from the Foothill community meeting with SSD Daly on Oct 28th and four blocks from Jim Huddle's partner in Terra Nova Produce. The victim had received hang up phone calls, and a few weeks prior to the attack had come home to find her house *locked*—when she had left it unlocked. Pickles inside the refrigerator had been moved and a photo of the victim was removed during that break in.

Saturday, December 10, 1977 - Sacramento: *The Bee* reported that the remains of Linda Sue Kuykendall and Christine Riley were found the day before by a nature photographer. The location was a ravine off Latrobe Road, near El Dorado Hills. *(Unsolved; 8/18/77, above)*

Sunday, December 11, 1977 - Sacramento: Three typed originals of a poem, appearing on legal-sized, onion skin paper and titled "*Excitement's Crave,*" were received by the editor of *The Sacramento Bee*; the Sacramento Mayor, and KVIE 6 TV from "*your East Area Rapist.*" These copies were received by the EAR task force on the 13th.

Saturday, January 28, 1978 - Carmichael: DeAngelo attacked 14- and 15-year-old sisters while their parents were out of town for the weekend.

Wednesday, February 1, 1978 - Auburn: The *Journal* ran a front page story about Kenneth Lane's murder trial being delayed. Lane's attorney had asked to withdraw from the case because of the burden on his small office.

Thursday, February 2, 1978 - Rocklin & Roseville: The *Placer Herald* also ran a story on the front page about Lane's attorney asking to be replaced; the *Roseville Press Tribune* covered the same story, but reported that the presiding judge had, in fact, released the attorney and appointed a public defender to continue Lane's defense.

Thursday, February 2, 1978, 9:00 pm - Rancho Cordova: DeAngelo chased, shot, and killed 20-year-old Katie and 21-year-old Brian Maggiore as they walked their dog on La Gloria Way. A witness saw them being chased by a masked man, and pre-tied bindings were found dropped at the scene.

Thursday, February 16, 1978 - Sacramento: *The Bee* published the first composite drawings of possible suspects in the Maggiore case.

Friday, March 17, 1978 - Sacramento: *The Bee* ran an update story on the Maggiore homicides titled "*Officers Return to Murder Scene Hunting for Clues.*" A dozen investigators went door to door talking to residents on La Gloria and La Algeria streets, hoping to find new leads in the case.

Saturday, March 18, 1978, 1:00 am - Stockton: DeAngelo attacked a 24- and 29-year-old couple.

Wednesday, March 29, 1978, 3:20 am - Rancho Cordova: DeAngelo attacked a 32-year-old woman alone with two sleeping children.

Friday, April 14, 1978, 9:50 pm - Sacramento: DeAngelo attacked a 15-year-old babysitter; Sacramento PD jurisdiction.

Sunday, April 16, 1978 - Sacramento: *The Bee* published a new set of composite drawings of possible suspects provided by a new witness in the Maggiore murders.

Monday, May 22, 1978 - Visalia: Tulare County Superior Court Judge Bradley complied with an order from the Fifth Circuit Court of Appeals, ordering that Oscar Clifton's death sentence be modified to life imprisonment.

Tuesday, May 30, 1978 - Roseville: The Press Tribune reported on the granting of Kenneth Lane's motion for change of venue. No decision was made as to where the trial would be held. The judge ruled that stories about the ballistics, the hypnotized witness, and evidence concerning the death of Lane's dog could taint the jury pool.

Monday, June 5, 1978, 2:00 am - Modesto: DeAngelo attacked a 27- and 24-year-old couple in their home.

Wednesday, June 7, 1978, 3:50 am - Davis: DeAngelo attacked a 21-year-old woman alone in her apartment. The victim was badly beaten; she suffered a broken nose and a concussion.

Friday, June 23, 1978, 1:30 am - Modesto: DeAngelo attacked a couple in their home.

Friday, June 23, 1978 - Modesto: A .357 caliber handgun, matching serial number to one stolen during the above EAR attack, was found in an irrigation canal 1.5 miles from the scene.

Saturday, June 24, 1978, 3:15 am - Davis: DeAngelo attacked a couple in their home.

Thursday, July 6, 1978, 2:50 am - Davis: DeAngelo attacked a 33-year-old female alone with her children.

Saturday, July 22, 1978 - Sacramento: The *Union* newspaper reported a "*new working relationship*" between Visalia PD and Sacramento PD, which included sharing the EAR reports withheld by SSD. After reading the additional reports, and meeting with Sacramento PD, Vaughan and McGowen were quoted: "Now that the Visalia sergeant is again privy to reports on the East Area Rapist through the Sacramento Police Department, he is 'more convinced than ever that they are the same man.' … McGowen, whose life was spared when the Ransacker's bullet hit McGowen's flashlight, agrees, 'I am convinced they're the same guy' he says. 'We will never stop trying to find and convict him.'"

Sunday, July 23, 1978 - Sacramento: *The Bee* ran a front page story titled "*Sheriff Department Attacks Newspaper Rapist Story.*" SSD Spokesman Bill Miller was quoted: "Our people worked with them [Visalia police] over a year ago," the obviously angry Miller said in response. "Our investigators looked at their case and of nine m.o. [method of operation] factors involved; we totally discounted six of them. There was no similarity."

"It appears to me," he charged, "that these investigators in Visalia were looking for publicity—and it's not there. That is really irresponsible," Miller said. He later repeated his charge against the Visalia police, adding: "What they did was unprofessional and irresponsible."

Saturday, October 7, 1978, 2:30 am - Concord: DeAngelo attacked a 26- and 29-year-old couple.

Wednesday, October 11, 1978 - Placer County: The *Auburn Journal* and *Roseville Press Tribune* had front page stories on the Kenneth Lane trial. They focused on "*Investigators Ignored Evidence in Murder Case,*" which included cigarette papers, a pack of cigarettes (Lane was not a smoker), soda and beer cans, a shotgun shell, and a "notebook"—none of which were collected at the homicide scene by PCSO. The

Sacramento Bee ran a large story on B-3 titled "*Murder Case: Police Admit Error in Trial Testimony.*" PCSO admitted that screws that they claimed came from the murder gun were actually excluded. The star eyewitness was questioned about the fact that the description of the man she claimed to see pick up the girls did not match Lane, especially since Lane had a dark, bushy beard on the day of the murder.

Friday, October 13, 1978, 4:30 am - Concord: DeAngelo attacked a 29- and 30-year-old couple.

Saturday, October 28, 1978 - Sacramento: *The Bee* covered an alternate suspect in the Best and Sinclair homicides that the judge had excluded from the Kenneth Lane trial.

Sunday, October 29, 1978, 4:30 am - San Ramon: DeAngelo attacked a 23- and 24-year-old couple.

Friday, November 3, 1978 - Placer County: The *Auburn Journal* and *Roseville Press Democrat* both ran front pages stories about the Kenneth Lane trial. The topic was the alternate suspect in the case. A former neighbor of Lane's had reportedly told a witness that he had taken Lane's truck from his driveway while Lane was at school on the day of the homicides. The *Sacramento Bee* also covered the same story in their A section that day.

Saturday, November 4, 1978, 3:45 am - San Jose: DeAngelo attacked a 34-year-old female with a child in the house.

Sunday, December 3, 1978, 4:30 am - San Jose: DeAngelo attacked a couple.

Friday, December 8, 1978 - Auburn: The *Journal* printed a front page story on the cost of the Kenneth Lane trial to the budget of Placer County.

Saturday, December 9, 1978, 2:00 am - Danville: DeAngelo attacked a 32-year-old woman in her home six blocks from the new home of a prior EAR victim *(October 1976, Sacramento).*

Monday, February 5, 1979-Wednesday, March 21, 1979 - Santa Rosa: Kenneth Lane's second trial was held in Santa Rosa. The jury deadlocked and the judge declared a mistrial.

Wednesday, March 7, 1979, am - Auburn: The *Journal* had a lengthy story about the start of Kenneth Lane's second trial. It included three witnesses who saw the girls in Auburn, near the intersection of Lincoln and Foresthill Road, in the morning and again later in the afternoon— times that Lane was in class and buying sand at the gravel yard with his girlfriend, respectively.

Thursday, April 5, 1979, 1:00 am - Fremont: DeAngelo attacked a couple.

Friday, June 1, 1979 - Auburn: The *Journal* gave front page coverage to the start of Kenneth Lane's *third* murder trial. The story mainly discussed the prosecutor's attempt to discredit the testimony of two eyewitnesses who saw the girls in Auburn on the day that they were killed, rather than in Sacramento *(according to the hypnotized witness).*

Saturday June 2, 1979, 11:34 pm - Walnut Creek: DeAngelo attacked a 17-year-old babysitter.

Friday, June 8, 1979 - Auburn: The *Journal* had another front page story on the third Kenneth Lane trial, which was scheduled to take twice as long as either of his two previous trials. The multiple hypnosis sessions of the main witness against Lane were discussed in detail.

Monday, June 11, 1979, 4:00 am - Danville: DeAngelo attacked a couple.

Friday, June 22, 1979 - Auburn: The *Journal* returned the Kenneth Lane story to the front page, with the sole focus on Lane's alibi that he was in classes at American River College, with his girlfriend having lunch, and traveling to the gravel yard with her that afternoon. The story also discussed the prior burglary Lane had reported at his home on September 20, 1977, which was supported by Lane's calls to the insurance adjustor on the day the girls were murdered.

Monday, June 25, 1979, 4:15 am - Walnut Creek: DeAngelo attacked a 13-year-old girl in her home. The girl's father and 16-year-old sister were asleep in the house.

Monday, July 2, 1979 - Santa Rosa: Lane jury deadlocked in the third trial, and another mistrial was declared.

Monday, July 2, 1979 - Citrus Heights: DeAngelo was arrested for attempting to shoplift a can of dog mace and a hammer. The items had been hidden in his pants, and were retrieved by Pay 'n Save store security, who were forced to tie DeAngelo to a chair to await SSD. The store was located at Sunrise and Greenback. DeAngelo was criminally charged.

Wednesday, July 4, 1979 - Santa Rosa: The *Auburn Journal* reported that the third trial against Kenneth Lane for the murder of Kimberly Best and Paige Sinclair had ended with a mistrial.

Thursday, July 5, 1979, 3:50 am - Danville: DeAngelo's last documented EAR attack in Northern California. The couple fought back, and DeAngelo dropped shoelaces at the scene.

Monday, August 27, 1979 - Auburn: Following a citation being issued by SSD for the July 2 shoplifting incident, DeAngelo was terminated by APD Chief Nick Willick.

Monday, October 1, 1979 2:15 am - Goleta: DeAngelo attempted an EAR-style attack on a 33-year-old couple. Both victims managed to escape, and they alerted their neighbor, an FBI agent. DeAngelo escaped the scene on a bike he had stolen from a nearby garage, and the FBI agent gave chase in his car, but lost DeAngelo when he ditched the bike and hopped over a fence.

Friday, October 26, 1979 - Sacramento: Following testifying on his own defense, DeAngelo was convicted of misdemeanor shoplifting by a jury during a three-day trial. He was fined $100, and given six months of probation.

Tuesday, November 6, 1979 - Auburn: DeAngelo withdrew his pending appeal for his Auburn PD termination. The appeal was scheduled to be heard by the Personnel Board on 11/9/79.

Sunday, December 30, 1979, 3:00 am - Goleta: DeAngelo killed 35-year-old Dr. Alexandra Manning and 44-year-old Dr. Robert Offerman in their home.

Thursday, February 26, 1980 - Sacramento: *The Bee* published a story about the Goleta homicides entitled "*Link to East Area Rapist Probed in Couple's Slaying.*" The article noted the similarities in prior robberies and burglaries in the Goleta area near the double homicide "*that seem to go beyond mere coincidence.*" After expressing doubt that the EAR could be linked to the Offerman/Manning homicides, SSD Spokesman Bill Miller identified how the EAR link was first established—another MO match in the CII system: "Information that a similarity existed between the methods of operation of the 'Goleta Valley Killer' and the 'East Area Rapist' originally came from the California Department of Justice."

Thursday, March 13, 1980 - Sacramento: *The Bee* published a story entitled "*Police Debate Tie Between East Area Rapist, Killings.*" Both

Santa Barbara Sheriff William Baker and SSD Lt. Ray Root agreed that the EAR was not the person who killed Drs. Manning and Offerman: "Root said that the factor that convinced him there was no connection was the apparent ineptitude exhibited by the killer in Santa Barbara... Root said that scenario does not fit the East Area rapist, who never lost control of a situation."

Sacramento PD detective Sgt. James D. Bevins disagreed, and stated that he felt there was a "*strong possibility*" it was the same man. Bevins was circulating copies of the footprint evidence collected at the Offerman/Manning scene within his department.

Thursday, March 13, 1980 11:30 pm - Ventura: DeAngelo murdered 43-year-olds Charlene and Lyman Smith in their home on High Point Drive. *(NOTE: This was the same day as the news story described above.)*

Friday, April 11, 1980 - Citrus Heights: Joe and Sharon DeAngelo purchased their new home on the 8300 block of Canyon Oak Drive.

Tuesday, August 19, 1980, 11:30 pm - Dana Point: DeAngelo murdered 28-year-old Patrice and 24-year-old Keith Harrington in their residence located in a private, gated community on Cockleshell Drive.

Thursday, February 5, 1981 2:00 am - Irvine: DeAngelo murdered 28-year-old Manuela Witthuhn in her home on Columbus Way.

Monday, July 27, 1981, 3:30 am - Goleta: DeAngelo murdered 35-year-old Cheri Domingo and 28-year-old Greg Sanchez in a residence on Toltec Way adjacent to the San Jose Creek connecting the Goleta homicides.

Wednesday, September 9, 1981 - Sacramento County: DeAngelo's oldest child was born.

Friday, December 3, 1982 - Sacramento: Sharon Huddle was admitted to the California Bar.

Sunday, May 4, 1986 11:30 pm - Irvine: DeAngelo murdered 18-year-old Janelle Cruz in her home located on Encina Court.

Wednesday, November 26, 1986 - Los Angeles County: DeAngelo's middle child was born.

Sunday, May 14, 1989 - Sacramento County: DeAngelo's youngest child was born.

1989 - Roseville: DeAngelo started work as a truck mechanic at Save Mart Distribution Center, located in Roseville Industrial Area East.

Monday, November 4, 1991 - Sacramento County: Family court action filed by DeAngelo.

Friday, August 6, 1993 - Placer County: Sharon filed for dissolution of marriage. It was later dismissed on April 24, 2006 for "lack of prosecution."

Friday October 29, 1993 - Roseville: Sharon closed on the purchase of a separate residence; Joe DeAngelo signed documents waiving his community property interest.

Friday, July 28, 1995 - Sacramento County: DeAngelo got into a dispute with a gas station attendant. DeAngelo said that he believed that he was owed a refund for un-pumped gas, but the clerk reported it to the police as an attempted robbery.

Tuesday, April 16, 1996 - Sacramento County: DeAngelo was arrested in a warrant sting, and booked into jail. The warrant stemmed from the above incident at the gas station. The charges were dropped, and DeAngelo's civil suit against the gas station was settled in March 1998.

Saturday, August 21, 2010 - Exeter: DeAngelo's mother died.

Monday, February 18, 2013 - Oscar Clifton died in prison.

2017 - Roseville: DeAngelo retired from Save Mart.

Tuesday, April 24, 2018 - Citrus Heights: DeAngelo was arrested for twelve homicides, and for crimes as the East Area Rapist and Visalia Ransacker *(the Snelling homicide was added by amended complaint; 8/21/2018).*

Monday, June 29, 2020 - DeAngelo entered guilty pleas for all pending charges and admitted responsibility for the uncharged rapes, attempted rapes, kidnapping, and attempted murder that were past the applicable statutes of limitation.

Afterword

"I hear much of people's calling out to punish the guilty, but very few are concerned to clear the innocent."

—Daniel Defoe, *An Appeal to Honor and Justice*, 1715.